Russia's Arctic Strategies and the Future of the Far North

Russia's Arctic Strategies and the Future of the Far North

Marlene Laruelle

M.E.Sharpe
Armonk, New York
London, England

The EuroSlavic fonts used to create this work are © 1986–2014 Payne Loving Trust.
EuroSlavic is available from Linguist's Software, Inc.,
www.linguistsoftware.com, P.O. Box 580, Edmonds, WA 98020-0580 USA
tel (425) 775-1130.

Library of Congress Cataloging-in-Publication Data

Laruelle, Marlene, author.
  Russia's Arctic strategies and the future of the Far North / by Marlene Laruelle.
    pages : maps ; cm
  Includes bibliographical references and index.
  ISBN 978-0-7656-3500-6 (hardcover : alk. paper) — ISBN 978-0-7656-3501-3 (pbk. : alk. paper)
  1. Russia, Northern—Strategic aspects. 2. Geopolitics—Russia, Northern. 3. Arctic Coast
(Russia)—Strategic aspects. 4. Geopolitics—Russia (Federation)—Arctic Coast. I. Title.

DK501.2.L37 2014
320.60947'1—dc23   2013021593

Printed in the United States of America

The paper used in this publication meets the minimum requirements of
American National Standard for Information Sciences
Permanence of Paper for Printed Library Materials,
ANSI Z 39.48-1984.

IBT (c)   10   9   8   7   6   5   4   3   2   1
SP (p)   10   9   8   7   6   5   4   3   2

Contents

List of Maps and Tables

Maps

Tables

Introduction

Long dismissed as a frozen wasteland, the Arctic has recently come under increasing scrutiny, for better and for worse. Moving from the realm of the unknown to the known, from the marginal to at times central, it has been bumped up to front-page treatment, replete with superlatives: the most northerly region, the coldest one, the region with the longest nights and longest days, the world's most fragile ecosystem, the region richest in hydrocarbons, and so on. The hype is often backed up with multiple historical references, as though the new configurations of the twenty-first century need to be explained in familiar terms in order to be understood. Strategic issues are thus framed using historical journalistic parallels. These include the conquest of the West (Arctic as *the New Western Frontier*), the Cold War (*the Ice Cold War*), or the Great Game in Central Asia at the end of the nineteenth century (Arctic as *the New Great Game*). The economic drivers, often presented without taking into account changes in the market, new technologies, and knowledge of private actors, are evoked using the filter of the Gold Rush (*the Rush to the Arctic*).[1]

At the other end of the spectrum, that of environmental concerns, the messages target emotional sensitivity to nature and wildlife, such as a National Geographic photo of a polar bear, the quintessential symbol of the Arctic, trapped on a melting ice floe.[2] Expected climate change is indeed an important driver in the global picture of the Arctic. It already heavily impacts human activities in this region and will continue to do so, either encouraging more human presence, or making the region increasingly inhospitable and unpredictable. The future of the Arctic in international affairs is not, however, limited to debates on climate change. Once the hype has ended, the Arctic will certainly remain important in world affairs. Various countries' warships and submarines will continue to cross paths in the Arctic Ocean; the fragile ecosystems of local populations and wildlife will need international oversight and protection; potentially profitable exploitation of the subsoil or of water resources could begin despite extreme conditions; and use of the "Trans-Arctic Air Corridor" by the air traffic linking North America, Eurasia, and

Asia will increase because the circumpolar route saves time and fuel. Since the publication of one of the pioneering books, *The Age of the Arctic: Hot Conflicts and Cold Realities* by Gail Osherenko and Oran R. Young (1989), the situation in the polar regions has drastically changed, yet the "hot conflict versus cold realities" paradigm remains one of the keys to understanding the current challenges in addressing Arctic issues.

The Many Actors of the Arctic Debate

The Arctic debate has several distinctive features. Like discussions on climate change, it is a globalized forum, with interested parties coming not only from North America and Europe, but also from Asia, Latin America, and Africa. The Arctic discussion is even more multidisciplinary than that on climate change, with climatologists, geographers, oceanologists, scholars from the human and social sciences, and security specialists all in the mix. The public voices on the Arctic also epitomize the wide diversity of people involved in the debate: scientific groups, indigenous communities, politicians and the military, NGOs with environmental agendas, and private business interests are all invited to hear and take into account other points of view. The growing dissonance between advocates of environmental protection and natural resource development is but one aspect, albeit the one perhaps most hyped by the media, of a broader, more complex dispute.

But the Arctic is also distinctive in the way that it stimulates our imaginations. As the last *terra incognita* on Earth—after the great marine depths—it is apt to evoke romantic and utopian clichés. The two poles remain still largely unknown and untamed spaces. People have their own visions of the Arctic region, influenced by readings from childhood and the accounts of the great polar expeditions of the nineteenth and early twentieth centuries.[3] The Arctic is also eminently visual. Sometimes more than words, photos play a key role in raising public awareness and demanding respect for "Mother Earth." Another striking visual element of the Arctic is maps. To understand the region, one must look at the globe from a very different and unusual angle. Visual representations have a direct impact on self-perceptions of identity, place in the world, and security. But they are also capable of distorting reality and power relations.[4]

A great number of arguments and viewpoints must be taken into account when discussing the Arctic. As such, collecting information is sometimes challenging. Journalistic reports are abundant, and tend to overshadow academic works, which are usually deeply rooted in their own disciplines with little cross-referencing. Interdisciplinary connections between the natural sciences, human sciences, and security studies are still largely underdeveloped.

Moreover, most of the information is presented from the point of view of particular countries. American and Canadian publications are largely focused on their bilateral issues (Northwest Passage, Beaufort Sea, and Alaska), while Nordic countries and Russians focus likewise on their own regional issues. The importance of the Arctic in the transatlantic partnership is as yet rarely discussed, and Russia is conspicuous by its general absence in Western discussions. All the Arctic states have published their own strategies in regard to the Arctic, with Norway and Canada being the first, and the United States the last, but civil society pronouncements on Arctic-related subjects are almost exclusively Western. Non-Arctic states such as China also want to promote their points of view, and many international organizations are part of the picture: the International Maritime Organization (IMO) and other UN entities, NATO, the European Union, the Arctic Council, and the Barents Euro-Arctic Council (BEAC). Everyone—states, institutions, individuals, firms, and civil society—wants to participate in the Arctic narrative, making it a truly globalized issue.[5]

Defining the Arctic: A Geographical, Political, and Institutional Landscape

There is currently no universally accepted definition for the spatial scope of the Arctic. Climatologists, oceanologists, historians, and security experts all lay out their own criteria. Some definitions only take into account the Arctic Ocean, which is the smallest of all the oceans with only 3% of the world's total ocean surface area and 1% of its volume. Although it is classified as an ocean because of its size (14 million square kilometers), it is also reminiscent of the Mediterranean Sea, being mostly surrounded by land. The Arctic Ocean's distinctive feature is a very extensive continental shelf, covering about one-third of the seabed and reaching a width of 1,200 kilometers in Siberia. A vast number of islands rise up from the shelf, considerably limiting opportunities for deep-draft vessels.[6] Even Arctic maritime internal delimitations differ. The U.S. National Oceanic and Atmospheric Administration (NOAA) has defined 17 large marine ecosystems in the Arctic,[7] whereas the UN Food and Agriculture Organization (FAO) classifies the Arctic waters in a different way, according to the purposes of fisheries.[8]

Other definitions are land based, in which case the criteria of delimitation are even more complex. Biotic regions are often the leading criterion, taking into account the natural borders where vegetation ceases to grow (the tree line) or the zones whose mean daily temperatures do not exceed 10° Celsius in July. The range of possible definitions is therefore very large. The Arctic Monitoring and Assessment Programme (AMAP) and the Arctic Human

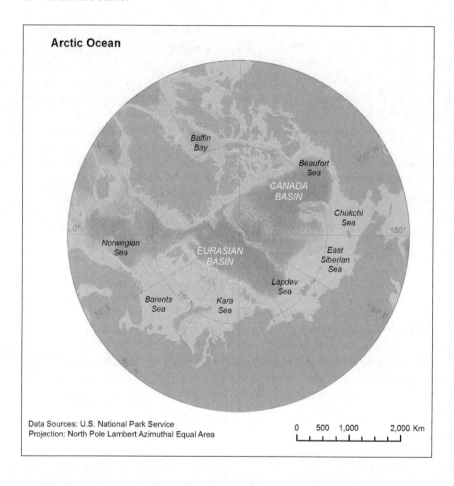

Arctic Ocean

Baffin Bay
Beaufort Sea
CANADA BASIN
Chukchi Sea
Norwegian Sea
EURASIAN BASIN
East Siberian Sea
Lapdev Sea
Barents Sea
Kara Sea

Data Sources: U.S. National Park Service
Projection: North Pole Lambert Azimuthal Equal Area

0   500   1,000   2,000 Km

Development Report (AHDR) consider the Arctic zone to encompass parts of territories that lie below the Arctic Circle, such as Greenland and the Faroe Islands, as well as the Aleutian Islands. The AMAP-defined borders are more extensive than the AHDR ones, except in some places where the AHDR definition includes some areas of Canada's Quebec province and Alaska's islands along the Canadian coastline. This inclusive definition, which thwarts all attempts at precise boundary delimitation and accepts a multiplicity of possible borders, is the one that has been accepted by the Arctic Council.[9] However, if one takes into account criteria measuring extreme climatic conditions, especially permafrost, then almost all of Siberia and a large part of Canada can also be classified as Arctic. The borders could extend still further; China tests its polar scientific advances on the high plateaus of Tibet, which it considers its own "High North." Everyone seems,

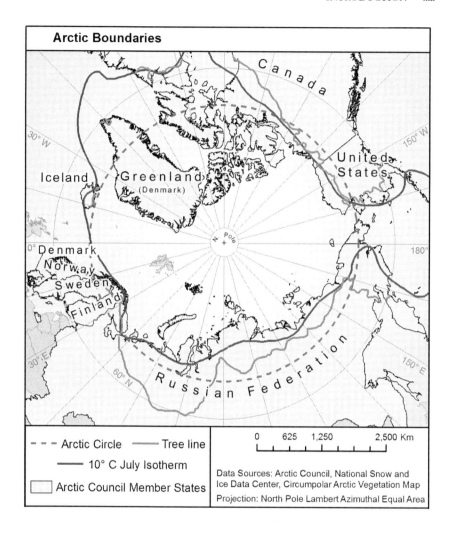

Arctic Boundaries

- - - Arctic Circle   ——— Tree line

——— 10° C July Isotherm

☐ Arctic Council Member States

0   625   1,250   2,500 Km

Data Sources: Arctic Council, National Snow and
Ice Data Center, Circumpolar Arctic Vegetation Map
Projection: North Pole Lambert Azimuthal Equal Area

therefore, to have their own set of definitions. The question of the Arctic's southern borders is not a matter of a simple debate among scientists: it may have direct consequences on the level of analysis and on the decision-making process. Even the terminology used to describe the Arctic differs, such as Far North, Circumpolar North, and Polar regions. The differences are often poorly defined and depend primarily on national traditions.[10]

However, the Arctic is not merely a geographic space. It is also a political space, with its already fuzzy borders further distorted by state-centric mind-sets. Five states, known as the Arctic Rim, have coastal Arctic waters: the United States, Canada, Denmark, Norway, and Russia. For two of them—the

United States and Denmark—the coastal waters are not geographically contiguous with the mainland. While Alaska is still part of the North American continent, Greenland is a specific, isolated component of the Kingdom of Denmark. Three other states have part of their territory beyond the polar circle but lack direct access to the Arctic Ocean: Iceland, Finland, and Sweden. Although accustomed to cooperation, the five coastal states and the three non-coastal ones have divergent views on the importance of the geographic criterion of access to the Arctic Ocean. Hence, in the 2008 Ilulissat Declaration, the five Arctic Rim countries announced their cooperation on high-level ocean policy issues without the participation of the three other states, which protested their exclusion from the decision-making process.[11]

These eight states are all members of the Arctic Council. Established in 1996, it is an intergovernmental forum designed to build consensus on issues concerning the environment and sustainable development, as well as to monitor pollution, disseminate information, and promote cooperation among the eight Arctic nations. It was born out of the Arctic Environmental Protection Strategy (AEPS), which was founded in 1991 to deal with the threat of polar pollution. It includes the four initial AEPS working groups[12] and two additional groups: one on sustainable development (Sustainable Development Working Group, or SDWG)—particularly active after the 2004 Arctic Climate Impact Assessment—and the other on the Arctic Contaminants Action Program (ACAP). The Arctic Council has worked in particular to improve the membership status accorded to the Arctic's indigenous peoples, making their nongovernmental organizations (NGOs) permanent participants equal to the states. The council works mainly on issues related to environmental protection and sustainable development and excludes matters linked to hard security.[13] In the absence of a permanent secretariat, the work of the Arctic Council is heavily influenced by the priorities of whichever state is chairing the two-year rotating presidency.

A second regional organization has been established for part of the Arctic region, the Barents Euro-Arctic Council (BEAC). The foreign affairs ministries of Finland, Norway, Sweden, Russia, Denmark, Iceland, and the European Commission formally instituted the BEAC in 1993. Today, Canada, France, Germany, Italy, Japan, the Netherlands, Poland, the United Kingdom, and the United States also participate as observers. The BEAC engages in manifold activities, such as managing spent nuclear fuel and radioactive waste, simplifying border crossings, cooperating on the environment and emergency search and rescue, and strengthening the history and cultures of the region with the involvement of indigenous peoples.[14] To this day, the Barents region remains Europe's largest in terms of interregional cooperation with non-EU actors, and is a driver of interaction with Russia. A third, regional organization should be mentioned, namely the Nordic Council, which includes Iceland, Norway, Sweden, Denmark, and Finland, and welcomes as observers the three post-Soviet Baltic states (Lithuania, Latvia, Estonia), as well as the Faroe Islands, the Åland Islands, and Greenland.

Moreover, several larger institutions are involved in the future of the region, including the North Atlantic Treaty Organization (NATO), the European Union (EU), and the G8 (Group of Eight) nations.[15] All the Western Arctic Ocean states are members of NATO (the United States, Canada, Iceland, Denmark, and Norway). The joint presence of the United States and Russia in the Arctic and the memories of the Cold War complicate the Arctic debate, as well as perceptions of threat in the region. The EU is also represented. Although Denmark, Finland, and Sweden are EU members, Norway is not, which means that the EU encompasses Arctic territory but has no Arctic coastline. The geographical absence of the EU on the shores of the Arctic Ocean also has consequences for policymaking processes, because some states have been very reticent about according the EU full member status in the Arctic Council.[16] And whereas Iceland and Norway are members of the European Free Trade Association (EFTA), Greenland is not; it opted out of the European Economic Community (EEC) which preceded the EU. Furthermore, Greenland and the Faroe Islands may well proclaim their independence from Denmark in the years to come, becoming new independent players and thereby reducing Copenhagen's role. Finally, three Arctic states are members of the G8: the United States, Russia, and Canada. All three are federations that have granted some autonomous rights to their sub-administrative units and their indigenous peoples.

The Arctic is often presented in the media and public opinion as a new "Wild West," in which international law is either nonexistent or not applied by the rival players. However, the Arctic has many complex legal charters, which sometimes overlap, and some specialists believe, on the contrary, that there is too much rather than too little of a legal framework. Because the Arctic Ocean possesses no special status, it is subject to the decisions of the International Maritime Organization (IMO). Moreover, it is also subject to the United Nations Convention on the Law of the Sea (UNCLOS), which was signed in 1982 and came into force in 1994. The convention has been ratified by more than 150 states including all the Arctic coastal states except the United States, and therefore has significant legal influence over the region.[17] According to UNCLOS, all states, coastal or not, possess legitimate rights and interests regarding the high seas as well as the deep seabed, in the Arctic as in the other oceans, and are therefore able to participate in decision-making, a fact that some states have been quick to point out. Accordingly, in May 2013 six countries were granted observer status, which does not give them a right to vote, but allows them to be present in all the debates and, over the longer term, to hope for a greater role.[18]

Among the six new observer states, five are Asian countries: China, India, Japan, South Korea, and Singapore—striking evidence of the growing internationalization of the Arctic theater. All are striving to become institutionalized Arctic players, for multiple reasons: first, they hope that their power aspirations will be confirmed through an Arctic status; second, they want to gain access to Arctic shipping because all are greatly exposed to the geopolitical risks associated with dependence on energy shipments through the straits of Hormuz and Malacca; and third, they are interested in Arctic fishing resources. Thus far their visibility in the region derives above all from their polar scientific activities, which are effectively follow-ons, of lesser scale, of projects they have undertaken in Antarctica for many years. They are also involved in strategies to enhance their technological knowledge on the Arctic, and both the Korean and Chinese shipping industries are booming.[19]

If the ambitions of Japan and South Korea are no cause for concern, China's are perceived more ambiguously. Not being a coastal state, it is now presenting itself as a "near-Arctic state" and claims to be a stakeholder just like any other, on the pretext that the melting icecap will have an environmental impact of global dimensions. Beijing is anxious about the rapid evolution of the situation in the Arctic: the progressive attribution of the continental shelf to the coastal states could drastically reduce its prospects of gaining access to Arctic resources. The Chinese strategy has thus been to internationalize the region in order to weaken the oversight rights of the eight Arctic states, and to obtain legal recognition of the rights of non-Arctic states.[20] This aggressive stance has perturbed some members of the Arctic Council, in particular Russia and the United States,[21] but Norway supported China's candidacy.

Beyond self-assertive declarations, China remains an Arctic actor of modest proportions. The vast majority of its polar expeditions take place in the Antarctic, even as Beijing's activities in the North Pole are on the rise. Since 2004 it has acquired a polar base for climate research in Ny-Ålesund, on the island of Spitsbergen in Norway's Svalbard archipelago. In 2010, the main Chinese polar research vessel and the world's largest icebreaker, the *Xuelong*, carried out a mission lasting almost three months in the Russian Arctic,[22] a mission that was repeated in the summer of 2012. A new, high-tech polar expedition research icebreaker is expected to be operational in 2014, and an international Arctic cooperation and research institute is to open in Shanghai, with backing from Iceland.[23] Chinese firms are also seeking, albeit timidly, to make their presence felt in the Arctic, or sub-Arctic, regions (the Alberta oil sands, an iron ore mine in Greenland, and geothermal production and eco-resorts in Iceland), and each attempt they make, whether successful or not, provokes worried commentaries in the Western media. China seems to have focused on a privileged partnership with Iceland, but massive Chinese investments could also be of interest to Russia and Canada. In terms of fishing, the China Ocean Shipping Company (COSCO) has thus far shown little interest in Arctic navigation, but in 2010 China leased the right to use North Korea's Rajin port, which provides it direct access to the Sea of Japan, and in theory it could become China's northern base for Arctic shipping.

Despite the existence of an Arctic legal framework, many experts stress the fact that these regulatory systems and supervisory institutions are founded on soft-law status, an *ad hoc* funding system, and consensus. A 2011 report titled *A New Security Architecture for the Arctic: An American Perspective,* published by the Washington-based Center for Strategic and International Studies (CSIS), thus speaks of "an abundance of governance, [and] a scarcity of capabilities" to describe this paradox.[24] Indeed the legislation and institutional mechanisms do not seem fit to manage any serious tensions that may arise. For instance, the Arctic Council has no regulatory mandate and cannot enforce its decisions on member states. To date, only two genuinely circumpolar agreements have been signed—the 1974 Agreement for the Protection of Polar Bears, and the 2011 Agreement on Cooperation on Aeronautical and Maritime Search and Rescue (SAR). Impending climate change is pushing all participants to consider a more consistent normative framework, inasmuch as the Arctic Council is currently unable to do much to ensure the sustainability of the region. The EU and an increasing number of states are questioning whether the council is able to perform the tasks expected of a forum in charge of managing a region that is undergoing such significant transformation. However, in Ilulissat, Greenland, the five Arctic Rim states declared that they saw no need to form a new comprehensive international legal regime for the region, opting instead to address the potential challenges of the Arctic Ocean by virtue of their sovereignty and jurisdiction over large areas of the ocean.[25]

For several years, the idea of an Arctic Treaty based on the model of the 1959 Antarctic Treaty and the 1983 Madrid Protocol on Environmental Protection to the Antarctic Treaty has been suggested by some experts and politicians as a means of giving the region a stronger institutional structure, but with no tangible result. As of now, only the Antarctic is governed by a legally binding regime. It is clear that the Arctic and the Antarctic are fundamentally different geographically; one is largely an ice-covered ocean, the other is an ice-covered continent; and one has human inhabitants, whereas the other does not. But they are also very different in legal terms. Much of the Arctic falls under the sovereignty of various states, whereas claims to the Antarctic have been frozen.[26] The Antarctic model is therefore not particularly relevant for a regional, legally binding system in the Arctic, and other ideas must be explored.[27]

The Arctic: Not a New Geopolitical Pivot, But a Balance-Shifter?

The Arctic region feeds the strategic imagination. Some hasten to predict an Arctic completely altered by climate change, auguring a sudden growth in population, providing an unregulated haven for international terrorists, and transforming itself into the next Suez Canal in terms of shipping and the future Middle East in terms of hydrocarbons. However, this vision distorts drastically the realities of the Arctic, and it also neglects to compare the opportunities to be found there with those found in other regions of the world. Will the emergence of the Arctic necessarily bring about a drastic change in the twenty-first century global balance of power? Is it a new geopolitical pivot similar to the one announced by Sir Halford Mackinder (1861–1947) centered on Siberia and Central Asia? While the previous *Heartland*—the pivotal point between the so-called continental and maritime powers—was found in the expanses of Eurasia, will the new one be the Far North? Will "whoever controls the Arctic controls the world" become the maxim of the twenty-first century?

The viewpoint defended here is that the Arctic is not the new geopolitical pivot point, but it could be one of the *balance-shifters* in the global equilibrium of power. It does not change the fundamental order, but it adds new weight for various states. It could contribute to reshaping some geopolitical axes such as transatlantic commitments, the Nordic Europe—Russia partnership, or Asia-Russia, and specifically the China-Russia pairing. But the Arctic above all offers new spaces for the expression of state power, of a type that no longer pertains to the assertion of classical military supremacy. The new Arctic power is going to be a soft type of power, based on logistics, technology, and science: the powerful will be those able to master the seas for commercial shipping as much as for rescue missions, to launch observation and communications satellites, and to produce knowledge on the region. The Arctic is also an important nation-branding tool, as can be seen in the hyped, self-assertive declarations of some Russian and Canadian politicians. A state that has succeeded in integrating private actors and civil society organizations in its management of Arctic issues will better promote its brand. The Arctic will thus partly set the tone for evolving relations between twenty-first century actors—states, private actors, NGOs, populations, and supranational organizations.

In the second half of the 2000s, the geostrategic uncertainty in the Arctic region gave rise to a proliferation of discourses predicting its transformation into a warlike zone. Having been a central area for U.S.-Soviet opposition during the Cold War and the site of numerous incidents that could have led to an escalation of the conflict, the Arctic could potentially be added to the long list of "hot" or "frozen" conflict zones. Indeed, the great world powers have long rubbed shoulders here, while the rising Asian powers— China followed by India—do not conceal their interest in the region. The changing status of NATO, as it tries to redefine its missions in a post-Cold War world, combined with the ups and downs of NATO-Russia relations, certainly complicates the Arctic security debate. This conflict-oriented vision has been reinforced by the sometimes aggressive rhetoric voiced by some of the coastal states. Accordingly, certain politicians and public figures have fanned the flames through statements such as "we will not give the Arctic to anyone"—attributable to Artur Chilingarov, the Russian president's special representative for the Arctic and Antarctic—or the slogan "use it or lose it" by the Canadian Prime Minister Stephen Harper. Although their rhetoric was aimed primarily at domestic public opinion, it may have international repercussions.

In 2008, NATO expressed the view that the Northern Alliance needed to expand its military activities in the Arctic and discuss the issue of securitizing this quickly evolving theater. The same year, the U.S. Northern Edge exercise, led by the Alaska Command, was widely discussed in Russia as a symbol of the resumption of the United States' "aggressive activities" in the Arctic.[28] Russian military exercises were thus organized close to Svalbard involving the cruisers *Marshal Ustinov* and the *Severomorsk,* and the plan is now to hold these exercises at regular intervals. In 2009, Russia organized military exercises at the Pemboy test range in the Komi Republic, while NATO conducted "Cold Response" training in northern Norway, its biggest exercise that year, involving more than 7,000 soldiers from 13 countries.[29] Russia also continues to undertake large-scale military exercises in the western part of its Arctic, such as in the vicinity of Lake Ladoga in 2009, with scenarios involving the protection of oil and gas installations in northwest Russia.[30] The same year, the U.S. Navy released a new roadmap for its activities relating to the Arctic for the next five years.[31]

However, the global tendency has very clearly been one of de-securitization, as the Arctic region no longer forms part of the precarious nuclear balance of the Cold War. Despite the revival of a modest level of military activity, the region is increasingly viewed as a space of cooperation where the central stakes pertain to soft security, environmental challenges, and human security.[32] Multiple patterns of cooperation exist: in 2013, Russia's Northern

Fleet took part in several international exercises, especially the POMOR one, the most extensive joint action involving Norwegian and Russian forces. More importantly, no littoral state has expressed a desire to redraw Arctic land boundaries. Claims on the continental shelf have all been presented peacefully within the framework provided by UNCLOS. Additionally, more than 80 percent of the coveted offshore resources are located in the exclusive economic zones of the various states, and therefore do not present any potential for conflict.[33] As Alison J. K. Bailes rightfully notes, because Arctic challenges are intersectoral, multi-functional, and multi-institutional,[34] they push toward geopolitical cooperation and legal innovation.

Although the Arctic faces no risk of imminent conflict, it is a legitimate security concern.[35] First, a global geo-strategic uncertainty may push states toward proactive policies in order to diminish this uncertainty. Second, the potential for accidents—collisions between ships or submarines, with oil platforms, or oil spills—as well as small-scale localized tensions over mineral or fish stock resources that could suddenly escalate, and the possibility that different players' actions may be misinterpreted, has to be taken into account. Finally, some states may have subjective feelings of marginalization or of having been deprived of their international rights. Perceptions of threats and projections of power therefore constitute major elements in the Arctic security debate. All of these elements combined confirm that security, understood as an "inter-subjective speech act," is definitely an issue in the Arctic.[36]

Russia: The Least Known Arctic Player, But the Most Determined

Russia is probably the least known Arctic player. The literature devoted to it and available in Western languages is still minimal. Three monographs by Terence Armstrong, Pier Horensma, and John McCannon are devoted to the Soviet Arctic,[37] and two collective volumes edited by Helge Blackkisrud and Geir Hønneland and by Elana Wilson Rowe have discussed the post-Soviet Arctic situation, especially the center-periphery relations.[38] This lack of literature is in the process of changing thanks to the growing number of interdisciplinary approaches being explored, especially through the pioneering works that, for the most part, have been done in the Nordic countries, in particular in Norway, and by individual scholars such as Elana Wilson Rowe on political aspects, Timothy Heleniak on demographic ones, and Katarzyna Zysk on strategic ones. Russian scholarship—among others Aleksandr Pelyasov, Valery Konyshev, and Aleksandr Sergunin[39]—is quite obviously the most developed, but is largely carried out in Russian, and within disciplinary confines so that there is no comprehensive assessment encompassing all aspects of the problem in a holistic way.

Despite this partial absence in the literature, Russia dominates the Arctic region geographically, conquered it historically very early on, and is setting the tone on strategic issues. Geographically, it encompasses half of the Arctic coastline, 40% of the land area beyond the Arctic Circle, and three quarters of the Arctic population—about three million of the total four million. Economically, as much as 20% of Russia's gross domestic product (GDP) and of its total exports is generated north of the Arctic Circle.[40] In terms of resources, about 95% of its gas, 75% of its oil, 96% of its platinum, 90% of its nickel and cobalt, and 60% of its copper reserves are found in Arctic and sub-Arctic regions. To this must be added the riches—often estimated but rarely proven—of the continental shelf, seabed, and the water itself, ranging from rare earth minerals to fish stocks. Historically, Russia is far and away the first European power to have ventured into the North and to have controlled both Arctic land and sea routes.

In the twentieth century Moscow has played a key role in the Arctic strategic balance. During the Cold War, the Soviet Union, on a par with the United States, was an engine of the region's militarization, but it has also facilitated strategic de-escalation and the promotion of international cooperation. Mikhail Gorbachev's famous speech in Murmansk in 1987 inspired the negotiations for an Arctic environmental protection strategy that began two years later. He called for a series of wide-ranging proposals to be adopted on regional cooperation, including restrictions on naval activities, the establishment of a nuclear weapons free zone in Northern Europe, and the development of trans-border cooperation.[41] Russia disappeared from the Arctic security landscape in the 1990s, subsequent to the Soviet Union's disintegration and the partial collapse of the state authority. With the country's reassertion in the 2000s, it once again occupies a major place in all Arctic debates, even though it is still a modest player in terms of environmental issues and those related to indigenous populations. Today the Arctic is again considered vital to the Russian Federation's national security. It constitutes its most dynamic border with NATO (much more so than the Bering Strait); it forms a large part of the border with the EU; provides it access to the Atlantic Ocean; and offers convenient locations for nuclear and other strategic deterrence systems.

Since the traumas of the 1990s, Russia has viewed the world through the prism of its fear of being confined to the periphery of international decision making. Russian decision makers think—probably rightfully—that maintenance of the status quo in terms of strategic equilibrium has largely been unfavorable to Moscow over the past two decades. For this reason, although

Russia's foreign policy is fundamentally reactive, its policy in the Arctic is proactive—a new approach for Moscow thought to be better suited to advancing its interests.[42] Nation-branding, prestige on the international scene, and acknowledgment by the main Western powers and especially by the United States of its status as a great power thus have particular importance in Russia's perception of Arctic issues. In the forthcoming decades the country will have to face many dilemmas in defining its strategic priorities. As stated by John W. Parker,[43] Russia can either be a "mediocre power"—an international player *by default* due to its nuclear capabilities, its veto power in the UN Security Council, and its size and location, but without the capacity to promote a "Russian voice" in the world order—or it can become a bit more of a Euro- and partly Asia-centric, medium-sized power, with limited ambitions and regional capacities, but more success. In this context the Arctic region opens up new options, and could furnish Moscow with a more dynamic and innovative role on the international stage.[44]

The Kremlin interprets the Arctic as fostering a potentially drastic shift in Russia's long-term geostrategic identity. The frozen Arctic Ocean constituted a key element of geopolitical containment for Russia's competitors, while at the same time forming a major domestic route for the Soviet Union's shipping and navy. Despite U.S. submarine traffic in Arctic waters and regular encounters with the Norwegian navy, Moscow felt the Far North was secure and could thus focus on securing its western, southern, and eastern frontiers. Today, this self-representation has deeply changed. Russia can now present itself, at least on paper, as a maritime state, breaking its encirclement in a direction until now underused, but at the same time it finds itself with a new border to protect.[45] By transforming the Arctic Ocean into a sea transit route, Russia's immense Siberian continental hinterland, hitherto cut off from southern routes such as the Trans-Siberian, can potentially connect to the rest of the world. Improved access to the North Pacific could shift the geopolitical and economic domestic order by emphasizing the strategic value of Russia's Pacific frontage, which opens onto the dynamism of Asia. The spatial projection of Russia in general and of landlocked northern Eurasia in particular would therefore emerge drastically modified by the prospect of free circulation in Arctic waters.

In addition, the Arctic offers theoretically unique opportunities that would enable the Russian economy to guarantee itself several decades of ample revenues. Moscow is thus planning somewhat optimistically to transform the region into the "Russian Federation's leading strategic resource base."[46] Russia's strategies for the Arctic therefore by no means only reflect its relationship with the major international powers or regional institutions. The Arctic is above all a domestic issue: it is an economic resource, a strategy for Siberian regional development, and an opportunity for new population settlement and human capital formation. Russia's reading of the Arctic is therefore based on *potentialities:* seen from Moscow, the Arctic is not the country's back door, but rather its potential twenty-first-century front door. However, what may seem obvious on a map or on paper is not necessarily destined to become a reality. At the beginning of the twentieth century, the Norwegian polar explorer Fridtjof Nansen (1861–1930) called the Russian North "the land of the future."[47] A century later, Russia still stands on the cusp of multiple potential Arctic futures.

The purpose of this book is to offer a comprehensive assessment of Russia's strategy in the Arctic. It investigates the multiple facets making Arctic questions a revelatory prism through which to view Russia's current changes and future challenges, and attempts to assemble them together into a coherent whole. The first chapter analyzes the Kremlin's formulation of its Arctic policies and the place of the region in its new nation-branding exercise on the international scene. The second chapter discusses the place of the Far North in Russia's statehood, especially the issue of a specific status for the Arctic regions and their population. The third investigates Russia's main domestic challenges, i.e., a fragmented territory and demographic crisis, and their implication for Arctic developments. The fourth looks briefly at expected climate change in the Arctic globally, and in Russia specifically, and at Moscow's ambiguous stance on climate change. The fifth chapter delves into the Russian position on territorial delimitation in the Arctic and the juridical conquest of the continental shelf. The sixth discusses the hard security issues and Russia's options for enhancing its strategic presence in the Arctic theater. The seventh examines the Arctic as a new economic Eldorado, as well as the relevance of Russian strategy in terms of hydrocarbons, minerals, and the fishing industry. Lastly, the eighth and final chapter scrutinizes hopes for transforming the Northern Sea Route into an international shipping line and an engine of Siberia's revival.

I would like to thank the Institute for European, Russian, and Eurasian Studies (IERES) at George Washington University, and its Arctic Research Group, for the extensive support provided in the making of this work, in particular the organizing of a "book incubator" session. I am particularly grateful to Oleg Anisimov, Caitlyn Antrim, Dmitri Gorenburg, Timothy Heleniak, Robert Orttung, Nikolay Shiklomanov, Dmitri Streletski, and Elana Wilson Rowe for their comments on the manuscript. I am also deeply thankful to Kelsey Nyland and Tim Swales, in the GW Geography Department, for their enthusiasm and commitment to creating the large majority of maps that illustrate the book.

Notes

1. R. Howard, *The Arctic Gold Rush: The New Race for Tomorrow's Natural Resources* (London and New York: Continuum, 2009). Several recent works examine the Arctic in the context of potential geopolitical and legal conflict. Cf. R. Sale, and E. Potapov, *The Scramble for the Arctic: Ownership, Exploitation and Conflict in the Far North* (London: Frances Lincoln, 2010); A. Anderson, *After the Ice: Life, Death, and Geopolitics in the New Arctic* (New York: Smithsonian Books, 2009); M. Byers, *Who Owns the Arctic? Understanding Sovereignty Disputes in the North* (Vancouver: Douglas and McIntyre, 2009); D. Fairhall, *Cold Front: Conflict Ahead in Arctic Waters* (London, New York: I. B. Tauris, 2010); B. Scott Zellen, *Arctic Doom, Arctic Boom? The Geopolitics of Climate Change in the Arctic* (Santa Barbara, Denver, Oxford: ABC Clio 2009). Note that many of these works deconstruct the region's potential for conflict.

2. Blog at WordPress.com, Jason Schaeffer, http://jasonschaeffer.wordpress.com/category/green/ (accessed November 12, 2012).

3. R. McGhee, *The Last Imaginary Place. A Human History of the Arctic World* (Chicago: The University of Chicago Press, 2005).

4. D. Wood, *The Power of Maps* (New York: The Guilford Press, 1992); J. Black, *Maps and Politics* (London: Reaktion Books Ltd., 1997); M. Monmonier, *Drawing the Line: Tales of Maps and Cartocontroversy* (New York: Henry Holt & Co., 1996).

5. C. Emmerson, *The Future History of the Arctic* (New York: Public Affairs, 2010).

6. *North Meets North. Navigation and the Future of the Arctic* (Reykjavik: Iceland Ministry for Foreign Affairs Working Group, 2005): 11.

7. NOAA, *State of the Arctic,* October 2006, http://www.pmel.noaa.gov/pubs/PDF/rich2952/rich2952.pdf (accessed November 14, 2012).

8. Fisheries and Aquaculture Department, FAO Major Fishing Areas, Arctic Sea (Major Fishing Area 18), http://www.fao.org/fishery/area/Area18/en (accessed November 12, 2012).

9. Arctic Council, maps, http://www.arctic-council.org/index.php/en/resources/other-resources/maps (accessed June 24, 2013).

10. See chapter 2.

11. T. Koivurova, "Governance of Protected Areas in the Arctic," *Utrecht Law Review* 5, no. 1 (2009): 128–159.

12. The Conservation of Arctic Flora and Fauna (CAFF), the Protection of the Arctic Marine Environment (PAME), Emergency Prevention, Preparedness, and Response Group (EPPR), and the Arctic Monitoring and Assessment Program (AMAP).

13. Koivurova, "Governance of Protected Areas in the Arctic," 128–159.

14. "The Barents Euro-Arctic Region Cooperation and Visions of the North," no date, http://www.bd.lst.se/publishedObjects/10000666/barentsbroschyr.pdf (accessed November 12, 2012).

15. A.J.K. Bailes, "Options for Closer Cooperation in the High North: What Is Needed?" in S.G. Holtsmark and B.A. Smith-Windsor, eds., *Security Prospects in the High North: Geostrategic Thaw or Freeze?* (Rome: NATO Defence College, 2009): 47–48.

16. A. Staalesen, "EU Eyes Breakthrough in Arctic Council," *Barents Observer,* September 10, 2012, http://barentsobserver.com/en/arctic/eu-eyes-breakthrough-arctic-council-10-09 (accessed November 12, 2012).

17. D.R. Rothwell, and C.C. Joyner, "Polar Oceans and the Law of the Sea," in A.G. Oude Elferink and D.R. Rothwell, eds., *The Law of the Sea and Polar Maritime Delimitation and Jurisdiction* (Leiden, Boston: Martinus Nijhoff Publishers, 2001), 1–22.

18. Steven Lee Myers, "Arctic Council adds 6 nations as observer states including China," *The New York Times*, May 15, 2013, http://www.nytimes.com/2013/05/16/world/europe/arctic-council-adds-six-members-including-china.html?_r=0 (accessed June 23, 2013).

19. L. Jakobson, "Northeast Asia Turns Its Attention to the Arctic," *NBR Analysis Brief,* December 2012.

20. L. Jakobson, "China and the Arctic: Cautious but Determined." Paper presented at the International Studies Association (ISA) Convention, San Diego, April 1–4, 2012.

21. C. Campbell, "China and the Arctic: Objectives and Obstacles," U.S.-China Economic and Security Review Commission Staff Research Report, April 13, 2012, http://origin.www.uscc.gov/sites/default/files/Research/China-and-the-Arctic_April 2012 (accessed November 15, 2012).

22. L. Jakobson, "China Prepares for an Ice-Free Arctic," *SIPRI Insights on Peace and Security,* no. 2, 2010; J. Spears, "The Snow Dragon Moves into the Arctic Ocean Basin," *China Brief* 11, no. 2 (2010), http://www.jamestown.org/single/?no_cache=1&tx_ttnews%5Btt_news%5D=37429 (accessed November 15, 2012).

23. "China to Open Int'l Institute for Arctic Studies," *English.news.cn*, August 18, 2012, http://news.xinhuanet.com/english/sci/2012–08/18/c_131793870.htm (accessed November 15, 2012).

24. H. Conley, T. Toland, J. Kraut, and A. Østhagen, "A New Security Architecture for the Arctic. An American Perspective" (Washington, DC: Center for Strategic and International Studies, CSIS Europe Report, January 2012): 13.

25. Ilulissat Declaration, May 28, 2008, http://www.sikunews.com/News/International/The-Ilulissat-Declaration-4833 (accessed May 23, 2011).

26. T. Koivurova, "Alternatives for an Arctic Treaty—Evaluation and a New Proposal," *European Community & International Environmental Law* 17, no. 1 (2008): 14–26.

27. O.R. Young, "Arctic Governance—Pathways to the Future," *Arctic Review on Law and Politics*, no. 1 (2010): 164–185.

28. A. Slizhevskii, "Arktika: eshche odna kholodnaia voina? [The Arctic: Again a Cold War?]," *Nezavisimoe voennoe obozrenie,* March 26, 2010, http://nvo.ng.ru/wars/2010–03–26/1_arctic.html (accessed November 18, 2012).

29. "Russian Air Force Exercise," *Barents Observer,* March 19, 2009, http://www.barentsobserver.com/russian-air-force-exercise.4568703–16149.html.

30. "Large Russian Military Exercise in Baltic Sea Area Involves Tens of Thousands of Troops," *Helsinki Sanomat,* August 20, 2009, http://www.hs.fi/english/article/Large+Russian+military+exercise+in+Baltic+Sea+area+involves+tens+of+thousands+of+troops/1135248663305 (accessed November 18, 2012).

31. *The U.S. Navy Arctic Road Map,* November 2009, http://www.navy.mil/navy-data/documents/USN_artic_roadmap.pdf (accessed November 18, 2012).

32. O. Tunander, "Geopolitics of the North: Geopolitik of the Weak. A Post–Cold War Return to Rudolf Kjellén," *Cooperation and Conflict* 43, no. 2 (2008): 164–184.

33. Howard, *The Arctic Gold Rush,* 70–71. See also M.H. Nordquist, J. Norton

Moore, and A.S. Skaridov, eds., *International Energy Policy, the Arctic and the Law of the Sea* (Leiden, Boston: Martinus Nijhoff, 2005); and K.N. Casper, "Oil and Gas Development in the Arctic: Softening of Ice Demands, Hardening of International Law," *Natural Resources Journal* 49 (2009): 825–881.

34. Bailes, "Options for Closer Cooperation in the High North: What Is Needed?" 32.

35. H. Conley, and J. Kraut, "U.S. Strategic Interests in the Arctic. An Assessment of Current Challenges and New Opportunities for Cooperation," *CSIS Europe Program Working Paper,* April 2010, http://csis.org/files/publication/100426_Conley_US Strategic Interests_Web.pdf.

36. For the Copenhagen school on securitization, see H. Stritzel, "Towards a Theory of Securitization: Copenhagen and Beyond," *European Journal of International Relations* 13, no. 3 (2007): 357–383.

37. Terence Armstrong, *Russian Settlement in the North* (Cambridge, UK: Cambridge University Press, 1965); Piers Horensma, *The Soviet Arctic* (London: Routledge, 1991); J. McCannon, *Red Arctic. Polar Exploration and the Myth of the North in the Soviet Union, 1932–1939* (New York: Oxford University Press, 1998).

38. H. Blakkisrud and G. Hønneland, eds., *Tackling Space: Federal Politics and the Russian North* (Lanham, Oxford: University Press of America, 2006); E. Wilson Rowe, ed., *Russia and the North* (Ottawa: University of Ottawa Press, 2009).

39. V.N. Konyshev, A.A. Sergunin, *Arktika v mezhdunarodnom politike. Sotrudnichestvo ili sopernichestvo?* [The Arctic in International Affairs. Cooperation or Competition?] (Moscow: RISI, 2011).

40. Speech of then Russian president Dmitri Medvedev at a meeting of the Russian Security Council on Protecting Russia's National Interests in the Arctic, September 17, 2008, http://eng.kremlin.ru/ text/speeches/2008/09/17/1945_type-82912type82913_206564.shtml (accessed February 24, 2010).

41. K. Åtland, "Mikhail Gorbachev, the Murmansk Initiative, and the Desecuritization of Interstate Relations in the Arctic, Cooperation and Conflict," *Journal of the Nordic International Studies Association* 43, no. 3 (2008): 289–311.

42. P. Baev, *Russia's Race for the Arctic and the New Geopolitics of the North Pole* (Washington, DC: The Jamestown Foundation, October 2007).

43. J.W. Parker, "Russia's Revival: Ambitions, Limitations, and Opportunities for the United States," *INSS Strategic Perspectives*, no. 3 (2011), 1.

44. P. Baev, and D. Trenin, *The Arctic. A View from Russia, 2010* (Moscow, Carnegie Center, 2010).

45. C.L. Antrim, "The Next Geographical Pivot. The Russian Arctic in the Twenty-first Century," *Naval War College Review* 63, no. 3 (2010): 15–37.

46. *Osnovy gosudarstvennoi politiki Rossiiskoi Federatsii v Arktike na period do 2020 g. i dal'neishuiu perspektivu* [Principles of State Policy of the Russian Federation in the Arctic up to 2020 and beyond], *Sovet Bezopasnosti Rossiiskoi Federatsii*, September 18, 2008, http://www.scrf.gov.ru/documents/98.html (accessed December 12, 2012).

47. F. Nansen, *Through Siberia—The Land of the Future* (New York: Frederick A. Stokes Co., 1914, republished by Books for Libraries Press, 1972).

Russia's Arctic Strategies and the Future of the Far North

Chapter 1

Russia's Arctic Policy and the Interplay of the Domestic and International

The Arctic does not constitute a specific domain of Russian policy. The region—in contrast, for example, with the North Caucasus—has not been singled out for special treatment and is largely integrated into countrywide processes. In fact, Arctic policy provides a very relevant example of the general processes of change under way in contemporary Russia: a recentralization of political authority to the detriment of the regions; collusion between political and economic interests in Putin's inner circle; an oscillation between the use of hard power and soft power tools; and the extensive interplay of the domestic and international environments. If Russia's policy for the Arctic is somehow unique, this is due to the high degree of symbolism that the region assumes for the authorities. Being an Arctic player is considered a matter of prestige and of recognition, often undermined, of Moscow's aspirations to great power status. The state-produced narrative on the role of Russia in this region of the world is therefore, like Janus, double faced: on the one hand, the rhetoric designed for domestic public consumption relies on older ideological sources, inspired by the Soviet legacy and the Cold War decades; on the other, that aimed abroad seeks to capitalize on the Arctic as a brand. This brand enables the Kremlin to position itself as an actor in touch with the international community, to renegotiate bilateral relations with the other Arctic players, and to advance mechanisms of legitimization based on soft power.

Discursive and Bureaucratic Production

In the 1990s, Moscow lost interest in the Arctic regions. Boris Yeltsin's offer to "take as much sovereignty as you can swallow," the first war in Chechnya, and the collapse of revenues and of state authority gave rise to a massive, chaotic, and quasi-spontaneous process of decentralization. The regions were forced to learn how to govern themselves.[1] Those that had the advantage of having extractive industries—for example, Tyumen'—were able to generate some public financing, whereas the others watched their budgets collapse and the industrial crisis turn into a general, social, and demographic crisis. The Arctic regions continued to receive the Northern deliveries (*severnyi zavoz*), mostly fuel and food products at a discounted rate, albeit markedly downsized in volume, and the state remained in charge of managing the railway system, but the majority of other state services vanished. At the administrative level, the State Committee for the Socio-economic Development of the North, the *Goskomsever*—created in 1992 but derived from an older Soviet structure—was charged with reformulating Russia's Arctic policy in the context of the transition to the market economy. Lacking in influence, its administrative fate was revealing of the authorities' persistent wavering. The State Committee was quickly downgraded, in 1993, to a simple Committee, *Roskomsever*, then integrated into the Ministry of Nationalities and Regional Policies, then reestablished as an autonomous entity, and was even abolished for a few months between 1998 and 1999.[2]

During Vladimir Putin's first two terms (2000–2008), Moscow brought to heel regional elites deemed to be bucking the system, and reasserted "the vertical of power" as the central mechanism of state functioning.[3] For the regions, the first concrete consequence was the end of the reign of the provincial barons, but equally a shifting of tax revenues to the federal state. The administrative recentralization led to a certain bureaucratic rationalization and to the progressive disappearance of the Ministry of Nationalities and other bureaucratic entities in charge of nationalities policy, also a legacy of the previous regime. The management of affairs in the Far North was then essentially the portfolio of the Ministry of Economic Development and Trade, before being transferred to the Ministry of Regional Development in 2004. Within this latter body, different administrative entities—committees, agencies, ad hoc groups—all share responsibility for various Arctic issues.[4] They are preoccupied with the day-to-day management of the Soviet legacy and are therefore not influential as sites in the production of a new strategy.

Since 2000, the Kremlin's revived interest in the Arctic region essentially has been manifest in a great deal of technocratic activity, resulting in a profusion of policy guidelines that were complemented by detailed programs under various ministries and governmental agencies. Russia's main Arctic policy documents above all took strategic and economic considerations into account.[5] A first state strategy for the Arctic was published in 2001, and although it was not implemented, it signaled that the region was once again included in Moscow's global security concerns. During his second term, Vladimir Putin re-emphasized the Arctic's strategic importance for Russia, with among other things a report completed in 2004 by the Russian State

Council Working Group on National Security Interests in the Far North. Finally in 2008, a second Arctic Strategy of the Russian Federation through 2020—drafted under the auspices of the Security Council—defined the main goals and strategic priorities of Russia in the Arctic, including socioeconomic development, military security, environmental security, science, technology, and population challenges.[6] In this document the Arctic is explicitly presented as "the main strategic base for Russian natural resources" in the twenty-first century.[7] The National Security Strategy of the Russian Federation through 2020, released in 2009, also emphasizes the quest for energy resources, which are considered to be the potential means for Russia to remain a great power. The document confirms Russia's interest in the Arctic, which is elevated to the status of the Caspian Sea and Central Asia as one of the main energy battlegrounds of the future.[8]

Russian projections of power in the Arctic (or rather articulations thereof) progressed rather distinctly throughout the 2000s.[9] The first Arctic Policy of 2001 outlined traditional military tensions in the region, projected as a new zone of conflicts of interest and of rivalry for spheres of influence among great powers. The 2008 second Arctic Policy departed from the belligerent rhetoric of its predecessor. It notably mentions the multitude of nontraditional risks and the need for international cooperation among coastal countries, in particular in terms of search and rescue systems.[10] Under the auspices of the project launched by then President Dmitri Medvedev for a revised European security architecture, the Arctic was presented as a region requiring cooperation between Europe and Russia.[11] Potential tensions with NATO were relegated to the background, and only materialized in terms of the nuclear deterrent, and to a lesser extent naval capabilities. The National Security Strategy for 2020 also advances more nuanced and subtle arguments, reflecting Russia's changed perception of the international security environment. The concept defines security much more broadly, and includes energy security, soft security challenges, the environment, health, education, technologies, and living standards.[12]

As a result of these renewed strategic interests, several other legal texts were adopted: a new Russian maritime doctrine through 2020; many decrees on the modernization of the Russian Armed Forces, development plans for naval construction, maritime transport, and the fishing industry; a state policy for maritime military activities; and a defense strategy for state borders, inland waters, territorial seas, the continental shelf, and exclusive economic zones. Russia's Arctic strategy can be compared to Norway's in terms of its holistic character, a feature that is less evident among the other Arctic players.[13] However, as often in Russian history, this bureaucratic production only impacted in a marginal way the realities on the ground, and many of the texts remained "dead letters." Despite the creation of a Russian Arctic Council in 2007 (tasked with coordinating the multiple policies toward the region), federal ministries, agencies, committees, and region-level administrations and programs still face difficulties in interacting with one another.[14] However, the recentralization of administrative authority among federal bodies, the fundamental changes of the center-periphery relationship, the revival of key sectors linked to the military-industrial complex, and the dynamism of the Russian economy in the 2000s, boosted by the elevated prices of hydrocarbons, all have altered the Arctic order. There have been many failures, but several projects have borne fruit, and the (positive) difference between today's Arctic regions under development and the 1990s Arctic regions in crisis, is palpable.

Russia's Decision Making Regarding Arctic Affairs

The four key elements below define the current decision-making process on Arctic affairs in Russia.

Arctic Policy Is a Centralized Process

Arctic decision making relies mostly on the presidential administration and the Security Council of the Russian Federation, thus confirming the priority accorded to a strategic reading of the region. Economic considerations are also central, but the input from the Ministry of Natural Resources is limited; major Russian firms all have direct access to Putin's inner circle without any need for mediation by the ministry. Regional development, social, indigenous, and environmental issues are situated far lower on the list of priorities. They are not ignored, but instead must find a place within the grand design constructed by the Kremlin. The input of the regional elite, as well as circles of experts, is even more limited.

Arctic Policy Is Plural

Several different Arctic policies coexist, often poorly coordinated. For Arctic affairs, as for everything else, the Russian decision-making chain is complex. Decisions made in high places do not necessarily make their way back down the administrative pyramid.[15] The local elite along with their bureaucracies have a strong power of inertia, which affords a way for them to resist changes they do not support. Conversely, local needs are difficult to articulate at higher levels of the administrative hierarchy, and are often not properly taken into account. Success in implementing efficiently any decision therefore depends on personal connections: those regions with their own associates in Putin's inner circle and/or the presidential administration are able to make themselves heard and have their needs considered. The republic of Yakutia-Sakha was, for example, able to assume a privileged status thanks to Mikhail Nikolayev, its president from 1991 to 2002, who was a close associate of Boris Yeltsin. However, in the 2000s, these "feudal presidents" were progressively replaced and access to the central administration went through the oligarchs: Russia's fifth richest person, Roman Abramovich, served as governor of Chukotka from 2000 to 2008, and the former Noril'sk Nickel CEO Aleksandr Khloponin was governor of the Krasnoyarsk region from 2002 to 2010. Thanks to them, both regions were able to voice their concerns in Moscow. But the political game in some Arctic regions is shifting: the presidential party United Russia, already weakened in Moscow and Saint Petersburg, is not always in a position of strength. Influential in the Yamalo-Nenets district of Tyumen', it will likely have to contend with social discontent in the regions of Murmansk and Arkhangel'sk.[16] These political shifts intensify the absence of policy coordination.

Two Differing Arctic Strategies Discerned

Schematically speaking, at least two Arctic strategies can be discerned. The first one focuses on a "security-first" reading of the region. This is the one defended by the Security Council, the Armed Forces, and the military-industrial complex, as well as by security services such as the FSB (Federal Security Service, successor of the KGB), and it enjoys Vladimir Putin's direct patronage. This "security-first" strategy endorses the Arctic as the main outpost of Russia's reassertion as a great power—as a theater where Russia's revival of great power status can be forcefully expressed. The exploitation of resources is not forgotten in this strategy, but it is subjected to security imperatives, and foreign presence must be curbed.

The second approach, "cooperation first," is essentially motivated by an economic reading of the Arctic. Under this strategy, in order to develop its potential, Russia must be open to foreign influence, both in terms of investment and with respect to sharing expertise; and private actors, whether Russians or foreigners, have to play an increasingly important role, because the state alone cannot provide all the necessary support. This is the view promoted by the Ministry of Natural Resources as well as by several Russian economic actors, and it has the support of less influential Arctic circles, such as the Ministry of Regional Development. During Dmitri Medvedev's presidency (2008–2012), one may have been led to think that the new president advocated this second strategy, given his greater sensitivity to issues related to Russia's need for "modernization." However, his return to the subordinate status of prime minister has deprived this second strategy of its herald.

Arctic Policy Is Driven by Leading Figures and their Corporate Strategies

Arctic affairs are by no means unique, and on the contrary are part of the mainstream of Russia's current political system. Those societal sectors considered as non-strategic—i.e., those that do not involve the country's sovereignty, security, or political stability—function in a relatively democratic, decentralized manner. Conversely, domains judged strategic are tightly controlled and are ordered according to informal pyramids of power.[17] Numerous parallel institutions created in the 2000s—what Richard Sakwa has called the Putin regime's para-constitutionalism (the seven federal districts affiliated with the presidency, the State Council, the Presidential Council for the realization of national projects, the Public Chamber)[18]—make it possible to appoint figures from the private sector or from the security services to important positions, without having to subject such appointments to an election or legislative approval. Putin's inner circle maintains close supervision over economic activities in multiple ways: this can occur via their occupying government positions, but also by being board members of energy companies, as well as through family networks or informal schemes.

Many facets of the Arctic make it part of Putin's "personal business," which in part explains the renewed interest in the region and the centralization of decision making that affects it. First, the main figures of Putin's inner circle, Viktor Zubkov, Sergei Ivanov, Igor Sechin, Sergei Naryshkin, and Dmitri Medvedev, all have multiple relations with the main state corporations, including: in the energy domain, Gazprom, followed by Rosneft and Rosneftegas; in the electricity sector, Inter RAO-UES and Rosatom; in the defense industries, Rostekhnologii, the military holding company Almaz-Antey, and United Aircraft Corporation; and in the transport domain, United Shipbuilding Corporation, Aeroflot, and Sovcomflot. Several of these companies are active in the Arctic region. Second, Putin's personal circles, built around the Ozero Cooperative in the second half of the 1990s, also include Vladimir Yakunin, CEO of the Russian Railways (a key actor in Arctic transportation) and such personalities as Gennadi Timchenko, and Yuri and Mikhail Kovalchuk.[19] This node is the most "business-oriented," the most connected to the private sector, and also the least bureaucratic, in the sense that its key figures, the Kovalchuk brothers and Timchenko, do not have any position in the government. Through the Rossiya Bank, they have personal (both direct and indirect) assets in Nord Stream AG, which manages Gazprom's

North European Gas Pipeline project; Lentransgaz, a Gazprom subsidiary currently in charge of the very strategic Yamal-Europe gas pipeline; the Vyborg shipbuilding yard; the Clearlake Shipping company, the Ust-Luga oil terminal; Transoil (Russia's largest oil transporter by rail); Stroytransgaz (Russia's largest contractor in the construction of gas infrastructure); and some assets in the oil trading company Surguteks and in Novatek, Russia's largest private natural gas producer.[20] Putin's inner circle's interest in the Arctic development is thus partly shaped by private interests.

The Arctic as a Flagship for Putin-Style Statehood

The Russian state's renewed interest in the Arctic is also part of a larger context—the reassertion of patriotism as a tool fostering political legitimacy. During Vladimir Putin's first two terms, the Kremlin institutionalized patriotism as the new ideological matrix of the presidential party, United Russia.[21] State patriotic education programs and the return of large historical commemorations have worked to cultivate a sense of national pride, and the revival of the Russian *derzhavnost'* ("great powerness") has been presented as a unifying political program. In an address to the Federal Assembly in April 2005, Putin acknowledged that "the collapse of the Soviet Union was the greatest geopolitical catastrophe of the century,"[22] a statement approved by more than three-fourths of the Russian population, although long regarded as politically incorrect during Yeltsin's decade in power. While the desire to regain the geopolitical power lost in 1991 is openly stated, Soviet symbols have not been restored for their ideological value—communism itself has not been rehabilitated—but because they are part of a cultural background common to a large part of the population and are seen as an indication of normalcy. The Soviet Union indeed enjoys a positive image in Russian public opinion.[23]

From the Kremlin's viewpoint, the return to a great power status materializes via Russia's reassertion of its role in the international arena, and via the revival of sectors that classically define a great power, such as the military-industrial complex, in particular aviation and the navy. This Soviet-style "great power" model goes hand-in-hand with the domestic legitimacy strategies put in place by Putin since the start of the 2000s. Kremlin-fostered patriotism promotes masculine and virile values, embodied by Putin himself, who presents himself as a hardened sportsman, military man, and outdoor enthusiast who appreciates the harshness of nature.[24] However, under the presidency of Dmitri Medvedev, state propaganda changed its tack by emphasizing the need for "modernization." This narrative essentially underscored Russia's need for innovative industries, information technologies, and nanotechnologies, and also implied that changes in Russia's economic structures would naturally impact its political system.[25] This modernization narrative did not really come to life, however, and since Putin's third term starting in 2012 has in any case been set aside, because the new/old president is again giving priority to the classical, militarized symbols of power. For the Arctic focus, this change has had little immediate impact: the two competing paradigms—that of triumphant military industries and that of new technologies, that of hard power or soft power—both accord very well with the Arctic, as manifest in the classic symbols of the industrial-military complex as much as through the modernization narrative.

Transforming the Arctic into a flagship for Russia's new nationhood crystallized as a Kremlin strategy during the second half of the 2000s, at the same time as increasing international debate came to focus on the region. The Kremlin first chose to favor a bellicose discourse in which the Arctic was presented as the future site of a new Cold War. This strategy was embodied in the president's special representative for cooperation in the Arctic and Antarctic, the famous polar explorer Arthur Chilingarov, a member of United Russia and close associate of Putin. During the Polar Year in 2007, he organized a helicopter flight to the South Pole and the Amundsen-Scott station in the company of Nikolai Patrushev, then director of the FSB, and led the highly publicized Russian expedition to the North Pole. The nuclear icebreaker *Rossiia* and research ship *Akademik Fedorov* reached the North Pole, where two deep-water submersibles, Mir-1 and Mir-2, were launched to plant a Russian flag on the Arctic seabed, at a depth of about 4,300 meters.[26] Chilingarov stated that "we have exercised the maritime right of the first night,"[27] while in 2009, he again bluntly asserted that "we will not give the Arctic to anyone."[28] Although his remarks do not correspond with the legal position of the Russian state, whose claims strictly respect international laws, they have never been rejected by the Kremlin. Putin is in fact perfectly happy with the provocative character of Chilingarov, whose declarations are essentially addressed to a domestic audience.

Presenting the Arctic as the scene of a new race among great powers makes it possible to portray Russia once again as a besieged fortress, caught in a viselike grip by the advance of NATO. The comments of Russian officials on the Arctic are thus marked by old patterns of resentment toward the West and especially the United States. In 2009 the FSB director Nikolai Patrushev stated that "the United States, Norway, Denmark, and Canada are conducting a united and coordinated policy of barring Russia from the riches of the shelf. It is quite obvious that much of this doesn't coincide with the economic, geopolitical, and defense interests of Russia, and constitutes a systemic threat to its national security. . . . Further into the future it will be simply too late, they will drive us away from here."[29] The idea that there is a "united and coordinated" alliance of the other Arctic coastal states against Russia is part of a conspiracy narrative that is widespread in the country.[30] In 2010, Dmitri Medvedev himself mentioned, without qualifying what he had in mind, that "Regrettably, we have seen attempts to limit Russia's access to the exploration and development of the Arctic mineral resources. . . . That is absolutely inadmissible from the legal viewpoint and unfair given our nation's geographical location and history."[31]

This Cold War memory is broadly prevalent in all the publications devoted to the Arctic.[32] Russian experts on issues of maritime territorial delimitations all harbor feelings of resentment. The dominant opinion among them is that Russia lost or ceded much more territory than it had to. According to some of them, about 3 million square kilometers of land in North America (including Alaska and California) had been sold for a negligible amount in the nineteenth century.[33] A large area of the Bering Sea was also ceded too easily to the United States in 1990, as were territories in the Barents Sea to Norway in 2010. According to Alexander Oreshenkov, expert in Arctic international legislation, "the sphere of Russia's jurisdiction over the continental shelf within the limits of its polar sector could be expanded by about 1.5 million square kilometers even without any request if it used the norms of international law and national legislation more expediently."[34] Other researchers, such as G.K. Voitolovsky, a member of the Scientific Advisory Council of the Maritime Board under the Government, have asked that Russia withdraw its 2001 claims to the UN Commission on the Limits of the Continental Shelf (CLCS, see below) and refuse any territorial restrictions as long as the United States does not play by the same rules and the coastal states have not settled their border disputes—this so that an international Arctic zone does not appear that would encroach on potential Russian territory.[35]

The will to turn the Arctic into a component of the state-centric patriotic narrative was reinforced in 2009 by the decision to revive the Russian Geographical Society, itself born in 1845 as part of the imperial drive for territorial expansion and exploration of the country's natural resources, and to turn it into one of the Kremlin's flagships. The then Minister of Emergency Situations, Sergey Shoigu, was appointed its president, while Putin assigned himself the post of Council of Trustees' chairman. Putin has not concealed his desire to have the activities of the Geographical Society focus on the main state-sponsored projects: "The Society can offer practical support to our plans to develop East Siberia and the Far East, Yamal and the north of the Krasnoyarsk region, to participate actively in further research projects in the Arctic and Antarctica, as well as environmental support of the Olympic Games in Sochi."[36] As it is directly connected to the Kremlin, the society benefits from privileged grants, and is seeking to coordinate scientific projects on the Arctic. Its mission is not so much to engage in fundamental research as to perform applied research on projects that have been decided upon by the authorities.[37]

Despite this institutional enhancement via the Geographical Society, the Arctic remains a theme that is little discussed in Russian public space. Between the Kremlin's media hype concerning the "Arctic race" and the articles of experts published for limited circulation in specialized academic journals, the public does not have much to read. General yet serious articles are far and few between, and the journal *Russia in Global Affairs,* run by Fedor Lukyanov, is practically the only one that regularly discusses the issue's importance for Russia.[38] The formation of public opinion that is correctly informed and able to decide whether it wishes to engage in a financial, technological, and human commitment to Arctic conquest has not yet taken shape. The Arctic continues to be a concern of the state elites, not of the Russian society as whole.

An Internationally Recognized "Brand" for Russia

During Putin's first two terms, Russian leaders have openly voiced their disillusionment and frustration with their European and American partners. They have also desired that Russia be resurrected and counted as a great power, with no obligation to limit its own interests in the name of any solidarity with the West. As with other international issues, President Vladimir Putin has been sending mixed messages on the Arctic to the international community. Moscow played an undeniable role in the escalation of self-assertive rhetoric when the Russian flag was planted on the Arctic seabed in 2007, giving voice to Chilingarov's provocative speeches. However, since 2008–2009, Moscow has been noticeably focused on creating a highly cooperative "Arctic brand" and positioning itself as the co-leader of any prospective international cooperation on the region. At the time of the Arctic Forum in September 2010, then Prime Minister Putin stated that:

> While we are taking care of a steady and balanced development of the Russian North, we are working to strengthen our ties with our neighbors in our common Arctic home. And we think that preserving the Arctic as a zone of peace and cooperation is of the utmost importance. It is our conviction that the Arctic area should serve as a platform for uniting forces for genuine partnership in the economy, security, science, education and the preservation of the North's cultural heritage.[39]

The creation of this Arctic brand is part of a more general reflection on the question of nation-branding. In Russia the general feeling is that formerly the Soviet Union, and now the Russian Federation, has systematically lost the information war and has been unable to succeed in its "conquest for hearts and minds." This has led to the consideration of new mechanisms of influence and soft power, something that the country has not mastered since the great era of Soviet propaganda. The idea that the West's appeal is in decline throughout the world, and that the global competition between world powers has acquired a "civilizational dimension," as expressed in the Foreign Policy Concept of 2008,[40] have structured the logics of promoting Russia abroad. This can be seen in the English-language TV channel *Russia Today*, the Paris- and New York-based Institute for Democracy and Cooperation, and the *Russkii Mir* foundation headed by Kremlin-connected Viacheslav Nikonov, which promotes Russian language and culture beyond Russia's borders and tries to associate the Russian-speaking diaspora with the reassessment of the Russian state.[41] This idea of Russia as a brand that can be capitalized on abroad among countries and peoples that are critical of "American domination" is particularly present among the pro-presidential youth movements. One such youth movement, the Nashi affiliate *Stal'* (Steel), has for instance made its main objective to "develop pro-Russian networks abroad, with the goal of creating a positive image of Russia, and this will give us a strategic superiority. We will change the world, turning ignorance and incomprehension of Russia into respect and even into a fashion[able image] for [Russia]."[42]

In this context, the Arctic presents itself an opportunity not to be squandered. The media focus is considerable, with the issue enjoying international visibility, involving countries from the West, rising powers, first and foremost China and India, but also Latin America, the Middle East, and Africa. The Arctic also makes it possible to modify Russia's image as a polluting industrial power for which environmental issues are unimportant, and that has no definite public stance on climate change. It offers unique possibilities for Russia to turn its competition with the United States to its advantage, particularly given the latter's non-ratification of the Kyoto Protocol. In this vein, polluting Russia is cast as a thing of the past, something that was part of the Soviet heritage, whereas the new Russia, the Russia of the future, projects itself as a clean power. The need to participate in a world narrative about preserving nature is also visible in the growing interest that the Russian Geographical Society grants to these questions, clearly inspired by the model of the National Geographic Society in the United States. In 2010 Putin has announced the creation of a "Russian Arctic" national park to develop ecological tourism in the Far North.[43]

The Russian official narrative has thus evolved toward a celebration of the Arctic region as a space of international cooperation. Putin, Medvedev, and the Minister of Foreign Affairs, Sergey Lavrov, have continuously strived to cultivate a discourse promoting a "dialogue of cultures" in the Arctic. This can be explained by the evolution of the international context (the Obama administration's "reset policy" or Medvedev's softer discourse as compared to Putin's), but also because the Kremlin has understood the potential of the Arctic topic as a strategic communication tool. The first international forum "The Arctic: Territory of Dialogue," held in Moscow in September 2010, was an occasion to play this card with success, in particular thanks to Prince Albert of Monaco and President of Iceland Ólafur Ragnar Grímsson, whose presence guaranteed that the event was in the international media spotlight.[44] This event is now repeated almost every year in the hope of promoting not an *Arctic Race* between great powers, but a *Polar Saga* of humanity, among other things, under Russian co-leadership.

This cooperative pattern is based on the already long and positive role played by Russia in Arctic institutions. Even though Moscow has traditionally been disdainful of multilateral organizations with exclusively consultative functions,[45] it is a determined actor both in the Arctic Council and in the Barents Euro-Arctic Council. It played a very constructive role in the discussions on joint research and sea rescue systems (SAR),[46] and in developing scientific cooperation. In the framework of international debates concerning the delimitation of the continental shelf, Russian scientists have shared the charts, maps, and data used in their 2001 submission to the UN Commission on the Limits of the Continental Shelf and have declassified some materials collected by the armed forces. Despite state competition, Russian and Canadian scientists are exchanging information on the Lomonosov Ridge. In 2007, Canadian, Danish, and Russian officials, all of them representatives of their respective ministries or departments of natural resources, discussed deepening their collaboration in the Arctic.[47]

If cooperation patterns are clearly dominant and Russia has succeeded in building, at least in part, an internationally recognized brand for itself on the Arctic issue, it remains an actor whose agenda is not fully in harmony with that of the other Arctic players. Russia indeed defends its own strategic and political objectives and considers it has no reason to yield to the majority opinion on several points. First, Moscow remains negative about NATO's potential role in the Arctic region. Regular declarations by Sergey Lavrov on NATO's having no role to play in the region illustrate the Russian viewpoint,[48] as does the 2009 National Security Strategy, according to which NATO involvement in the region would amount to a return to a Cold War logic.[49] Second, Russia's position is conservative concerning the status granted to non-Arctic states and institutions within the Arctic Council: it is reluctant to provide full observer member status to the European Union and is even more disturbed by the growing role demanded by China. Moscow is a status quo power in the Arctic in terms of institutional design and does not desire to strengthen the existing portfolio of regional organizations.

Third, Russia's position is at odds with the international community's concerning indigenous peoples' rights and voices. For reasons that are as much historical as demographic and political, Russia's perception of the Arctic devotes little attention to indigenous peoples and does not view them as actors who should enjoy any privileged status.[50] The Russian Association of Indigenous Peoples of the North (RAIPON) is the main institutional body, working as an umbrella organization for smaller associations representing 41 indigenous groups whose total population is roughly 300,000. RAIPON enjoys significant international visibility, which is not always to the liking of the Russian authorities. It has permanent participant status in the Arctic Council's Indigenous Peoples' Secretariat, is a member of the United Nations Economic and Social Council, the UN Permanent Forum on Indigenous Issues, the UN Expert Mechanism on the Rights of Indigenous Peoples (EMRIP), and the UN Working Group on the issue of human rights and transnational corporations and other business enterprises, and is an observer in the Governing Council/Global Ministerial Environment Forum of the United Nations Environment Program.[51]

RAIPON thus has several international platforms through which to apply pressure on Moscow and to express its concerns about environmental degradation and insufficient indigenous autonomy. Relations between the Russian authorities and RAIPON are difficult and have deteriorated over recent years. In November 2012, the Ministry of Justice ordered the closure of the association on the grounds that it does not fulfill the very strict conditions imposed by the new legislation on NGOs.[52] It was authorized to continue its activities after some legal changes and a turn over at the highest level of the organization. If RAIPON's difficulties are indeed part of the general context of Russia's hardening stance toward civil society, other, more specific motives also are in play: the association is criticized off the record for its high levels of corruption, and it seems to have voiced its concerns a little too loudly against certain large Russian companies involved in developing new industrial infrastructure in southern Siberia.[53]

The Arctic: A Soft Power Tool for Bilateral Relations?

Russia's bilateral relationship with other Arctic players is built on a game of mirrors. The gamut of its positions is therefore very wide, ranging from the reciprocally bellicose exchanges with Canada, its competition/collaboration with the United States for the title of "Arctic knowledge power," up to the multitude of pragmatic forms of cooperation that it has put into place with

European countries. Globally, the Arctic is positioned as one of the regions in which the opportunities for cooperation between Russia and Western countries are the greatest: the feeling of having contradictory geopolitical agendas here is far less than in the other post-Soviet spaces (Ukraine, the Caucasus, and Central Asia), and the perception of long-term threats there is largely similar.

The Canada-Russia relationship has become increasingly focused on the Arctic question in recent years. In the 1990s and early 2000s, Ottawa took it upon itself to integrate Russia more firmly into the concert of Arctic nations working on environmental issues and the participation of indigenous people.[54] In 2007, however, Canadian politicians took a dim view of the planting of the Russian flag on the Arctic seabed and of Chilingarov's provocative declarations. Canadian Foreign Affairs Minister Peter MacKay stated that humanity was no longer living in the Middle Ages and that it was not sufficient to plant a flag to lay claim to the possession of a territory, while Prime Minister Stephen Harper declared in Nunavut that "Canada's new government understands that the first principle of Arctic sovereignty is: use it or lose it."[55] In the Canadian press, discourses on Russia's warmongering have multiplied, in particular when reporting the flights of Russian bomber planes above the Arctic, regardless of the fact that they do not violate Canadian airspace. The legal debates over whether the Lomonosov and Mendeleev Ridges belong to the North American or the Eurasian continent have sharpened this conflictual reading of things, and the Nanook military exercises in the Canadian High North have been revived at a steady rate.

As a new flagship of Canadian nationhood, the Arctic issue led Ottawa to take a more assertive position on the question of ownership of the Northwest Passage. In 2009, the decision—approved almost unanimously by the House of Commons despite protests from Inuit communities—to change the name of the Northwest Passage to the "Canadian Northwest Passage" confirmed state sensitivity with respect to territorial sovereignty in the Arctic.[56] The narrative on the Arctic as Canada's last frontier has not gone unnoticed in Russia, most of whose self-assertive discourses are targeted at Ottawa, whether by name or not.[57] This deterioration of the bilateral relationship in the name of nation-making symbols is especially harmful, as the two countries have never had strong geopolitical antagonisms. Canada is seeking to assert itself on the international scene independently of the United States,[58] and both Russia and Canada have a shared view on the question of the Northwest and Northeast Passages as national waters. Far from the narrative posted up for domestic public opinion, Russian-Canadian cooperation in the Arctic has developed in recent years and should continue to improve further in the years ahead.

Russia's relationship with the United States is by definition more ambivalent, because several elements external to the Arctic as such intervene to disrupt the discussion. The old Cold War antagonisms have not yet departed the collective mindset. Several current elements can be added to this. On the Russian side, a refusal to ratify the treaty of territorial delimitation in the Bering Sea keeps alive tensions with Washington and fuels the memory of the humiliating years of *perestroika*.[59] On the US side, the non-ratification of UNCLOS by the world's foremost maritime power confirms Russians' perception of the United States as a unilateral power that refuses to apply any binding agreements to itself, but is bent on applying them to the rest of the world.[60] The Russian elites also consider that the refusal of Western capitals and of NATO to discuss openly questions of Arctic security, soft and hard, opens the door to a strategic uncertainty that obliges Moscow to react in a defensive way. Moreover, the state of Alaska at times speaks out loudly against any enhancement of US-Russia cooperation in the Arctic, and this impedes the White House and fuels anti-American narratives on the Russian side. Despite the common projects such as the Joint Russian-American Long-term Census of the Arctic (RUSALCA), the number of bilateral scientific and cultural activities remains at a low level.[61] However, the United States is cultivating its image as a knowledge power on the Arctic, a title to which Russia also aspires. Fields of cooperation in this domain are therefore multiple, and Moscow hopes the United States will truly appreciate and value its academic and applied knowledge on the Far North.

With Europe, and more precisely with the Nordic countries, Russia has managed to construct a more privileged and pragmatic relationship. This is a notable departure from the Cold War, when the North Sea-Baltic Sea zone constituted an area of considerable tension between the two blocs. The Scandinavian countries are far from being pro-Russian, for historical (old historical rivalry between the Czarist empire and the Kingdom of Sweden; tensions with Helsinki relating to the low level of autonomy of Finland during the Soviet period and memories of the war of 1939–1940; and for Norway, geopolitical tensions between NATO and the Warsaw Pact), political (criticisms of Putin's regime), and geopolitical (the debate surrounding Russia's Nord Stream natural gas pipeline in Sweden) reasons. Nonetheless, Norway, Finland, and Sweden all have succeeded in developing multiple bilateral projects with Russia, as much at the state level as between border regions; this is the case despite some clashes of perceptions.[62]

Finnish and Norwegian experiences from border management and cross-border cooperation with Russia are considered as best practices that can be exported to other European border regions.[63] The cross-border flows between Karelia, Murmansk, and Arkhangel'sk on one hand and Finnmark, Lapland,

and Finnish Karelia on the other have grown rapidly and have positively altered the daily relations between border populations. Both Norway and Finland issued a record number of Schengen visas to Russian border populations in 2012. The small Norwegian city of Kirkenes has become an important tourist and shopping center for Russians on the other side of the border. Furthermore, cultural exchange programs, including student exchanges (for instance between the Arkhangel'sk-based Northern Arctic Federal University and Tromsø University), and regional collaboration in the environmental, shipping, and fishing domains have all flourished.[64] For Russia, the Nordic dimension constitutes an increasingly important element of its relationship with Europe, not least as the Scandinavian countries have become familiar and predictable neighbors. For Europe as a whole (i.e., the European Union, its member states, and non-EU European countries such as Norway), the capacity to build partnerships with Russia in the Baltic Sea–North Sea–Arctic regions is a positive engine of the global Europe-Russia partnership, which has been weakened by many problems, from establishing a visa-free system to energy cooperation.

Within only a few years, the Arctic has become a component—one among many others—both of Kremlin-led domestic policies and legitimacy strategies, and of Russia's renewed international brand. The authorities' difficulties in realizing the numerous policy documents adopted for the development of the Arctic region highlight broader problems, mainly the state's inefficiency in implementing decisions. Often projects promulgated by the central authorities see the light of day only thanks to personal, business-related connections. To circumvent these problems, Putin's inner circle has engineered micromanagement mechanisms for the issues it considers crucial, whether Arctic projects, the APEC summit in Vladivostok in September 2012, or the staging of the 2014 Winter Olympics in Sochi.[65] The Kremlin's management of the Arctic in this sense is nothing special, inasmuch as it has encountered the same types of problems afflicting all Russian policy, and has employed some of the same solutions to overcome them.

But the Arctic is also an ideological symbol for the Kremlin both on the domestic scene and in the international arena. The thundering declarations of Artur Chilingarov on the "Arctic race" and muscle-flexing by the main figures of Putin's inner circle are part of the classic arsenal of political communication in Russia today. The region provides a magnificent stage on which to employ these tools of communication. In the international arena, Russia's stance is more nuanced, and varies depending on the topics under discussion. It is in an awkward position on some elements on which it has a divergent agenda from the other Arctic players (the role of NATO, indigenous issues, the claims of non-Arctic players), but Russia otherwise aims to harmonize with the international community by displaying its support for polar knowledge, the need for a coordinated search and rescue system, and its concerns for preserving the fragile Arctic ecosystems. Multilateralism and sustainability have thus become part of the Russian thematic arsenal on the Arctic, even if questions can be raised about Moscow's real desire to take environmental issues into account. The Arctic framework, more cooperative than confrontational, has probably acted as a process for Russia's "socialization," defined in international relations as the transmission of the rules and guidelines to states and their leaders concerning how they are supposed to behave in the international system.[66]

Russia's Arctic policy also makes it possible to renegotiate its bilateral relations. In this process, Moscow seems to define its strategy by mirroring its partners, as evidenced by its bellicose rhetoric against Canadian self-assertiveness, its hesitation toward its American ally/rival, and its constructive neighborhood partnerships with the Nordic countries. Why this multiplicity of facets? Russia's main agenda in the Arctic is to be recognized as a key stakeholder. As long as it perceives that it is not being marginalized, it privileges a cooperative rather than a competitive framework with the other Arctic states, an approach that is less costly and from which Moscow indeed stands to gain some advantage. Arctic issues therefore occupy a paradoxical position in Russia's new statehood, both overestimated and under-discussed. It is a way of simultaneously affirming Russia's uniqueness and its desire to be viewed as a "normal" country by the international community, repeating old patterns of being the *other* Europe.[67]

Notes

1. G.P. Herd and A. Aldis, *Russian Regions and Regionalism: Strength through Weakness* (London: Routledge, 2002).

2. P.D. Waisberg, "Emerging Configurations of Indigenous Status in Post-Soviet Russia." Paper presented at the Annual Meeting of American Association for the Advancement of Slavic Studies, Pittsburgh, November 21–24, 2002.

3. R. Sakwa, *Putin, Russia's Choice* (London: Routledge, 2007).

4. H. Blakkisrud, "What's to Be Done with the North?" in Blakkisrud and Hønneland, eds., *Tackling Space: Federal Politics and the Russian North*, (Lanham, Oxford: Oxford University Press, 2006), 25–51.

5. For details, see K. Zysk, "Russia's Arctic Strategy: Ambitions and Constraints," *Joint Force Quarterly,* no. 57 (2010): 103–110.

6. *Osnovy gosudarstvennoi politiki Rossiiskoi Federatsii v Arktike na period do 2020 g. i dal'neishuiu perspektivu* [Principles of State Policy of the Russian Federation in the Arctic up to 2020 and beyond], *Sovet Bezopasnosti Rossiiskoi Federatsii,* September 18, 2008, http://www.scrf.gov.ru/documents/98.html (accessed December 12, 2012).

7. "Vystuplenie na zasedanii Soveta Bezopasnosti, 'O zashchite national'nykh interesov Rossii v Arktike' [Address at session of the Security Council 'On protecting the national interests of Russia in the Arctic']", *Kremlin.ru*, September 17, 2008, http://www.kremlin.ru/transcripts/1433 (accessed October 24, 2012).

8. On the "National Security Strategy of the Russian Federation until 2020," *Russian Analytical Digest*, no. 62 (2009).

9. R. Kefferpütz, "On Thin Ice? (Mis)interpreting Russian Policy in the High North," *CEPS Policy Brief*, no. 205, February 2010; K. Roberts, "Jets, Flags, and a New Cold War? Demystifying Russia's Arctic Intentions," *International Journal*, Autumn (2010): 957–976.

10. K. Zysk, "Russia's Arctic Strategy: Ambitions and Constraints," 103–110.

11. B. Lo, "Medvedev and the New European Security Architecture," *CER Policy Brief*, July 2009, http://www.cer.org.uk/pdf/pbrief_medvedev_july09.pdf (accessed October 24, 2012).

12. S.J. Main, *The Mouse that Roared, or the Bear that Growled? Russia's Latest Military Doctrine* (Wiltshire: Defence Academy of the United Kingdom, 2010).

13. Cf. *The Norwegian Government's High North Strategy*, Norway Ministry of Foreign Affairs, 2011, http://www.regjeringen.no/upload/UD/Vedlegg/strategien.pdf (accessed October 4, 2012).

14. Interview with Alexander Pelyasov, Moscow, October 25, 2010.

15. A.V. Ledeneva, *Can Russia Modernise? Sistema, Power Networks and Informal Governance* (Cambridge: Cambridge University Press, 2012).

16. P. Baev, "Russia's Arctic Policy and the Northern Fleet Modernization," *Russie. Nei.Visions*, no. 65 (2012), 8, http://www.ifri.org/?page=contribution-detail&id=7264 (accessed October 25, 2012).

17. N. Melvin and E. Klimenko, "Russia's Arctic Strategy in the Context of Its Eurasian Security Policies." Paper presented at the Annual Meeting of the International Studies Association (ISA), San Diego, April 1–4, 2012.

18. R. Sakwa, "Putin's Leadership: Character and Consequences," *Europe-Asia Studies* 60, no. 6 (2008): 879–897.

19. V. Pribylovskii, *Kooperativ Ozero i drugie proekty Vladimir Putina* [The Ozero Cooperative and other projects of Vladimir Putin] (Moscow: Algoritm, 2012).

20. "Skhema vzaimodeistviia Piterskogo okruzheniia Putina i Al'fa-Grupp" [Scheme of interaction of Putin's Petersburg network and the Alfa-Group circle], http://scilla.ru/works/raznoe/pitralfa.html (accessed May 2, 2012).

21. The Kremlin had already revived the unifying theme of the motherland in 1995–1996, when Boris Yeltsin set about promoting Russian national identity and quickly lifted the ideological ban imposed on patriotic themes. See M. Laruelle, *In the Name of the Nation. Nationalism and Politics in Contemporary Russia* (New York: Palgrave, 2009), 120–134.

22. V. V. Putin, "Poslanie Federal'nomu Sobraniiu Rossiiskoi Federatsii," *Kremlin. ru*, April 25, 2005, http://www.kremlin.ru/appears/2005/04/25/1223_type63372type-63374type82634_87049.shtml (accessed October 25, 2012).

23. Laruelle, *In the Name of the Nation*, 154–155 and 188–191.

24. See, for instance, A. Blomfield, "Vladimir Putin Hailed as Virile Vampire," *The Telegraph*, June 19, 2008, http://www.telegraph.co.uk/news/worldnews/europe/russia/2158556/Vladimir-Putin-hailed-as-virile-vampire.html (accessed October 25, 2012).

25. R. Sakwa, *The Crisis of Russian Democracy. The Dual State, Factionalism, and the Medvedev Succession* (Cambridge: Cambridge University Press, 2011).

26. T. Parfitt, "Russia Plants Flag on North Pole Seabed," *The Guardian*, August 2, 2007, http://www.guardian.co.uk/world/2007/aug/02/russia.arctic (accessed October 25, 2012).

27. A. Chilingarov, "Arktika—nash rodnoi krai [The Arctic—our native land]," *Regnum.ru*, July 7, 2007, http://www.regnum.ru/news/867158.html (accessed October 25, 2012).

28. "SShA i Rossiia razdeliaiut Arktiku [The USA and Russia divide up the Arctic]," *Pogranichnik.ru*, January 14, 2009, http://forum.pogranichnik.ru/index.php?showtopic=10737 (accessed October 25, 2012).

29. N. Patrushev, "Arkticheskie territorii imeiut strategicheskoe znachenie dlia Rossii [The Arctic territories have strategic importance for Russia]," *Rossiiskaia gazeta*, March 30, 2009.

30. M. Laruelle, "Conspiracy and Alternate History in Russia: A Nationalist Equation for Success?" *The Russian Review* 71, no. 4 (2012): 565–580.

31. "Sovet bezopasnoti RF provel zasedanie po problem izmeneniia klimata [RF Security Council holds session on the problem of climate change]," *Climate Change*, March 17, 2010, http://www.climatechange.ru/node/423 (accessed October 26, 2012).

32. More details can be found in S.J. Main, *If Spring Comes Tomorrow . . . Russia and the Arctic* (Shrivenham: Defence Academy of the United Kingdom, 2011).

33. Author's interviews with anonymous Russian experts on Arctic legal issues, Moscow, October 2010.

34. A. Oreshenkov, "Arctic Square of Opportunities," *Russia in Global Affairs*, December 25, 2010, http://eng.globalaffairs.ru/number/Arctic-Square-of-Opportunities-15085 (accessed October 25, 2012).

35. G.K. Voitolovsky, "Nereshennye problemy Arkticheskogo morepol'zovaniia [Unresolved problems of Arctic Navigation]." *Vestnik MGTU*, no. 1 (2010): 90–104, http://vestnik.mstu.edu.ru/v13_1_n38/articles/17_voitol.pdf (accessed October 25, 2012).

36. M. Antonova, "State Lays Claim to Geography Society," *The St. Petersburg Times*, November 20, 2009, http://www.sptimes.ru/story/30332.

37. See the Society's information portal, http://www.rgo.ru/, and its institutional website, http://www.rgo.ru/rgo/ (accessed October 25, 2012).

38. The journal *Russia in Global Affairs* has published at least four articles on the Arctic; see its website at http://eng.globalaffairs.ru.

39. "Prime Minister Vladimir Putin Addresses the International Forum—'The Arctic: Territory of Dialogue'," September 23, 2010, http://premier.gov.ru/eng/events/news/12304/ (accessed October 25, 2012).

40. *The Foreign Policy Concept of the Russian Federation*, July 12, 2008, http://archive.kremlin.ru/eng/text/docs/2008/07/204750.shtml (accessed October 25, 2012).

41. L. March, "Nationalism for Export? The Domestic and Foreign Policy Implications of the New 'Russian Idea,'" *Europe-Asia Studies* 64, no. 3 (2012): 401–425.

42. See http://steelastra.ucoz.ru (accessed January 18, 2011).

43. "Putin sozdast gosuchrezhdenie po arkticheskomu turizmu [Putin creates state institution for Arctic tourism]," *Rosbalt*, December 14, 2010, http://www.rosbalt.ru/main/2010/12/14/800534.html (accessed October 25, 2012).

44. Agenda of the meeting at The Second International Arctic Forum in

Arkhangel'sk, "The Arctic–Territory of Dialogue," http://www.arctic.ru/forum (accessed October 25, 2012).

45. E. Wilson Rowe, "Russian Regional Multilateralism: The Case of the Arctic Council," in E. Wilson Rowe and S. Torjesen, eds., *The Multilateral Dimension in Russian Foreign Policy* (London: Routledge, 2008), 142–152.

46. See chapters 4 and 6.

47. E. Riddell-Dixon, "Canada and Arctic Politics: The Continental Shelf Extension," *Ocean Development & International Law* 39, no. 4 (2008): 351.

48. "Opening Remarks and Answers by Russian Foreign Minister Sergey Lavrov at Press Conference Following Talks with Icelandic Foreign Minister Ossur Skarphedinsson," Ministry of Foreign Affairs, November 29, 2011, http://www.mid.ru/brp_4.nsf/0/910EA870582BC0F344257959001DACE9 (accessed October 28, 2012).

49. K. Zysk, "Geopolitics in the Arctic: The Russian Security Perspective," *Climate of Opinion. The Stockholm Network's Energy and Environment Update*, no. 12 (2009), http://www.stockholm-network.org/downloads/publications/Climate_of_Opinion_12.pdf (accessed October 28, 2012).

50. See chapter 2.

51. See the RAIPON website, http://www.raipon.info/en/.

52. A. Staalesen and T. Nilsen, "Moscow Orders Closure of Indigenous Peoples Organization," *Barents Observer*, November 12, 2012, http://barentsobserver.com/en/arctic/moscow-orders-closure-indigenous-peoples-organization-12-11 (accessed November 18, 2012).

53. "Narod tol'ko meshaet. Vpervye v etom zaiavleno otkryto [The people only impede. For the first time this can be stated openly]." *Novaia gazeta*, November 15, 2012, http://www.novayagazeta.ru/economy/55433.html (accessed November 18, 2012).

54. N. Sciullo, "Canada and Russia in the North Pole: Cooperation, Conflict, and Canadian Identity in the Interpretation of the Arctic Region," *Crossroads* 8, no. 1 (2008): 93–109.

55. M. Wyrzykowska, "*Use It or Lose It*: Canadian Arctic Sovereignty Heats Up," *The Atlantic Council of Canada*, September 9, 2010, http://atlantic-council.ca/?p=1928 (accessed October 28, 2012); R. Macnab, "Use It or Lose It in Arctic Canada: Action Agenda or Election Hype?" *Vermont Law Review* 34, no. 1 (2009): 1–14.

56. R. Boswell, "Arctic Sea Route to Be Renamed Canadian Northwest Passage," *Canwest News Service*, December 3, 2009, http://www.vancouversun.com/news/Arctic+route+renamed+Canadian+Northwest+Passage/2300092/story.html (accessed October 28, 2012).

57. P. Whitney Lackenbauer, "Mirror Images? Canada, Russia and the Circumpolar World," *International Journal*, Autumn (2010): 879–897.

58. The use of U.S. ice-breakers in Canadian polar expeditions, however, contributes to Russian views that Canada is still too prone to American interests. For more, see E. Piskunova, "Russia in the Arctic. What's Lurking behind the Flag?" *International Journal*, Autumn (2010): 851–864.

59. See chapter 5.

60. Anonymous interviews with Russian experts at the Moscow State Institute of International Relations (MGIMO), the Institute of World Economy and International Relations (IMEMO), and the Council for the Study of Production Forces (SOPS), Moscow, September 2010.

61. Russian-American Long-term Census of the Arctic (RUSALCA), 2009. Expedition to the Bering Strait and Pacific side of the Arctic Ocean, http://www.arctic.noaa.gov/aro/russian-american/2009/ (accessed October 28, 2012).

62. B. Solum Whist, "Norway and Russia in the High North: Clash of Perceptions," *Security Brief*, no. 1 (2008), http://www.atlanterhavskomiteen.no/files/atlanterhavskomiteen.no/Publikasjoner/KortInfo/Arkiv/2008/kortinfo_1_2008.pdf (accessed October 28, 2012).

63. See *Cross-Border Cooperation on the EU's Eastern Border—Learning from Finnish and Norwegian Experience* (Prague: Institute of Stability and Development, 2012), http://exborealux.isd-network.org/ (accessed October 28, 2012).

64. See, for instance, on environmental issues, "Norwegian-Russian Environmental Cooperation," http://www.regjeringen.no/en/dep/md/Selected-topics/svalbard_og_polaromradene/Norwegian-Russian-environmental-cooperation.html?id=451246/ (accessed October 28, 2012).

65. B. Judah and A. Wilson, "The End of the Putin Consensus," *ECFR Policy Memo*, March 2012, http://ecfr.eu/page/-/Putin_final.pdf (accessed October 28, 2012).

66. T. Risse, S.C. Ropp and K. Sikkink, eds., *The Power of Human Rights: International Norms and Domestic Change* (Cambridge: Cambridge University Press, 1999).

67. I. Krastev, "Russia as 'the Other Europe'," *Russia in Global Affairs*, July-August (2007): 42.

Chapter 2

A Territory or an Identity? The Far North in Russia's Statehood

If the Arctic lies at the intersection of the domestic and the international, this is also because the region has a paradoxical identity for Russian statehood. The Arctic is at once overvalued in the state-run ideological production, and undervalued in many other respects, especially social, economic, and demographic. This disjunction is rooted in the importance often accorded, in Russia, to the territory as defining state identity. Vladimir Putin has worked this vision in his own way and has not concealed the direct link he sees between the revival of Russia's great power and geography: "When we say great, a great country, a great state—certainly, size matters. . . . When there is no size, there is no influence, no meaning."[1] Putin's emphasis on the link between *size* and *meaning* highlights the messianic paradigms still present in the political rhetoric of today's Russia.[2] The country's territorial immensity, and above all its continental nature, landlocked and northern, have been apprehended both as a burden and a blessing: a blessing for the classic affirmation of superpower status, for the resources provided by its subsoil, for the autarkic policies of the previous authoritarian regime; a burden for developing connectedness within one and the same country, due to its harsh climatic challenges, and to the costs it presents for human activities. This paradox, already manifest in the imperial and above all Soviet treatment of the Arctic region, is being amplified today. This point is amply illustrated by the uncertainties of Russian federal policy concerning attributing a particular status to the Far North, the handling of the question of the indigenous peoples, and the role of the region in the Russian nationalist imaginary.

The Imperial and Soviet Memory of the Arctic

The Arctic is fully a part of Russian history. Throughout many centuries, it was seen as the northern shore of Siberia and conceived exclusively in relation to the conquest and development of the Siberian mainland. From the medieval republic of Novgorod, Russian merchants ventured deep into Karelia, toward the White Sea, and the Urals, seeking furs to sell to Hanseatic traders. After the capture of Kazan' and Astrakhan' by Ivan the Terrible, in 1552 and 1556, respectively, Moscow sought to "reunify" Russian lands through its campaign to conquer the ancient territory of the Golden Horde. The Urals were crossed in 1581, the Yenisei River in 1628, the Pacific Ocean was reached in 1680, and Alaska fell under Russian authority in 1741.[3] This multidirectional advance, to the north, east, and south, was not actually driven by the Russian state itself, but by diverse groups: the Arkhangel'sk region was conquered by merchants who were after furs; the Pomors, Russians from the White Sea region, had navigated in Arctic waters since the seventeenth century; Siberia was traversed by the Cossacks and by agents of important merchant families; and Alaska was run by the private Russian-American Company.

In the eighteenth century, Peter the Great (1672–1725), inspired by the great European maritime discoveries, financed numerous expeditions to the Kamchatka Peninsula. Thanks to imperial funds, Danish Captain Vitus Bering (1681–1741) led one of the greatest maritime expeditions of his time, the Great Northern Expedition (1733–1743). It resulted in the mapping of most of the Arctic coast of Siberia and some parts of North America, and confirmed to Peter the Great's descendants that it was indeed possible to reach the American continent via the Arctic seas along the Siberian coast.[4] St. Petersburg's interest in the Arctic, however, was subject to vacillations, and often disappeared in the face of more pressing issues in Central Europe, the Balkans, the Caucasus, and Central Asia.

In the second half of the nineteenth century, and despite the discovery of Franz-Josef Land in 1872, Russian popular and scientific fascination for the polar region remained relatively muted. Whereas Western European public opinion exalted the expeditions to the North and South Poles, the topic was not very popular among the cultivated Russian classes.[5] But the Swedish advances at Spitsbergen, and Germany's on Bear Island forced the Tsarist authorities to defend their interests in the region. In 1899, St. Petersburg sent the first seagoing icebreaker in the world, the *Yermak,* to Svalbard, in order to assert its rights over the archipelago. Russian jurists also sought to demonstrate the status of the partially enclosed Kara Sea, with the aim of declaring Novaya Zemlya a Russian territory. Vice-admiral of the Imperial Navy and oceanographer Stepan O. Makarov (1849–1904) and the famous chemist Dmitri I. Mendeleyev (1834–1907) fought to convince the Tsarist authorities to build an icebreaker fleet in order to secure the Arctic route during the summer months, but without success.[6] The government's disinterest bore great costs during the Russo-Japanese War of 1904–1905; lack of an

Arctic navy forced the Russian fleet, stationed in the Baltic, to traverse the globe in order to defend the Pacific shores of the country.

All this changed radically in the Soviet period. From the early 1920s, the Bolshevik elites developed a robust interest in the Far North, endowed the indigenous populations with cultural and linguistic rights, attempted to solidify their sovereignty, which was under threat in the Far East, and sought to enhance the Northern Sea Route (NSR, or *Sevmorput'*). The Murmansk research station, which had been chiefly focused on fishing, was rapidly transformed into the Northern Scientific Industrial Expedition (*Sevekpeditsiia*), and a Floating Sea Research Institute (*Plavmornin*) was tasked with taking a census of all Siberian rivers and their connections to the Arctic Ocean. Rapid aeronautical progress fostered Arctic discoveries, and the young Soviet Union did not want to lag behind in the developing field of trans-Arctic aviation. The rescue expedition organized by the *Krasin* in 1928 to save the second Italian Polar Expedition (*Italia*) confirmed the effectiveness of Soviet icebreakers and boosted Moscow's interest in establishing control over the Northern Sea Route.[7]

Moscow's interest in the Arctic grew steadily during the First Five-Year Plan, launched in 1928, which signaled the entry of Stalin's Soviet Union into a period of forced collectivization and massive industrialization. The latter presupposed having a large quantity of mineral resources, which marked the beginning of a reading of the Arctic as mainly a zone of natural resources. In the 1930s, priority was given to the exploitation of coal from Vorkuta, metals from the Kola Peninsula, and oil and gas from Ukhta. In the 1940s, metals from the Noril'sk region became Moscow's priority. The Committee of the Northern Sea Route (*Komseveroput'*) then began to support Arctic navigation, first around the Kara Sea and then farther to the east. The first shipments of timber and minerals were organized along the Northern Sea Route; the port of Igarka on the Yenisei River was developed, as was the Kolyma-Indigirka region.[8] Severely lacking in manpower, the regime used the penitentiary industry as the engine for Arctic development: from the *Gostroy* project that built the city of Noril'sk from scratch to the infamous *Dal'stroy*—the Main Administration for the Construction in the Far North—of Kolyma, the Gulag was at the core of the system for the conquest of the Arctic regions.

The idea that the Arctic is a specific region, to be run by a sole organ gathering together all powers in order to exploit it in conformity with Stalinist standards, gave rise to the Main Administration of the Northern Sea Route or *Glavsevmorput'* (*Glavnoe upravlenie severnogo morskogo puti*), which John McCannon has quite appropriately described as "one of the Soviet Union's greatest experiments in hypercentralization."[9] The *Glavsevmorput'* was a state within the state, controlling a territory of two million square kilometers and employing as many as 100,000 persons.[10] It was responsible for Arctic research, shipping, mineral production, shipyards, aviation, agricultural development, and population management—Russians as well as indigenous groups. The experiment, however, did not last long. In 1938, *Glavsevmorput'* was dismantled.

The years of High Stalinism resulted in numerous technical and human feats in the Arctic. In 1932, the International Polar Year, the Soviet icebreaker *Sibiriakov* became the first vessel to cross the Northern Sea Route in a single summer. Its captain, Otto Schmidt, became a Soviet hero, and was subsequently put in charge of all the major Arctic exploration projects. A Soviet flag was planted on Victoria Island for the occasion. In 1934, Soviet polar aviators rescued passengers from the *Cheliuskin* as it sank in the Chukchi Sea. Between 1934 and 1937, Soviet Arctic flights multiplied and became part of the legend of world aviation. In 1937, Soviet planes set the world record for long-distance aviation by crossing the North Pole from Moscow to the United States. In the same year, the Soviet Union became the first nation to land aircraft at the North Pole as part of the Papanin expedition, and therefore the first to establish a scientific outpost there.[11]

These incredible years of discovery gave rise to a central myth of Soviet popular culture, that of the "Red Arctic." Stalin himself considered Arctic literature as a central propaganda tool. Exalted in newspapers like *Vokrug sveta*, novels, films, and radio broadcasts, the epic of the "Red Arctic" deeply marked Russian culture, among both the elites and broader society. The Arctic came to be presented as the forepost of Soviet civilization, an authentic *tabula rasa* on which to build socialism. This made it possible to celebrate the Stalinist values of patriotism (Russia was portrayed as having been an Arctic power since the Varangians, without historical discontinuity), heroism, human and technological prowess, and to underscore the extraordinary industrial capacities of socialism, as it conquered one of the world's most extreme natural environments.[12]

The Red Arctic topic faded from view with de-Stalinization. From the 1950s on, the great Soviet pioneering fronts shifted farther to the south: the Bratsk aluminum smelter in East Siberia during the 1950s, West Siberia for oil and gas in the 1960s, and the Angara industrial complex and the Baikal-Amur Magistral' (BAM) railway in the 1970s.[13] The management of the Far North was decentralized, each ministry given a share of the portfolios, and the Northern Sea Route was more modestly turned into a section of the Ministry of the Marine Fleet, with the Far East and Murmansk shipping companies in charge of its commercial aspects.[14] The Arctic workforce policy was no longer based on prison labor, but rather involved the use of financial incentives to attract a voluntary labor force to the area—the so-called

Northern benefits (*severnye l'goty*) could be as much as 250% higher than the average Soviet salary, and also included earlier retirement age, higher pensions, rehousing priority, and so on.[15] Growing human settlements in the Arctic and their normalization after the Stalinist excesses were supported by Northern deliveries, which came to constitute the main supplies of subsided fuel and food during winter months. After de-Stalinization, the "Red Arctic" motif fell into discreet oblivion—neither rejected, nor exalted—and was revived only on specific occasions, such as the construction of the BAM.[16] But the memory of this Soviet past has left deep imprints in contemporary perceptions, and was revived in the 2000s with the Kremlin's "resumption" of Arctic mythology.

What Administrative Status for Arctic Regions?

As during the Soviet period, Moscow's current policy toward its Arctic regions is hesitant and shifting. First, the geographical definition of what constitutes Russia's Arctic is fuzzy: if Russian Arctic's western and eastern boundaries are defined by a border with Norway and Finland on one side, and the Bering Sea on the other, and the broad northern border is naturally the Russian sector of the Arctic Ocean (including its islands), the southern border remains imprecise; however it is the one that is crucial, where the interconnections with the domestic territories and economic logics are manifest.

The terminology itself is uncertain. In Russian tradition, the *North* (*sever*) defines the regions extending from Karelia to the White Sea, thus including Arkhangel'sk, the first Russian Arctic port, built in the sixteenth century, and sometimes, depending on the definitions, Kotlas and Perm' farther east. Although this region was historically populated by Finno-Ugric peoples largely assimilated with the Russians, it occupies a particular place in the national imaginary. Considered as a reservoir of Russian authenticity in terms of folklore and arts and crafts, the region is often labeled the "Russian North" (*Russkii sever*). This created many memory debates between Finno-Ugric groups, who wish to emphasize their status as indigenous peoples, and Russian populations, in particular local elites aiming to create commercial and tourist brands promoting the Russian North.[17]

As far as the regions farther east were concerned, the Soviet regime defined an area stretching from the Urals to Chukotka as the "Far North" (*Krainyi Sever* or *Dal'nii sever*). Although the boundaries of what has come to be included in it have shifted, the "Far North" and the "Russian North" are often seen as distinct entities, as the latter is judged to be peripheral and remote, whereas the former is better integrated into "mainland" Russia.

Until recently the term *Arctic* (*Arktika*) was reserved only for the ocean of the same name and its shores. The situation changed progressively in the 2000s as the Kremlin sought to be recognized as a key actor in *Arctic* affairs. To communicate effectively with the international community, it is indeed necessary to speak its language. The term *Arctic*, a noun as much as an adjective, thus entered into Russian usage, and today tends to replace the Far North, and to include the Russian North, as evident in the 2008 Arctic policy, which refers to "Russia's Arctic zone."[18]

Multiple administrative definitions of the Arctic/Far North coexist today. In the 1960s Moscow provided the first geographical definition of what constitutes the "Far North."[19] It has never attributed this status according to purely climatic criteria, but one notes that the farther east one goes, the farther south the southern border of the Arctic extends. The presence of permafrost thus constitutes an important criterion, but it is accompanied by other more economically related elements, such as distance from the more densely populated regions of the country and transportation remoteness (e.g., inaccessibility by land for at least half of the year). Regions classified as belonging to the "Far North" received prioritized deliveries and their inhabitants specific benefits. Until the fall of the Soviet Union in 1991, the "Far North" only continued to grow geographically, as many regions and municipalities lobbied for inclusion within it. A second category of so-called "territories equivalent to those of the Far North" (*mestnosti, priravnennye k raionam Krainego Severa*) also took into account remoteness and climatic conditions. In practice, almost all of the immense Siberian landmass east of the Urals was and is still considered as either the "Far North" or as part of the territories equivalent to it, even when the southern boundary of these regions extends well below the Arctic Circle and runs along the borders of Mongolia and China.

In its 2008 Arctic policy, the Russian government provided a more restrictive definition of "Russia's Arctic zone," based on the definition provided by the 1989 USSR Council of Ministers' State Commission on Arctic Affairs. It mentions three autonomous republics (Karelia, Komi, and Yakutia-Sakha); two provinces (*krai*: Kamchatka and parts of Krasnoyask); two regions (*oblast'*: Murmansk, and Arkhangel'sk); and three autonomous districts (*okrug*: Chukotka, Nenets and Yamalo-Nenets). Added to these are all the islands of the Arctic Ocean, as well as those of the Bering and Okhotsk Seas mentioned in the 1926 law.[20] Some regions are therefore considered by the Russian administration as "Far North" (Irkutsk, Magadan, Sakhalin, Tuva, Khabarovsk) or are equivalent to it (Altay, Amur, Perm', and parts of the Tomsk and Tyumen' regions), but are not listed as "Arctic" in the 2008 policy.

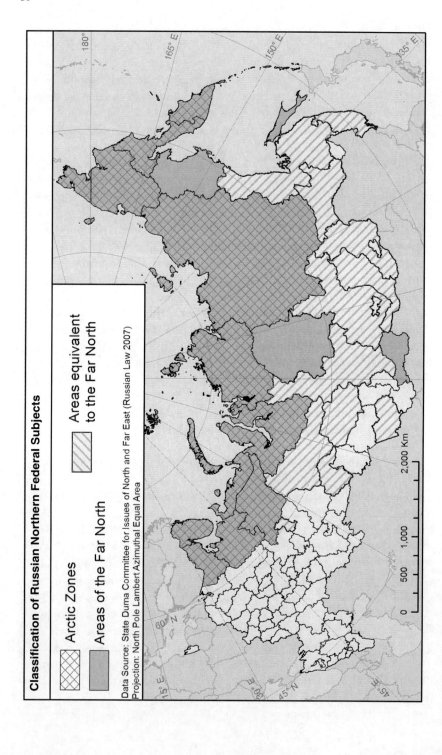

Classification of Russian Northern Federal Subjects

Arctic Zones

Areas of the Far North

Areas equivalent to the Far North

Data Source: State Duma Committee for Issues of North and Far East (Russian Law 2007)
Projection: North Pole Lambert Azimuthal Equal Area

0 500 1,000 2,000 Km

Even in the more restricted definition in force in the 2008 Arctic policy, there is no unified administrative entity encompassing all of Russia's Arctic regions, which straddle multiple federal districts: the Northwest, Urals, Siberia, and Far East. Both their names and borders reflect a history of conquest and a Moscow-centric view, inasmuch as the administrative criterion used is the degree of distance from the capital. This territorial division overlaps more or less geographical realities, in particular watersheds. The Urals, Siberia, and the Far East districts intersect the three major river basins—the Ob', the Yenisei, and the Lena—that link the Arctic coasts respectively to the Ural Mountains, Kazakhstan, and Mongolia. As all of Siberia is drainage-based, the large amount of coordination required to navigate between the rivers and the Arctic Ocean has been a driving force behind all local economic development.

A division in accordance with population and economic patterns, never recognized by the Russian administration, would insert a border between the north and south of the Siberian hinterland, separating "Trans-Siberian Russia" from "Northern Sea Route Russia." The relatively highly populated Siberian south has some larger populations of indigenous ethnic groups as well as ancient Russian rural settlements. These settlements follow the Trans-Siberian Railroad, and run along the borders with Kazakhstan, Mongolia, and China as far as Vladivostok. They are also better developed economically, better integrated in terms of transportation, and today involved in the trade and investment dynamics emanating from the Asia-Pacific region, especially growing linkages with China.[21] Conversely, Arctic and sub-Arctic Siberia has a very dispersed pattern of human settlement. It is the least populated region in the country, with a population density of less than one inhabitant per one hundred square kilometers. Indigenous populations pursuing traditional ways of life are in the minority compared to European populations residing in urban environment. Economically, the north of the Eurasian continent is an immense isolated mass, which can be considered as an enclave, as its only opening is onto the Arctic Ocean. However, this north-south division has no historical tradition in Russia.

The administrative complexities do not stop there. The federalism in force in Russia is equally ambiguous and shifting. Imperial Russia was not a federation, properly speaking, but it attributed a wide variety of statuses to the conquered territories and to the populations living in them, in accordance with the modality of their integration into the empire, with the existence of national elites able to formulate autonomy claims, and with what was considered the state of advancement or backwardness on the ladder of civilization.[22] The Soviet regime turned federalism into one of its central mechanisms for managing national diversity and center-periphery relations. All federated republics, autonomous republics, and autonomous districts created over the course of Soviet history were founded on the recognition, by the central administration, of the existence of a specific ethnic group, classified on the Marxist-Leninist scale then in force according to a status of tribe (*plemia*), nationality (*narodnost'*), or nation (*natsional'nost'*).[23]

Upon the disintegration of the USSR, the Russian Federation thus inherited a very complex administrative fabric, the chaotic character of which intensified during the Yeltsin years and the "parade of sovereignties." In the 2000s, the Kremlin embarked upon a recentralization of powers and was not inclined to endow regions with new forms of special status. Weighing heavily in Moscow's thinking was the realization that such status did not lead to greater success in implementation issues; quite the contrary, during the 1990s, the "sovereignties" acquired during *perestroika* were transformed into feudal fiefs controlled by local governors.

For the Arctic regions, Russia's federalism is therefore challenging. Does an Arctic identity exist that ought to be reflected in the Russian territorial administrative system? If so, then based on what criterion: the autonomy of indigenous peoples or the mode of economic development? The majority of Russian experts who have campaigned for years to have the Arctic recognized as a new federal district have advanced socioeconomic arguments, not cultural ones. The issue here concerns state's access to resources. The acquisition of an administrative status guarantees better access to public subsidies or at the very least to channels of influence.[24] At the start of 2013, the Duma was still discussing the issue of passing a state program on "Regional Politics and Federal Relations" that might recognize the Arctic regions as having a specific status.[25] A rather timid Arctic lobby organized itself in the Duma, demanding that a special law be passed to provide assistance to Arctic regions, but this has been blocked by lobbying from the southern regions, especially the North Caucasus Federal District, whose livelihood depends on massive handouts from the federal budget.[26]

The scope of a potential Arctic Federal District stretches far beyond the competition for budget funding. It would be interpreted as signifying the recognition of an identity. Some experts and high-ranking officials do not hesitate, for instance, off the record, to question the pertinence of the considerable financial support provided to the North Caucasus, insofar as the region seems to be "lost" to Moscow. They assert that refocusing on the Arctic would allow Russia to escape from the North Caucasus quagmire and give the current Russian nationhood a more peaceful and Europeanized space on which to project itself.[27] Regardless of the territorial definition of the Arctic selected by the authorities, and the likely occurrence of future changes, Russia's Arctic is above all continental and not maritime. This takes into account the historical, economic, and social specificities of the region and pointedly differentiates Russia's strategies from those of the other Arctic states, whose prism is essentially maritime and coastal.

Indigenous Peoples as Marginalized Stakeholders?

Russia's Arctic policy accords little importance to the ethnic identity of the region, although it is home to many indigenous peoples. The European Arctic region, which stretches from the Kola Peninsula to the Ural Mountains, hosts Finno-Ugric peoples with populations numbering in the several tens or even hundreds of thousands. These include the small Sami population on the Kola Peninsula close to the Norwegian border; the more numerous Karelians along the border with Finland; Mordvins, Udmurts, and Mari around the Urals; and the Komi in the autonomous republic of the same name. In close contact with Slavic populations for several centuries, these groups are largely Russified linguistically (rates of retention of their national languages are low and Russian is dominant) and religiously (many are Orthodox Christians even if some, such as the Mari, also practice traditional shamanist rites). Whether they live in an urban milieu or work the land, their ways of life are closer to those of Russians than to those of the Siberian peoples, who still practice reindeer herding, fishing, and hunting.[28] Farther east, ethnic groups range from a few tens of thousands to just a few individuals. Khants and Mansi reside in the Khanty-Mansi autonomous district; Nenets in the Yamalo-Nenets autonomous district; Dolgans, Nenets, Nganasan, Evenk, and Enets in the Taimyr autonomous district; and Chukchi, Koriaks, Inuits, and Yugakirs in Chukotka and on the Kamchatka Peninsula.

However, Moscow does not consider the Arctic as an "ethno-region." The indigenous peoples living there are largely in the minority and have been acculturated to an ethnic Russian population; the lifestyle of the region is mostly urban, not "traditional"; and the stakes are economic and strategic, thereby falling within Moscow's remit. The fact that RAIPON is under the jurisdiction of the Ministry for Regional Development is revealing of this order of priorities. Moreover, Russia's reading of the Arctic is still very much shaped by the imperial past and memory of an easy conquest of territories deemed "unpopulated."

Under the Soviet regime, central policies toward indigenous populations varied greatly, in keeping with the twists and turns of Soviet nationalities policy. Massive phases of acculturation to Russian/Soviet culture, seen as superior and civilizing of backward peoples, were followed by phases in which a greater degree of autonomy was permitted and traditional ways of life

34

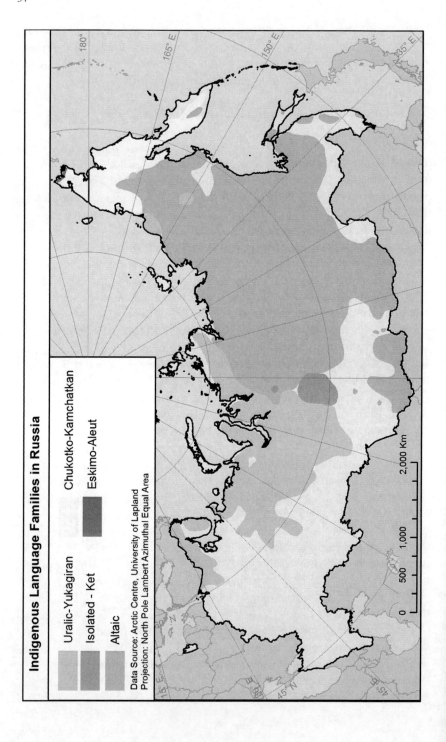

Indigenous Language Families in Russia

Uralic-Yukagiran
Isolated - Ket
Altaic
Chukotko-Kamchatkan
Eskimo-Aleut

Data Source: Arctic Centre, University of Lapland
Projection: North Pole Lambert Azimuthal Equal Area

2,000 Km

1,000

500

0

could be better preserved. [29] In the 1920s, the *Goskomsever* was tasked with protecting the rights of the first national districts and assisting the indigenous peoples to become full-fledged citizens, mainly through literacy programs. In the second half of the 1930s, the idea of preserving national specificities faded, the autonomous districts were abolished, and Russification became obligatory. In the 1960s, Moscow made a show of its desire to change traditional modes of economic production and pushed for collectivization. At the end of the Soviet period, only the Nenets still had schools in their national language. After the Soviet collapse, indigenous populations are essentially left to themselves. Many resumed their traditional activities in the 1990s when the subsidies sent from Moscow abruptly ceased. Indigenous peoples' life expectancy is often around 10 years less than the Russian average, and they suffer from many more diseases, including psychological ones. [30] Alcoholism is the major social scourge, unemployment is very high, and youth seek to escape to the large towns. [31]

Today's Russian Federation comprises more than 80 administrative subjects, including 20 autonomous republics and 10 autonomous districts bearing the name of a titular population, even if that population often forms only a minority. [32] These administrative entities have been granted an autonomy that is limited to the cultural and linguistic rights of the titular populations—local identity symbols are promoted, schools offer courses in national languages, the national language can be used in administration, and titulars are given priority in the civil service. But in terms of all political and economic decision making, Russia is a centralized state that leaves the regions little margin for maneuver. Although some have managed to negotiate with the center and obtained a certain degree of autonomy, they have mainly been those primarily populated by ethnic Russians. Among the national territories, only Tatarstan and the North Caucasus republics have been given greater autonomy: Tatarstan's, though, is being drastically reduced today, while the ongoing autonomy of the North Caucasus republics can essentially be explained by the Kremlin's inability to manage the local political situation and its delegating of power to the local elites in a zone adjudged to be highly problematic. [33]

For the Arctic region as defined by the 2008 policy, only the Sakha, Komis, and Karelians have their own autonomous republic. Four other groups have their own autonomous districts (*okrugs*): the Chukchi (Chukotka autonomous district), the Khants and the Mansi (Khanty-Mansi autonomous district), and the Nenets (Yamalo-Nenets autonomous district and Nenets autonomous district). The Dolgans, Evenks, some Nenets, and the Koriaks lost their administrative entities during Putin's administrative recentralization, the aim of which was to merge entities deemed not economically viable. Hence, in

Table 2.1

Arctic Indigenous Groups in the 2010 Population Census

Yakut-Sakha	478,085
Komis (and Komi-Permiaks)	329,111
Karelians	60,815
Nenets	44,640
Evenks	37,843
Khants	30,943
Evens	22,383
Chukchi	15,908
Mansi	12,269
Koriaks	7,953
Dolgans	7,885
Veps	5,936
Nivkhi	4,652
Selkups	3,649
Itelmens	3,193
Kamchadals	1,927
Sami	1,771
Inuits	1,738
Yukagir	1,603
Chuvantsy	1,002
Nganasan	862
Aleuts	482
Entsy	227
Kereki	4
Alyutors	—

Source: 2010 Census of the Population of the Russian Federation, vol. 4, http://www.perepis-2010.ru/results_of_the_census/.

2005 the Komi-Permiak district merged with the Perm' region; and in 2007 the Taimyr (Dolgan) and Evenki districts joined the Krasnoyarsk region, and the Koriak district joined the province of Kamchatka.[34] The merging of administrative entities could proceed further in the years ahead, but seems for the moment to have slowed.

This paradoxical ethno-federalism is hampered by several factors. First, the titular populations are almost all minorities in their autonomous entities and ethnic Russians the majority. Only Yakutia-Sakha can claim an almost equivalent number of ethnic Russians and of Yakuts. Second, many indigenous groups straddle several administrative entities or are a minority in an entity established to represent another titular group. Third, for the most part these entities have only very restricted decision-making powers, and have to accept generalized understandings of the rules decided at the federal level, which essentially revolve around the exploitation of resources.

The fuzziness of ethnic categorizations and their administrative territorialization works to reinforce the limitations of promoting the Arctic as an area with an indigenous identity. As the inheritor of sophisticated categorizations from the Soviet tradition, contemporary Russia distinguishes many different population groups. From the 1920s on, the key concept was that of small-numbered indigenous peoples (*korennye malochislennye narody*), a concept validated by the Russian government in 2000, insofar as it passed several decrees guaranteeing these peoples a specific status, such as the right to organize as a community (*obshchina*), and the right to a traditional use of nature.[35] The list compiled in 2000 includes 45 groups, of which 21 live in the Arctic zone, while the others are spread throughout the regions of Sakhalin, Khabarovsk, Vladivostok, in south Siberia, and the North Caucasus. Aleuts, Alyutors, Itelmens, Kamchadals, Kereki, Koriaki, Chuchki, Chuvantsy, Inuit, and Yukagirs all live in the province of Kamchatka; the Evens and Evenks in Yakutia-Sakha and in neighboring regions; the Dolgans, Nganasan, Selkups, and Entsy in the Taimyr Peninsula and further south toward Krasnoyarsk; the Mansi and Khanty in their own eponymous district; the Nenets in their autonomous districts of Yamalo-Nenets, Nenets, Khanty-Mansi, and the Republic of Komi; and the Sami around Murmansk, and Veps in Karelia. All these groups meet the criteria defined by the Russian law for consideration as small-numbered indigenous peoples: they live in their historical territory, preserve their traditional ways of life, define themselves as separate ethnicities, and do not exceed 50,000 persons.[36]

The Komi, Karelian, and Sakha populations are all far larger in number and so are not included in this categorization. They belong to the bigger set of indigenous peoples (*korennye narody*), but in this case it is not a matter of legal status. The Sakha (Yakuts), although the largest in number with close to one-half million persons, have even a much more precarious symbolic status. Unlike the Komi and the Karelians, Russian historiography and ethnology considers them as colonizers—similar to the Russians themselves—and not as natives of the territory on which they live today. In fact, the Sakha originally came from southern Siberia and are Turkic-speakers, and thus related to the Altay-Mongolian world. Being recognized as having the particular status of "native of the north" has therefore turned into a political issue. This situation leads to tensions between the Yakut establishment, which wishes to be recognized as indigenous, in order to promote national revival and the autonomy of the republic, and groups classified as small-numbered indigenous peoples, who are legally protected.[37]

The term *indigenous peoples* is not specific to the Arctic and includes all groups who are recognized as national minorities—i.e., non-ethnic Russians, from the Tatars to the Chechens. Moreover, its semantic reach is more complex than the term *native* in English. In fact, the distinction between newcomers and natives is made difficult by the history of Russian conquest, which stretched out over several centuries. Hence the Russians settled in the Altay and around the perimeters of Lake Baikal from the seventeenth century also consider themselves to be *korennye*, and define themselves as Siberians, *sibiriaki*. Moreover, for some years now, with the growth of xenophobia in Russia, the term *native population* (*korennoe naselenie*) is used increasingly in the media and by politicians, with Vladimir Putin leading the way, to define all Russian citizens in opposition to migrants, or else all Russian citizens living in their "traditional regions" in contrast to internal migrants, in particular from the North Caucasus.

Russia has not ratified the 1969 ILO convention on Indigenous and Tribal Rights—which is binding for only 17 countries, mainly in Latin America. It is opposed to the clause on property rights, which would necessitate long negotiations about the territories occupied by the massive industrial combines and would undermine the assets of the Russian state or of its administrative subjects.[38] Contrary to what its federal structure might lead some to believe, and in contrast to Canada, Denmark, and Norway, Russia does not grant its indigenous peoples any political autonomy, nor does it consult them about subsoil exploitation. Traditional knowledge, patterns of land use for traditional means of subsistence such as reindeer herding, and access to non-polluted rivers are not respected by major resource development companies, whether public or private. Decision-making in the energy and minerals sector is particularly centralized, resting in the hands of a few figures within Putin's inner circle. The regional administrations may obtain good subsidies from large companies, often primary resources (e.g., low-priced gas and oil), or receive large transfers in the form of taxes. Thus, Khanty-Mansiisk, the capital of the autonomous region of the same name, has a higher GDP per capita (nearly US$40,000 in 2007) than Moscow, and is on a par with that of the United States.[39] But those who stand to gain from it are mostly the Russian urban populations, not the indigenous ones.

The indigenous problem is rather acute in two regions: the former Taimyr autonomous district (today merged into the Krasnoyark region), where the vast rangeland for reindeer surrounding the mining complex and city of Noril'sk has been degraded by pollution; and the Yamalo-Nenets autonomous district, where indigenous groups must herd their reindeer in such a way as to avoid gas wells and pipelines. In both cases, the Nenets have had regular confrontations with Gazprom and Noril'sk Nickel. Their associations have organized protests thanks to which they have become among the most widely media-covered indigenous populations in all of Russia.[40] Given Moscow's participation in the Arctic Council and international pressures surrounding the question of indigenous peoples, the Kremlin has had to soften its position and encourage Gazprom, Noril'sk Nickel, and Rosneft to show a certain interest in the issue. Today relations have improved and the large Russian resource consortia have developed contacts with indigenous representatives.[41] Shareholders of the Sakhalin-2 consortium have committed to supporting Sakhalin's indigenous people, the Nivkhi,[42] while Gazprom provides compensation to the Nenets for pasture degradation and land withdrawal, and employs some of them as well. The main resource extraction companies also offer special study grants, housing facilities, schooling opportunities for children, and helicopter transport. But the subsidies from intense subsoil exploitation continue to be essentially soaked up by central and local governments.[43] And as the 2012 crisis within the Arctic Council has showed (see Chapter 1), the Kremlin does not consider RAIPON to be an essential interlocutor. As seen from Moscow, the indigenous component of its Arctic policy is minimal and is often viewed with disdain as a "fashion" from the West.

The Nationalist Reading of the Arctic: Russia's New *Lebensraum*

The dominant Russian view of the Arctic is one of a Russian national territory and not of an "ethno-region." This view is strengthened by the maintenance of historical memory about the conquest of Siberia, the revival of *Red Arctic* symbolism, and the recent enthusiasm of Russian nationalist movements for the Arctic theme. These movements have seized upon the myth of the Far North, something they did soberly in the 1990s, before becoming more vocal in the 2000s. Since the Soviet collapse, they have actually produced many discourses that can be defined as "geographical metanarratives."[44] These metanarratives advance a supposedly comprehensive and teleological explanation of Russia through a master idea—territorial size and location in space are the drivers of Russia's mission in the world, and of the nature of the Russian state and culture. Three main geographical metanarratives circulate in contemporary Russia, all of them arguing that a specific element gives the country its uniqueness among nations: Russia's territory is *larger* than other countries in the world and forms a specific continent (Eurasianism); Russia is going *higher* in the universe (Cosmism); and Russia is going *farther* north (Arctic mythology). In their own ways, these three metanarratives all incorporate spatial criteria: the territorial dimension and the location between Europe and Asia for Eurasianism; the conquest of space as providing a new mode of continuing territorial expansion (Cosmism); and the northern location of Russia as the revenge of territory over history and of space over politics (Arctic mythology).

Some nationalist groups see the Arctic above all as a crucial element in the revival of Russia's great power status and are therefore focused on geopolitical competition with the West, and in particular with the United States. Popularizations such as Artur Indzhiev's book *The Battle for the Arctic: Will the North Be Russian?*, which was published by one of the major nationalist publishers, have depicted the onset of a sort of Third World War in which a weakened Russia will have to prove its heroism in order to safeguard its rights in the Arctic against aggressive Western powers.[45] Others put forward a more spiritual view of the role of the Far North in the construction of Russian identity and the pursuit of its traditional messianism. In both cases, the Arctic is presented as Russia's "last chance," and as a possible way to take "revenge on history." The notion that Russian expansion into the Arctic could attenuate the consequences of territorial losses linked to the Soviet Union's collapse has become a recurrent theme: the Arctic is presented as rightful compensation for the hegemony lost with the disappearance of the Soviet Union.

The famous geopolitician Alexander Dugin has been one of the most virulent defenders of a Russian Arctic. According to his explosive formulation "[t]he purpose of our being lies in the expansion of our space. The shelf belongs to us. Polar bears live there, Russian polar bears. And penguins live there, Russian penguins."[46] This passage, cited by *Der Spiegel*, became famous in the West both for its radicality as well as for its blunder (there are no penguins in the Arctic). Inspired by the Eurasianist tradition, Dugin also borrows from the Germanic one, especially the idea of Hyperborea as the last unknown continent. He states that Eurasia is giving birth to a new political and spiritual continent, which he calls *Arctogeia*, and bases his argumentation on Aryan references inspired by the European New Right, Nazi theories, and René Guénon's esoterism.[47] He defines the Hyperborean continent as the birthplace of the Aryans, of whom the Russians are the purest descendants. In his *The Mysteries of Eurasia*, he elaborates a cosmogony of the world, in order to make Siberia the last "empire of paradise"[48] after Thule, the instrument of his geopolitical desire for domination of the world, justified by Russia's "cosmic destiny."[49] As for the Eurasianist Youth Movement that lays claim to Dugin's thinking, it has organized several demonstrations in support of Russian territorial claims in the Arctic, calling for the continental shelf to be automatically integrated into the borders of the Russian state and to be transformed into a new federal district. The movement's then leader, Alexander Bobdunov, has claimed that "the North is not only a base of economic resources, our future in the material sense, but also a territory of the spirit, of heroism, and of overcoming, a symbolic resource of central importance for the future of our country."[50]

The Arctic theme has not left the Communist movements indifferent either, and notably not their main theoretician, Alexander Prokhanov. In his project to legitimate Russia's claims to lead the new Arctic race, he combines pragmatic arguments with revivalist theories on the Russian nation. He remarks that "for more than fifteen years immense spaces have been excised from Russia to the south. The Russian people have become more and more northern. The Ukrainian black lands have been taken away, as has access to the seas of the south, and Belorussia."[51] The new, post-Soviet Russia will therefore be destined to look north, no more to the south, to find its "radiant future." But Prokhanov also sees a renewal of Russian messianism in what he calls "the Russian march toward the north" and the assertion that the Arctic Ocean is domestic water for Russia.[52] Not without humor, he designates Gazprom as "the corporation of all the Russias" (on the model of the "Church of all the Russias") and notes that the Arctic is likely to become the source of both Russia's material and spiritual power, because "the Arctic civilization requires an incredible concentration of force in all domains. It will become, then, a sanctified 'common good,' in which the peoples of Russia will rediscover their unity, conceived by God as those to whom he destines great missions."[53]

A new movement of so-called "white world" doctrinaires has also developed in the 2000s.[54] It groups different theoreticians of a Northern/European/white race under one and the same umbrella in order to propagate the idea that Russia was founded by Aryans and that the imperial structure of the country constitutes the apogee of "white" political thought. The movement was able to develop some political connections through the Rodina party, leads a small but influential group called White World (*belyi mir*), hosts websites for so-called white and Slavic audiences, and participates in neo-Slavophile literary circles, notably in the International Fund for Slavic Writing and Culture.[55] In 1999, it decided to start a collection, the Library of Racial Thinking (*Biblioteka rasovoi mysli*), which publishes works on physical anthropology of some Russian, but more so Western, authors from the turn of nineteenth-twentieth centuries, and openly claims the legacy of racial anthropology.

The broad dissemination of Aryan and neo-Pagan themes in contemporary Russia also helps familiarize the public with the notion of the Arctic as Russia's destiny. The Russian version of the Aryan myth stems back to the nineteenth century, but was strengthened in its neo-Pagan aspect during the 1920s–1950s by debates on the false manuscript *The Book of Vles (Vlesova kniga)*, presented by Russian and Ukrainian nationalist émigrés as an indisputable historical source evidencing Slavic pre-Christian antiquity, but also as a book of prayers and hymns to ancient gods to be adhered to in practice.[56] Numerous ethnic faith movements (*rodnoverie*) that are seeking to restore the pre-Christian and

Aryan religion of the Slavs promotes this Aryan motif. Moreover, since the end of the Soviet Union, numerous meta-historical publications on the Aryan past have flooded the shelves of Russian bookshops and libraries, for instance Valery Demin's works.[57] Because of the general public's interest in Slavic prehistory, Aryan doctrinarians have been able to permeate historiography, books for children, and textbooks. According to them, the Aryan homeland was located in ancient Atlantis, a bygone Nordic country whose descendants allegedly managed to migrate to Russia. Far from being marginal, this meta-history about Russia's Aryan past and future represents the basis for a form of popular knowledge of ancient history.

The Far North has also become a fashionable topic as the result of a revival of interest in the history of Alaska. Since the 1990s, historical and fictional publications about the Russian conquest of Alaska and its sale to the United States in 1867 have multiplied. The idea of a former Russian Empire stretching from Finland to California fuels nationalist resentment, focused as it is on the importance of geography in the assertion of Russian great power. This makes it possible to cultivate conspiracy theories about the West's supposed desire to fragment Russia. Many works lament the corruption of the Russian elites who decided to sell California and then Alaska for financial gain, setting these historical events in parallel with Russo-American negotiations over the Chukchi and Bering Seas in 1990.[58] These texts elevate the natural character of the Russian advance in Alaska as the logical consequence of that into Siberia, the spiritual understanding between Russians and the indigenous peoples, and the key role of Orthodoxy in Alaska. These arguments are presented in counterpoint to American history, which is marked by the alleged destruction of indigenous peoples.[59] Regrets concerning the sale of Alaska are not only expressed by so-called nationalist authors, but can also be found among high-ranking officials with links to Arctic questions.[60]

The Arctic metanarrative is well received in a Russian society marked by a growing xenophobia and identification with a "white " identity.[61] The public discourse, fed by both politicians and the media, about "threats" coming from the South—including instability in the North Caucasus, migrations from Central Asia, and a form of Chinese "yellow peril" in Siberia and the Far East—reinforces a spatial representation of Russia in which the "south" is the region from where all danger arises, while the "north" is the place where the Russian nation will be able to take refuge and preserve itself. The growing Europeanization of identity narratives in Russia therefore opens new niches for a Nordic/Arctic metanarrative to develop.

The place of the Far North in Russia's statehood may appear paradoxical, wedged as it is between technocratic debates on territorial divisions, vested interests fighting for the acquisition of state subsidies and specific rights, and the national imaginary of regeneration of great Russian power through a kind of Arctic rebirth. However, all these juxtaposed debates are rooted in longstanding ambiguities that have marked Russian history since the start of the eighteenth century and have widely influenced the construction of modern Russian statehood. The central question, in imperial times as well as, in an altered form, during the Soviet period, and indeed even more so today, is the following: should the Russian territory be the defining feature of the identity of state and of the nation? If the response is affirmative, then which administrative structure is the most judicious: empire, federalism, or a centralized state? Moreover, should recognition, in whatever form it takes, of the diversity of territories be based on ethnic criteria or economic interests? If ethnic criteria are selected, then should autonomy have a territorial basis, or should it rather be linked to individual identity, echoing the past debate between Austro-Hungarian and Russian Marxists?[62] In what way is any ethnic autonomy compatible with the dominant identity of "ethnic Russians," who represent more than 80% of the population, and is this not likely to lead to secessionist demands in certain regions such as the North Caucasus? Further, how is this autonomy to be materialized, for instance in the distribution of tax revenues, a sensitive topic that the Arctic regions consider to be crucial? If the Russian state decides to endow the Arctic with the status of federal district, what are the political and identity implications of this move, and will it impact the priority that has been hitherto granted to the North Caucasus?

To all these questions, the state bodies and political circles have no ready answers. An open debate, stating clearly the issues involved in determining Russia's federal identity and the criteria for that determination, is not the order of the day. The Putin regime is built on consensus, the cult of the smallest common denominator, and a refusal to return to the ideological divisions of the 1990s, which imperiled state unity. Although the legitimacy of the regime is increasingly contested, it is highly unlikely that the Kremlin will decide to foster any such debate, insofar as it would probably incite polemics over the policies conducted in the North Caucasus. Moscow prefers instead to continue to manage the ambiguities and to postpone making any strategic decisions, even if the cost is a loss in efficiency.

Notes

1. M. Antonova, "State Lays Claim to Geography Society," *The St. Petersburg Times,* November 20, 2009, http://www.sptimes.ru/story/30332 (accessed December 2, 2012).

2. M. Laruelle, "Larger, Higher, Farther North . . . Geographical Metanarratives of the Nation in Russia," *Eurasian Geography and Economics* 53, no. 5 (2012): 557–574.

3. A. Kappeler, *The Russian Empire: A Multi-Ethnic History* (New York: Longman, 2001).

4. O. Frost, *Bering: The Russian Discovery of America* (New Haven and London: Yale University Press, 2003).

5. J. Nurminen and M. Lainema, *A History of Arctic Exploration: Discovery, Adventure, and Endurance at the Top of the World* (London: Conway, 2010).

6. P. Horensma, *The Soviet Arctic* (London: Routledge, 1991), 19.

7. Ibid., 21–34.

8. Ibid., 35–52.

9. J. McCannon, *Red Arctic: Polar Exploration and the Myth of the North in the Soviet Union, 1932–1939* (Oxford: Oxford University Press, 1998), 6.

10. Ibid., 38.

11. See *North Pole Drifting Stations (1930s–1980s)*, Beaufort Gyre Exploration project, http://www.whoi.edu/page.do?pid=66677 (accessed December 2, 2012).

12. For more details, see McCannon, *Red Arctic*, 81–144.

13. See A. Wood, ed., *Siberia: Problems and Prospects for Regional Development* (London: Croom Helm, 1987).

14. Horensma, *The Soviet Arctic*, 139–150.

15. P. Thorez, "La Route maritime du Nord. Les promesses d'une seconde vie, [The Northern Searoute: promise of a second life]," *Le Courrier des Pays de l'Est*, no. 2 (2008): 55.

16. Arctic territories are therefore integrated, in the Russian imagination, in the epic of Siberian conquest.

17. N. Zamiatina, and A. Yashunskii, "Severa kak zona rosta dlia Rossiiskoi provintsii [The North as a place of growth for Russia's provinces]," *Otechestvennye zapiski*, no. 5 (2012): 227–239.

18. "Osnovy gosudarstvennoi politiki Rossiiskoi Federatsii v Arktike na period do 2020 g. i dal'neishuiu perspektivu [Fundamentals of state policy of the Russian Federation in the Arctic for the period to 2020 and longer-term prospects]," *Sovet Bezopasnosti Rossiiskoi Federatsii*, September 2008, http://www.scrf.gov.ru/documents/98.html (accessed December 2, 2012).

19. H. Blakkisrud, and G. Hønneland, "The Russian North. An Introduction," in H. Blakkisrud and G. Hønneland, eds., *Tackling Space: Federal Politics and the Russian North* (Lanham, Oxford: University Press of America, 2006), 9.

20. "Osnovy gosudarstvennoi politiki Rossiiskoi Federatsii v Arktike na period do 2020 g. i dal'neishuiu perspektivu." On the 1926 law, see chapter 5.

21. J. Forsyth, *A History of the Peoples of Siberia: Russia's North Asian Colony 1581–1990* (Cambridge: Cambridge University Press, 1994).

22. F. Hirsch, *Empire of Nations. Ethnographic Knowledge and the Making of the Soviet Union* (Ithaca: Cornell University Press, 2005).

23. T. Martin, *The Affirmative Action Empire. Nations and Nationalism in the Soviet Union, 1923–1939* (Ithaca, London: Cornell University Press, 2001).

24. Information provided to the author by anonymous Russian experts at MGIMO, IMEMO, and SOPS, Moscow, September 2010.

25. "Proekt novoi gosprogrammy Minregiona predusmatrivaet sozdanie uslovii dlia razvitiia Arktiki [Draft of a new state program by the Ministry of Regions foresees the creation of conditions for development of the Arctic]," *Arctic.info*, January 17, 2013, http://www.arctic-info.ru/News/Page/proekt-novoi-gosprogrammi-minregiona-predysmatrivaet-sozdanie-yslovii-dla-razvitia-arktiki (accessed December 2, 2012).

26. Author's interview with anonymous Russian experts at MGIMO, IMEMO, and SOPS, Moscow, September 2010.

27. Ibid.

28. A. Heinapuu, "Finno-Ugric peoples in Russia. Territorial or Cultural Autonomy," in *2004 Estonian Ministry of Foreign Affairs Yearbook* (Tallinn: Foreign Affairs Ministry, 2004), 71–75.

29. Yu. Slezkine, *Arctic Mirrors. Russia and the Small Peoples of the North* (Ithaca, London: Cornell University Press, 1994).

30. For details, see M. Feshbach, *Russia's Health and Demographic Crises: Policy Implications and Consequences* (Washington, DC: Chemical & Biological Arms Control Institute, 2003). See also S.A. Crate, "Co-Option in Siberia: The Case of Diamonds and the Vilyuy Sakha," *Polar Geography* 26, no. 4 (2002): 418–435.

31. A.N. Petrov, "Lost Generations? Indigenous Population of the Russian North in the Post-Soviet Era," *Canadian Studies in Population* 35, no. 2 (2008): 269–290.

32. P. Söderlund, *The Dynamics of Federalism in Russia* (Helsinki: Åbo Akademi University Press, 2006), and on contemporary issues, A. Makarychev, "New Challenges to Russian Federalism," *PONARS Eurasia Policy Memo*, no. 75, 2009.

33. C. Ross, and A. Campbell, *Federalism and Local Politics in Russia* (London: Routledge, 2010).

34. M. Derrick, "The Merging of Russia's Regions as Applied Nationality Policy: A Suggested Rationale," *Caucasian Review of International Affairs* 3, no. 3 (2009): 317–323.

35. I. Øverland, and H. Blakkisrud, "The Evolution of Federal Indigenous Policy in the Post-Soviet North," in H. Blakkisrud and G. Hønneland, eds., *Tackling Space. Federal Politics and the Russian North* (Lanham, Oxford: University Press of America, 2006), 175–176.

36. "Postanovlenie Pravitel'stva Rossiiskoi Federatsii 24 marta 2000 N° 255 'O edinom perechne korennykh malochistlennykh narodov Rossiiskoi Federatsii' [Decree No. 255 of the Government of the Russian Federation of March 24, 2000 'On a unified enumeration of small-numbered indigenous peoples of the Russian Federation']," http://demoscope.ru/weekly/knigi/zakon/zakon047.html (accessed December 2, 2012).

37. For a brief assessment see UNHRC, *Assessment for Yakut in Russia*. United Nations Human Rights Council, Minorities at Risk Project, December 31, 2003, http://www.refworld.org/cgi-bin/texis/vtx/rwmain?page=topic&tocid=463af2212&toid=469f2eff2&publisher=&type=COUNTRYREP&coi=&docid=469f3acac&skip=0 (accessed December 2, 2012).

38. I. Øverland, "Indigenous Rights in the Russian Far North," in E. Wilson Rowe, ed., *Russia and the North* (Ottawa: University of Ottawa Press, 2009), 165–186.

39. J.-R. Raviot, "Géographie politique de la Russie en 2010 [Political geography of Russia in 2010]," *Hérodote*, no. 138 (2010): 171.

40. See, for instance, "Indigenous Peoples—Excluded and Discriminated," *Human Rights Report,* no. 43 (2006): 14–18.

41. More in T.N. Vasil'kova, A.V. Evai, E.P. Martynova, and N.I. Novikova, *Korennye malochislennye narody i promyshlennoe razvitie Arktiki* [Indigenous small-numbered peoples and the industrial development of the Arctic]. (Moscow: Shchadrinskii dom pechati, 2011) and E.P. Martynova, and N.I. Novikova, *Tazovskie nentsy v usloviiakh neftegazovogo osvoeniia* [The Taz Nenets under conditions of oil and gas development] (Moscow: RAN, 2012).

42. See *Sakhalin Indigenous Minorities Development Plan. First Five-Year Plan*

(2006–2010), Sakhalin Energy Investment Company Ltd., 2006, http://www.sakha-linenergy.com/en/documents/doc_lender_soc_4.pdf (accessed December 2, 2012).

43. Anonymous interviews with Russian experts on the Arctic, MGIMO and IM-EMO, September 24 and 26, 2010.

44. This section is largely based on the material appearing in Laruelle, "Larger, Higher, Farther North . . . Geographical Metanarratives of the Nation in Russia."

45. A. Indzhiev, *Bitva za Arktiku. Budet li sever russkim?* [The Battle for the Arctic. Will the North be Russian?] (Moscow: Iauza, Eksmo, 2010).

46. M. Schepp, and G. Traufetter, "Riches at the North Pole. Russia Unveils Aggressive Arctic Plans," *Der Spiegel*, January 29, 2009, http://www.spiegel.de/international/world/0,1518,604338,00.html (accessed December 2, 2012).

47. A. Dugin, *Giperboreiskaia teoriia. Opyt ariosofskogo issledovaniia* [Hyberboreal theory. An experiment in ariosophic investigation]. (Moscow: Arktogeia, 1993).

48. A. Dugin, *Misterii Evrazii* [The mysteries of Eurasia]. (Moscow: Arktogeia, 1991), 78.

49. Ibid., 26.

50. "ESM piketiroval MID za Arktiku [Eurasianist Youth Movement picketed Foreign Ministry over Arctic]," *Rossiia 3*, September 27, 2010, http://www.rossia3.ru/news/1612484841d0b8b954a7f4c9179bfda7 (accessed December 2, 2012).

51. D. Steshin, "Rossiia vernulas' v Arktiku [Russia returns to the Arctic]," *Komsomol'skaia pravda*, January 23, 2008, http://kp.by/daily/24036/96268/ (accessed December 2, 2012).

52. A. Prokhanov, "Ledovityi okean—vnutrennee more Rossii [The Arctic Ocean—Russia's internal sea]," *Zavtra*, August 8, 2007, http://www.zavtra.ru/cgi/veil/data/zavtra/07/716/11.html (accessed December 2, 2012).

53. A. Prokhanov, "Severnyi marsh Rossii [Russia's northern march]," *Zavtra*, April 25, 2007, http://www.arctictoday.ru/analytics/704.html (accessed December 2, 2012).

54. V. Shnirelman, *"'Tsepnoi pes rasy': divannaia rasologiia kak zashchitnitsa 'belogo cheloveka'* ["The watch dog of race": A couch-based raciology in defense of the "white man"]" (Moscow: SOVA, 2007).

55. See the website http://www.slavfond.ru/ (accessed October 27, 2010).

56. K. Aitamurto, "Russian Paganism and the Issue of Nationalism: A Case Study of the Circle of Pagan Tradition," *Pomegranate: The International Journal of Pagan Studies* 8, no. 2 (2006): 184–210.

57. V. Shnirelman, *Intellektual'nye labirinty: ocherki ideologii v sovremennoi Rossii* [Intellectual labyrinths: Essays on ideology in contemporary Russia] (Moscow: Academia, 2004).

58. S. Pykhtyn, "Kak prodavali Aliasku: temnaia storona russko-amerikanskikh otnoshenii s 1824 po 1867 g. [How Alaska was sold: The dark side of Russian-American relations from 1824 to 1867]," *Moskva*, no. 8 (2005): 144–165.

59. A. Znamenski, "History with an Attitude: Alaska in Modern Russian Patriotic Rhetoric," *Jahrbücher für Geschichte Osteuropeas* 57, no. 3 (2009): 346–373.

60. Author's anonymous interviews with experts of Russia's legal claims on the Arctic, Moscow, September–October 2010.

61. M. Laruelle, "The Ideological Shift on the Russian Radical Right: From Demonizing the West to Fear of Migrants," *Problems of Post-Communism* 57, no. 6 (2010): 19–31.

62. M. Löwy, "Marxists and the National Question," *New Left Review* I, no. 96 (1976), http://newleftreview.org/I/96/michael-lowy-marxists-and-the-national-question (accessed December 2, 2012).

Chapter 3

Russia's Spatial and Demographic Challenges

Not all the Arctic states share the same relationship with the Arctic portion of their territories; for some it is marginal, for others it is more central. For the United States and Denmark, their Arctic territories, Alaska and Greenland, respectively, are geographically detached from the rest of the country. Excepting Svalbard and the islands of the Canadian Arctic Archipelago, the Arctic regions of Canada and Norway are territorially contiguous, but are granted diverse administrative levels of autonomy on behalf of their indigenous populations. For Russia, however, the polar lands form an integral part of the Siberian mainland.

This is reinforced by the long history of European settlement—the region was colonized in the sixteenth century—and the numerical importance of the populations residing there. According to its maximal definition, Russia's Far North totals about 30 million inhabitants; taken in a more restricted sense—that of the Arctic Council—it has a little less than 3 million inhabitants. Even the more modest figure, though, means Russia has the largest Arctic population in the world, with about three-quarters of the total (2.9 million out of 4).[1] Another unique feature is that indigenous groups constitute only a very small percentage of the total figure. Indigenous peoples represent 80% of Greenland's population, 50% of Canada's, 20% of Alaska's, and 15% of Arctic Norway's, but they make up less than 5% of that of Arctic Russia. The Russian Arctic is therefore populated by Europeans living in an urban environment. Five major towns stand out: Murmansk (320,000 habitants), Arkhangel'sk (350,000), Noril'sk (170,000), Vorkuta (80,000), and Novyi Urengoi (113,000), the latter being the last town of more than 100,000 inhabitants to have been built above the Arctic Circle in the 1980s. For Russia the urban character of its Arctic settlement presents totally different challenges to those of the other Arctic countries.[2]

Moscow also faces its own set of issues related to larger trends affecting the country, mainly a population crisis and drastic changes in territorial management. The Russian Federation is a fragmented territory in terms of population, access to wealth, human development indicators, and economic strategies. Within the space of two decades it has become a de facto archipelago. While some modern and wealthy "islands" are developing among its immense landmass, other areas are being emptied of their populations, are economically impoverished, contain secessionist elements (the North Caucasus), or are increasingly disconnected from the rest of the country (the Far East). Russia is also the only country in the world to be undergoing such a demographic crisis in peacetime, and the only developed country to be experiencing a crisis in terms of the lack of a skilled and educated workforce—this despite the fact that it is second in the world after the United States as a destination for migration flows. This immense demographic and territorial ferment impacts directly on the viability of Russian strategies in the Arctic. How is it possible to make mineral development a viable proposition when the Arctic regions are depopulating? Where is the labor force—ranging from manual laborers to executives—going to come from? How can Moscow reshape the human geography of a country experiencing economic fragmentation?

"Archipelago Russia": A Fragmented Territory

Territory is a key, and long-term, element of state identity. It shapes geo-political strategies and perceptions of the world; it is used as a symbol of the nation through cartographic representation; and more concretely, it has a major influence on the economic capacities of a country. In Russia, the reference to territory has always been part of identity narratives.[3] Ever since the Church Chronicles were written in the Middle Ages, the geographical position of Muscovy, situated at the junction between Europe and Asia and to the north of Byzantium, has been presented as an explanatory element of its history. In the eighteenth century, the major historians of the Russian empire, such as Nikolai Karamzin (1766–1826), insisted on the unique dimension of the Russian territory. Such observations were taken up and reformulated in the nineteenth century, in endless variations, by the Slavophiles and their descendants, for whom the psychological traits of the Russian people and the imperial nature of Russia owe much to geography. In Soviet times, the accent was put on the country's feats in exploiting the soil and on its territorial diversity, which made it possible to present the homeland of socialism as humanity in miniature, including almost all the various climate types and landscapes of the earth.

The Soviet Union's collapse accentuated the complex interplay between nationhood and territory. Although Russia remains the largest country in the world, with close to one-sixth of the earth's land surface, the feeling of territorial hypotrophy dominates current self-representations.[4] The disintegration of the Soviet Union deprived the Russians of fertile southern lands, mainly those in Ukraine and Kazakhstan, of access to ports in temperate waters like the Caspian and Black Seas, and has pushed back the western borders of the country farther to the east, while at the same time, the population is leaving parts of Siberia and the Far East to return to the country's European regions. In such a context, a focus on the Arctic has suddenly reopened a national mental atlas of forgotten or marginalized spaces. Whereas Russia was withdrawing into itself territorially for the first time in a millennium, the Arctic seems to revive an *expansive*, and no longer *retractive*, vision of the country; a potential new space is opening up to it. This reading of the Arctic is particularly operative in the military circles, which see this region as being Russia's most important "reserve of space" (*prostranstvennyi rezerv*).[5]

Apart from the still traumatic loss of the Soviet borders, Russia has additionally faced, for more than two decades now, a considerable reshaping of its territory, with living standards that are increasingly dissociated by region. The principle of "unity in diversity," which stamped Russian history for many centuries, was born of a traditionally centralizing autocratic regime combined with large-scale territorial expansion and decentralization in the management of daily activity. With the implosion of the Soviet Union, the unity/diversity balance fractured, and the country is now undergoing an extreme fragmentation of its territory in terms of population, access to wealth, human development indicators, and economic strategies.[6] The European regions, including the Urals, which constitute only 25% of the territory of the Russian Federation, are home to 78% of the population.[7] In addition to the special case of Moscow city, which saw an exceptional rise in its population of 28% between 1989 and 2008, only three regions have received a large influx of people: the Moscow region (*oblast'*), the Central Federal District, and the Southern Federal District, all three of which have experienced net migration inflows of between 12 and 17%. The rest of Russia is depopulating. Wealth is also concentrated in the European regions: Moscow, with 7.4% of the population, produces 23% of the country's GDP; the Tyumen' region, with 2.4% of the population, provides 18% of the country's tax revenues, while Siberia and the Far East account for 66% of Russian territory but produce only 15% of the country's GDP.[8]

Several Russias coexist within one country. Leslie Dienes likened the highly concentrated pattern of population density and heightened economic activity in post-Soviet Russia to an "archipelago" set within a sea of emptiness and neglect.[9] The French political scientist Jean-Robert Raviot has identified three such archipelagos. "Metropolitan Russia"—Moscow, St. Petersburg, Yekaterinburg, Novosibirsk, and to a lesser extent, Rostov on Don, Nizhnii-Novgorod, Samara, Kazan, and Omsk—is distinguished by its high level of revenues, of inhabitants with tertiary degrees, and its many opportunities of access to services. The university and science towns can also be added to this list, such as Tomsk and Krasnoyarsk, which have lower revenues but a high degree of access to the outside world. A second, "rent archipelago"— Tyumen', Surgut, and Khanty-Mansiisk—has the highest revenues per capita in the country, and offers its inhabitants very generous social policies and broad access to technologies. The "archipelago of the Black Earth"—situated between Kursk, Tambov, Volgograd, and Krasnodar—is the only region to record both economic and demographic growth. With a leading role given to agriculture, the region has a high population density and a level of connected-ness close to Central European standards. While the standard of living there is not as high as in metropolitan Russia, the quality of life has improved.[10] The rest of the country can be defined as "second-class Russia," characterized by abandoned industrial towns in full crisis, high unemployment rates, the pauperization of the former Soviet middle classes, agricultural wastelands, very poor access to transport, and an acute demographic crisis. The North Caucasus Federal District is a case in point. Though one of the poorest areas of the country, with a high unemployment rate and very low GDP per capita, it also displays demographic dynamism, ethnic diversity, increasing political volatility, and considerable outmigration.

Russia is therefore an archipelago of wealthy, urban, economically dy-namic islands in an ocean of sparsely populated and undeveloped hinterland. The social inequalities are above all regional inequalities.[11] The country's extreme regional, social, economic, and ethnic disparities are difficult to reconcile with the traditional strong tendencies toward centralization of authority in Moscow. In this context, the Arctic is simultaneously present and forgotten. Forgotten because it is part of second-class Russia in terms of population, wealth, and connection to the rest of the country, a predica-ment that is exacerbated by the harsh climate with which its inhabitants must contend. However, the Arctic is simultaneously presented by the political authorities as Russia's future, especially in terms of resources. This paradox is not new and has its roots in the former Soviet paradigm of Siberia as a space that is both over- and underdeveloped.

The theory of Siberia's general mismanagement under the Soviet regime resides at the core of the economic analysis conducted by Fiona Hill and Clifford Gaddy in their book *The Siberian Curse: How Communist Plan-ners Left Russia out in the Cold* (2003). They established a contested way of calculating the "cost of the cold,"—i.e., the technical, financial, and human cost of developing regions that are unfavorable to modern human settlement. To this end, they developed a "temperature per capita" system that calculated a cost of living four times higher than in the more temperate regions of the Soviet Union.[12] While Canada and Australia have never sought to link subsoil exploitation to permanent settlements and conceived the development of their immense territories through shift work, the Soviet Union projected its territorial development as extensive and not intensive. It relied largely on the work of Gulag prisoners for achieving its goals of industrialization, and it subsidized unprofitable industries, as the populations based in Siberia and the Arctic achieved a low rate of productivity compared to the other regions of the country. This financial and human burden probably played a major role in the Soviet collapse, which was marked by the misallocation of resources.

Today, the debate over the "cost of cold" arises anew with each evocation of grand plans for Arctic development by high senior officials. The Soviet heritage of extensive development is not the only thing that has come into question. The former imperial system of "mastering" or "settling"(*osvoenie*) the land still draws Moscow into making an intrinsic link between economic development and large settlements. New development programs for the Far East are, for instance, based on the *osvoenie* narrative and Soviet mechanisms: heavy industrialization projects and new incentives for the population to stay and even to migrate there.[13] For the Arctic region, the authorities seem more hesitant and manifest contradictory logics. Some regional experts, as well as firms exploiting Arctic resources, encourage the application of the Canadian or Australian model, and thus the development of non-permanent population settlements operating in a shift-work system. But the official discourse often remains one of economic conquest by *osvoenie*, massive population settlement. Hence the intrinsic—but contestable—link created by Moscow between Arctic resources and demographic issues.

Russia's Demographic Puzzle

The demographic crisis affecting Russia is not new. Throughout the twentieth century, the Russian population had to contend with political crises of such magnitude—years of civil war, Stalinist purges, the Second World War—that they strongly impacted on its demography in terms of falling birth rates, increases in mortality, and massive emigration. All these events had a cumulative effect, since the smaller generations of the 1920s–1950s had statistically fewer children. After the 1970s, a new demographic trend with political and cultural repercussions became apparent when Soviet statistics began to register a demographic slowdown among its Slavic and Baltic

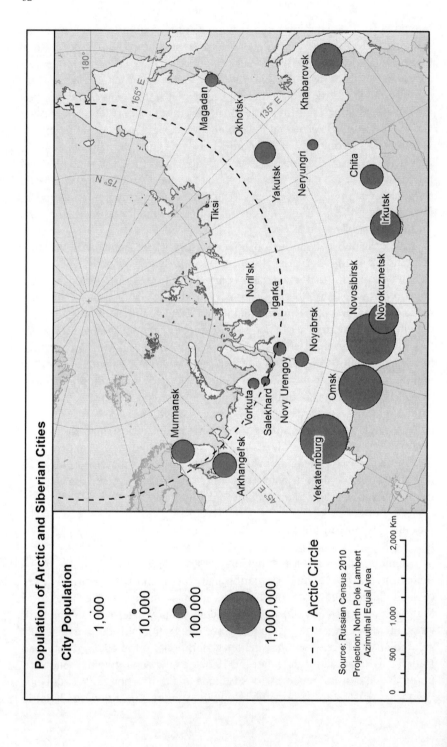

Population of Arctic and Siberian Cities

City Population

1,000

10,000

100,000

1,000,000

– – – Arctic Circle

Source: Russian Census 2010
Projection: North Pole Lambert
Azimuthal Equal Area

0   500   1,000   2,000 Km

populations relative to the continued rapid growth of the Central Asian and Caucasian peoples.[14]

This negative trend intensified in the 1990s, with the Russian population dropping from 148.5 million in 1992 to 141 million in 2009.[15] During the first 15 years of its independence, the country lost about 770,000 persons per year. Since 2007, the trend line began to flatten, or even to invert: while the net loss of population was "only" 478,000 persons during that year, it decreased to 362,000 in 2008,[16] 248,000 in 2009, and 241,000 in 2010, before registering net increases of 191,000 and 243,000, respectively, in 2011 and 2012.[17] At the end of 2012 the authorities announced a total of 143 million citizens, the increase being mainly explained by the natural-ization of immigrants and not merely by improved birth rates. Despite the partial reversal of the population decline in recent years, Russia's overall demographic figures remain particularly poor for a developed country. Between the 1960s and the launch of *perestroika* in the mid-1980s, life expectancy barely increased; it then plummeted to a mere 60 years for men and 73 for women, 15 and 10 years less, respectively than life expectancies in Western Europe. In 2006, average life expectancy was lower than it had been in 1959 during the Khrushchev years.[18] This demographic collapse is unprecedented, as Russia is the only state to experience such depopulation in peacetime, at the same level as some African countries.

There are several explanatory factors. First, the ratio of births to deaths has drastically changed. Between 1992 and 2007, there were only 22 million births in Russia, but close to 35 million deaths, which represents a decrease by one-third and an increase of 40% respectively, compared to Soviet times, and amounts to a total natural population decline of about 13 million since the fall of the Soviet Union.[19] Today, the birth rate per woman (total fertil-ity rate) is around 1.3 to 1.4, which is much lower than the rate required for natural regeneration (2.1), albeit on a par with those found in some European countries, such as Germany. Until the mid-2000s, there were many more abortions than births: an average of 121 abortions per 100 births, one of the highest figures in the world.[20] This ratio balanced out in 2006, and now there are about the same number of births and abortions, due to better knowl-edge of chemical contraception. However, the mortality rate of young women has not stopped rising due to declining social conditions.

Although the weak Russian birth rate is not unique by European standards, and is even higher than the Japanese one, the exceptionally high death rate is. The major explanation for such high peacetime mortality is linked to the level of premature deaths for males through violence and because of accidents (crimes, domestic accidents, accidents at work, road accidents). Deaths due to external causes in Russia appear to be on a par with Burundi,

Liberia, Sierra Leone, Angola, and the Congo.[21] The health of the younger generations is worse than during the Soviet decades. Birth weights and heights were lower for children born in the 1990s than during the Soviet period; but fortunately an increase in the standard of living during the 2000s has somewhat mitigated this phenomenon. Infectious and parasitic diseases have increased. Alcohol abuse, the high rates of smoking, poor diets, and the deterioration of the health care system also in part explain the low life expectancy. Last but not least, Russia has the unenviable status of being the world's leading consumer of heroin, using 70 tons per year, or around 21% of world consumption according to the United Nations Office on Drugs and Crime (UNODC).[22] The country has between four and six million drug users, mainly young people in both urban and rural areas, according to these calculations; this figure has increased by more than nine-fold over the last decade.[23] Russia's Federal Drug Control Service estimates that each year 10,000 Russians die from overdoses and that another 70,000 deaths are drug-related.[24] Moreover, this consumption has a major effect on the spread of the HIV virus because the country has banned methadone treatment and needle exchange programs. According to the UNODC, Russia now has a 1% HIV prevalence rate among its young people and the fastest growing HIV/AIDS epidemic in the world.[25]

This Russian demographic collapse, however, is not uniform and essentially affects the Slavic populations. Of the 20 regions of Russia that have registered positive rates of population growth, 19 are republics or autonomous districts populated in part by non-Russian populations. In Ingushetia, the rate of natural population increase reached 1%, and in Chechnya 2%.[26] Other areas experiencing positive population growth are Dagestan, the Yamalo-Nenets autonomous district, the Khanty-Mansi autonomous district, Tuva, Chita, Tyumen', Altay, and Kabardino-Balkaria. Generally, and with some exceptions, these represent two categories of regions: those of the North Caucasus, from a Muslim tradition, and those of southern and northern Siberia, many of which with a Buddhist tradition. These figures must, however, be seen in context. Although Chechnya has the highest birth rate in Russia, with 3.18 children per woman, the figure is nonetheless low for Muslim populations more globally.[27]

Between the two censuses of 1989 and 2002, the so-called "Muslim populations"[28] increased by 26%. This very high figure is due not only to their higher birth rates but to processes of ethnic re-identification that work to their advantage: the rights accorded to titular populations in the republics or autonomous regions, as well as the symbolic valorization of the local culture are pushing those inhabitants with multiple possible identities to declare their affiliation with the titular nationality. The demographic balance is therefore unfavorable to "ethnic Russians." Between the two censuses, their share of the country's total population dropped from 81.5% to 79.8%, a net decrease of four million persons. However, the figure is probably larger at around eight million, since it was compensated for by the arrival of several million Russians from the Near Abroad (former Soviet republics of the USSR), who emigrated to Russia during the 1990s.[29] The "Muslim population" constitutes about 14 million people (10% of the population),[30] although some calculations put this figure at close to 20 million, or about 15% of the population. This figure takes into account only Russian citizens, not migrants, who are largely undocumented.

The projections of the United Nations Development Programme (UNDP), the U.S. Census Bureau, and the Russian State Statistics Service (*Rosstat*), despite their divergent methods of calculation, all agree that Russia's population will continue to decline in the decades to come. It is forecast that the country will have between 122 and 135 million inhabitants by 2030, a figure that could collapse to about 100 million by the middle of the twenty-first century. Upon Putin's arrival in power and even more so during his second term as president, the demographic question became a central one for the Kremlin, and was presented as a challenge to national security. Accordingly, in the Concept of Demographic Policy for the Russian Federation by 2025, released in 2007, the authorities set the goal of achieving a stabilized population of 145 million people with a life expectancy of 75 years.[31] If the figure of 145 million is easy to attain thanks to the naturalization of migrants, a life expectancy of 75 years requires genuine improvement in health care policies at the federal level.

So far the measures implemented to respond to the demographic challenge seem to have been rather ineffective. The focus has been placed on the birth rate, rather than on the mortality rate. A "baby bonus" of close to $10,000 was implemented in 2006 to provide financial and home-related incentives for women to have a second child. If this measure led to a rise in the birth rate, it is mainly the improvement in the living standards of the middle classes that explains the inversion of the curve. Russia's birth rate increased by 100,000 annually in 2011 and in 2012.[32] Every year since 2009, the authorities have mounted a large self-congratulatory campaign, boasting of Russia's natural population increases. Nevertheless, demographic factors work against the incentives and programs put in place to arrest the declining number of births. Even if Russian women of childbearing age do start having more children, the overall number of such women will decline by 20% by around 2025, which can only lead to a decrease in the number of births. Russia no longer has enough young people to maintain the population level. In 2009, the 15–19 age group was only 4.5 million, and both the 5–9 and 10–14 age groups taken together totaled only 6.5 million persons.[33] The number of births will thus decrease again when the tiny cohort born during the 1990s enters the prime childbearing years. In addition and more importantly, the measures taken to fight against the real scourge that is male mortality are practically nonexistent. With the exception of a campaign against traffic accidents and fatalities, the authorities do not seem to have come to grips with the loss of such a considerable proportion of working-age men to violent deaths. Reviving births through financial mechanisms is easier to do than making significant social changes to address the issue of violent male deaths, whose explanatory factors are much more complex.

These demographic trends have a direct impact on the workforce. The average age in Russia will rise from the 2005 figure of 40 years to 46 years by 2030, which is only 15 years less than current male life expectancy and 10–15 years less than the legal age of retirement (55 years for women and 60 for men). Today Russia has 2.5 persons of working age for every person over working age, but it will have less than two by 2025. The phenomenon of population aging, also very pronounced in Western Europe and Japan, will take on a special dimension in Russia given the small size of the young cohorts and the massive poverty among the retired population. The population of those between 15 and 34 years will fall to 35% of the total by 2030. The 55–64 age cohort is the only one that will increase—but will largely not be part of the labor force.[34]

The U.S. Census Bureau has predicted a decrease in manpower availability in Russia of 16% between 2009 and 2025.[35] A study conducted by the Russian Regional Policy Institute revealed that by 2020 the country is expected to create seven million new jobs thanks to the industrial projects under way, but that it will lose a million persons of working age each year. The replacement of Soviet generations entering retirement is thus by no means guaranteed. By 2020, the working-age population could decrease from nearly 90 million to 77 million, and the country could face an accumulated shortage of educated workers of up to13 million.[36] Contributing to this shortage is the astonishing decrease in the student population. The total number of high school students fell by almost half between 1998 and 2009, dropping from 20 million to 13 million. University student numbers, moreover, are expected to decrease from the current 7.5 million to 4 million in the 2013–2014 academic year.[37] According to the calculations of the UNDP, to compensate for the declining population over the first half of the twenty-first century, Russia will need a cumulative net immigration of 25 million persons before 2050, and 32 million if it is to maintain its working-age population.[38]

Russia lacks not only cheap labor but also a qualified workforce. Paradoxically, education standards are high but the level of human capital low.

It is the only country in the world where the comparatively high number of graduates is at such odds with the very low GDP per capita, declining labor productivity, few new patents, and where so-called social capital (participation in voluntary associations, trust in society, subjective well-being, level of self-assessed degree of personal control over one's own life) is so weak.[39] In 2009, a group of leading businessmen led by Severstal' Group CEO Aleksey Mordashov launched an appeal to President Medvedev for skilled workers. According to their surveys, 54% of Russian CEOs view staff shortages as the biggest impediment to growth.[40] This trend hampers the development potential of the Arctic regions, which necessitate advanced technologies and highly specialized knowledge.

Evolving Patterns of Arctic Demography and Mobility

To these countrywide demographic trends can be added profound changes in patterns of population mobility. The collapse of the Soviet system has had a huge impact on the Arctic and Siberian economic development. Between 1987 and 2000 economic output fell by four-fifths in Yakutia-Sakha and Chukotka, some mining centers and industrial settlements were totally abandoned, and several military bases were closed. The downsizing of the Northern benefits accelerated the exodus of population from the region. The absence of work prospects, of a future for their children; the exorbitant prices of basic goods; the chronic shortage of heating, gas, and electricity; and the declining transportation attenuating linkages with the rest of the country have pushed millions of Russians to migrate to the European regions.[41] The majority have migrated outside of any state-organized framework. As noted by Timothy Heleniak, between 1993 and 2009 the High North "had a population decline of 15.3%, consisting of 17.1% decline from net out-migration, compensated for by a 1.8% increase from the region having more births than deaths as a result of having a younger age structure than the country."[42]

Between 1989 and 2006, one out of six emigrated from the Far North.[43] Between the censuses of 1989 and 2002, the regions of Magadan and Chukotka lost more than half of their populations, Taimyr 30%, Yamalo-Nenets 25%, and even the Murmansk region lost more than 20% of its population. Yakutia escaped relatively lightly, with a depopulation of only 12%.[44] The port towns of Igarka and Tiksi lost about half of their inhabitants between 1987 and 2005, while Dikson lost four-fifths of its population. In the Magadan region, more than 40 settlements were declared "without inhabitants" in the 2002 census. Ghost towns have grown in number, creating poverty gaps in which the remaining populations do not have enough money to migrate.[45] The Far East as a whole lost 17% of its population in the space of two decades, declining from eight million inhabitants in 1990 to 6.4 million in 2010.[46] The case is similar for the Siberian Federal District, although the decline is less steep.[47] Arctic Siberia today is the least inhabited area in the world after Antarctica and the Sahara Desert.

Russia's Arctic became an immense terrain in movement. Internal migrations between Arctic regions have been considerable.[48] Small towns and rural settlements have been abandoned and their inhabitants have moved to larger towns, which are able to provide a wider range of services. But one also notes north-south and south-north movements, as the large cities of the Siberian south, such as Krasnoyarsk, attract youths born in the north, who come mainly for their studies before "returning" to their regions of origin. Objectively difficult living conditions alone are not enough to make the inhabitants relocate outside the Arctic region. In the first half of the 2000s, the Russian government launched the Northern Restructuring Project thanks to a loan from the World Bank. The goal was to assist the voluntary resettlement of Chukotka's non-working population to more southerly towns; but the success has been limited, and those resettled have experienced difficulties in adapting.[49] Indeed place-specific social capital is not easy to rebuild and many people have refused to leave the region where they have built their lives, despite the deterioration in living conditions. Arctic identity and a feeling of belonging to the region have played an important role in the refusal of some to move.[50]

A more detailed analysis of Arctic mobility yields a less negative and more diverse demographic picture. Just as during the Soviet period, the Arctic population is younger than the national average (30 compared to 37 years of age in the 2002 census), because the oil and gas fields attract youths with a dearth of career opportunities, and because the indigenous peoples have a higher birth rate. However, again similar to the Soviet period, life expectancy there is also shorter, both among indigenous peoples and ethnic Russians.[51] Moreover, despite the bigger picture of depopulation, closer analysis reveals that towns linked to the mineral resource extraction sector have experienced positive migration rates during the 2000s. The Khanty-Mansi and Yamalo-Nenets districts, which account for about 60% of the entire economic output of the North, remain attractive to both Russian and foreign migrants.[52]

The Arctic region remains one of Russia's most "mobile," with young generations ready to migrate for secure employment as well as job opportunities. It is therefore necessary to distinguish between at least two Arctics: regions in crisis that are losing population and where Russians and indigenous populations alike experience deteriorating living conditions; and those regions in full economic boom, whose populations are more educated, younger, more prone to migrate, and which attract an increasing number of

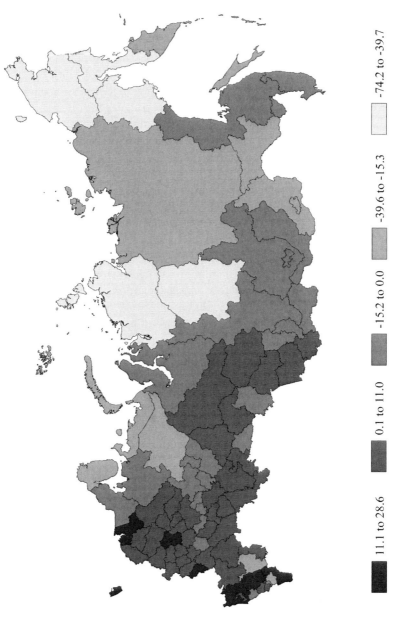

Net Migration by Region in Russia, 1989 to 2008 (percent of 1989 population)

11.1 to 28.6

0.1 to 11.0

-15.2 to 0.0

-39.6 to -15.3

-74.2 to -39.7

foreign migrants. In the latter Arctic zones, migration has more to do with labor market turnover than a one-way exodus as in the former.[53]

Is Migration the Future of the Arctic Workforce?

The future development of the Arctic presupposes a labor force that, in view of the country's demographic dynamics, is lacking today. The recourse to immigration already presents itself as a key engine of Russia's current economic growth. Although the data on migration are difficult to collect and interpret, all experts are in agreement that Russia has become the second-largest receiving country of migrants in the world, after the United States.[54]

According to Russian statistics, between 1992 and 2006, 3.1 million persons emigrated from and 7.4 million immigrated to Russia, yielding a net positive migration balance of 4.3 million inhabitants.[55] The figures compiled by the UNDP and the U.S. Census Bureau are higher and, depending on the calculations used, show a migration surplus of about 6 million people in the first 15 years following the Soviet Union's collapse. The majority of Russian emigrants left for Western Europe, Israel, Canada, and the United States, while the majority of immigrants came from among the 25 million ethnic Russians of the Near Abroad who left their republics to settle in Russia.[56] However, the prevailing pattern of "repatriation" or "ethnic return" of Russians in the 1990s changed in the 2000s, during which time fewer Russians in the Near Abroad immigrated, while the number of post-Soviet citizens belonging to the titular nationalities increased. Requests for Russian citizenship today come mainly from Central Asian or Azeri populations, especially as Russian law has simplified the procedures for obtaining citizenship for all former Soviet citizens, without distinction between ethnic Russians and non-Russians. Thus data from the census of 2002 show that the growth in the foreign-born population from the southern areas of the former Soviet Union has literally exploded: 70% growth for citizens born in Uzbekistan, Kyrgyzstan, and Azerbaijan, and 150% for those from Tajikistan.[57]

The Russian media and politicians have systematically sought to inflate the number of foreign migrants, and the topic has become one of the most debated in the public sphere, as it has in Europe or the United States. Estimates vary from 5 to 15 million migrants, but a range of between 7 and 10 million would seem to be most likely.[58] The distinction between legal and illegal migrants is very complex in Russia, since the country has a visa-free system with most CIS countries. It is therefore not illegal to cross the border, but it is illegal to stay for work without registering with the appropriate authorities. But Russian bureaucracy, because of its complexity and corruption, plays a key role in making migrants undocumented by complicating the registration procedures. As in Europe, companies gain from employing illegal workers and do not want the processes of legalization to be reformed. The majority of these migrants are from Central Asia (Tajikistan, Uzbekistan, and Kyrgyzstan) and the Caucasus (mainly Azerbaijan), speak Russian with varying degrees of proficiency, and organize their migration through family and regional networks.[59] Other migrants require a visa to enter the country. One notable group is the Chinese (but also the Vietnamese), who reportedly number about half a million, and who for the most part reside in the Far East.[60]

As in the United States or Europe, migration has become the main source of labor in some economic sectors. The extractive industries, construction sites, the public service sector (waste management, and road, rail, and water works), and other services (domestic staff, security personnel, cooks, and restaurant and cafe staff) are all large users of migrant labor. Russian citizens tend to disregard these professional niches, deeming the salaries insufficient, working conditions too difficult, and social prestige too low. Russia's migrants are widely distributed geographically. Moscow and its broader region largely dominate and attract the largest number of them due to the quality of life and better prospects for jobs. This is followed by large cities such as St. Petersburg and Yekaterinburg, industrial sites in the Urals, the south of the country where many migrants are increasingly working in agriculture, and lastly the Far East, where they face some competition from Chinese and Vietnamese migrants.[61] Although Arctic regions experience net out-migration with the rest of Russia, they do benefit from a simultaneous massive net immigration from foreign countries.[62]

In the 1990s, companies working the large oil deposits of the Tyumen' region were the only ones that continued to pay profitable salaries and thus readily attracted labor from outside the region. In the following decade, the gap between the rise of revenues and the quality of life widened between the European regions and the rest of the country. Consequently, fewer qualified Russians moved to West Siberia to take up the offers made by the large companies, which then turned massively toward foreign migrants. The oil and gas regions of Tyumen' and Khanty-Mansi have quickly become privileged destinations for Central Asians and Caucasians, in particular Azeris, and some Kazakhs seeking employment at extraction sites, while Tajiks and Uzbeks are massively involved in the construction sector. Already at the start of the 2000s, foreigners made up half of the workforce on some construction sites in the Far East; in the Tyumen' region they constituted about two-thirds of salaried workers.[63] Developing the Yamal megaproject is expected to require about 50,000 workers, and there are reportedly already nearly 20,000 foreigners working there on infrastructure construction sites.[64] The state nuclear agency Rosatom has been criticized for employing illegal migrants in its nuclear power plants, for not only do these migrants work in unsafe conditions for low wages, but they are untrained and thereby pose a safety risk at the plants.[65] Lastly, the city of Noril'sk has by some estimates a population of 50,000 migrants, mainly from Azerbaijan, Dagestan, and Central Asia.[66] The Arctic's difficult working conditions, and in particular the increase in shift-work (*vakhtovyi metod*, short-term tours of duty on extraction sites from a base city), necessitate finding undemanding workers that come for the financial incentives offered and not for the quality of life.

The foreign migrants living in the Arctic fall into two broad categories: those who work on the main industrial sites, and those who of their own initiative move into the private sector, mostly into trade and small-size services. As for now only two CIS countries are able to supply Russia with qualified labor: Ukraine, where there is high unemployment among graduates, especially in the engineering sectors, and Azerbaijan, where oil-related expertise and professions have long been established. It is likely that Kazakhstan will also become a supplier once its main gas and oil sites become fully operational, as they will require fewer personnel. In 2010, and then in 2012, Moscow made a decision to relax migration policy with respect to CIS countries, which are the main source countries for migrants, but this alone will not be sufficient to meet the needs of the national economy.[67] Large Russian companies today lobby in favor of a proactive migration intake policy, albeit discreetly because of the xenophobic atmosphere: being perceived as too pro-migrant could tarnish the corporate brand.[68] In any case, a favorable migration policy for the CIS countries will not be enough to compensate for shortages of qualified labor, as most workers arriving from Central Asia and the Caucasus are unskilled. In coming years the Russian economy will require a targeted policy, as in Canada and Australia, of inviting graduates from Asia, the Middle East, or perhaps Central and Southern Europe, on the condition that it is able to offer attractive living conditions and salaries. The need to adopt a major policy drive to train engineers and management staff at Russian universities is also apparent, in order to offset the departure of Soviet-trained specialists from the workforce.

It remains difficult at present to ascertain what long-term role the immigrating populations will play in Russia, and particularly whether they will settle permanently. Although for the moment a large share of the migrants either adopt seasonal strategies or wish to stay in Russia for only a few years while accumulating the financial resources that will allow them to return home, the European and U.S. experience shows that a large number eventually do settle in the host country and build new lives there.[69] These migrants are therefore destined to form a growing share of the Russian population, and indeed of its workforce. Regardless of whether all of the Arctic industrial projects currently projected become a reality, or whether the demand for labor recedes after infrastructure construction is completed and the deposits have become operational, the urban fabric has already been profoundly modified by interaction with migrants. Built in 1998 in Noril'sk, the Nurd Kamal Mosque, the northernmost mosque in the world, can be viewed as a symbol of the presence of Islam in the Arctic. Since the 1970s, numerous Azeri, Tatar, and Bashkir engineers have settled in the northern regions, and Islam has quickly become a part of the local scenery, a trend strengthened today by Central Asian immigration. It is also possible that Chinese migrants, already based in the Far East, might look to settle farther north. Two migratory spurts, one involving Chinese and the other Central Asians, might thus come into competition with one another. This is already the case in the cities of the Far East, where construction sites in Chinese hands have been taken over in recent years by Central Asians.[70] The capacity of the Russian state to formulate a new civic identity and to integrate its growing migrant community therefore will be crucial for the country's future, and for local Arctic identities.

Russia must contend with multiple domestic dilemmas. Some relate to the collapse of the Soviet framework, as well as to the social dynamics and economic legacy bequeathed by the preceding regime; others, probably the most challenging, are yet to come. One of these is the population issue. If the aging of the population is not a phenomenon unique to Russia, the country nonetheless is burdened by many demographic particularities: a rate of male mortality unacceptable for a developed country; a dearth of younger generations and women of childbearing age; and a glaring lack of skilled workers, and universities poor at creating engineering expertise and technological innovation. Added to this is the immigration challenge: thus far, Russian public policies have had little visible success in better integrating the millions of migrants (providing them with legal rights, protecting them against violence and arbitrary corruption, and so on), or in creating a new civic identity. The Russian social fabric is therefore significantly destructured and unbalanced.

The second dilemma is related to the management of Russia's territory. Russia has always been a centralized state, despite some decentralizing trends in the nineteenth century, in the 1920s, and then in the 1990s during Yeltsin's presidency. The current territorial polarization weighs heavily on Russia's self-representation, but also on its political legitimacy and the country's social unity. The conjunction of these two dilemmas—population and territorial management—is central to the future of the Russian Arctic: Moscow's grand ambitions for its northern regions will not become a reality unless a joint solution is found to address both problems. But this would require the country to undergo deep identity, social, and political transformations. Russia's spatial representation of itself is destined to change: the North Caucasus has, for all intents and purposes, become a "foreign" region; the demographic dynamism of the Buddhist populations of southern Siberia has strengthened their specificity and identity; and the feeling of a lack of control over the Far East is also growing. Russian territorial identification has withdrawn into a space stretching from the borders of the EU to the Urals, from St. Petersburg to Stavropol'. Will the Arctic form part of these areas where Russia's future identity will find itself "at home," or of those zones left abandoned? Which Arctic regions will be integrated, and which forgotten?

Notes

1. "Socio-demographic Situation in the Arctic," August 30, 2010, http://int. rgo.ru/arctic/arctic-overview/socio-demographic-situation-in-the-arctic/ (accessed December 4, 2012).

2. See the "Arctic Research Coordination Network: Building a Research Network for Promoting Arctic Urban Sustainability," George Washington University, http://www.gwu.edu/~ieresgwu/programs/ARCN.cfm (accessed December 4, 2012).

3. M. Bassin, C. Ely, and M.K. Stockdale, eds., *Space, Place, and Power in Modern Russia: Essays in the New Spatial History* (DeKalb: Northern Illinois University Press, 2010).

4. J. O'Loughlin, and P. Talbot, "Where in the World is Russia? Geopolitical Perceptions and Preferences of Ordinary Russians," *Eurasian Geography and Economics* 46, no. 1 (2005): 23–50; J. O'Loughlin, G. Toal, and V. Kolossov, "The Geopolitical Orientations of Ordinary Russians: A Public Opinion Analysis," *Eurasian Geography and Economics* 48, no. 2 (2006): 129–152.

5. See for instance S. Koz'menko, and S. Kovalev, "Morskaia politika v Arktike i sistema national'noi bezopasnosti [Maritime policy in the Arctic and the national security system]," *Morskoi sbornik* 8 (2009): 57.

6. B.A. Ruble, J. Koehn, and N.E. Popson, eds., *Fragmented Space in the Russian Federation* (Washington, DC: Woodrow Wilson International Center for Scholars and Johns Hopkins University, 2011).

7. J. Radvanyi, *La Nouvelle Russie. Géographie économique, régions et nations, géopolitique* [The new Russia. Economic geography, regions and peoples, geopolitics] (Paris: Masson, Armand Colin, 1996), 60.

8. J.-R. Raviot, "Géographie politique de la Russie en 2010 [The political geography of Russia in 2010]," *Hérodote*, no. 138 (2010): 169.

9. L. Dienes, "Reflections on a Geographic Dichotomy: Archipelago Russia," *Eurasian Geography and Economics* 43, no. 6 (2002): 443–458.

10. Raviot, "Géographie politique de la Russie en 2010."

11. T. Heleniak, "Growth Poles and Ghost Towns in the Russian Far North," in E. Wilson Rowe, ed., *Russia and the North* (Ottawa: University of Ottawa Press, 2009), 134.

12. F. Hill and C. Gaddy, *The Siberian Curse: How Communist Planners Left Russia out in the Cold* (Washington, DC: Brookings Institution Press, 2003).

13. United Russia's Regional Conference on "The Strategy for Social and Economic Development of the Far East until 2020," http://premier.gov.ru/events/news/13223/ (accessed December 4, 2012).

14. See H. Carrère d'Encausse, *L'Empire éclaté: la révolte des nations en URSS* [The broken empire: The revolt of nations in the USSR] (Paris: Flammarion, 1978).

15. T. Heleniak, "Population Perils in Russia at the Beginning of the 21st Century," in S. Wegren and D. Herspring, eds., *After Putin's Russia: Past Imperfect, Future Unknown* (Lanham: Rowman & Littlefield, 2009), 133–158.

16. N. Eberstadt, "Russia's Peacetime Demographic Crisis: Dimensions, Causes, Implications," *NBR Report*, May 2010, 28. The majority of the demographic information in this section is taken from this report.

17. Data are from the Russian State Statistics Service, http://www.gks.ru/bgd/free/B12_00/IssWWW.exe/Stg/dk11/8–0.htm (accessed December 4, 2012).

18. Eberstadt, "Russia's Peacetime Demographic Crisis," 67.

19. Ibid., 11.

20. Ibid., 44.

21. N. Eberstadt, "The Security Consequences of Democratic Decline," International conference on "Matching Ambitions and Realities: What Future for Russia?", Canadian Security Intelligence Service (CSIS), Ottawa, May 6–7, 2010.

22. *World Drug Report 2010* (Vienna: UNODC, 2010), 41 and 45.

23. *Illicit Drug Trends in the Russian Federation* (Vienna: UNODC, April 2008), 10.

24. *International Narcotics Control Strategy Report—2008*, US Embassy in Russia, 2008, http://moscow.usembassy.gov/incsr2008.html (accessed December 4, 2012).

25. *Illicit Drug Trends in the Russian Federation*, 6.

26. Eberstadt, "Russia's Peacetime Demographic Crisis," 22.

27. Ibid., 37.

28. Russian censuses do not ask any religion-related questions. One cannot therefore use religious criteria to classify the population. The use of the term "Muslim populations" defines only people whose traditional and most practiced religion is Islam, but not individual religious practices.

29. Ibid., 24.

30. T. Heleniak, "Regional Distribution of the Muslim Population of Russia," *Eurasian Geography and Economics* 47, no. 4 (2007): 426–448.

31. "Kontseptsiia demograficheskoi politiki Rossiiskoi Federatsii na period do 2025 g. [Concept of demographic policy of the Russian Federation by 2025]," October 9, 2007, http://www.demoscope.ru/weekly/knigi/koncepciya/koncepciya25.html (accessed December 4, 2012).

32. "Russian Birth Rate to Rise to 1.8 Million as New Year Rings In," *Russia Today*, December 21, 2012, http://rt.com/politics/russia-demographics-population-babies-crisis-538/ (accessed December 4, 2012).

33. "On Russia's Brief Population Increase," *Demography matters*, January 30, 2010, http://demographymatters.blogspot.com/2010/01/on-russias-brief-population-increase.html (accessed December 4, 2012).

34. Eberstadt, "Russia's Peacetime Demographic Crisis," 250.

35. Ibid., 286.

36. O. Kolesnikova, "Stop, kadry. V 2010–2020g. obostroitsia bor'ba za trudovye

resursy [Stop, cadres. In 2010–2020 the struggle for labor resources will become more intense]," *Rossiiskaia gazeta*, June 6, 2008; "Dostatochno li v Rossii professional'nykh kadrov dlia investitsionnogo rosta? [Are professional personnel sufficient in Russia for investment growth?]," *Polit.ru*, October 30, 2008, http://www.polit.ru/research/2008/10/30/demoscope349.html (accessed December 4, 2012).

37. "On Russia's Brief Population Increase."

38. Eberstadt, "Russia's Peacetime Demographic Crisis," 171.

39. Ibid., 220–245.

40. "Staff Shortages Cripple Russian Business," *Russia Today*, April 9, 2008, http://rt.com/business/news/staff-shortages-cripple-russian-business/ (accessed December 4, 2012).

41. T. Wites, "Depopulation of the Russian Far East. Magadan Oblast, a Case Study," *Miscellanea Geographica* 12 (2006): 185–196.

42. T. Heleniak, "Population Change in the Periphery: Changing Migration Patterns in the Russian North," *Sibirica: Interdisciplinary Journal of Siberian Studies* 9, no. 3 (2010): 17–18.

43. Heleniak, "Growth Poles and Ghost Towns in the Russian Far North," in Wilson Rowe, *Russia and the North*, 129.

44. T. Heleniak, "Out-migration and Depopulation of the Russian North during the 1990s," *Post-Soviet Geography and Economics* 40, no. 3 (1999): 281–304.

45. Y. Andreinko, and S. Guriev, *Determinants of Interregional Mobility in Russia: Evidence from Panel Data*. (Moscow: New Economic School, 2003). See also N. Thompson, *Settlers on the Edge: Identity and Modernization on Russia's Arctic Frontier* (Vancouver and Toronto: University of British Columbia Press, 2008).

46. "Population Statistics of the Russian Far East," *Russian Analytical Digest*, no. 82, July 2010, 11.

47. Eberstadt, "Russia's Peacetime Demographic Crisis," 191.

48. T.S. Heleniak, "Changing Settlement Patterns across the Russian North at the Turn of the Millenium," in M. Tykkyläinen and V. Rautio, eds., *Russia's Northern Regions on the Edge: Communities, Industries, and Populations from Murmansk to Magadan* (Helsinki: Aleksanteri Institute, 2008), 25–52.

49. N. Thompson, "Administrative Resettlement and the Pursuit of Economy: The Case of Chukotka," *Polar Geography* 26, no. 4 (2002): 270–288. See also the project funded by the BOREAS scheme of the European Science Foundation, "Moved by the State: Perspectives on Relocation and Resettlement in the Circumpolar North (MOVE)."

50. T. Heleniak, "The Role of Attachment to Place in Migration Decisions of the Population of the Russian North," *Polar Geography* 32, no. 1–2 (2009): 31–60.

51. I. Øverland and H. Blakkisrud, "The Evolution of Federal Indigenous Policy in the Post-Soviet North," in H. Blakkisrud and G. Hønneland, eds., *Tackling Space: Federal Politics and the Russian North* (Lanham, Oxford: University Press of America, 2006), 181.

52. Heleniak, "Growth Poles and Ghost Towns in the Russian Far North," 146–148.

53. Ibid., 137–138.

54. A. Mansoor and B. Quillin, eds., *Migration and Remittances: Eastern Europe and the Former Soviet Union* (Washington, DC: The World Bank, 2006).

55. Eberstadt, "Russia's Peacetime Demographic Crisis," 153.

56. A. de Tinguy, *La Grande Migration. La Russie et les Russes depuis l'ouverture du rideau de fer* [The great migration. Russia and the Russians since the opening of the Iron Curtain] (Paris: Plon, 2004).

57. Eberstadt, "Russia's Peacetime Demographic Crisis," 163.

58. G. Ioffe and Zh. Zayonchkovskaya, *Immigration to Russia: Why It Is Inevitable, and How Large It May Have to Be to Provide the Workforce Russia Needs* (Washington, DC: National Council for Eurasian and East European Research, January 2011).

59. M. Laruelle, ed., *Migration and Social Upheaval as the Face of Globalization in Central Asia* (Leiden: Brill, 2013).

60. M. Repnikova, and H. Balzer, "Chinese Migration to Russia: Missed Opportunities," *WWICS Eurasian Migration Paper*, no. 3 (2010): 13–15.

61. Zh. A. Zaionchkovskaia, O.I. Vendina, N.V. Mkrtchyan, E.V. Tyurkanova, T.D. Ivanova, and V.G. Gelbras, *Immigranty v Moskve* [Immigrants in Moscow] (Moscow: Tri kvadrata, 2009); Zh.A. Zaionchkovskaia and G.S. Vitkovskaia, eds., *Postsovetskie transformatsii: otrazhenie v migratsiiakh* [Post-Soviet transformations and their impact on migrations] (Moscow: Tsentr migratsionnykh issledovanii, 2009).

62. Heleniak, "Growth Poles and Ghost Towns in the Russian Far North," 138.

63. Hill and Gaddy, *The Siberian Curse,* 179.

64. "Investitsii v cheloveka [Human investments]," *Rossiiskie regiony*, no. 4, 2009, http://www.gosrf.ru/journal/article/64 (accessed December 4, 2012).

65. A. Ozharovskii, "Rossiiskie AES stroiat gastartbaitery-nelegaly [Illegal guest workers—illegals are building Russian nuclear power plants]," *Bellona*, February 14, 2011, http://www.bellona.ru/articles_ru/articles_2011/Rafshan.

66. Information given by Russian experts on the Arctic, SOPS, Moscow, October 25, 2010.

67. "Rossiia snimaet bar'ery dlia gastarbaiterov iz stran SNG [Russia removes barriers for CIS guest workers]," *Trud*, May 19, 2010, http://www.trud.ru/article/19–05–2010/242381_rossija_snimaet_barjery_dlja_gastarbajterov_iz_stran_sng.html (accessed December 4, 2012).

68. Anonymous information provided by Russian experts, MGIMO, IMEMO and SOPS, Moscow, September 2010.

69. C. Bonifazi, M. Okolski, J. Schoorl, and P. Simon, eds., *International Migration in Europe: New Trends and New Methods of Analysis* (Amsterdam: Amsterdam University Press, 2008).

70. Personal observations during fieldwork in Vladivostok, October 2010.

Chapter 4

Climate Change and Its Expected Impact on Russia

There is substantial evidence that global warming of some significance will occur during the twenty-first century. The fourth Intergovernmental Panel on Climate Change (IPCC) has drawn up several scenarios that envisage what impact global warming might entail. In all scenarios, the northerly latitude of the Russian territory—especially its Arctic regions—means that it will be more greatly affected than more temperate parts of the globe. Indeed, more than the tropical or temperate regions, the northern zones of the globe have proved especially sensitive to climate change, and warming in Northern Eurasia is expected to be well above the global mean. However, in contrast with Europe, Japan, and the United States, Russia will be the only developed country that stands to benefit economically from climate change. Indeed, being the most northern of countries with a developed economy, it should see some sectors such as agriculture and hydroelectric production gain from more advantageous climatic conditions. However, such predictions are linked only to changes in temperature. Through several other interrelated aspects of climate change, the Russian territory will also endure negative effects, ranging from the thawing of permafrost to large-scale droughts. Reflecting the ambiguous character of the expected impacts, the Russian state's stance on the issue of climate change is in many ways contradictory and has been evolving for some years now. Skeptical on the whole, and tending to interpret the most pessimistic predictions as reflecting a Western penchant for "decline" theories, Moscow above all is looking to protect its economic interests, ready only to engage in limited processes of adaptation, but not of mitigation, and prepared to make concessions under the proviso that the United States is also willing to come to the party.

Framing Climate Change Debates

Debates over climate change probably constitute one of the most intense scientific controversies of the century. This is the case for three reasons.

The first is globalization, the exchange of information is no longer confined within national borders, which means that Indian, Chinese, African, and Latin American researchers are just as involved in the debate as are their Western colleagues. Second, the consequences of a prospective drastic climate change will affect the entire planet, from the richest to the poorest countries. And lastly, these debates involve making decisions on the global evolution of humanity, and therefore on forging international mechanisms in which the balance between developed and developing countries is under permanent negotiation.

The quasi totality of scientists recognizes that the Earth's climate is evolving: the planet is a living organism, and its climate continues to change as it previously had for millennia, the time scale of the Earth being different from that of the human species. A large number of the scientists agree that there was an increase in the overall temperature of the Earth of 0.7°C during the twentieth century, probably because the concentration of carbon dioxide and other greenhouse gases in the atmosphere has increased since the start of the industrial era, added to which is the related question of stratospheric ozone depletion. This consensual—but far from unanimous—opinion has been expressed by the IPCC, which, as of 2001, has maintained that "an increasing body of observations gives a collective picture of a warming world and other changes in the climate system. . . . There is new and stronger evidence that most of the warming observed over the last fifty years is attributable to human activities."[1] Those who reject the idea that there is a tendency toward global warming now find themselves in the minority. The question of the role played by human activity in climate change is the subject of even more bitter debate. While majority opinion thinks that this change is mainly, but not solely, manmade, others maintain that it has more to do with natural cycles over which humans do not have control, among other solar activity, which seems to play a key role in the Earth's global climate.[2]

The difficulty involved in taking a stance can be explained by the multiplicity of analytical criteria, their highly technical nature, as well as the diversity of possible interpretations. Each scientific discipline constructs its own norms, modes of calculation, and verification, and what is true in meteorology is not necessarily so in oceanology. Climate change theories must therefore take into account multiple assessments from different disciplinary perspectives, while providing a global meta-narrative that is in conformity with each.[3] Moreover, the debates are not devoid of ideology. Some lobbies have vested interests in promoting a doomsday reading of the climate question or, on the contrary, in playing down its importance, or indeed denying it altogether. Those groups convinced of the major role of human-induced climate change denounce the role of the industrial lobbies, in particular those linked to the extraction of fossil fuels and automobile production, which do not want to see their mode of production, or the profits they gain from it, undermined.[4] The skeptics, however, are concerned about the possible emergence of a "green" political newspeak, shaped by movements such as Greenpeace, and more still about an ideology of "de-growth" that rejects even the idea of sustainable development.[5] Lastly, the division between science and politics is tenuous, and the same scientific arguments can be interpreted differently along national lines. Even among those who believe in manmade climate change, competing logics of responding to this new challenge exist. One appeals to procedures of mitigation that argues for reducing greenhouse gas emissions into the atmosphere by modifying patterns of economic activity. The second insists on adaptation, claiming that climate change cannot be stopped and so the resiliency of human societies must be increased. This debate is fundamental, as it implies contradictory strategies of development.[6]

Among the multiple difficulties encountered in framing climate change debates is the question of the scale (geographical as well as temporal) of the predictions. Studying global patterns common to the entire planet does not necessarily make it possible to devise frameworks of prediction at finer scales such as that of a region or a country. Temporality is also a key question. Climate change models are based on long-term data, for the purpose of obtaining an overview of the climate several decades from now, essentially in the second half of the twenty-first century. Intense debate is ongoing regarding the capabilities and methods needed to create such models—that is, the mathematical formulae and information utilized—and lies beyond the scope of this book.[7] However, all recognize that medium-term modeling (20–30 years) of climate change is particularly difficult and that interpretation becomes more complicated at small temporal scales. It is even more a complex matter to prove the causal relation between any particular climatic event, such as the immense bush fires that occurred in Russia in the summer of 2010, or the increase of the number of floods or hurricanes, and climate change as such. The link between perceptions of climate change at the micro-level—that of an individual human life—often bears no major connection to planetary processes, which take place on a temporal scale measured in millions of years.[8]

Despite these limitations, knowledge on the evolution of climate has multiplied many times over the last 10 years. While the future is by definition unknown, and the predictions can always be contested, the past certainly is known, as is the present, at least in general terms, and both confirm changes of great magnitude are occurring. The climate change prognoses made in the 1980s and at the beginning of the 1990s have nearly all been rendered inaccurate: the changes visible today are much greater and have occurred much more rapidly than predicted by forecasts 20 years ago. As early as 2007, the National Center for Atmospheric Research (NCAR) recognized that the scenarios established for the Arctic were too conservative.[9] The next IPCC report, to be published in 2014, will paint an even bleaker picture of the planet's change in terms of pollution, extreme weather, sea level rise, changes in the Arctic, and impacts on fauna, flora, and food production.[10] It seems that three main feedback mechanisms (i.e., chains of cause and effect) are accelerating climate change: the modification of oceanic circulation by meltwater; the release of carbon dioxide and methane by thawing permafrost; and the worldwide disappearance of ice.

Climate Change in the Arctic

Different parts of the planet will be affected unevenly by climate change. Both polar regions are particularly fragile in environmental terms, and are deemed to be the most susceptible to changes in climate; the Arctic is considered to be even more fragile than the Antarctic. In 2004, the Arctic Climate Impact Assessment (ACIA), a joint project of the Arctic Council and the International Arctic Science Committee, published a detailed report on the consequences of climate change in the Arctic region. The work, involving the collaboration of more than 300 researchers, formed the first comprehensively researched and independently reviewed evaluation of Arctic climate change and its impacts on the region and the world. It was followed by a National Oceanic and Atmospheric Administration report completed in 2006, and now updated yearly. These reports are complemented by others, such as *Arctic Climate Impact Science—An Update since ACIA*, which was carried out by the World Wildlife Fund in 2008. The fourth IPCC also quickly became one of the most quoted reference texts, as much for its state of the art modeling in the physical sciences as for its forecasts on impacts, adaptation, vulnerability, and steps to be taken concerning mitigation.[11]

Today the Arctic is considered the region to have been the most affected by climate change. Air temperatures have risen at almost twice the global average rate over the past few decades. The interaction between different components here is more inextricably linked, creating a cumulative effect with feedback processes called "Arctic amplification."[12] The symptoms of climate change are multiple, including a noted rise in summertime temperatures, a shorter and warmer winter season, and an increase in precipitation in the spring. In Alaska and western Canada, mean wintertime temperatures have risen by 3 to 4°C over a period of 50 years.[13] During the record year of 2007, some surface water ice-free areas were as much as 5°C higher than

72

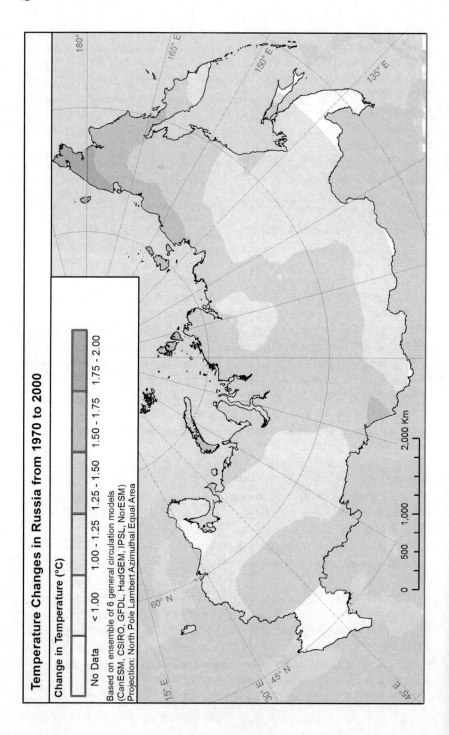

Temperature Changes in Russia from 1970 to 2000

Change in Temperature (°C)

No Data   < 1.00   1.00 - 1.25   1.25 - 1.50   1.50 - 1.75   1.75 - 2.00

Based on ensemble of 6 general circulation models
(CanESM, CSIRO, GFDL, HadGEM, IPSL, NorESM)
Projection: North Pole Lambert Azimuthal Equal Area

0   500   1,000   2,000 Km

the long-term average.[14] Temperatures in the Arctic have already warmed globally as much as 4°C over the last few decades, and the extent of ice cover has been greatly affected: the area covered with perennial sea ice receded significantly in 2010, falling to nearly half the area observed in 2005. There has been a reduction of at least 10% in the Arctic snow cover since the 1980s; a sharp decrease in the extent of Arctic sea ice in all seasons, with summer sea ice declining the most dramatically; and a reduction of the thickness of sea ice, as well as thawing of permafrost, diminishing lake and river ice, and rising river flows.[15] The Greenland Ice Sheet has been especially affected. The melting of mountain glaciers has also accelerated. Retreating glaciers in Alaska, where melting began long ago, have more recently been joined by the glaciers of Scandinavia and Svalbard.

The transformation of the Arctic is now occurring at a pace not anticipated even a few years ago. For the year 2010, the NOAA report confirmed a general tendency toward more rapid than predicted change in the Arctic.[16] That same year Greenland's climate was marked by record-breaking high air temperatures, ice loss by melting, and marine-terminating glacier area loss. The year also saw record warm air temperatures across the Canadian Arctic, record snow cover decreases, and the loss of thick multiyear ice in the Beaufort Sea during summer. The combination of warm spring air temperatures and low winter snow accumulation led to a new record minimum in springtime snow cover duration over the Arctic. The first half of 2010 saw a near record with monthly positive temperature anomalies of over 4°C in northern Canada. At the end of the summer of 2010, sea ice extent reached a minimum of 4.6 million square kilometers, at the time, the third-lowest recorded since 1979, surpassed only by 2008 and the record low in 2007. The active layer (zone of seasonal thawing) of Arctic permafrost is becoming progressively deeper.

In 2012, the official U.S. monitoring organization, the National Snow and Ice Data Center based in Boulder, Colorado, announced that Arctic sea ice had shrunk 18% that year relative to the previous record set in 2007. In September, at the end of the melt season, ice extent was at the lowest level ever recorded in the satellite survey (3.41 million square kilometers), with sea ice covering just 24% of the surface of the Arctic Ocean.[17] Moreover, the disappearance of thick, multiyear ice makes summer more vulnerable to storms such as the cyclone experienced in the region in 2012.[18] Experts confirm that ice extent is declining at a rate of 4.6% per decade relative to the 1981–2010 average. This situation affects the entire Northern Hemisphere, which has seen snow cover drop to its lowest levels in 45 years; the Greenland ice sheet has been the most affected, with more than 90% of its surface area experiencing melting conditions in summer of 2012.[19] Given the accelerating rate of shrinkage, some scientists suggest that the Arctic Ocean may be totally ice free during summer as early as 2015 or 2016,[20] an opinion which, however, is not unanimously shared.[21]

These trends are not uniform, and several Arctic sub-regions can be identified in terms of their responses to climate change: one from eastern Greenland to western Russia, the Siberian shelf, one from Chukotka to the Western Canadian Arctic, and one from the Central Canadian Arctic to West Greenland.[22] Russia encompasses (entirely or in part) three of these four climatic sub-regions of the Arctic. In addition to impacts on snow, ice, and permafrost, climate change also has a pronounced influence on bio-systems. Arctic vegetation zones are likely to shift; wetland may disappear in one area yet appear in others; the tree line will move farther north; new forms of agriculture will be possible; insect infestations and forest fires in the taiga zones are expected to increase; and the diversity of fauna and flora will decline, as the natural habitats of polar species are threatened.[23] Nor will human habitats be spared. Storms and floods will increase in number; soil erosion will accelerate (e.g., in coastal areas as sea level rises); thawing permafrost will endanger human and industrial settlements; and indigenous communities will have to confront drastic changes.[24]

These phenomena are not restricted solely to the Arctic region; their impact will be global for three main reasons. First, the reflectance of solar radiation will change, as snow and ice reflect more (and thereby absorb less) solar radiation than water, which is darker. Thus as snow-covered surfaces and ice caps shrink, more solar radiation will be absorbed (contributing to increase warming of the Earth's surface). Second, melting glaciers will lead to rising sea levels and, due to the differing temperatures and salinity levels of meltwater and seawater, possibly to a change in the directions and flow volumes of major ocean currents. Warmer water will enter the Arctic Ocean from the Pacific and Atlantic Oceans, and fresh water flowing from melting Arctic ice will enter the world's seas.[25] Third, warming temperatures will induce changes in the amounts of greenhouses gases emitted into the atmosphere. A large amount of methane is frozen in permafrost and in the methane hydrates found in ocean sediments. Thawing of these frozen substrates could therefore release large volumes of methane, a powerful greenhouse gas, into the atmosphere.[26]

Climate Change in the Russian Federation

Despite its immense size and high northern latitude, Russia is often a forgotten player in Western studies of the impact of climate change in the Arctic, the reason being that there is much more information available on the North

American continent or Northern Europe, and it is readily accessible. There are nonetheless many Russian teams working on climate issues, but they by and large publish in Russian. Two of the major Russian climate modeling centers, the Institute for Numerical Mathematics and the Obukhov Institute of Atmospheric Physics at the Russian Academy of Sciences, regularly submit simulation data as part of the IPCC assessment process, and Oleg Anisimov, from Roshydromet, is the coordinating lead author for IPCC chapter on polar regions. A third center, the St. Petersburg V.A. Fock Institute of Physics, has also developed its own research instruments. Roshydromet, the Federal Service for Hydrometeorology and Environmental Monitoring, and its 1,600 meteorological stations, is the leading scientific institute for meteorology in Russia. It works mainly with the Atmosphere-Ocean General Circulation Models (AOGCMs), which it considers "the main and the most promising tool for prediction of future climate changes due to internal interactions between different components of the climate system and external forcing of natural and anthropogenic origin."[27]

In terms of temperatures, studies by Roshydromet show that localized warming in Russia is greater than global warming as a whole. Russia experienced a rise of 1.29°C in average temperature over the last 100 years (1907–2006), whereas global warming for the same period was only 0.74°C. Furthermore, mean warming in the country was 1.33°C over the last 30 years (1976–2006).[28] Russia's average temperature is therefore rising almost twice as fast as the global average. Winter temperatures in Siberia have increased by 2 to 3°C over the last century, with recent strong springtime warming witnessed in the Urals and West Siberia. During the 1990s and 2000s alone, Russia's mean surface air temperature increased by 0.4°C. In the Russian Arctic, surface air temperatures have warmed 0.2°C per decade over the past 30 years, precipitation has increased, and summers are also warmer. Russia accounts for the greater part of the so-called "poles" of temperature increase, located in the Altai, Chita, and Irkutsk regions, and elsewhere in southern Siberia. In his *Report on the Distinctive Features of Climate on the Territory of the Russian Federation in 2011*, the Director of Roshydromet, Aleksandr F. Frolov, notes that the year 2011 was among one of the hottest ever recorded in the country, with a temperature elevated above the normal by 1.5°C.[29] In the winter of 2012–2013, large parts of the Kara and Barents Seas remained ice free.

Forecasts emphasize the acceleration of these trends. Projections suggest that average winter temperatures for the country as a whole will have increased by an additional 1°C by 2015. According to Roshydromet, by 2020 temperature increases in the country will exceed the multi-model spread (standard deviation), which is 1.1 ± 0.5°C. By the middle of the century, the temperature rise will be even greater (2.6 ± 0.7°C), particularly in winter (3.4 ± 0.8°C).[30] Maximum temperature changes are expected to occur in the winter, with a significant increase in precipitation in Eastern Siberia. The temperature increase will be smaller during the summer, except in southern regions, where it could reach 2–3°C by the middle of the twenty-first century. According to the World Wildlife Fund assessment, a 30% increase in winter precipitation totals is expected on the Taymyr Peninsula by 2050, and a 15–20% increase in Chukotka and the Barents Sea region.[31]

From 1978 to 1996, the Siberian Arctic experienced a reduction in summer sea ice of 17.6% per decade in the Barents and Kara Seas, and a 3.7% reduction per decade in the Chukchi, East Siberian, and Laptev Seas. Observations also indicate that the area of winter fast ice in the Russian Arctic decreased by 11.3% from 1975 to 1993 and that the influx of multiyear ice from the Central Arctic Ocean decreased by 14% from 1978 to 1998.[32] Rising sea levels are also problematic. Projections show sea level rise will occur mainly in the Baltic Sea, the Gulf of Finland, and the White Sea, which will increase the dangers of serious flooding for Kaliningrad and St. Petersburg. It is projected that there will be a high risk of flooding in St. Petersburg before 2030.[33] The level of the Black Sea has been rising significantly since the 1980s, and if this trend continues, it will affect Novorossiisk, Russia's main warm-water port, where dry cargoes, crude oil, and refined petroleum products are exported. It would also impact Sevastopol', Russia's main Black Sea military base, situated in Ukraine.[34] For the Pacific coast, the forecasts of sea level rise are more moderate, but the probabilities of tsunamis occurring will be much greater, with Vladivostok being potentially endangered. Lastly, in terms of the Arctic coastline, the key question will concern coastal erosion, although Murmansk may also be subject to flooding.

Many studies focus on land-based changes in the Arctic. Russian and international researchers have noted changes in vegetation patterns: (shifting of the borders of the tundra and of different types of taiga,[35] the recession of mountain glaciers in Novaya Zemlya and the Caucasus), and increased soil erosion. The most recent information on the latter, however, comes mainly from the mid-1980s.[36] It is also difficult to dissociate the impact of direct human activity from the global impact of climate change on this erosion process. The excessive agriculture, deforestation, and mining organized on a large scale by the Soviet economic system have seriously damaged the soils and accelerated wind erosion. More is known about changes in river water levels. Between 1936 and 1999 the average annual discharge of fresh water from the six largest Eurasian rivers (Yenisei, Lena, Ob', Kolyma, Pechora, and Severnaia Dvina) into the Arctic Ocean increased by 7%. The duration of river ice cover is expected to decline by 15 to 27 days and ice cover to be 20 to 40% thinner,[37] which will increase the discharge of fresh water, also affecting sea ice distribution and the circulation of Arctic waters.

Covering 65% of the country, permafrost is of special importance to Russia.[38] The mean annual ground temperature has increased by 1.0°C in many parts of the permafrost zone of western Siberia and by 0.8 to 1.0°C in the northwestern regions.[39] Studies reveal that, since the 1970s, there has been a tendency toward temperature increases in the top layers of frozen ground of between 0.22 and 1.56°C. A 30–40% increase in active layer thickness for most of the permafrost area is projected. Seasonal thaw depths are predicted to increase by more than 50% in the northernmost permafrost regions, and 30–50% elsewhere, by around 2050.[40] In the Russian European North, the southern boundary of continuous permafrost has retreated northward by 30 to 40 kilometers in the Pechora lowland and by 70–100 kilometers in the foothills of northern Urals.[41] By 2100, it is predicted that almost 60% of the current permafrost zone may thaw and freeze on a seasonal basis, and that near-surface permafrost may decline. Thawing of permafrost will lead to increases in landslides, mudflows, and other abrupt changes in the landscape. It will also lead to a relatively large increase in emissions of carbon dioxide and methane along the Arctic coast, as well as in central Siberia and Yakutia, with the expected feedback effect.[42] Indeed methane hydrates contained in this permafrost are 26 times more potent than carbon dioxide molecules in terms of their greenhouse warming effect.[43] The 2012 UN Environment Programme (UNEP) report discussed the threat in an alarmist tone: warming permafrost could emit 43 to 135 gigatons of carbon dioxide equivalent by 2100 and 246 to 415 gigatons by 2200. Yet, it observed, this additional major contribution to global warming has not been factored into current climate predictions.[44]

Calculating the Impact of Climate Change on the Russian Economy

Expected climate change could drastically impact the Russian economy. The most obvious argument seems to be that warming temperatures could lead to a drop in energy consumption for heating. The Russian Federation's Fourth National Communication under the UN Framework Convention on Climate Change predicted that a reduction in heating requirements would result in a net fuel savings of 5 to 10% nationwide by 2025.[45] However, the analysis continues to be contested. Even if the heating season becomes shorter, the consumption of other categories of energy, for instance electricity, could increase, even if only for air-conditioning during the summer months.

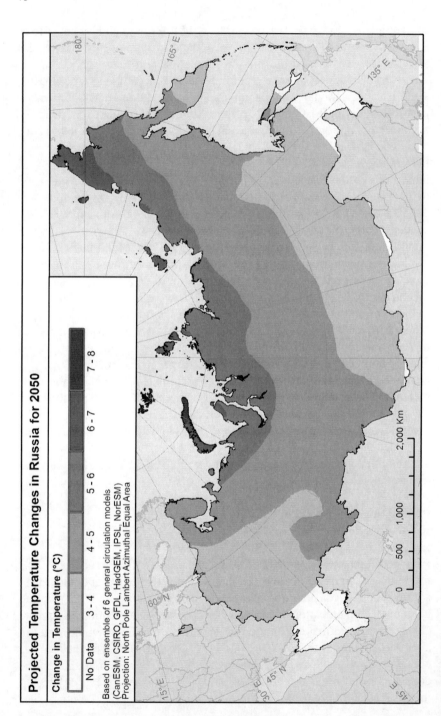

Projected Temperature Changes in Russia for 2050

Change in Temperature (°C)

| No Data | 3 - 4 | 4 - 5 | 5 - 6 | 6 - 7 | 7 - 8 |

Based on ensemble of 6 general circulation models
(CanESM, CSIRO, GFDL, HadGEM, IPSL, NorESM)
Projection: North Pole Lambert Azimuthal Equal Area

0   500   1,000   2,000 Km

Climate change will probably modify agricultural patterns. The growing season will be longer, conditions for growing winter crops will improve, new agricultural lands further to the north will be exploitable, and new crops, such as cotton, grapes, tea, and citrus, will be able to be cultivated in the North Caucasus and southern Volga regions.[46] Conditions for growing corn in the Stavropol' region have already improved. From 1970 to 2000, the growing season lengthened by an average of 5–10 days in many of the agricultural regions in European Russia. In the Central Black Earth and Volga regions, the frequency of very cold winters decreased by an average of 18–22% in the period up to 1990.[47] However, this change also implies that Russian agriculture will become increasingly reliant on irrigation.[48]

Other changes will present more complex problems. The northward migration of plant species will modify biodiversity patterns; an increase in the number of wildfires may accelerate the reduction of Russia's forested area, the largest in the world after the Amazon; and an increase in insect infestations, such as locusts, mosquitoes, and ticks, may pose a public health threat. The middle, or Black Earth, regions of the country, which are known as Russia's "breadbasket" and which enjoy a temperate climate, will be beset by more extreme climate processes: heavy precipitation, droughts, and reduced springtime river runoff. The southern regions of the country, those of the North Caucasus Federal District, will experience extensive periods of drought. Droughts have already resulted in reductions in crop cover by more than two million hectares.[49] These regions will experience declines in yields of about 20% by 2020.[50] This drop in production will be compensated, albeit insufficiently, by increasing grain yields in more northerly regions. Periods of drought in key agricultural regions are expected to be 50–100% more frequent by 2025,[51] which will impact Russia's cereals export strategy.

The question of water is also central. Annual river discharge in the western regions of Russia increased by 15–40% in the period 1978–2005 relative to that of 1946–1977.[52] The majority of Russian territory, in particular Siberia and northwest regions, will experience increased water flows due to glacial melting and growing precipitation, which implies more river ice jams and flooding. By 2015, there is likely to be more flooding in river basins in the Arkhangel'sk region, the Komi Republic, the Urals area, and in the Yenisei and Lena basins.[53] At the same time, other regions of Russia will experience water shortages, especially in the Black Earth lands, which are already experiencing chronic water stress. The situation will be even worse in the southern regions (Kalmykia, Krasnodar, Stavropol', and Rostov), which will likely have to contend with water supply reductions on the order of 5–15%.[54] The drinking water supply of the major Russian cities, and in particular the Moscow metropolis, will become a significant issue. By 2015, it is expected that "zones of environmental discomfort" will have shifted northward by about 60 kilometers in northwestern Russia (Komi Republic and Arkhangel'sk region), by about 150 kilometers in the Khanty-Mansi and Evenk autonomous areas, and by about 250 kilometers in the Republic of Sakha-Yakutia, in northern parts of the Irkutsk region, and in Khabarovsk.[55]

The hydroelectric sector will probably expand, thanks to a projected 8–10% increase in water volume by 2015.[56] The growing availability of water in the main Russian rivers will therefore be able to be used to produce more energy. According to Roshydromet, the Volga-Kama Cascade will experience a net increase of 10–20% in water flows, and the Siberian power dams along the Angara-Yenisei, Vilyui, Kolyma, and Zeya should have a 15% increase.[57] But the contrary situation is also likely to be the case in southern Russia—because extreme downpours will be difficult to manage and production owing to reduced river flows will drop. Moreover, the Russian electricity system will have to contend with complex situations linked to increased risks of flooding and winds, which are projected to be about 20% stronger in the Arctic and North Caucasus regions.[58]

Last but not least, the progressive thawing of the permafrost will present major challenges to Russia's infrastructure, because it will result in the creation of thermokarst and unstable soil conditions such as solifluction.[59] The Russian railway system, in particular the Baikal-Amur Mainline (BAM), will be undermined in the Far East; the possibility of the permafrost thawing was not a consideration during its construction. Similarly, electric transmission lines were not built to withstand changes in soil structure, or thawing and refreezing of the upper soil layer. The Russian road network, already very inefficient and the least developed of the G8 countries, will have more manageable snow cover conditions, but will have to contend with an increase in weather variability, which will result in downpours, mudslides, soil erosion, floods, and so on. In Siberia and the Far East, the traditional use of seasonal ice roads will become more problematic due to the shorter cold season, which will further limit already reduced travel links between towns. The well-developed river transport system will be positively affected, although the challenges of weather instability will have to be taken into account, as will the drop in water levels in the Don River basin.[60]

The stability of existing urban and industrial infrastructure will be put into serious question, as thawing not only reduces the stability of the ground underlying building foundations but also increases the corrosion of foundation materials, which, moreover, date predominantly from the Soviet period and thus are often already in a poor state. The impact of climate change on housing is already visible. In the 1990s–2000s, the rate of reported damage to buildings due to soil instability increased by about 42% in Noril'sk , 61% in Yakutsk, and 90% in Amderma. About 21% of reported damage to West Siberian pipelines occurs because of the thawing of underlying permafrost.[61] More than 7,000 accidents related to the thawing of permafrost and soil degradation in West Siberia were reported in 2007 alone. While builders in the United States and Canada have preferred to use components made of wood and aluminum in the polar zone, Soviet construction continued to rely on reinforced concrete and poor quality steel, both of which are ill-suited to very low temperatures. Structural damage is common not just in areas of low population density. About 60% of all industrial infrastructure of the Usa Basin, a very populated area by northern Russian standards, is located in a high-risk permafrost zone.[62] In addition, about 30 so-called impact zones, with high levels of atmospheric pollution, degradation of vegetation and soil, and incidence of disease among the local population, have been identified in the Russian Arctic region. There is also a potential danger of radioactive contamination in several places. Each year the mining company Apatit stores approximately 30 million tons of waste on the Kola Peninsula. Many radioactive waste storage sites are located in permafrost areas, for instance on Novaya Zemlya, and some aging spent nuclear fuel storage facilities are no longer secured.[63]

The energy sector, which forms the backbone of the Russian economy, will be among the first to encounter risks associated with expected climate change; 93% of natural gas and 75% of oil production occurs in permafrost zones. In addition to the aging extraction infrastructure, constructed mainly in the 1970s, the transport system is not adapted to deal with changes in soil stability. Above-ground pipelines are not designed to cope with the seasonal thawing of permafrost and can be destabilized by increased water flow. It will thus be necessary to build new and much more costly pipelines with deeper foundations to avoid structural damage from subsidence. The question of hydrocarbon transport to export and consumption centers will have to be rethought, as well. Despite the possible emergence of a commercially navigable Northern Sea Route, transportation may become more difficult. The zones to be crossed from the key extraction sites in West Siberia and the Volga-Urals region to Europe will be subject to drastic changes in soil stability. Accessing the main gas deposits of the future will also become more challenging. There are, for instance, mounting concerns that the entire low-lying Yamal Peninsula could disappear due to subsidence from permafrost thawing.[64]Access to extraction sites via road transit also will become more problematic, as roads will be compromised by unstable soils.

Russia's Domestic Actors on Climate Change

In Russia, environmental issues, and especially those concerning climate change, are rarely debated in public. To date, the media has done very little to investigate such topics which, compared with other publicly discussed issues, have by and large been relegated to the background. In 2009, a world survey revealed that Russians—in this way similar to Americans but in contrast to Europeans—felt much less concerned by climate change, with a majority of the opinion that they were not affected by it.[65] About 85% of the people surveyed declared they were aware of climate change, but only 39% perceived it as a serious personal threat.[66] This situation, however, changed with the forest fires in 2010. Even if there is no direct relation between these events and climate change projections, the public viewed them as proof that climate change could turn out to be a destructive force. However, the debate remains dominated by a few stakeholders; the private sector is not fully involved beyond pushing for Joint Implementation project approvals (the right to sell carbon credits under the Kyoto Protocol [see below]), and it is unlikely that Russian "civil society" will be able to pressure public opinion and the government into becoming more engaged in its understanding of climate change. The nongovernmental organizations (NGOs) have for the most part been silenced, especially those working on environmental questions, and public opinion remains focused on other short- and medium-term issues.

Environmental themes are generally not as prevalent in the Russian media as they are in Western Europe or the United States. Russian scientists are the main figures to have made any statements on the subject. The Soviet school of climatology, which had enjoyed many good decades with excellent research conditions in Arctic regions, focused mainly on the question of climate evolution, defined by long, natural cycles of cooling and heating. Debates concerning the role of anthropogenic elements in climate evolution have occurred in Soviet Union since the 1970s, but never came to inform the majority opinion.[67] Then, the disintegration of the USSR significantly hindered Russian research. In the 1990s, the high level of state disorganization and the lack of public funding drove tens of thousands of scientific workers to emigrate to the West, change professions, or retire early. The financial situation by and large turned around in the 2000s, but by that time the damage had been done. Large gaps persist in the intergenerational transmission of knowledge, equipment dating from the Soviet era has aged, and Russian teams, very competent, remain sometimes poorly integrated into international consortia.

The present-day Russian school of climatology can be schematically divided into three major currents: those who maintain that there is no human-induced global warming and that such warming can be attributed to natural processes; those who think that global warming exists but that it will bring net positive benefits for Russia and who are defined by Elana Wilson Rowe as "causally agnostic"[68] in terms of anthropogenic responsibility; and those who believe in human-induced climate change and are convinced of the dangers it poses. The first two viewpoints largely predominate in the Russian scientific institutions. Yuri Izrael, director of the Institute of Global Climate and Ecology, and Vladimir Melnikov, director of the Russian Institute on the Earth's Cryosphere, are the main voices on climate change; they either deny its human origin or deem that the change will be positive for Russia.[69] A similar viewpoint has long been advanced by institutions such as Roshydromet, the All-Russia Research Institute of Agricultural Meteorology, the Voeikov Main Geophysical Observatory, the Hydrometeorological Center of the Russian Federation, the Research Center for Space Meteorology, and by other institutions linked with Arctic exploration, such as the Arctic and Antarctica Research Institute and the Institute for Cultural Heritage.

Nevertheless, opinion began to change in the second half of the 2000s. Russian scientific institutions acknowledged that warming seemed to be occurring, and that this was in part due to anthropogenic factors.[70] In 2006, for example, Roshydromet published a *Strategic Prediction for the Period up to 2010–2015 of Climate Change Expected in Russia and its Impacts on the Sectors of the Russian National Economy*. The report puts special emphasis on the severe rise in extreme weather events and environmental hazards linked with agriculture, and on the need to begin preparing for them.[71] This point of view was backed up by a new document published in 2008 titled the *Assessment Report on Climate Change and Its Consequences in the Russian Federation*. The document states that "a comparison of simulated and observed variations of surface air temperature provides convincing evidence supporting the anthropogenic nature of observed climate warming."[72] However in December 2009, just before the UN Climate Change Conference COP-15, the director of the Ministry of Energy's research institute claimed that global warming could be attributed to the slowing of the Earth's rotation, and the Institute of Oceanography issued a report stating that human activity is not a major factor in climate change.[73] Some Russian think tanks have even decided to directly attack European discourse on climate change. The Institute of Economic Analysis claimed for instance the British Meteorological Office used statistics from only those weather stations in Russia that fitted its theory of global warming, but ignored the data of the three-quarters of them that did not.[74]

The role of Russian scientists in framing the climate change debate in Russia is important. They play the role of the interface between domestic institutions and international debates, in large part though their participation in international reports, such as the IPCC. However, their influence on decision making is limited, and they rather seem to intervene *a posteriori* than *a priori*, without directly contributing to political choices. The only players involved in finalizing the decisions on Russia's international role are Putin's inner circle, the Security Council of the Russian Federation, and the main industrial consortia.[75]

Russia's Hesitant Climate Change Policy

The official position of the Russian state on climate change has generally turned around over recent years. In 2003, during the World Climate Change Conference in Moscow, Russia took a distinctly skeptical position. Russian politicians have been very vocal on the climate issue, viewing it as a Western fantasy or an object of anti-Russian propaganda. President Vladimir Putin stated, for instance, that a warming of 2–3°C would be a good thing for Russia, joking that it would no longer be necessary to wear fur coats and that agricultural production would be boosted.[76] In 2010, after drought and immense fires had ravaged one quarter of Russia's grain crop, Putin visited a meteorological station on the Lena, where he implied that human activity probably played no great role in global warming.[77] As Sergei Mironov, the speaker of the Federation Council explained, in 2007, "the impact of greenhouse gas emissions on the climate had not been studied sufficiently to push for a change of economic strategies."[78] In 2010, Mironov reiterated his skepticism by implying that Western countries were trying to hamper the Russian economy by exerting pressure on it in the name of environmental concerns.[79]

Although domestic political discourse continues to be dominated by the idea that Russia stands to gain from climate change, or at least that it has less to lose than other developed countries, the discussion has changed in recent years to become more attuned with that of the international community. In 2009, in preparation for the Copenhagen Climate Conference, Minister of Natural Resources and Ecology Yuri Trutnev unveiled Russia's Climate Doctrine for 2030–2050 that outlines the country's response to climate change, in a drastically different tone. Rather than putting the usual emphasis on the benefits of climate change, the doctrine warns of serious climate-induced challenges, even at the level of individuals' daily lives. It calls for the creation of an institution to supervise climate change, for environmental regulations, and for legislation to be updated in order to bring Russia in line with international norms on climate change; for the stimulation of responsible resource use and efficiency; and for increased resilience in key economic sectors such as agriculture, transport, and energy. The minister himself recognized that climate change could cause up to a 5% reduction in Russia's GDP.[80]

The Climate Doctrine marks the first attempt at institutionalizing a climate change policy in Russia; however, its text provides no precise strategy and remains purely declarative. It is thus difficult to say whether it was drafted specifically for Copenhagen, or whether it reveals a real change in the perceptions of part of the ruling elites.[81] Some of Dmitrii Medvedev's statements suggest the latter. In February 2010, the then Russian president delivered a highly unusual speech on climate change, in which he insisted on its negative impact and the dangers for humanity. He issued a wake-up call to heads of state and social organizations, and requested the creation of economic incentives to address climate change, pointing out that Russia is still quite a long way behind most developed countries in monitoring and forecasting climate change. He repeated these ideas in a speech to the Security Council and issued a presidential instruction to the government to approve a package of measures for implementing the doctrine by the end of 2010. For the first time, climate change was discussed as a threat to national security by the Security Council.[82]

The Russian Federation's role in the international negotiations over climate change follows these zigzagging policies. After the collapse of the Soviet Union, Moscow repeated incessantly that it would not slow down its economic revival out of unwarranted concern for environmental issues. Russia did, however, play a key role in the implementation of the Kyoto Protocol to the United Nations Framework Convention on Climate Change (UNFCCC), initially adopted in 1997. Following the refusal of the United States to sign the document, the number of collected signatures was insufficient to reach the minimum threshold (signatory nations should account for 55% or more of global carbon emissions). As the third-largest source of global carbon emissions, Russia's agreement to ratify the protocol in 2005 was thus decisive, transforming it into a legally binding commitment for developed countries and some transition economies. Agreeing to comply with the protocol's target posed no challenge for Russia. The text is based on a 1990 level of global carbon emissions that, following the post-Soviet industrial collapse, guaranteed that Russia would not reach its maximum emissions threshold until 2020 (in 2009, it was still 40% below the base line). Moscow therefore signed the protocol in the anticipation of financial gains as a potential seller of carbon credits.[83] It had more than 50% of the world's Joint Implementation projects market, with a total greenhouse gas reduction potential of over 150 MtC (million tons of carbon). In addition, ratifying the protocol served as a "currency exchange" in its negotiations with the European Union concerning its bilateral World Trade Organization

(WTO) accession protocol, and it worked to enhance Russia's international image, in particular relative to that of the United States.[84]

Despite its ratification of the Kyoto Protocol, Moscow believes it does not have to accept any binding agreement that would be damaging to its economy, especially as the United States refuses to submit to it. Russia remains thus a passive actor in the construction of the international climate regime. It asserts that the decline of greenhouse gas emissions is the country's major contribution to global climate mitigation, whereas in reality this has nothing to do with a policy outcome, but rather is the result of the severe economic downturn following the USSR's disintegration. In 2009, during preparatory negotiations for the post-Kyoto era, Medvedev declared that Russia was ready to become more active, and proposed a 20 to 25% further drop in greenhouse gas emissions from the 1990 baseline (eventually it committed to a 15 to 25% reduction). Russia did not demand to transfer the quota surplus (equal to over 3 billion tons of $CO2$) it had accumulated under Kyoto, but argued that carbon sinks from its forests—the largest national terrestrial carbon pool is associated with the boreal forest of Northern Eurasia—be taken into account in calculations of its overall emissions.[85] Russia also tried to reclassify itself as an emerging economy, entailing less binding agreements.[86] At the Copenhagen and Durban conferences, the Russian authorities clearly stated that they would not enter into the second commitment period of the Kyoto Protocols and called for a new global agreement that obliged all major emitters to participate.[87]

The impact of the 2008 economic crisis contributed to an increased awareness among the ruling elites about the huge possible energy savings to be gained through greater efficiency, but Moscow's environmental policy still remains very limited. The incomplete data for the various industrial and forest sectors make it difficult to measure Russia's implementation of (and compliance with) the Kyoto Protocols.[88] It is the fourth-largest emitter of carbon dioxide ($CO2$) behind China, the United States, and India, although it is only the world's eighth-largest economic power. It is one of the highest energy consumers among the industrial powers, which is attributable to its astounding lack of energy efficiency that runs the entire gamut from households to large corporations. Russia consumes six times as much energy as the United States for each dollar of GDP (measured in purchasing power parity),[89] and its growing per capita emissions appear poised to approach U.S. levels by 2030. This can be partly explained by its cold climate, but above all reveals a large amount of energy waste in industrial processes. Indeed, the consumption of energy in Russia's industrial sectors is unparalleled. The depreciation of capital stock exceeds 46% in the natural resource extraction sector, 53% in transportation, 70% in the thermal power sector, and 80% in hydropower.[90] The World Bank and the Russian Center for Energy Efficiency found that Russia could save 45% of its total primary energy consumption if it were to implement reforms. *It could save* around 200 million tons of oil equivalent (Mtoe) annually, equal to 30% of its consumption, if it were to apply the same measures of energy efficiency as the main OECD countries, including Canada, the country with which it shares the most climatic similarities.[91] However, only some of the largest companies have started to address carbon issues and have released detailed information about their greenhouse gas emissions.[92] The 2009 Climate Doctrine has thus not been followed up with concrete measures. In 2010 the government set a target of reducing the energy intensity of the Russian economy by 40% by 2020, but it remains largely unimplemented.[93]

Russia's climate change policy is relatively consistent, but aimed at short-term benefits. It remains subordinated to domestic economic imperatives, which are themselves centered on fossil fuels. The fact that the environment comes under the portfolio of the Ministry of Natural Resources clearly shows what Russia's priorities are. Furthermore, Moscow feels it should be excused insofar as times of brutal post-Soviet socioeconomic change mean that priority cannot be given to environmental concerns. Moreover, the country advocates adaptation, but not mitigation, a stance that emerges very clearly from the 2009 doctrine, which does not seek to address the root causes of climate change. From the Russian viewpoint, strategies of mitigation are considered irrelevant and useless, impossible to implement, or too costly. Even though the opinion of the ruling elites on climate change appears to be changing, Russia is likely to keep maintaining that the world is dealing with a *fait accompli* that cannot be resisted, that it is necessary to continue to rely on fossil fuel production, and that all climate policy ought to be limited to alleviation efforts and adapting the economy and society to the new challenges climate change presents.

Even by focusing on adaptation and not mitigation, the capacities of the Russian state are questionable. In theory, Russia has a higher capacity for climate resilience than other developed countries; it also potentially stands to gain economically from climate change, mainly in the agriculture and hydro-electricity sectors. However, the price to pay for this change, and the balance of advantages/disadvantages, are largely unknown. Given Russia's aging infrastructure, and the high costs—already apparent in the Soviet period—of its economic development in harsh climatic regions, the price of managing climate change in terms of economic development, urban sustainability, and human security might turn out to be higher than the optimistic predictions still holding sway among the Russian authorities. This cost will be added to other challenges that Russia will have to manage in the decades to come, including those of its demography, knowledge capacity and competence-building, and the reorientation of its overall economic structure. The more Russia delays in moving toward a greener economy, and addressing its energy inefficiency, the wider the gap will become in its levels of competitiveness as compared to Western countries.[94] In addition, the main problem is perhaps not so much the price that will have to be paid as the ability to prepare oneself to anticipate the changes and therefore to reduce their financial and human costs. The Concept for the long-term Social and Economic Development of Russia until 2030 notes that the emergence of climatic problems may impede economic growth, but it does attempt to take this possible cost into account in its projections of social and economic development.[95]

Notes

1. J.T. Houghton, Y. Ding, D.J. Griggs, M. Noguer, P.J. van der Linden, X. Dai, K. Maskell, and C.A. Johnson, eds., *Climate Change 2001: The Scientific Basis. Contribution of Working Group I to the Third Assessment Report of the Intergovernmental Panel on Climate Change* (Cambridge: Cambridge University Press, 2001).

2. M. Hulme, *Why We Disagree About Climate Change: Understanding Controversy, Inaction and Opportunity* (Cambridge: Cambridge University Press, 2009).

3. M.A. Parsons, Ø. Godøy, E. LeDrew, T.F. de Bruin, B. Danis, S. Tomlinson, and D. Carlson, "A Conceptual Framework for Managing Very Diverse Data for Complex, Interdisciplinary Science," *Journal of Information Science* 37, no. 6 (2011): 555–569.

4. J. Hoggan and R. Littlemore, *Climate Cover-Up: The Crusade to Deny Global Warming* (Toronto, Vancouver: Greystone, 2009).

5. This movement, based on environmentalist, anti-consumerist, and anti-capitalist ideas, is well-developed in Europe, and especially in France and Italy. On this theory, see "Economic Degrowth for Sustainability and Equity," *Degrowth.net*, January 28, 2009, http://www.degrowth.net/ (accessed June 16, 2012).

6. For more on this issue, see the journal *Mitigation and Adaptation Strategies for Global Change.*

7. S. Solomon, D. Qin, M. Manning, Z. Chen, M. Marquis, K.B. Averyt, M. Tignor, and H.L. Miller, eds., *Contribution of Working Group I to the Fourth Assessment Report of the Intergovernmental Panel on Climate Change* (Cambridge: Cambridge University Press, 2007).

8. G. Schmidt and J. Wolfe, *Climate Change: Picturing the Science* (New York: W.W. Norton & Company, 2009); A. Dressler and E.A. Parson, *The Science and Politics of Global Climate Change: A Guide to the Debate* (Cambridge: Cambridge University Press, 2010).

9. "Arctic Ice Retreating More Quickly Than Computer Models Project," UCAR (University Corporation for Atmospheric Research), April 30, 2007, http://www.ucar.edu/news/releases/2007/seaice.shtml (accessed June 16, 2012).

10. M. Le Page, "Climate Change: It's Even Worse than We Thought," *New Scientist,* no date, http://www.newscientist.com/special/worse-climate?cmpid=

NLC%7CNSNS%7C2012–1911-GLOBAL%7Cworseclimate&utm_medium=
NLC&utm_source=NSNS&utm_content=worseclimate (accessed June 16, 2012).

11. See the *IPCC Climate Change 2007: Synthesis Report,* http://www.ipcc.ch/
publications_and_data/publications_and_data_reports.shtml#1 (accessed June 16,
2012).

12. WWF, *Arctic Climate Feedbacks: Global Implications* (Oslo: WWF International Arctic Program, 2009).

13. ACIA Report, *Impacts of a Warming Arctic,* 22.

14. WWF, *Arctic Climate Feedbacks: Global Implications*, 10.

15. More details in NOAA, *State of the Arctic* (October 2006), 15–27.

16. NOAA, *Arctic Report Card: Update for 2010* (2010), www.arctic.noaa.gov/
reportcard/ (accessed June 16, 2012).

17. See the National Snow and Ice Data Center, http://nsidc.org/arcticseaicenews/
(accessed June 16, 2012).

18. I. Simmonds and I. Rudeva, "The Great Arctic Cyclone of August 2012,"
Geophysical Research Letters 39, no 23 (2012).

19. J. Vidal, "Arctic Ice Shrinks 18% against Record, Sounding Climate Change
Alarm Bells," *The Guardian,* September 19, 2012, http://www.guardian.co.uk/environment/2012/sep/19/arctic-ice-shrinks (accessed September 24, 2012).

20. J. Vidal, "Arctic Expert Predicts Final Collapse of Sea Ice within Four Years,"
The Guardian, September 17, 2012, http://www.guardian.co.uk/environment/2012/
sep/17/arctic-collapse-sea-ice (accessed September 24, 2012).

21. A. Doyle and N. Chestney, "Arctic Summer Sea Ice Might Thaw by 2015—or
Linger for Decades," *Reuters,* August 30, 2012, http://in.reuters.com/article/2012/08/30/
climate-arctic-idINL6E8JTH2620120830 (accessed September 24, 2012).

22. ACIA Report. *Impacts of a Warming Arctic,* 18–19.

23. J.C.J. Nihoul and A.G. Kostianoy, eds., *Influence of Climate Change on the
Changing Arctic and Sub-Arctic Condition* (New York: Springer, 2009).

24. ACIA Report. *Impacts of a Warming Arctic,* 92–97.

25. M.L. Parry, O.F. Canziani, J.P. Palutikov, P.J. van der Linden, and C.E. Hanson,
eds., *Contribution of Working Group II to the Fourth Assessment Report of the Intergovernmental Panel on Climate Change* (Cambridge: Cambridge University Press,
2007), chapter 15 on "Polar regions (Arctic and Antarctic)," 664–665.

26. ACIA Report. *Impacts of a Warming Arctic,* 34–39.

27. Roshydromet, *Assessment Report on Climate Change and Its Consequences in
the Russian Federation. General Summary* (Moscow: Roshydromet, 2008), 11.

28. Ibid., 7.

29. A.F. Frolov, *Doklad ob osobennostiakh klimata na territorii Rossiiskoi Federatsii za 2011 god* [Report on the distinctive features of climate on the territory of
the Russian Federation in 2011] (Moscow: Roshydromet, 2012).

30. Roshydromet, *Assessment Report on Climate Change and its Consequences
in the Russian Federation,* 13.

31. WWF, *The Impact of Climate Change on the Russian Arctic and Paths to Solving the Problem* (Moscow: WWF, 2008), 12.

32. W. Ostreng, "Looking Ahead to the Northern Sea Route," *Scandinavian Review*
90, no. 2 (2002): 78.

33. I.E. Chestin and N.A. Colloff, eds., *Russia and Neighbouring Countries:
Environmental, Economic and Social Impacts of Climate Change* (Moscow: WWF
and Oxfam, 2008), 14.

34. Roshydromet, *Assessment Report on Climate Change and its Consequences in the Russian Federation,* 17.

35. R. Perelet, S. Pegov, and M. Yulkin, "Climate Change. Russia Country Paper," in *Fighting Climate Change: Human Solidarity in a Divided World. Human Development Report* (Washington, DC: United Nations Development Programme, 2008), 23.

36. For more details, see *Climate Change in Russia: Research and Impacts* (London: Climate Change Risk Management, May 2008), 54–77.

37. *Russia. The Impact of Climate Change to 2030. A Commissioned Research Report* (Washington, DC: National Intelligence Council, 2009), 16.

38. O. Anisimov, A. Velichko, P. Demchenko, A. Eliseev, I. Mokhov, and V. Nechaev, "Effect of Climate Change on Permafrost in the Past, Present and Future," *Atmospheric and Oceanic Physics* 38, no. 1 (2002): 25–39.

39. Roshydromet, *Assessment Report on Climate Change and its Consequences in the Russian Federation,* 8.

40. *Climate Change in Russia: Research and Impacts,* 6.

41. D. Streletskiy, N. Shiklomanov, and E. Hatleberg, "Stability of Arctic Urban Infrastructure through the Prism of Ground Thermal Regime," in R. Orttung, ed., *Russia's Arctic Cities: State Policies, Resource Development, and Climate Change,* forthcoming.

42. For more details, see Chestin and Colloff, *Russia and Neighbouring Countries: Environmental, Economic and Social Impacts of Climate Change,* 22–25.

43. C. ZumBrunnen, "Climate Change in the Russian North. Threats Real and Potential," in E. Wilson Rowe, ed., *Russia and the North,* 69.

44. UNEP, *Policy Implications of Warming Permafrost,* 2012, http://www.unep.org/pdf/permafrost.pdf.

45. *Russia: The Impact of Climate Change to 2030. Geopolitical Implications* (Washington, DC: National Intelligence Council, 2009), 19.

46. Roshydromet, *Strategic Prediction for the Period up to 2010–2015 of Climate Change Expected in Russia and its Impacts on the Sectors of the Russian National Economy* (Moscow: Roshydromet, 2006), 17.

47. N. Lemeshko and M. Nikolaev, "Climate Change, Vulnerability, and Adaptation in Agriculture. The Situation and State of Art in Russia," in *ADAGIO International Symposium,* Sofia, March 10–11, 2008; N. Lemeshko, "Climate Change, Vulnerability, and Adaptation in Agriculture. The Situation and State of Art in Russia," in *ADAGIO International Symposium,* Vienna, June 22–24, 2009.

48. N. Dronin and A. Kirilenko, "Climate Change and Food Stress in Russia: What If the Market Transforms as It Did during the Past Century?" *Climatic Change* 86 (2008): 123–150.

49. Chestin and Colloff, *Russia and Neighbouring Countries: Environmental, Economic and Social Impacts of Climate Change,* 19.

50. J. Dobrolyubova, *Climate Change Effects and Assessment of Adaptation Potential in the Russian Federation* (Moscow: Russian Regional Environmental Centre, November 19–20, 2007).

51. *Russia: The Impact of Climate Change to 2030. A Commissioned Research Report,* 27.

52. Roshydromet, *Assessment Report on Climate Change and its Consequences in the Russian Federation,* 8.

53. Roshydromet, *Strategic Prediction for the Period up to 2010–2015 of Climate Change Expected in Russia,* 18.

54. Ibid., 19.

55. Ibid., 15.

56. Ibid., 8.

57. Ibid., 13.

58. *Russia: The Impact of Climate Change to 2030. A Commissioned Research Report*, 20.

59. More details in *Climate Change in Russia: Research and Impacts*, 36–45.

60. *Russia: The Impact of Climate Change to 2030. A Commissioned Research Report*, 28.

61. O. Anisimov and S. Reneva, "Permafrost and Changing Climate: The Russian Perspective," *Ambio* 35, no. 4 (2006): 169–175.

62. G. Mazhitova, N. Karstkarel, N. Oberman, V. Romanovsky, and P. Kuhry, "Permafrost and Infrastructure in the Usa Basin (Northeast European Russia): Possible Impacts of Global Warming," *Ambio* 33, no. 6 (2004): 289–294.

63. Yu. Morozov, "The Arctic: The Next 'Hot Spot' of International Relations or a Region of Cooperation?" Carnegie U.S. Global Engagement Program, December 16, 2009, http://www.carnegiecouncil.org/resources/articles_papers_reports/0039.html (accessed June 16, 2012).

64. ZumBrunnen, "Climate Change in the Russian North. Threats Real and Potential," 69.

65. "Russian Public Opinion on Climate Change and Climate Policy in International Comparison," *Russian Analytical Digest*, no. 79, 2010, based on representative polls of the population organized by WorldPublicOpinion.Org, conducted in September and October 2009, www.worldbank.org/wdr2010/climatepoll (accessed June 16, 2012).

66. A. Pugliese and J. Ray, "Top-Emitting Countries Differ on Climate Change Threat," *Gallup*, 2009, http://www.gallup.com/poll/124595/top-emitting-countries-differ-climate-change-threat.aspx.

67. See M. I. Budenko, *Vliianie cheloveka na klimate* [The influence of mankind on climate] (Leningrad, 1972). I would like to thank Oleg Anisimov and Nikolai Shiklomanov for their comments on this section and for bringing Budenko's works to my attention.

68. E. Wilson Rowe "Who is to Blame? Agency, Causality, Responsibility, and the Role of Experts in Russian Framings of Global Climate Change," *Europe-Asia Studies* 61, no. 4 (2009): 602.

69. Ibid., 593–619.

70. M. Kulakovskaia, "Izmenenie klimata: gipotezy i fakty [Climate change: Hypotheses and facts]," *Golos Rossii*, August 26, 2010, http://rus.ruvr.ru/2010/08/25/17231067.html (accessed June 16, 2012).

71. Roshydromet, *Strategic Prediction for the Period up to 2010–2015 of Climate Change Expected in Russia*, 24.

72. Roshydromet, *Assessment Report on Climate Change and Its Consequences in the Russian Federation*, 12.

73. As quoted in "Russia's Lackluster Record on Climate Change," *Russian Analytical Digest*, no. 79 (2010): 15.

74. "Russian Weather Data Cherry Picked by UK Climatologists," *Russia Today*, December 18, 2009, http://rt.com/news/data-cherry-picked-climatologists/ (accessed June 16, 2012).

75. E. Wilson Rowe, "International Science, Domestic Politics: Russian Reception

of International Climate Change Assessments," *Environment and Planning D: Society and Space* 30, no. 4 (2012): 711–726.

76. "German Scientist Refutes Putin on Climate Change," *The Local*, August 23, 2010, http://www.thelocal.de/sci-tech/20100823–29349.html (accessed June 16, 2012).

77. "Scientist Scorns Putin's Climate Musings," *The Sydney Morning Herald*, August 25, 2010 http://www.smh.com.au/environment/climate-change/scientist-scorns-putins-climate-musings-20100824–13qba.htm (accessed June 16, 2012).

78. S. Shuster, "Mironov Tells Kyoto Experts the World Is Getting Cooler," *Moscow Times*, May 28, 2007.

79. See Mironov's speech, April 28, 2010, http://mironov.info/events/9993.php (accessed June 16, 2012).

80. S. Charap and G.I. Safonov, "Climate Change and Role of Energy Efficiency," in A. Aslund, S. Guriev, and A. Kuchins, eds., *Russia after the Global Economic Crisis* (Washington, DC: Peterson Institute for Internal Economics, 2010), 130.

81. A. Korppoo, "The Russian Debate on Climate Doctrine, Emerging Issues on the Road to Copenhagen," *FIIA Briefing Paper*, no. 33, June 5, 2009.

82. N. Kozlova, "Strashnei vsego—pogoda v dome. Sovet bezopasnosti ob ugrozakh i problemakh, kotorye neset izmenenie klimata [The most fearful of all—the weather at home. Security Council on the threats and problems which climate change brings]," *Rossiiskaia gazeta*, no. 136(57), March 19, 2010, http://www.rg.ru/2010/03/19/klimat.html (accessed June 16, 2012).

83. A. Korppoo, "Russia and the Post-2012 Climate Regime: Foreign Rather than Environmental Policy," *FIIA Briefing* Paper, no. 23, November 24, 2008.

84. For more details, see A. Korppoo, J. Karas, and M. Grubb, eds., *Russia and the Kyoto Protocol. Opportunities and Challenges* (London: Chatham House, 2006).

85. S. Charap, "Russia's Lackluster Record on Climate Change," *Russian Analytical Digest*, no. 79 (2010): 14; E. Lioubimtseva, "Russia's Role in the Post-2012 Climate Change Policy: Key Contradictions and Uncertainties," *Forum on Public Policy*, Spring 2010, 1–18, http://www.forumonpublicpolicy.com/spring2010.vol2010/spring2010archive/Lioubimtseva.pdf (accessed June 16, 2012).

86. A. Korppoo, "Russia's Climate Policy Fails to Raise Hopes," Finnish Institute for International Affairs, June 19, 2009, http://www.fiia.fi/se/news/683/rysslands_klimatpolitik_ar_inte_agnat_att_inge_forhoppningar/ (accessed June 16, 2012).

87. A. Korppoo and A. Vatansever, "A Climate Vision for Russia. From Rhetoric to Action," *Carnegie Policy Outlook*, August 2012, http://carnegieendowment.org/2012/08/01/climate-vision-for-russia-from-rhetoric-to-action/d4tq (accessed June 16, 2012).

89. ZumBrunnen, "Climate Change in the Russian North. Threats Real and Potential," 77–78. More details are available in McKinsey and Co., *Pathways to an Energy and Carbon Efficient Russia* (Moscow, McKinsey & Co. Inc., 2009).

90. Data from the Russian State Statistical Agency for 2009 and Audit Chamber report on RAO UES investment program 2006, quoted in S. Charap and G.I. Safonov, "Climate Change and Role of Energy Efficiency," 140.

91. International Energy Agency, *World Energy Outlook 2011 Factsheet*, http://www.worldenergyoutlook.org/media/weowebsite/factsheets/factsheets.pdf (accessed June 16, 2012).

92. *Carbon Disclosure Project*, "Public Procurement Programme 2010," London, AEA Europe 2010, http://media.blueprint.tv/cdp/public-procurement-report-2010/ (accessed June 16, 2012).

93. A. Korppoo and A. Vatansever, "A Climate Vision for Russia. From Rhetoric to Action."

94. B. Porfiryev, "Climate Change and Economy. A Risk for or a Factor of Development?" *Russia in Global Affairs*, July 7, 2010, http://eng.globalaffairs.ru/number/ Climate_Change_and_Economy-14899 (accessed June 16, 2012).

95. "Osnovnye tendentsii i prognoznye otsenki sotsial'no-ekonomicheskogo razvitiia Rossii na period do 2030 g. [Basic trends and forecasting estimates of the socio-economic development of Russia during the period to 2030]," Ministry of Energy, http://minenergo.gov.ru/aboutminen/energostrategy/ch_3.php (accessed June 16, 2012).

Chapter 5

The Russian Stance on Arctic Territorial Conflicts

The polar regions have often been considered as unique with regard to international law—multiple sets of regulations are applied to them, with important historical changes occurring in conjunction with the exploration of the ocean depths and the discovery of deep-sea resources.[1] Since the end of the World War II, the authority granted to coastal states over the adjacent waters and seabed has substantially expanded. Customary international law has been codified by the United Nations Convention on the Law of the Sea (UNCLOS), which recognizes that each state has the right to 12 nautical miles of territorial sea, 24 nautical miles of contiguous zone, and 200 nautical miles of exclusive economic zone (EEZ). On territorial seas, sovereignty is exercised over the airspace, water column, seabed, and the subsoil. Within the 200 nautical miles of the EEZ, each state has sovereign rights over all living and non-living resources in the water column, seabed, and subsoil, but the passage of foreign ships must be guaranteed. Beyond these 200 nautical miles, state jurisdiction can no longer be applied to the water columns, which are defined as high seas subject to free navigation. It can, however, be applied to a continental shelf if UNCLOS recognizes a territorial contiguity of up to 350 nautical miles or 100 nautical miles beyond the 2,500-meter isobath. Beyond this, the deep seabed is regarded as the heritage of humanity and is managed by the International Seabed Authority.[2]

The majority of bilateral disputes between states concern the delimitation of their respective EEZs. There have been eight disputes over Arctic EEZs: (1) between the United States and Canada over the Beaufort Sea (the bone of contention centers on the delimitation of hydrocarbon-rich waters lying between the Yukon Territory and Alaska); (2) between Canada and Denmark/ Greenland involving the Davis Strait (the issue was settled in 1973 despite continuing disagreement over Hans Island); (3) between Denmark/Greenland and Iceland over the Fram Strait (settled in 1997); (4) between Denmark/

Greenland and Norway over Svalbard (settled in 2006); (5) between Iceland and Norway over the island of Jan Mayen (settled in 1993–1995); and (6) between Denmark/Greenland and Norway over Jan Mayen (settled in 1981). The Soviet Union/Russia has been involved in two disputes: (7) one with the United States over the Bering Sea; and another (8) with Norway over the Barents Sea and Svalbard.

Interstate disputes can also involve other aspects of sovereignty in the Arctic, in particular the legal status of straits. Hence, Canada and Russia consider the Northwest Passage and the Northeast Passage, respectively, their territorial waters, and therefore claim the right to regulate the traffic of foreign ships, while the other states, especially the United States, consider them international waters.[3] Finally, a third category of disputes concerns the delimitation of the continental shelf. The shelf has been at the center of international attention right from the start of the twenty-first century, with the establishment of the UN Commission on the Limits of the Continental Shelf (CLCS). The commission is an especially important actor in Arctic issues, as the continental shelf occupies a much higher proportion of the Arctic Ocean floor than of any other ocean. Although the mushrooming interest in Arctic resources encourages the littoral states to stake out claims for sovereignty, all unequivocally uphold the importance of international law in the resolution of their jurisdictional disputes and none have tried to bypass it.

Given the length of its coastlines, Russia is very active in both theoretical and practical debates on the issue of Arctic territorial delimitation. It is involved in all three types of legal disputes: those concerning the delineation of EEZ boundaries, the delimitation of the continental shelf, and vessel transit in the straits. On these issues, Moscow pursues proactive policies, which is a sign of the importance that it assigns to them, as Russian international policies are traditionally quite reactive.

The Soviet Historical Referent: The 1926 Decree

The Russian legal tradition of delimitating Arctic waters is characterized by the notion of the sectoral line, that is, the line (meridian) of longitude that starts from the terminus of the land boundary and intersects with the North Pole. The division of the Arctic into national sectors began at the start of the twentieth century, when Canada first, in 1909, proclaimed its sovereignty over the lands stretching between its territorial border and the North Pole. Tsarist Russia quickly also adopted the Canadian criteria of sectoral division. Upon Imperial Russia's entry into World War I in 1914, St. Petersburg confirmed its 12-mile territorial waters in the Arctic, and in 1916 sent an official note to the Allied powers, announcing possession of a significant number of lands and islands in the Arctic.[4] The Bolsheviks' seizure of power during the October Revolution of 1917 had no impact on the Russian stance: the USSR endorsed the decisions of the Tsarist regime.

The new Soviet regime soon felt under threat in the Arctic because of Canada's occupation of Wrangel Island, which enabled Canadian and American expeditions to travel easily to Chukotka.[5] Concerned about the possible discovery of unknown lands by European countries that had better mastered aviation than the Soviet Union had, on April 15, 1926, the Central Executive Committee of the Communist Party issued a decree "On the Proclamation of Lands and Islands Located in the Northern Arctic Ocean as Territory of the USSR" (1926 decree). The decree stated that "all lands and islands, both discovered and which may be discovered in the future, which do not comprise at the time of publication of the present decree the territory of any foreign state recognized by the Government of the Soviet Union, located in the northern Arctic Ocean, north of the shores of the Union of Soviet Socialist Republics up to the North Pole between the meridian 32°04'35" E. long from Greenwich, running along the eastern side of Vaida Bay through the triangular marker on Cape Kekurskii, and the meridian 168°49' 30" W. long from Greenwich, bisecting the strait separating the Ratmanov and Kruzenstern Islands, of the Diomede group in the Bering Sea, are proclaimed to be territory of the Soviet Union."[6]

The territory defined in the decree is based on the internationally validated boundaries of the time: to the east, those between the United States and Russia defined in the 1867 Convention on Alaska; and to the west, the border between the Soviet Union and Norway. Moscow lays claim to sovereignty over all the territories between these two points along the meridian up to the North Pole. At a time when Russia regarded itself as surrounded by capitalist enemies characterized by their "imperialism," the objective of this decree was to prevent other states from proclaiming their sovereign will over unknown territories. Later, some Soviet researchers extended the scope of the decree, for example, V.L. Lakhtin, who published a monograph titled *Prava na severnye poliarnye prostranstva* (Rights on Northern Polar Spaces) as early as 1928. In it, he advanced two new arguments: first, that all lands and islands, regardless of who effectively occupied them, came under the sovereignty of the owner of a sector in accordance not with the contiguity theory but with the principle of "region of attraction" (*raion tiagoteniia*); second, that fast ice should be equated to land territory, that is, be incorporated within the sovereign part of a sectoral state, as well as the air space above it.[7]

The 1926 decree was designed to regulate questions over sovereignty of the Arctic Ocean, not to serve as a general principle for the demarcation of maritime borders. However, it was viewed within Soviet legal practice as a historical precedent and therefore led Moscow to propose a sectoral division of all maritime borders.[8] The Soviet Union stuck to this principle throughout its existence. Some Soviet maps showed state borders following meridians from the Kola Peninsula and the Bering Strait toward the pole, so that one-third of the Arctic Ocean was designated as lying within the USSR's territorial waters. But Soviet works remained divided in their interpretation of the decree's scope. Those that maintained a more restricted reading of the decree considered that only the islands of the sectoral zone constituted part of the territorial contiguity of the state, not the waters between the islands and the continent. Those who interpreted the decree more broadly claimed that the islands, the waters, and the air space must also fall under national jurisdiction.[9] In practice, Moscow did not uphold this broader interpretation of the 1926 decree and never perceived the border of the Arctic sector as its territorial border.

During the decades of the Cold War, however, these juridical ambiguities served to stoke tensions with the United States, which exercised its perceived right to freely navigate the oceans. U.S. submarines succeeded in not only reaching the North Pole (in 1958, the *USS Nautilus* was the first watercraft to reach the geographic North Pole), but also passed through Soviet-controlled Arctic waters and northern straits (achieved by the *USS Blackfin*), and even entered Soviet territorial waters (the *USS Gudgeon* in 1957 close to Vladivostok).[10] In April 1989, at the height of *glasnost*, the USSR Council of Ministers' State Commission on Arctic Affairs defined the country's Arctic zone: 3.1 million square kilometers of the landmass, and about 4 million square kilometers of continental shelf.[11]

Since the collapse of the Soviet Union, the Russian legal position has softened. In the course of its border conflicts with Kazakhstan and Azerbaijan over the Caspian Sea, Moscow yielded without demanding sectoral demarcation of the Caspian, in large part because demarcation using the principle of the median line provided it with zones rich in hydrocarbons. The oil factor was therefore most likely conclusive in Russia's decision to change its principle of delimitation, and this enabled peaceful settlements with both Astana and Baku.[12] Moscow also realized that by upholding the sectoral principle of demarcation, it was losing some potential territory in the Bering Sea. Moreover, this method of division has met with little international success. Denmark, Norway, and the United States have all publicly rejected it, and UNCLOS posits the median line as the basic principle of division of marine territories. This shift in Russia's legal position contributed to the 2010 agreement with Norway (see below).

Russian Claims on the Arctic Continental Shelf

Under UNCLOS, a coastal state has exclusive sovereign rights to explore and exploit the natural resources of its continental shelf up to 200 nautical miles from its shores. Beyond this limit, it has to provide scientific evidence to establish the extent of the legally defined continental shelf in order to exercise the same rights. These rights apply to the exploitation of living and non-living resources of that state's share of the shelf's seabed and subsoil, but do not extend to resources in the water column such as fish stocks, which are covered by a separate regime. Thanks to Soviet marine research that has been systematically carried out in the Arctic since the 1960s, in 2001 Russia became the first country to refer to the CLCS (see above), a review body of scientists created under UNCLOS. In so doing, it created a legal precedent, which other states hastened to follow.

After ratifying UNCLOS, each state has 10 years to submit an application for the recognition of its continental shelf; it can then make as many claims as it wishes once the first application has been made. The commission consists of 21 members chosen for their expertise in geology, geophysics, and hydrography, but they are also elected with due regard for geographic representation—having its own national member sitting in the body can be beneficial for a state submitting a claim. The commission's decisions require a two-thirds majority, but rulings cannot be made that disadvantage other states, even if the state in question has not submitted a claim but deems it is potentially disadvantaged.[13] This measure is designed to protect the weakest countries, which do not have the financial and technological means to submit a request. Known as Rule 5, this rule can be used to prevent the commission from issuing a verdict that would be binding. The commission is also unable to settle border disputes between states, except if the governments concerned request the arbitration of the commission. The scope for legal wrangling is therefore seemingly endless.[14]

In addition, the definition of the continental shelf as expressed in Article 76 of UNCLOS is composed of many technical and geological criteria that scientists often judge to be incomplete or contradictory. It leaves open some definitions that are likely to evolve in accordance with technological progress, even if scientific and technical guidelines are supposed to help interpret the terms used. UNCLOS states that "[t]he continental shelf of a coastal state comprises the seabed and subsoil of the submarine areas that extend beyond its territorial sea throughout the *natural prolongation* of its land territory to the outer edge of the continental margin."[15] Several criteria defining "natural prolongation" are thus to be taken into account: the thickness of sedimentary cover, a distance of 60 nautical miles from the foot of the continental slope, a distance of 350 nautical miles from the country's baseline, and/or 100 nautical miles from its 2,500-meter isobath. In addition, claims must first prove that the prolongation is not constituted by an oceanic ridge, as this term has a complex definition apt to be interpreted in multiple ways, and is not considered as a natural component of the continental shelf per se.[16]

In its claim, Russia argues that the Lomonosov Ridge and the Alpha-Mendeleev Ridge are both geological extensions of its continental Siberian shelf and, thus, that parts of the Central Arctic Ocean, as well as parts of the Barents Sea, the Bering Sea, and the Sea of Okhotsk, fall under its jurisdiction. Most of this area, amounting to about 1.2 million square kilometers of Arctic waters, is situated in a triangular zone, "the top of which is the North Pole, the eastern side is approximately the meridian 170°W, the western side is an irregular line running southward from the North Pole to the cross point with the EEZ outer limit (81°N, 120°E), and the base is the outer limit of the Russian EEZ."[17] The Lomonosov Ridge is a 1,800 kilometer-long submerged elevation joining the continental Eurasian and American platforms, while the Mendeleev Ridge is a 1,500 kilometer-long elevation between Wrangel Island and the Canadian Arctic archipelago. In 2002, the CLCS issued a recommendation about the additional data and information it needed, which Russia was to supply by 2009. With this in mind, Moscow organized the much-publicized 2007 Arctic expedition, during which the Russian flag was planted on the Arctic seabed, an act devoid of any legal significance but that incited the anger of other states. Still the information gathered for a renewed submission was not adequately detailed in its bathymetric analysis. In September 2012, Russia organized a new expedition to the Mendeleev Ridge to collect several hundred kilograms of geological material taken at depths of 2,000–3,000 meters, which will be analyzed during 2013.[18] The additional application should be submitted by early 2014.

A technical analysis of the Russian claims lies beyond the scope of this chapter and can in any case be conducted only obliquely, inasmuch as all claims are subject to confidentiality. Only the executive summaries have been made public, as have the appeals submitted by the other states, which thus make it possible, through the responses they provide, to surmise the approximate nature of the claims and the arguments put forward.[19] Since Moscow's initial submission, Canada, Denmark, Japan, Norway, and the United States have filed their responses to the executive summary of the Russian claims. Norway has issued official documents indicating that the Russian request infringes upon its own claims. As the commission cannot give rulings that disadvantage another state, it cannot issue a verdict inasmuch as the claims of the other states remained unexamined. Thus, after Norway placed a request for recognition of its continental shelf in 2006, including an expressed reservation of the right to claim additional territory, it came to light that both Moscow and Oslo claimed two zones, the Loop Hole and the Western Nansen Basin. In the absence of any territorial delimitation treaty between the two states until spring 2010, the commission was unable to rule in favor of either party, with both states invoking Rule 5, which safeguards against any prejudicial decisions. In 2008, the commission endorsed Norway's description of the seabed outside of its established border, thus allowing the country to widen its economic zone in the Arctic by 235,000 square kilometers, but without issuing a ruling on the two zones that, at that time, were still under dispute.[20]

Canada and Denmark stressed that the oceanographic data contained in the Russian executive summary was insufficient to permit them to determine their stance on Moscow's position. Nonetheless, the Canadian and Danish governments have been working together since 2005 to submit their own claims.[21] In 2006, both countries, considering that the stakes were of such importance, set aside their dispute over Hans Island and undertook a joint scientific expedition known as the Continental Shelf Project to collect bathymetric, seismic, and gravity data from the Lomonosov Ridge and to establish claims to territorial expansion.[22] Both states are involved in collecting data on the seabed north of Greenland and Ellesmere Island, and through the Lomonosov Ridge Test of Appurtenance (LORITA) Project hope to prove that the ridge, which passes through Greenland to Canada's Ellesmere Island, is a natural extension of the North American continent.[23] Canada and Denmark have until 2013 and 2014, respectively, to submit their claims.

The United States, although it has not ratified UNCLOS, submitted a document in 2002 contesting Russian claims on a scientific level, with detailed references to the technical aspects of the Russian submission. The U.S. document claims that the Russian text does not propose objective data sources concerning the location of the 2,500-meter isobath and the foot of the continental slope. The main scientific argument advanced by the United States seems to be that the Alpha-Mendeleev Ridge system is a geologic feature formed by volcanism (a submerged "hot spot"), and therefore cannot be considered a natural prolongation of the continental shelf or continental margin.[24] Regarding the Lomonosov Ridge, Russia seems to have more leeway with its potential claim for continental shelf expansion, but needs to provide sufficient arguments to prove the relationship between the ridge and the Russian continental shelf; otherwise the commission will define the ridge as an oceanic one. However, in 2002, U.S. State Department representatives mentioned that the U.S. view of Arctic geology was still evolving and that,

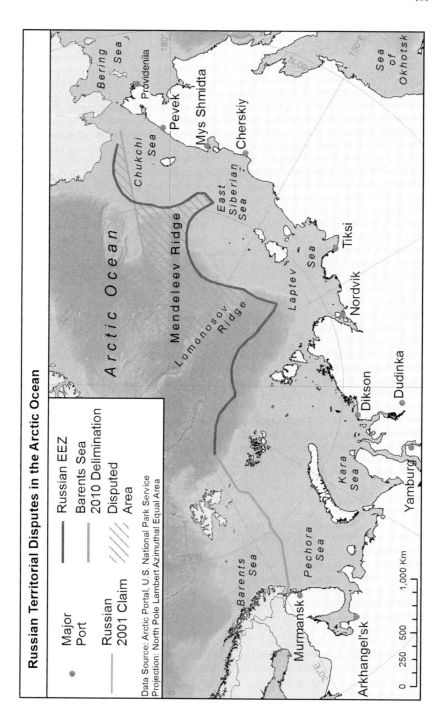

Russian Territorial Disputes in the Arctic Ocean

Major Port

Russian EEZ

Barents Sea
2010 Delimination

Russian
2001 Claim

Disputed
Area

Data Source: Arctic Portal, U.S. National Park Service
Projection: North Pole Lambert Azimuthal Equal Area

Arctic Ocean

Bering Sea

Providenia

Pevek

Mys Shmidta

Chukchi Sea

Cherskiy

East Siberian Sea

Mendeleev Ridge

Lomonosov Ridge

Laptev Sea

Tiksi

Nordvik

Dikson

Dudinka

Kara Sea

Yamburg

Pechora Sea

Barents Sea

Murmansk

Arkhangel'sk

Sea of Okhotsk

0 250 500 1,000 Km

in hindsight, their notification reflected an inadequate appreciation of the scientific complexities involved.[25]

In 2014, the CLCS could make a decision concerning Russia's claims on the Alpha-Mendeleev Ridge system and the Lomonosov Ridge. If a ruling is made, it will be binding and final. The CLCS may reject or accept the totality of Russia's claims, or make decisions only on some parts. But it is also possible that the CLCS will consider that the information obtained is insufficient to make a decision, and that it will ask that further research be undertaken. This would thus push back the delimitation of territorial borders on this part of the continental shelf by several years.

The Russian-U.S. Agreement on the Bering and Chukchi Seas

In the 1970s, the United States proposed to the Soviet Union that the two countries enter into negotiations over the length of their common maritime border (the longest in the world, more than 2,500 kilometers long) in order to settle points of disagreement: the EEZs of both countries intersected in the Bering Sea as well as in the Chukchi Sea, the two countries have competing claims to portions of their continental shelves, and part of the open sea was yet to be delimited. A provisional application for a forthcoming agreement entered into force in 1977 so that day-to-day issues could be regulated, particularly with respect to fishing. Long a zone of tensions during the Cold War, the negotiations on the Bering Sea resumed during *perestroika*, after Gorbachev's famous Murmansk Speech in October 1987. Both parties finally signed an agreement on July 1, 1990, resulting in the so-called Baker-Shevardnadze line, which is a compromise between a median line and a sectoral line.[26] The United States ratified the treaty in 1991 but, more than 20 years later, Russia has yet to do so. This refusal can be mostly explained by domestic political debates but is also related to the overall evolution of Russian-American relations.

Since the beginning of the 1990s, the Duma has refused to ratify the treaty, arguing that it harmed the interests of the Russian state in terms of fishing and potentially also of oil reserves. Opponents of ratification have put forward multiple arguments. In 1990, with the Soviet Union undergoing *perestroika* and rapid institutional changes, the decision-making system and legal procedures to ratify documents became blurred. Nikolai Ryzhkov, who at the time occupied the post of president of the Council of Ministers (Soviet Prime Minister), declared that neither the Politburo, nor the Council of Ministers, were able to examine the text of the treaty prior to its signature, which would render it invalid. But Foreign Affairs Minister Sergei Lavrov has stated, on the contrary, that the internal validation procedure in the Central

Committee had been followed.[27] Many also accused Eduard Shevarnadze of having ceded too easily to U.S. demands in order to obtain Washington's support.[28] Indeed, in 1990 Moscow was hoping to sign an entire package of agreements with the United States, including the withdrawal of missiles from Europe, and did not want to slow down the process by bringing the Bering Sea case before the UN International Court of Justice in The Hague, still decried as a "tool of capitalism." Moscow had also been in negotiations with Norway and had hoped to tip the balance on the sectoral line in its favor, provided that it first came to an agreement with Washington.

The issue returns regularly to center stage. In 1996, the Duma held new parliamentary readings on this subject, though it refrained from making a decision. In 2002, the Russian Audit Chamber provided a detailed opinion on the state of Russian fishing and concluded that because of this agreement, Moscow had lost between 1.6 and 1.9 million tons of fish in the 1990s.[29] The reports the Duma requested conclude that, of its own free will, the Soviet Union ceded three areas from its EEZ to the United States: one in the Bering Sea (23,000 square kilometers), one in the Chukchi Sea (7,700 square kilometers), and another in the Pacific Ocean (46,000 square kilometers). In exchange, Moscow was to secure guaranteed fish quotas for its fishermen, to obtain a small part of the American EEZ in the western sector, and to gain sovereignty over the islands of the Chukchi Sea, including Wrangel Island.[30]

In 2007, the director of the North American Department within the Ministry of Foreign Affairs declared that the text of the agreement did not harm the territorial interests of the Russian state, except in terms of fishing, and that negotiations were taking place with the United States in order to compensate for Russian losses,[31] but a solution has yet to be found. If fishing quotas indeed seem to be the main point of friction, it is possible in the future that new issues involving other natural resources could impede the resolution of the dispute. Indeed, it is likely that the zones ceded are rich in hydrocarbons, especially the Navarinsk and Aleut fields, even if the absence of offshore wells and lack of seismic data mean that such hypotheses cannot be verified for the time being. According to data gathered in 2006, the estimated total recoverable resources of the East Siberian and Chukchi Seas are more than eight billion tons of oil equivalent.[32]

In this dispute with the United States, the Soviet-Russian jurisdictional position has been weakened by its inconsistency. As a point of departure for the negotiations, Washington proposed to Moscow that the two sides adopt the same line of demarcation as that mentioned in the 1867 Convention on the Cession of Alaska, which determines a geographical line west of which all the territories are American, and to the east of which all are Russian. This line was mentioned in the 1926 decree delimiting the Soviet Arctic territories and corresponded more or less to the idea of a sectoral line as defended by Soviet jurisprudence. However, the 1867 agreement actually applied only to emerged territories (i.e., dry land), and not to seas, and was not intended for the delimitation of the EEZ or continental shelf. The Soviet Union could have pointed to the legal precedent, as an earlier decision made by a court of arbitration confirmed that the Convention on the Cession of Alaska did not concern seas, but despite this Moscow did not object to the U.S. request.

As stated by the Soviet jurist Alexander Vylegzhanin, the line of division chosen therefore brought 70% of the disputed areas of the Bering Sea under American jurisdiction.[33] If instead the median line principle had been applied, it could have provided the Soviet Union with an additional 25,000 square kilometers of sea.[34] Moreover, according to the U.S. statement on the Russian claim to the UN Commission on the Limits of the Continental Shelf, it appears that in its submission, Russia refers to the 1990 agreement on the Bering Sea, which in this case means that the country is now bound to the treaty even without having ratified it.[35]

Russia cannot legally undermine the 1990 agreement, even if ratification is necessary for it to enter into force. It can at best hope to negotiate some compensation to offset the losses incurred in fishing, to create new bilateral mechanisms to open American fishing zones to Russian vessels, or even to promote a more open status such as that of a natural park for the protection of biodiversity, and thus to settle the problem in a friendly way. It seems that the resolution of the question is intrinsically linked to the state of Russian-American relations in general. Washington, for its part, has to contend with criticism from the state of Alaska, which is a lot stricter in its negotiations with Moscow and would like to block any decisions that are taken without its participation.

The Issue of the Barents Sea and Its Resolution

The Russian-Norwegian territorial conflict over the Barents Sea has probably been the most complex. It was largely stamped by the Cold War geopolitical context (for many decades, Norway was the only member of NATO, along with Turkey, to share a common border with the Soviet Union), it also involved important economic questions (which, since the 1970s, have mainly related to fisheries but now increasingly concern the exploitation of hydrocarbons) and carries symbolic weight in terms of national sovereignty and nation-building for both countries.[36]

The sea border between Norway and the Soviet Union in the Varangerfjord area was agreed upon in a treaty signed in 1957; it was completed by a new treaty ratified in 2007 that specified the delimitation line for the territorial sea, the EEZ zone, and the continental shelf between Norway and Russia as farther north outside the mouth of the Varangerfjord. Negotiations concerning the delimitation of the other main maritime borders between the two countries began in 1974. In 1976–1977, however, both protagonists proclaimed their border in a unilateral manner. Norway based its claim on the principle of a median line between Svalbard, on the one hand, and Novaya Zemlya and the Franz Josef Land archipelago, on the other. The Soviet Union, although a signatory to UNCLOS, refused to accept this principle on the basis of the "special circumstances" clause provided by Law of the Sea. According to Moscow, the 1926 decree amounts to a historic precedent that makes provisions for a sectoral zone that starts out from Russian territory and proceeds in a straight line as far as the North Pole. As a result, about 155,000 square kilometers came under dispute, including the overlapping EEZs within this area. Added to this are the 20,000 square kilometers of overlapping claims farther north in the Arctic Ocean.[37] Since 1980, after the Soviet Union attempted to engage in oil extraction, both Moscow and Oslo agreed on a moratorium prohibiting oil and gas exploration and geological prospecting in the disputed area, which meant that fishing took center stage in the underlying economic debates on border division.[38]

Despite the impossibility of reaching a legal agreement, both countries quickly decided to cooperate over fishing. As early as 1978, an agreement concerning the so-called Grey Zone was signed. The 65,000 square kilometers of the Grey Zone includes the Loop Hole, a high seas triangle bounded by Russia's EEZ, the disputed waters between both countries, and the Svalbard Fisheries Protection Zone, but also encompassing 23,000 square kilometers of Norway's EEZ and 3,000 square kilometers belonging to Russia. The Grey Zone agreement, extended on a yearly basis, is a classic mechanism of enforcement and control in the management and conservation of fish stocks in international or disputed waters.[39] Throughout the 1990s and 2000s, regular tensions between the two countries arose over the inspection and boarding of Russian fishing boats by the Norwegian navy. For environmental reasons, Oslo has implemented strict rules to regulate the fishing industry and has fixed quotas on how many fish are allowed to be caught depending on the species, which it considers to be its duty to apply in its EEZ. The question of nuclear waste from Soviet nuclear plants on the Kola Peninsula and industrial pollution, mainly from nickel mining and smelting, in the Barents Sea is also a cause of disagreement. The lack of sustainable management of Moscow's maritime resources is part of the Norwegian mainstream narrative in the relationship with Russia.[40]

Despite elements of significant tension and a complex geopolitical context, Russian-Norwegian cooperation has been a success in terms of the everyday management of maritime relations.[41] Pragmatic cooperation has made it possible to overcome legal conflicts and to reach a definitive agreement, concluded in April 2010 during Dmitri Medvedev's visit to Norway, signed on September 15, 2010,[42] and ratified by the Russian Duma in March 2011. Norway has withdrawn some of its territorial claims, and Russia has consented to a shift of the 1926 demarcation line to share the 175,000 square kilometers in two almost equal parts defined by eight points.[43] The endpoint is still undefined because of the undefined edge of each party's continental shelves in the Arctic Ocean. Russia was granted EEZ rights in the area to the east of the boundary that lies within 200 nautical miles of the Norwegian mainland but more than 200 miles from Russian territory. The treaty is also accompanied by agreements on cooperation over fisheries and hydrocarbon activities in cases where oil or gas deposits extend across the delimitation line.[44] The Norwegian-Russian Joint Fisheries Commission will continue its activities, but the agreement effectively supersedes the Grey Zone fishing arrangement of 1978. On the Russian side, this decision was eminently political.[45] It was taken against the advice of the jurists in charge of the dossier at the Ministry of Foreign Affairs, who criticized Moscow for making excessive compromises.[46]

The Dispute over the Svalbard Archipelago and Spitsbergen

The 2010 Russian-Norwegian agreement leaves unresolved another point of contention, namely that of the Svalbard archipelago and its largest island, Spitsbergen. The archipelago, covering 61,000 square kilometers in the Barents Sea, is the object of a complex legal debate related to the limits of Norwegian sovereignty since its independence from Sweden in 1905. Despite the many conferences organized around this question in Oslo between 1910 and 1914, no solution was found and it was necessary to wait until the Paris Peace Conference in 1920 to attain the signing of a treaty that was favorable to Norway. The Svalbard Treaty, ratified by more than 40 states in the absence of the Soviet Union, which had no international legal recognition at the time, confirmed Norwegian sovereignty over the Svalbard archipelago, albeit under certain limits and conditions.

In 1924, still lacking international recognition, the Soviet Union finally accepted Norwegian sovereignty over Svalbard in exchange for the establishment of diplomatic relations with Oslo. In 1935, Moscow ratified the Svalbard Treaty, but continued to ask for joint jurisdiction over Svalbard itself and for the inclusion of Bear Island under Soviet jurisdiction. For this, it has requested that legal delimitation be decided according to the principle of equity, which supposes that factors of economic importance (fishing) and of historical precedence are to be taken into account.[47] The archipelago has allegedly been inhabited by Pomorian Russians since the seventeenth and eighteenth centuries, but the Russian villages were destroyed during the Crimean War, leaving only the Russian and Ukrainian population of the small mining town of Barentsburg. Lastly, Moscow also wanted to establish its sovereignty over a territory stretching to the Norwegian Tana River so as to rectify the provisions of the 1826 convention establishing the Norwegian-Russian border, which the Soviet Union found cumbersome.

The disputes concerning Svalbard/Spitsbergen are based on old legal texts, interpretations of which contemporary conditions have pushed in divergent directions. The Paris Treaty is sometimes unclear, and international maritime law underwent drastic changes in the second half of the twentieth century. Thus, at the time of the Paris Treaty, the international law of the sea did not recognize sovereign states' rights beyond a three-mile territorial sea, and defined a rectangle of land and sea, which has since come to be known as the "Svalbard box."[48] But the evolution of international maritime law has enabled Norway to increase its claims over the archipelago and its surrounding waters. In 1977, Oslo established a non-discriminatory Svalbard Fisheries Protection Zone of 200 nautical miles around Svalbard's islands, kept distinct from the main Norwegian EEZ. In 1985, the Petroleum Activities Act included the seabed and subsoil surrounding Svalbard as part of the Norwegian continental shelf, and the government announced that it was opening part of it for exploration by its oil companies—but no licenses have been granted. In 2003, Oslo decided to extend the breadth of its territorial waters to 12 miles around Svalbard, resulting in an increase of approximately 35% in the surrounding Norwegian territorial sea.[49] This change, which is in line with trends in the international law of the sea, was decided in a unilateral manner by Norway, without obtaining the consent of the signatory countries of the Paris agreement—only Canada and Finland recognize the change. According to the states most opposed to Norway's claims, such as Great Britain, the treaty does not authorize the establishment of maritime zones or enable coastal state jurisdiction beyond the territorial sea without the agreement of the signatory parties. Other states have staked out a middle ground. They recognize Norway's right to establish a fisheries zone and to exercise coastal state jurisdiction, but maintain the rights for the treaty's signatories.[50]

The treaty contains complex clauses stipulating that ships and citizens of contracting parties are permitted to undertake fishing and hunting on an equal basis on the lands and in the territorial waters of the archipelago, and that all signatory states have equal access to conduct economic activities there. The Svalbard mining code is favorable to foreign investors, so that the taxes paid promote the archipelago, but not the budget of the Norwegian state.[51] Russia challenges the Norwegian reading of the treaty at different levels. It claims that the historically shared sovereignty between Norway and Russia over the archipelago must be given legal precedence. It raises the fact that Norwegian lawmakers have no legislative grounds for invoking the "territorial sea"—a classical institution of contemporary international maritime treaty law—in order to mark off an EEZ around the archipelago or on its shelf.[52] Norwegian sovereignty is thus allegedly limited to the land—not the sea. Russia also criticizes the fact that Oslo applies Norwegian internal law to the archipelago, which restricts exploitation rights. Thus, the fisheries regime used by Oslo for Svalbard is more restricted in terms of permitted catch than in the EEZ. In addition, Norway has unilaterally imposed a mining code for the islands' geological shelf that contradicts the Paris Treaty. The Svalbard Environmental Protection Act, enacted by Oslo in 2001, could put into question the activities of the Russian state-owned mining company Trust Arktikugol, which exploits the promising coal reserves of the Coles Bay area. Moscow defends the economic interests of the mining town of Barentsburg and views Oslo's environmental discourses as a subterfuge to obstruct Russian activities on the archipelago.[53]

The 2010 Russian-Norwegian Treaty on the Barents Sea does not settle the question of Svalbard, which presents specific legal problems. One is the huge difference in taxation levels between Norway and the archipelago. Russian companies accessing the Svalbard continental shelf should enjoy the same right as the Norwegian companies, which would translate to taxes of less than 1% of the cost of the hydrocarbons produced. But as Russian jurist Alexander Oreshenkov explained, "If a deposit beginning within the limits of the archipelago's territory extends beyond its territorial waters, the Russian companies will be expected to observe the norms of Norway's continental mainland petroleum legislation, which means that 78% of their earnings from the hydrocarbons produced outside Norway's territorial waters will go away in tax payments to the Norwegian treasury."[54] These financial stakes are bound to be at the core of future negotiations.

Despite media depictions of a forthcoming "Ice Cold War," none of the five Arctic coastal states are involved in violent confrontation or unlawful occupation of disputed territories. State behavior is guided by the agreed rules of international law, and territorial disputes have been characterized as much by symbolic competition as by pragmatic cooperation. In 2009, Canadian and Russian diplomats raised the possibility of making a joint submission to the CLCS, possibly in cooperation with Denmark. In 2012, Vladimir Putin called for the creation of a joint scientific council with Canada to peacefully discuss potentially overlapping continental shelf claims. The patterns of co-operation are therefore clearly prevalent, even among competitors. Using the effective legal framework, all coastal states have been proposing innovative ideas in order to map out future areas of cooperation.

However, there is a basis for potential interstate tension. One is the growing demand by non-Arctic states—notably China—to participate in the debate over the Arctic and to be accorded specific rights. In addition, in the event of the CLCS's refusal to validate the claims made on the continental shelf, some states could be tempted to find loopholes in the law, but a unilateral annexation of the contested areas is very difficult to imagine. If the Lomonosov and Mendeleev Ridges are not recognized as part of the Russian continental shelf, Moscow, which has invested billions of dollars to collect the necessary scientific information, could toughen its discursive stance; it would be less likely to respect international law and may even be prompted to advocate for more binding structures for dispute resolution.[55] The Russian authorities are preparing their public opinion for the eventuality of a negative ruling, by regularly stating that the CLCS ruling will be decided not purely on scientific arguments, but also will reflect hidden political or geopolitical motives. On the contrary, should Russia receive a positive decision from the UN Commission, whether in part or justifying the entirety of its claims, it will achieve a territorial advantage on the Arctic continental shelf that the other Arctic states, especially Canada and the United States, will not be able to call into question. It would therefore modify the global geostrategic balance, as well as the prospects of economic exploitation, in Russia's favor.

Notes

1. D.R. Rothwell, *The Polar Regions and the Development of International Law* (Cambridge: Cambridge University Press, 1996).

2. Complete information is available on the website of the Commission on the Limits of the Continental Shelf at http://www.un.org/Depts/los/clcs_new/clcs_home.htm (accessed June 28, 2012).

3. A. Hakon Hoel, "The High North Legal-Political Regime," in S.G. Holtsmark and B.A. Smith-Windsor, eds., *Security Prospects in the High North: Geostrategic Thaw or Freeze?* (Rome: NATO Defense College, 2009), 87–93.

4. S.J. Main, *If Spring Comes Tomorrow . . . Russia and the Arctic* (Shrivenham: Defence Academy of the United Kingdom, 2011).

5. Horensma, *The Soviet Arctic* (London: Routledge, 1991), 21–34.

6. W.E. Butler, *International Straits of the World: Northeast Arctic Passage* (Alphen aan den Rijn: Sijthoff & Noordhoff, 1978), 72.

7. L. Timtchenko, "The Russian Arctic Sectoral Concept: Past and Present," *Arctic* 50, no. 1 (1997): 29–35.

8. A.G. Elferink, "The Law and Politics of the Maritime Boundary Delimitation of the Russian Federation, Part 1," *The International Journal of Marine and Coastal*

Law 10, no. 4 (1996): 525–561; A.G. Elferink, "The Law and Politics of the Maritime Boundary Delimitation of the Russian Federation, Part 2," *The International Journal of Marine and Coastal Law* 11, no. 1 (1997): 5–35.

9. Ibid., 32.

10. P. Sasgen, *Stalking the Red Bear: The True Story of a U.S. Cold War Submarine's Covert Operations Against the Soviet Union* (New York: St. Martin's Press, 2009).

11. See M. Shestopalov, "Vektor ustremlenii—Arktika [A vector of aspiration—the Arctic]," *Vozdushno-kosmicheskaia oborona,* no. 6 (2008) 16–24; S. Koz'menko and S. Kovalev, "Morskaia politika v Arktike i sistema natsional'noi bezopasnosti [Maritime policy in the Arctic and the national security system]," *Morskoi sbornik* 8 (2009): 57.

12. A. Wenger, S. Langenbach, and R. Orttung, "The role of hydrocarbons in maritime claim-making: patterns of conflict & cooperation," unpublished manuscript.

13. B. Spielman, "An Evaluation of Russia's Impending Claim for Continental Shelf Expansion: Why Rule 5 Will Shelve Russia's Submission," *Emory International Law Review* 23 (2009): 340.

14. Ibid., 317.

15. U.N. Convention on the Law of the Sea art. 76(1), Dec. 10, 1982, 1833 U.N.T.S. 397.

16. T. Górski, "A Note on Submarine Ridges and Elevations with Special Reference to the Russian Federation and the Arctic Ridges," *Ocean Development & International Law* 40, no. 1 (2009): 51–60.

17. Ibid., 51.

18. "Trilobity podtverdili kontinental'noe proiskhozhdenie arkticheskogo shel'fa RF [Trilobites confirmed the continental origin of the Arctic shelf of the RF]," *Voice of Russia,* October 31, 2012, http://rus.ruvr.ru/2012_10_31/Trilobiti-podtverdili-kontinentalnoe-proishozhdenie-arkticheskogo-shelfa-RF/ (accessed November 4, 2012).

19. More detailed comments on the Russian claim can be found in Spielman, "An Evaluation of Russia's Impending Claim for Continental Shelf Expansion," 309–350.

20. See the executive summary of the "Continental Shelf Submission of Norway in Respect of Areas in the Arctic Ocean, the Barents Sea, and the Norwegian Sea" at http://www.regjeringen.no/upload/kilde/ud/prm/2006/0374/ddd/pdfv/299461-sokkel.pdf; and "Limits of Norway's Arctic Seabed Agreed," *Barents Observer,* April 16, 2009, http://www.barentsobserver.com/limits-of-norways-arctic-seabed-agreed.4580729–16149.html (accessed June 28, 2012).

21. E. Riddell-Dixon, "Canada and Arctic Politics: The Continental Shelf Extension,", *Ocean Development & International Law* 39, no. 4 (2008): 343–359.

22. Ibid.

23. W. Jokat, G. Uenzelmann-Neben, Y. Kristoffersen, and T.M. Rasmussen, "Lomonosov Ridge—A Double-Sided Continental Margin," *Geology* 20, no. 10 (1992): 887–890.

24. Spielman, "An Evaluation of Russia's Impending Claim for Continental Shelf Expansion," 329.

25. B. Baker, "Law, Science, and the Continental Shelf: The Russian Federation and the Promise of Arctic Cooperation," *American University International Law Review* 25, no. 2 (2010): 270.

26. "Agreement between the United States of America and the Union of Soviet Socialist Republics on the Maritime Boundary," 1 June 1990, http://www.un.org/Depts/los/LEGISLATIONANDTREATIES/PDFFILES/TREATIES/USA-RUS1990MB. PDF (accessed June 28, 2012).

27. A. Oreshenkov, "Severnaia ledovitaia diplomatiia [Northern Arctic diplomacy]," *Rossiia v global'noi politike*, no. 4 (2009), www.globalaffairs.ru/number/n_13635 (accessed June 28, 2012).

28. L. Shebarshin, "Oni bez nas prozhivut, a my bez samikh sebia—net [They will survive without us, but we won't without ourselves]," *Ekonomicheskie strategii*, no. 6 (2000): 36–49.

29. N.G. Palamar, "Nekotorye aspekty pogranichnogo razgranicheniia mezhdu Rossiiskoi Federatsiei i SShA [Some aspects of boundary differentiation between the Russian Federation and the United States of America]," *Znanie, Ponimanie, Umenie*, no. 6 (2009), http://www.zpu-journal.ru/e-zpu/2009/6/Palamar_Boundary_Differentiation/index.php?sphrase_id=4718 (accessed June 28, 2012).

30. P. Prokhorov, "'Gaagskaia vaktsina' ot 'sindroma Siuarda' [The 'Hague vaccine' against 'Seward's syndrome']," *Sankt-Peterburgskie vedomosti*, no. 137, July 28, 2006, http://www.spbvedomosti.ru/print.htm?id=10237723 (accessed June 28, 2012).

31. "Interv'iu direktora Departamenta Severnoi Ameriki MID Rossii I.S. Neverova agentstvu Interfaks 2 dekabria 2007 o situatsii vokrug razresheniia spora mezhdu Rossiei i SShA. [Interview of director of the North American Department of Russia's Ministry of Foreign Affairs I.S. Neverov by the Interfax news agency on December 2, 2007 on the situation surrounding the resolution of the dispute between Russia and the United States of America]," http://www.mid.ru/brp_4.nsf/sps/9554B2AAAA2E844BC32573A8002BF76D (accessed June 28, 2012).

32. V. Verzhbitsky, E. Frantzen, T. Savostina, A. Little, S.D. Sokolov, and M.I. Tuchkova, "Russian Chukchi Sea," *GeoExpro*, September 10, 2008, http://www.geoexpro.com/TGS-Chukchi/ (accessed September 27, 2010).

33. A. Vylegzhanin, "Agreement between the USSR and the USA about the Line of the Demarcation of the Maritime Spaces of 1990: Different Assessments of Interim Application," unpublished manuscript. Translation by Caitlyn Antrim. I thank Caitlyn Antrim for sending me this document.

34. A. Oreshenkov, "Arctic Square of Opportunities," *Russia in Global Affairs*, December 25, 2010, http://eng.globalaffairs.ru/number/Arctic-Square-of-Opportunities-15085 (accessed June 28, 2012).

35. Spielman, "An Evaluation of Russia's Impending Claim for Continental Shelf Expansion," 339.

36. A. Moe, "The Russian Barents Sea: Openings for Norway?" in R. Gottemoeller and R. Tamnes, eds., *High North: High Stakes* (Bergen: Fagbokforlaget, 2008), 75–85.

37. I.V. Stepanov, P. Ørebech, and R.D. Brubaker, *Legal Implications for the Russian Northern Sea Route and Westward in the Barents Sea* (Oslo: Fridtjof Nansen Institute, 2005), 9.

38. P. Prokhorov, "How Do We Divide the Barents Sea?" Paper presented at the Northern Research Forum, October 4, 2006, 114–116.

39. "The Norwegian Exclusive Economic Zone," *Fisheries.no*, February 9, 2011, http://www.fisheries.no/resource_management/Area_management/economic_zone/ (accessed June 28, 2012).

40. L.C. Jensen and G. Hønneland, "Framing the High North: Public Discourses in Norway after 2000,"*Acta Borealia* 8, no. 1 (2011): 37–54.

41. O. Jensen and S. Vigeland Rottem, "The Politics of Security and International Law in Norway's Arctic Waters," *Polar Record* 46, no. 236 (2010): 75–83.

42. "Agreement between Norway and Russia on Maritime Delimitation," *Norway Mission to the EU*, April 27, 2010, http://www.eu-norway.org/news1/Agreement-between-Norway-and-Russia-on-maritime-delimitation/ (accessed June 28, 2012).

43. "Treaty between the Kingdom of Norway and the Russian Federation concerning Maritime Delimitation and Cooperation in the Barents Sea and the Arctic Ocean," September 15, 2010, in Russian at http://www.kremlin.ru/ref_notes/707, in English at http://www.regjeringen.no/upload/SMK/Vedlegg/2010/avtale_engelsk.pdf (accessed June 28, 2012).

44. T. Henriksen and G. Ulfstein, "Maritime Delimitation in the Arctic: The Barents Sea Treaty," *Ocean Development & International Law* 42, no. 1–2 (2011): 1–21.

45. A. Moe, D. Fjærtoft, and I. Øverland, "Space and Timing: Why Was the Barents Sea Delimitation Dispute Resolved in 2010?" *Polar Geography* 34, no. 3 (2011): 145–162.

46. Anonymous interviews with lawyers working on the Arctic at the Ministry of Foreign Affairs of Russia, Moscow, September 2010.

47. A. Oreshenkov, "Arctic Diplomacy," *Russia in Global Affairs*, no. 8 (2009), http://eng.globalaffairs.ru/number/n_14250 (accessed June 28, 2012).

48. T. Pedersen, "The Svalbard Continental Shelf Controversy: Legal Disputes and Political Rivalries," *Ocean Development & International Law* 37, no. 3–4 (2006): 339–358.

49. I. Caracciolo, "Unresolved Controversy: The Legal Situation of the Svalbard Islands Maritime Areas; an Interpretation of the Paris Treaty in Light of UNCLOS 1982." Paper presented at the International Conference on *Disputed Territory & Maritime Space*, Durkham University, April 2, 2010, http://www.dur.ac.uk/resources/ibru/conferences/sos/ida_caracciolo_paper.pdf (accessed June 28, 2012).

50. D.H. Anderson, "The Status under International Law of the Maritime Areas around Svalbard," *Ocean Development & International Law* 40, no. 4 (2009): 373–384.

51. Ibid.

52. A.N. Vylegzhanin and V.L. Zilanov, *Spitsbergen. Legal Regime of Adjacent Marine Areas* (Portland, OR: Eleven International Publishing, 2007), 57.

53. Oslo ended up excluding Coles Bay from the Protection Act. See K. Åtland and T. Pedersen, "The Svalbard Archipelago in Russian Security Policy: Overcoming the Legacy of Fear—or Reproducing It?" *European Security* 17, no. 2 (2008): 227–251.

54. Oreshenkov, "Arctic Square of Opportunities."

55. N. Matz-Lück, "Planting the Flag in Arctic Waters: Russia's Claim to the North Pole," *Göttingen Journal of International Law* 1, no. 2 (2009): 235–255.

Chapter 6

Projecting Military Power in the Arctic

The possible return of a strategic confrontation between Russia and NATO in the Arctic is probably one of the most debated subjects in Russia in relation to the Arctic, just as it is in the United States or in Canada. Similar to its English-speaking counterparts, the Russian press has been quick to put forward the image of a new "Ice Cold War."[1] Yet, all the major powers are cooperating closely in the Arctic, and assertive rhetorical declarations aside, the main trend is that of desecuritization. Compared to the nuclear tensions of the Cold War, the contemporary situation represents a clear de-escalation. However, the (very relative) military revival is part of a particular geopolitical context, one marked by the absence of Arctic institutions to deal with strategic issues, inasmuch as the Arctic Council expressly prohibits debate on military questions. This institutional vacuum has been interpreted by the bordering states as potentially opening the space up to a militarization of the region due to a lack of channels through which to debate security issues.[2]

The Arctic occupies a very unique place in Russian defense strategy. Since the 1950s, the region has been host to key industries and infrastructure related to the Russian nuclear deterrent, in particular the installations on the Kola Peninsula. The latter is indeed a very convenient location for launching ballistic missiles, for missile defense systems, missile early warning systems, and other elements of strategic deterrence systems. The Arctic Ocean also guarantees access to the Atlantic Ocean and is therefore vital to the Russian navy. Indeed, following the breakup of the Soviet Union, Russia lost the Estonian port of Paldiski and is having to lease the one at Sevastopol' from Ukraine, leaving the main Russian military port on the Black Sea subject to the multiple upheavals in Russian-Ukrainian relations, and reinforcing the importance of access to the open sea through the Arctic region.

The Russian military strategy in the Arctic as defined in official documents is ambitious, but the gap between rhetoric and reality (and between power projection and actual capabilities) is a recurrent feature of post-Soviet Russian military history. The Russian armed forces are faced with a number of complex challenges: current changes to the international security environment require adaptation to nonconventional threats; the country's demographic evolution calls for a transition toward a professional army; financial resources available to modernize the army corps and the military-industrial complex are lacking; and civil-military cooperation, privatization, and foreign participation have become essential drivers of the modernization of the Russian military-industrial complex. All these elements will drastically impact the outcome of Moscow's strategies in the Arctic region.

The Russian Army Still Lost in Transition

The Russian army was one of the major forgotten institutions during the economic liberalization of the 1990s; the Russian state spent almost nothing on it for almost a decade. Upon his arrival in power, Putin sought to redress this neglect, but the "modernization" rests on a narrative that has little impact on reality,[3] marked above all by the restoration of the Soviet legacy and mechanisms. Soviet military ranks were reintroduced, conscription was reaffirmed with alternatives rejected, and society was partly remilitarized through the resumption of training sessions for reserve officers and some general mobilization exercises. In May 2012, having only just been reelected for a third term, Putin signed a new presidential decree on the modernization of the Russian Armed Forces.[4] However, the sacking of the Minister of Defense, Anatoli Serdyukov, and of his vice-ministers, some months later (officially for corruption), even as they were attempting to implement ambitious and far-reaching reforms, was perceived as a possible victory for the anti-reform camp.

Budgeting or Reforming?

As always in Russia, the will to modernize is above all expressed in terms of budgetary increases. As such, between 2000 and 2008, the Russian military budget increased by 500%, especially in strategic sectors such as weaponry, the navy, and missiles. The Russian space program has also been relaunched,[5] and has become a driver of the technological modernization of the army, especially in the sector of satellite communications. The economic and financial crisis of 2008 impeded Russian ambitions, but the Kremlin seems resolved to stay the course and is giving priority to military spending. The current state of Russian military matériel remains indeed well below modern-day technological norms. With the exception of specific leading-edge sectors, armaments are largely outdated, obsolete, or nonfunctional. To meet the additional requirements for rearming ground troops, the navy, and air forces, Russia would need to triple the budgeted amount from now until 2020, supposing that it could actually be allocated in its entirety.[6] In March 2010, Dmitri Medvedev stated that he wished to see an annual equipment-renewal rate across the armed forces of 9 to 11%, compared with the current level of 2%,[7] but these projections seem overly ambitious.

For his third mandate Vladimir Putin is set on proceeding with an unprecedented rearmament of Russia, including a State Armament Program that earmarks more than $650 billion to renew two-thirds of Russia's military equipment by 2020. Thus, while state budgets for health and education are being cut, Moscow has announced an increase for defense spending of 25% between 2012 and 2013, with an additional 18% increase for 2014.[8] This choice in favor of the military has aroused fierce debates among elites, leading Aleksei Kudrin, the long-term Minister of Finance and embodiment of the financial orthodoxy, to resign to denounce the increasing military expenditures. Russian military spending is in fact about 3% of the national budget, a level of expenditure equivalent to that of such medium powers as France or Great Britain, but by no means comparable with the American or Chinese military budgets. However, Russian expenditure is in fact higher than the official amount reveals (insofar as some expenditures are not included in the publicly announced budget), and is undermined by corruption, particularly in relation to weapons acquisitions.[9]

While the sum to be invested in modernizing the Russian military's capabilities seems considerable, it remains modest in terms of meeting fundamental needs and would cover only those of the strategic nuclear forces, air defense, and the air force. The enormous investment plan includes the construction of eight nuclear submarines, 600 warplanes, 1,000 helicopters, and 100 naval vessels. But the domestic defense industry does not have this much production capacity, and the holding companies created by Putin to recentralize production—mainly United Shipbuilding, United Aircraft, and Rostekhnologii—are neither a sign of efficiency nor of modernization. Moreover, it seems that part of the funds provided in the State Armament Program will be allocated with a three-year delay and the best case scenario is that the most important sums of money will not be available before 2016.[10]

More importantly, the money that was pumped into the military sector during Vladimir Putin's first two terms as president does not in itself constitute reform. The military elite has had difficulty understanding the importance of recruiting conscripts in a country experiencing a severe demographic crisis and has failed to embrace the idea of alternative forms of service and professional recruitment. Hazing (*dedovshchina*[11]) goes largely unpunished, corruption among officers is massive, professionalism and discipline are in decline, and military methods in difficult terrain have shown no improvement between Afghanistan and the two wars in Chechnya. The August 2008 war against Georgia was won only because of the vast power differential between the two countries, rather than the tactical superiority of the Russian army. Russian deficiencies in terms of weaponry and the manifest unpreparedness of its air forces to conduct operations to neutralize adversary air defense systems have only served to confirm the armed forces' difficulties in coming to terms with new *modus operandi* in war.[12]

The reform plan announced at the end of 2008 by Defense Minister Anatoli Serdyukov anticipated a large, as yet unattained, transformation of the Russian armed forces. The reorganization process was largely completed: the brigade became the basic unit of the military, and traditional military districts were replaced by Unified Strategic Commands. However, combat-ready units are still limited in number; joint operations between different branches are not functional; and communications technologies are still lacking.[13] It is on the level of manpower that the difficulties are the most evident. Human resources have become scarce in Russia, and the generation gap in the armed forces is immense: the majority of high-ranking officers and qualified personnel of the industrial-military complex are 55 years old or more, and the younger generations have been poorly prepared for taking over the reins from their superiors. The Russian armed forces aim to have one million men in uniform, but are unable to attain even 800,000. They have had difficulties in attracting professional soldiers to serve on a contract basis—about 190,000 have been engaged, though the target is 425,000—while they have an excessively large officer corps. The reform envisaged scaling back the number of officers in favor of a more mobile, better trained, and better equipped army.[14] Between 150,000 and 200,000 men of the officer corps are thus destined for transfer to the reserve army,[15] which has provoked virulent reactions from high-ranking officials within the Defense Ministry.

But the most urgent problem remains recruitment. As stated by Dmitri Gorenburg only 400,000 of the men who reach 18 years of age each year are considered draft-eligible out of a total of 700,000, as the others enjoy exemptions for studies or are unsuited for health reasons.[16] This figure is likely to drop rapidly in the coming years: in 2015–2016, the draft pool will comprise only half the number of conscripts the army has been used to receiving.[17] Attempts to make military service more appealing, to draft students more rigorously by reducing the possibilities of evasion and extending the age of conscription, and to combat the massive corruption that enables young men to avoid enrollment are destined to remain unsuccessful.[18] Moreover, the ethnic composition of draftees will change rather significantly, with increasing numbers coming from the North Caucasus.

Regardless of the efficacy of the decision to dismantle an extensive infrastructure for mass mobilization (in preparation for a large-scale conventional war) in order to focus instead on operations and efficiency, the question of combat readiness and the disorganization of the chain of command remains problematic.[19] Moscow has to envisage a radical change in its military recruitment practices. It needs to give priority to a relatively small professional army, create a professional non-commissioned officer corps, and promote the employment of contract workers for terms of a few years. However, these decisions, among the most sensitive, have been postponed for the moment, with high-ranking officials in the Ministry of Defense resisting the Kremlin's desires to reform. The dismissal of Serdyukov, who had lost the support of his former father-in-law Viktor Zubkov,[20] seems to signal a return to the status quo, even if the new minister, Sergey Shoigu, is also a supporter of in-depth reforms.

Difficulties in Defining Strategic Capabilities

For two decades now, Russian military doctrine has been rather vague about how to define potential enemies, which impedes the reshaping of doctrines and practices.[21] At the beginning of the 2000s Russia's strategy was dominated by a classical schema, founded on hard military security, but the new Conception of National Security for 2020 changed the definition of enemies.[22] Some perspectives inherited from the Cold War still shape Russian perceptions: so-called U.S. unilateralism and NATO activities continue to be classified as threatening Russia, but "the West" is no longer perceived to be a real danger, and no military conflict is envisaged with Washington or Brussels.[23] Strategic uncertainties and non-traditional threats have become Russia's main concerns. Although many official sources refuse to admit it publicly, China is seen as a potential forthcoming danger in terms of strategic uncertainty and a growing imbalance of power in Eurasia.[24] Non-traditional threats come mostly from the south, including kinds of tension as different as those found in the North Caucasus, the South Caucasus, Central Asia, Afghanistan, and Iran.[25]

Russia's difficulties in elaborating a well-structured set of strategic objectives stem in part from the contradiction between its ambitions for global power and its more modest capabilities. Russia remains an international player thanks to its Soviet achievements: a nuclear balance of power with the United States and a seat on the UN Security Council. The latter gives it essential influence in all major international issues, from North Korea and Iran to Syria. Despite a very demonstrative interest in favor of developing new mechanisms that would transform it into a global power in the twenty-first century (BRIC forum, G20 forum, etc.), Russia will have a difficult time acquiring new tools of influence that it has not inherited from the USSR. Very sensitive to nation-branding, it wishes to become more engaged in international peacekeeping and humanitarian operations, but this is a costly strategy and the army is reluctant to expose its disciplinary and organizational problems (not to mention its limitations in terms of technology and capacity) to its Western counterparts.[26]

Several Russian officials and experts therefore have encouraged the country to set for itself more modest goals and to admit the essentially regional character of its strategic power. Former Minister of Defense Serdyukov stated on several occasions that the military bases outside the Russian Federation (in Kyrgyzstan, Tajikistan, Armenia, South Ossetia, and Abkhazia) are costly and that naval operations far from its borders, such as in the Gulf of Aden, ought to be downsized. The Maritime Doctrine of the Russian Federation for the Year 2020 outlined a regional, rather than global, role for the Russian navy. The navy is going to play a key role in securing energy resources and managing regional conflicts in East Asia and the Near Abroad, but will have a very limited capacity in terms of intervention in remote theaters or in repelling a large-scale conventional attack.[27] Things are similar for Russia's land forces, which have difficulties mounting operations far from Russia's borders: deficiencies in communications technologies are especially striking, and for the moment prevent any significant operations involving conventional forces outside the Near Abroad. Even in this region, the Russian army's intervention capabilities, whether unilaterally, bilaterally, or within the multilateral framework afforded by the Collective Security Treaty Organization (CSTO), are not proven.

New Trends: International Cooperation, Civil-Military Cooperation, and Private Actors

Other, more positive changes are under way. For instance, civil-military cooperation, which expanded in the 2000s, is set to become one of the main trends in future decades. The army's weakness in comparison to influential economic groups has altered power relations, and despite the revival of the Russian military sector, there can be no question of the Ministry of Defense ignoring the interests of companies like Gazprom, Rosneft, Lukoil, or Noril'sk Nickel, which all enjoy powerful support within the state administration and can counterbalance the military voice. These companies, whether state-controlled or private, and the army have come to the pragmatic conclusion that they are dependent on one another. The civil-military relationship is therefore in the process of changing profoundly, motivated not by reasons of principle concerning the control of civil society over the military, but by pragmatic economic interests that the army accepts and/or tries to turn to its own advantage.[28]

Moreover, Russia has fallen behind technologically and today can no longer modernize its army in an autarkic manner. It will therefore be forced to make radical changes that involve receiving massive amounts of equipment from foreign companies in order to obtain the latest in military technology. The purchase of French Mistral amphibious assault ships in 2010 confirmed that Russian industry lacks the technical expertise and capacity to build such complex vessels.[29] Even if some of the components are manufactured in Russia, the military-industrial complex will experience difficulties in bridging the technology gap with Western countries. Further indication of this gap is the fact that between 2000 and 2010, Russia launched only a few frigates and corvettes. What is more, fulfillment of the contract signed with India to refurbish and convert the former Soviet aircraft carrier *Admiral Gorshkov* took years longer than expected and has been more costly, given the extensive scale of the conversion. Foreign participation, mainly from Europe, Israel, and the United States, thus seems likely in future modernization efforts. This implies that the military-industrial complex will have to emerge, at least partially, from its secretive culture. As for the Kremlin, it will have to learn to manage the contradiction between the imperatives of competitiveness, which imply more openness to industrial partnerships with foreign companies, and considerations of sovereignty.

Another trend that is taking shape, a corollary of the preceding one, is the privatization of some companies in the Russian industrial complex, including some with military ties. In 2010, the government stated its intention to sell its shares in 10 large companies in order to raise $30 billion. Among the largest companies to be sold are Rusnano (nanotechnologies holding), Alrosa (diamond monopoly), Rosneft, Aeroflot, interRAO (electricity holding), RusHydro (Russia's biggest hydroelectric power producer), and several banks such as Sberbank. In the Arctic region, this privatization project includes Sovcomflot, the shipping group that owns the world's largest fleet of Arctic, Aframax, and ice-class LNG tankers; the Port of Murmansk, one of the jewels of the Russian fishing fleet, the Arkhangel'sk Trawler Fleet, and the mining company Apatit, near Kirovsk, a key enterprise on the Kola Peninsula.[30] The presence of private and/or foreign players is therefore set to develop further; this will have an impact on the strategic sector, as a series of arguments will come into play that are less subject to security decisions, and more favorable to profitability.

Upgrading the Northern Fleet and the Nuclear Deterrence

The most important component of Russia's defense capability is the Northern Fleet, accounting for about two-thirds of the Russian navy's global nuclear force. Based at Severomorsk near Murmansk on the northern Kola Peninsula, it remains the most powerful of the four Russian fleets before the Pacific, Black Sea, and Caspian, with the largest number of icebreakers and nuclear submarines. It is in charge of all operations undertaken in the Atlantic and is thus able to venture as far as the Caribbean or to conduct anti-piracy operations close to the Gulf of Aden. However, the Northern Fleet was hit hard by the collapse of the Soviet Union. In 1986, it possessed some 180 nuclear-powered submarines of various classes; however, by 2010 this figure had fallen by three-fourths, to just 42.[31] Its recent history has been marked by several failures. Four submarines have sunk, including the infamous *Kursk* in 2000, and its ballistic missile launches regularly misfire. The navy also faces numerous problems related to its aging fleet (the average vessel has been in service 20 years), the naval nuclear fuel cycle, the disposal of radioactive waste, and contamination issues. The naval nuclear reactors concentrated in the Kola region are dangerous, many of the nuclear submarines waiting to be decommissioned are poorly securitized, and large amounts of nuclear waste remain stored on vessels specifically designed for dumping at sea.[32]

The modernization efforts to be undertaken are therefore immense and multifaceted. Among the different branches of the armed forces, the navy was most severely affected by the drastically reduced military budgets of the 1990s. It saw its share of the defense budget drop from 23% to 9%. In addition, the modernization objectives mentioned in the two state programs for the armed forces (1996–2005 and 2001–2010) were never achieved. The Maritime Doctrine of the Russian Federation for the Year 2020 ambitiously plans to transform the navy into the second-most powerful in the world, after the U.S. Navy, in 20 to 30 years' time. In so doing, it puts great emphasis on issues such as the Arctic territorial disputes and undersea resources, and leaves aside the traditional security risks (a military attack from another state).[33] The third State Program for the Armed Forces (2007–2015) provided a financial and symbolic reassessment of the navy. For the first time in several decades, it has been placed on an equal footing with the other branches of the armed forces. The Russian government has allocated $132 billion for shipbuilding through 2020; in other words, about one-quarter of the total military budget is allocated to building new ships.[34] Although considerable, this amount is largely insufficient to modernize the entire fleet, and Moscow has had to learn how to organize its choices hierarchically. It has given priority to ballistic missile submarines and attack submarines, whereas surface combatants will only get a reduced share of the pie. No carrier, cruiser, or destroyer is currently being built, confirming that Russia does not envisage large-scale conflict with any of the world's major powers.[35]

The Northern Fleet has close to 80 operational ships of different categories, while around 30 are being repaired or are on stand-by.[36] The fleet's nuclear-powered submarines are divided into 11 ballistic missile submarines (SSBNs), 4 cruise missile submarines (SSGNs), and about 20 multipurpose attack submarines (SSNs). It also manages six missile cruisers, which Russia sees as key elements in the restoration of the strategic bastion concept in the Arctic. The Northern Fleet has two flagships at its disposal, the largest nuclear icebreaker in the world, *Fifty Years of Victory*, and the main nuclear-powered guided-missile cruiser, *Peter the Great*. After the latter's successful trip around the world in 2007, the Ministry of Defense announced that it would upgrade three other heavy nuclear-powered missile cruisers, the *Admiral Lazarev*, the *Admiral Nakhimov*, and the *Admiral Ushakov*, which are or will be undergoing modernization in terms of equipment and armaments.[37] Currently, only the aircraft carrier *Admiral Kuznetsov* operates with the Northern Fleet, hosting 20 planes on board and 10 anti-submarine helicopters.[38] The destroyer *Vice-Admiral Kulakov*, recently repaired, was integrated into the Northern Fleet in 2011.[39] Naval aviation includes about 200 combat planes and 50 helicopters.

As with the other fleets, the Northern Fleet is severely lacking in coastal ships and frigates able to conduct rapid intervention operations. Several are currently under construction, but the fleet's protection capabilities will be reduced during the interim.[40] The purchase of two Mistral assault ships from France and the project, routinely delayed, to build eight *Admiral Gorshkov*–class and six Krivak-class frigates, will not be adequate to renew Russia's ocean going surface ships. In the decades to come, the Northern Fleet will have to abandon single-function vessels in favor of more mobile and multipurpose ones as well as coastal vessels, especially corvettes, which guarantee the safety of the Russian coast.[41]

The future of the Northern Fleet is closely linked to the question of nuclear deterrence.[42] The older sea-based nuclear deterrent is in the process of being modernized. As of 2012, the Russian navy had six operational Delta III and six Delta IV strategic submarines that form the sea-based arm of its strategic nuclear deterrent. There are no plans to renovate the older Delta III–class submarines, which were built during the 1980s; they will be decommissioned in the years to come. Only the Delta IV submarines are presently being modernized. They will be equipped with a new sonar system and the new intercontinental ballistic missile (ICBM) Sineva, a third-generation liquid-propelled ICBM that entered service in 2007.[43] In 2010, the Northern Fleet acquired the *Karelia*, which has been modernized to augment its tactical and technical capabilities and equipped with the Sineva ICBM.[44] On October 11, 2008, during Northern Fleet military exercises, a Sineva rocket was fired from the nuclear submarine *Tula* that achieved its longest distance yet: more than 11,500 kilometers.[45] Russia is planning to equip its Delta IV–class submarines with at least 100 Sineva missiles, able to carry either 4 or 10 nuclear warheads. This system, which is to stay on alert status until 2030, enables missiles to be launched from under the ice while remaining invisible to hostile observation satellites until the last moment.[46]

Some typhoon-class strategic submarines—the world's largest, built in the 1980s—will also be rearmed to carry long-range cruise missiles. For the moment, only one, the *Dmitri Donskoy*, has been modernized and placed with the Northern Fleet. It conducts test firing for the Bulava system, a new generation solid-fuel submarine-launched ballistic missile (SLBM), designed to avoid possible future U.S. ballistic missile defense (BMD) weapons, and which can cover a distance of more than 8,000 kilometers. In the future, the typhoons will be replaced with the new Borey-class fourth-generation nuclear-powered strategic submarines. As the first strategic submarine to be built in Russia since the collapse of the Soviet Union, the first Borey-class submarine, the *Yuri Dolgorukii*, has been in operation since the end of 2012, while two others, the *Aleksandr Nevski* and the *Vladimir Monomakh*, are at a pier at the Severodvinsk shipyard.[47] They will be based at Gadzhievo, about 100 kilometers from the Norwegian border, where new infrastructure is being built to host them. This new generation of submarines is almost undetectable at deep ocean depths and can be used for multipurpose attacks. Thanks to its weaponry, including several types of cruise missiles and torpedoes, it will be able to carry out diverse missions, chase enemy aircraft carriers, and deliver massive missile strikes on coastal targets.[48] In total, the building of eight fourth-generation Borey-class submarines (half for the Northern Fleet, half for the Pacific one) is set for completion by 2020, which once again seems overly ambitious.

Together with Topol-M land-based ballistic missiles, the new Bulava system is planned to become the core of Russia's nuclear system and will be the only Russian sea-based ICBM after 2020–25. However, the Russian army has experienced unforeseen technological difficulties. In 2006–09, a long string of unsuccessful test launches (6 of 11) seemed to call into question the future of Bulava. However, since 2010 a new wave of launches has been more successful. The multiyear program of tests was completed in 2011,[49] and the system will be put into operational service in 2014. A key element of the Russian defense system for decades to come, the costs for developing the Bulava and the Borey submarines, and overcoming problems of their potential mismatch, have eaten up a large part of the military budget.[50] By focusing on nuclear armaments and parity with the United States, the Russian army has avoided any real doctrinal or strategic reform. Moscow's grand plans for the Arctic should therefore be analyzed in the context of the modernization difficulties experienced by the armed forces.

The missions of the Northern Fleet in the Arctic are bound to change considerably in the decades to come. They will be directly linked with protecting the growing economic interests of the Russian state in the region. Strengthened cooperation with energy firms has enabled the fleet to garner material advantages. For example, it currently benefits from cheaply priced fuel, offered to it by extraction companies, and some of its port infrastructure is renovated at the latter's expense. The energy companies, for their part, obtain the support of the Northern Fleet in implementing anti-terrorism protection systems, attaining authorization to extract hydrocarbons, and accessing existing port infrastructure, fuel storage sites, and the large naval construction sites in the Russian north. Gazprom, Lukoil, and Noril'sk Nickel have to contend not only with the lack of ice-free civil ports, but also with the absence of ports in deep water that are able to host 300,000-ton tankers. They would also like to take advantage of the military ships used for hydrographic and hydro-meteorological research, and coordinate a sea rescue system of considerable logistical complexity.

Many examples attest to this civil-military rapprochement of interests. In 2005, the Russian navy and Gazprom signed an agreement on the latter's use of auxiliary ships, ports, and naval military sites, including setting up a security and rescue system and maritime routes navigable by tankers, as well as establishing cooperation in terms of liquefied natural gas (LNG).[51] This enabled Gazprom to plan an LNG processing plant for the Shtokman field in the closed town of Vidiaevo, a submarine base and garrison on the northern shore of the Kola Peninsula. Further, in 2006, the Ministry of Defense agreed to provide Russian industry with previously classified geological and topological maps. Since the 1990s, the army has allowed Lukoil's Arctic tankers to use a military fuel storage facility at Mokhnatkina Pakhta, near Murmansk; but it has denied the oil company the right to build a refinery, judging its location to be too close to military installations. One can therefore note how, despite the projection of power, Russian objectives are much more pragmatic. The importance accorded to the energy sector means that the dictates of the market and profitability tend to take priority over security decisions.[52]

The increasing exploitation of Arctic resources, however, raises tactical and technical issues for which the Northern Fleet will have to find solutions. Being located at Severomorsk is not optimal for its monitoring role for the Northern Sea Route, the starting point of which lies farther east. The proliferation of platforms at sea, not to mention rigs, pipelines, and terminals on the coastlines, as well as the growth in maritime traffic, also represents a new challenge for the armed forces. Most oil facilities are not mobile, and this will force the Ministry of Defense to put in place the infrastructure to ensure their protection in the event of interstate conflict. Even if the Russian military considers these risks minimal, the potential for localized conflict must be taken into account. The securing of the platforms, pipelines, and ships against possible terrorist attacks accentuates the role of the special services deployed against nontraditional threats. It entails that defense be reoriented around mobile units able to react rapidly and equipped with high-technology hardware. The presence of foreign companies in resource extraction also implies that non-Russian interests may be involved, which will alter the strategic realities and the diplomatic flexibility available in cases of conflict. In addition, the presence of a large number of tankers traversing sensitive zones may impede the movement of military ships as well as submarines, which require space to maneuver, and increase the risks of collision. Finally, sonar emissions from drilling platforms and other oil industry installations will interfere with military radar systems.[53]

Russia's Renewed Security Activism in the Arctic

In the 1990s, Russia almost disappeared from the Arctic naval theater: the Russian authorities were focused on the Chechen war, and the army was in any case hardly in a position to conduct operations in a region that had so suddenly disappeared from the strategic agenda. The situation changed in the first decade of the twenty-first century with Russia's reassertion in the international arena and Vladimir Putin's will to revalorize the classic symbols of military power. In the second half of the decade, growing media interest in the Arctic pushed the Russian Armed Forces to recommit to the region. Apart from the nuclear deterrence strategy, the fear of being denied access to the open sea while harboring ambitions to re-create a "blue-water" navy remain important drivers of Moscow's activism. The Russian fleet cannot enter the Atlantic except by passing through Arctic choke points—between Svalbard, Bear Island, and mainland Norway; between Greenland, Iceland, and Norway, or between Greenland, Iceland, and the United Kingdom.[54] In 2008 and 2009, Russia revived erstwhile Soviet traditions by organizing several long-range patrols—the longest since the fall of the Soviet Union—in different parts of the world. This was epitomized by the patrols undertaken by the nuclear-powered guided-missile cruiser *Peter the Great* through the Mediterranean and Caribbean Seas, and the South Atlantic and Indian Oceans.[55]

In 2008, Russia confirmed that it was expanding its current level of operations in the Arctic. The navy resumed its warship presence, with military vessels patrolling near the Norwegian and Danish defense zones. It also increased the operational radius of the Northern Fleet's submarines, and under-ice training for submariners has become a priority task.[56] Moscow also pays particular attention to the situation in the Svalbard archipelago, which it interprets as indicative of tensions with NATO member states. Indeed, Norway and Russia have divergent understandings of the post–Cold war situation. Oslo wants to normalize the Finnmark province, which was previously heavily militarized when it was a border region with the Soviet Union. It has thus opened it up to public and collective military activities within the North Atlantic framework, but this development reinforced Russian concerns about the militarization of the zone. According to the Svalbard Treaty, Norway cannot establish bases on the archipelago for military purposes. However, Oslo considers that neither the Globus II radar in Vardø, on the Norwegian mainland, nor the space-related activities on the archipelago (the European Incoherent Scatter Scientific Association's radar, the Svalbard Satellite Station, and the Ny-Ålesund rocket range) can be considered military, while Moscow interprets them as part of (para) military activities. According to Kristian Åtland and Torbjørn Pedersen, Norway's decisions have accentuated Russian interpretations of a possible threat—fear of a Western conspiracy often continues to prevail in Russian readings of the Svalbard issue.[57] As far as the Russian navy is concerned, it is focused on increasing the protection of the Russian mining settlement at Barentsburg and on providing more effective protection for Russian fishermen. Director of National Fisheries (*Goskomrybolovstvo*) Andrei Krainin, for instance, has asked the armed forces to give "psychological support" to the Russian trawlers navigating close to Norwegian waters.[58]

Naval activism in the Arctic is accompanied by increasing activities in aviation. The air force is perceived by Moscow as a central element in its demonstration of power and its international legitimacy. The Russian aviation industry still occupies niches of excellence, such as in the production of aircraft for the strategic fleet used in the delivery, in tactical and strategic transport aircraft, and in ground-to-ground and ground-to-air missiles; however, the remainder of the stock is aging and obsolete, and very precise missile guidance weaponry is largely absent.[59] Flights of Russian military aircraft over the Arctic Ocean fell from 500 per year during the Soviet period, to only half a dozen in the 1990s and at the start of the 2000s. In 2007, Russian strategic bombers flew over the Arctic for the first time since the end of the Cold War.[60] Two Tu-95MS, based in Saratov at the Engels aviation base and with mid-flight refueling capability, now regularly patrol the Arctic.[61] Old turboprop Tu-95MSs are the mainstays of Russian Arctic aviation, but the air force also has 16 modern, long-range Tu-160 Blackjack bombers at its disposal. The shortage of midair refueling tankers remains the most serious problem affecting the operational capabilities of Russian strategic aviation.[62] Several Arctic air bases have been reactivated—such as at Anadyr', Monchegorsk, Olenii, Tiksi, and Vorkuta—albeit with only limited capacities. For the first time in 20 years, the air force also has organized supply missions for the Russian polar base Barneo, sponsored by the Russian Geographical Society.

As during the Soviet era, Arctic missions are flown via Scandinavia and toward the United Kingdom and Iceland, and on to the North Atlantic, or via the Arctic toward Alaska and Canada.[63] The British Royal Air Force conducted 21 intercepts of Russian bombers only between July 2007 and April 2008.[64] In 2007, there were 18 interceptions of Russian bombers in the proximity of American or Canadian airspace, 12 in 2008, and 17 in 2009, as compared with 11 for the entire period between 1999 and 2006.[65] These overflights drew criticism from Canada, which has accused Russia of coming too close to its territory. They are also closely monitored by Oslo. In 2010 alone, Russian strategic bombers carried out 10 missions in the vicinity of Norwegian airspace, compared with a total of 12 such missions in 2008 and 2009.[66] A pair of Tu-160 bombers covered a distance of 18,000 kilometers along a route that stretched from the Arctic to the Bering Strait, the Alaskan coast, the Japanese islands, Russia's southern borders, and Engels. In 2012, Norway identified a total of 71 Russian airplanes.[67] For the adjacent countries, the main risk of Russia's new air activism is not so much military conflict—these long-range flights are not belligerent in purpose and are exclusively reconnaissance missions—as of technical failure (the possible crash of one of its planes, and the absence of rescue system) or of errors in correctly interpreting their purpose, possibly leading to a defensive overreaction.

In the framework of the armed forces' reorganization, a new Arctic Center for Material and Technical Support (Tsentr MTO SF) was created in 2012, which, tasked with providing logistical and administrative support to all the Northern Fleet's naval bases, garrisons, and technical facilities, employs a staff of more than 15,000.[68] In addition to the Northern Fleet, several other military installations can be counted in the Arctic region. The Arkhangel'sk region hosts the firing range of Novaya Zemlya, where Russian nuclear weapons are tested, and the cosmodrome at Plesetsk, from where Soyuz, Cosmos-3M, and Tsyklon rockets are launched. The strategic missile forces are distributed across the Ural, Siberian, and Far East Districts.[69] Alexandra Land, in the Franz Joseph archipelago, is home to Nagurskaya, Russia's northernmost military base. Two motorized brigades are also based in Murmansk.

In 2008 Lieutenant General Vladimir Shamanov, then director of the Central Directorate of Military Training and Troop Services (GUBD) at the Ministry of Defense, announced plans to establish two so-called Arctic brigades, or special forces units (*spetsnazy*).[70] As Shamanov is known for his provocative declarations, these statements are difficult to interpret because they were made within a framework of ideological escalation. The Russian army's usual difficulties of putting into practice these calls for change suggest that the birth of Arctic brigades will probably be a long and chaotic administrative process. However, the direction has been set, and these embryonic Arctic brigades are in the process of being formed. A specific Arctic border guards section was created as early as 1994, the aim of which was to monitor the movement of ships and poaching at sea, prior to being reorganized in 2004–2005. In 2009, it was announced that new Arctic formations had been established in border guard units in the Arkhangel'sk and Murmansk regions, and were patrolling along the Northern Sea Route—for the first time since the early 1990s.[71] The 200th Independent Motorized Infantry Brigade, with specially trained soldiers equipped for military operations in the Arctic, will be based at Pechenga near the Norwegian border town of Kirkenes and be operational by 2016.[72]

Traditional armed forces are not the only security-oriented body to become more involved in Arctic matters, as the security services have also. The 2008 Arctic Policy mentions many nonconventional threats—the dangers of smuggling, potential illegal immigration, risks for aquatic biological resources, and obviously small-scale conflicts around energy deposits or transport facilities, without envisaging the possibility that they could degenerate into more widespread, interstate conflict.[73] Such as they are defined, the Arctic dangers therefore concern the Federal Security Service (FSB), its border guards section, and the troops of the Ministry of Emergency Situations more than they do the Ministry of Defense proper. The division of responsibilities between the navy and the coast guard nonetheless remains unclear. Provisions have therefore been made to strengthen FSB control over the region in order to deal with the new threats that have arisen from the development of the continental shelf and the proliferation of maritime traffic: border control systems, the introduction of special visa regulations for certain regions, and the implementation of technological controls over waterways and sites along the Northern Sea Route.[74] The Northern Sea Route is currently controlled from the air by FSB aircraft, and on the land and sea by the North-Eastern Border Guard Agency; the Russian border guard service further plans to establish a global monitoring network from Murmansk to Wrangel Island.[75]

Patterns of cooperation in soft security were boosted by the highly symbolic decision, taken by the Arctic Council in Nuuk in 2011, to create a Maritime and

Aeronautical Search and Rescue System (SAR). Mapped out by a task force co-chaired by Russia and the United States, the agreement commits all parties to monitor SAR areas for signals of distress, coordinating the response when the marine distress incident occurs and providing strategically located vessels to support the SAR operations.[76] Although several SAR exercises have already taken place—between Russia, the United States, and Canada in 1993, under the auspices of the NATO Partnership for Peace in 1996, and in a bilateral manner between Russia and Norway (Barents Exercise), and between Russia and the U.S. (Northern Eagle)—the 2011 document is the first binding agreement released by the Arctic Council. Each country is responsible for a part of the Arctic proportional to its territory, with Russia playing the preeminent role. The lobbying of Russia's Ministry of Emergency Situations and the coast guard in its favor was a decisive element of the signing, itself an indication of the positive role that can be played by the transition to soft security concerns.

There is no trend toward a global militarization of the Arctic: the majority of new structures, whether Russian, Canadian, or Norwegian, seek to patrol and protect national territories from nonconventional challenges, not to prepare for any kind of interstate conflict.[77] However, despite the hope that the Arctic will be desecuritized, geopolitical uncertainty and the lack of institutionalized channels of discussion on strategic matters are pushing Moscow to act in a pre-emptive manner. NATO is bound to remain a collective actor in the region, inasmuch as four of the five coastal states are its members. Neither the overall Russia-NATO global relationship, nor the ups and downs of the NATO-Russia Council, impacts directly on the Arctic security debate, but the region nonetheless lacks a collective structure that can serve as a platform for negotiations on security issues. The Russian military presence in the Arctic has increased since 2008, but this activism has to be compared not to the 1990s, when Russia was absent from the Arctic theater, but to the Soviet period. Retrospectively, the current Russian military presence in the Arctic is still minimal compared to that in the Soviet period. Norway itself has stated that Russian activities represent "a return to a more normal level of activity for a major power with legitimate interests in the region."[78]

Moreover, Russia's declared power projections are far removed from the actual capacity to act. The Russian armed forces have restored only a small fraction of the capability once possessed by the Soviet air force. Behind the nationalist-tinged discourse, which is sometimes fairly aggressive toward the West, Russia's goals are more pragmatic and domestically oriented. They include attempts to reform the army, upgrade the Northern Fleet, increase civil-military cooperation, and create mechanisms of cooperation with foreign and private firms. But modernization plans for the Russian army will be impossible to realize in the targeted time frame: the Soviet-style functioning of the military sector, as well as the usual administrative delays, corruption schemes, cost overruns, technical challenges, and declines in human capacity, will slow down any modernization program. Moreover, in Russia's definition of its strategic interests, "tactics prevail, medium-term thinking is just emerging, and no national interest worth the name has surfaced."[79] In the decades to come, Moscow will experience a fundamental alteration in its threat perceptions. On the one hand, conventional dangers, in particular in East Asia, will necessitate the maintenance of a traditional army. Further, nuclear deterrence will continue to be perceived as confirming Russia's status in the international arena, and also as a means by which to negotiate the geostrategic balance with NATO and the United States. On the other hand, increasing priority will be accorded to nontraditional threats.

These trends are bound to have an impact on the way in which Moscow formulates its strategic goals in the Arctic and tries to consolidate its power in the decades to come. The Arctic theater will be more subject to nontraditional threats than to classic military-centered conflicts. Security will have to be assured at least in part in a collegial manner through international cooperation. It will necessitate cutting-edge technology that Russia can only obtain from abroad, or via the private sector. Responsibility for soft security currently falls to the special forces (troops of the FSB, the Interior Ministry, and the Emergency Situations Ministry), but the future will call for changes in the Russian armed forces themselves. It implies a transition to a professional military with a rapid reaction capability, one that is trained in cutting-edge technologies, employs technologies from the private sector (telecommunications), or at least dual public-private ones, and engages in cooperation with foreign partners. Projected strategic power in the Arctic is thus part of the more global dilemma that the Russian military has faced since the fall of the Soviet Union. Its success or its failure will embody the more general fate of the deep transformations awaiting the Russian armed forces and strategic thinking in the years to come.

Notes

1. P. Dolatat-Kreutzkamp, "An Arctic (Cold) War: Alarming Developments or Empty Rhetoric?" *European Centre for Energy and Resource Security Newsletter*, no. 4 (2011): 1–5.

2. H. Conley, T. Toland, J. Kraut, and A. Østhagen, *A New Security Architecture for the Arctic. An American Perspective* (Washington, DC: Center for Strategic and International Studies, CSIS Europe Report, January 2012).

3. Z. Barany, *Democratic Breakdown and the Decline of the Russian Military* (Princeton: Princeton University Press, 2007).

4. "Podpisan Ukaz o realizatsii planov razvitiia Vooruzhennykh Sil i modern-

izatsii OPK [Decree signed on realization of plans to develop the armed forces and modernization of the military production complex]," *Kremlin.ru*, May 7, 2012, http://kremlin.ru/news/15242 (accessed May 28, 2012).

5. See *Russian Defense Industry and Arms Trade: Facts and Figures* (Moscow: Centre for Analysis of Strategies and Technologies, 2010), http://www.cast.ru/files/all-stats_eng.pdf (accessed May 28, 2012).

6. A. Golts, "The Disarmaments Program," *Ezhednevnyi zhurnal*, May 26, 2010.

7. D. Gorenburg, "Russia's State Armaments Program 2020: Is the Third Time the Charm for Military Modernization?" *Russia Military Reform*, October 12, 2010, http://russiamil.wordpress.com/2010/10/12/russia%E2%80%99s-state-armaments-program-2020-is-the-third-time-the-charm-for-military-modernization/ (accessed May 28, 2012).

8. T. Nilsen, "Russia to Boost Defence Budget by 25 Percent," *Barents Observer*, July 19, 2012, http://barentsobserver.com/en/security/russia-boost-defence-budget-25-percent-19–07 (accessed September 4, 2012).

9. A. Golts, "The Disarmaments Program."

10. D. Gorenburg, "Should We Panic about Russian Naval Modernization?" *Russia Military Reform*, January 1, 2013, http://russiamil.wordpress.com/.

11. F. Daucé and E. Sieca-Kozlowski, *Dedovshchina in the Post-Soviet Military. Hazing of Russian Army Conscripts in a Comparative Perspective* (Stuttgart: Ibidem Verlag, 2006).

12. C. Vendil Pallin and D. Westerlund, "Russia's War in Georgia: Lessons and Consequences," *Small Wars and Insurgencies* 20, no. 2 (2009): 400–424.

13. D. Gorenburg, "Challenges Facing the Russian Defense Establishment," *ISN International Relations and Security Network*, December 20, 2012, http://www.isn.ethz.ch/isn/Digital-Library/Articles/Special-Feature/Detail/?lng=en&id=156370&tabid=1453434465&contextid774=156370&contextid775=156366 (accessed January 5, 2013).

14. Ibid.

15. M. Sieff, "Makarov pledges to complete Russian army reform by 2012," *UPI.com*, February 9, 2009, http://www.upi.com/Business_News/Security-Industry/2009/02/09/Makarov-pledges-to-complete-Russian-army-reform-by-2012/UPI-95081234222215/ (accessed May 28, 2012).

16. Gorenburg, "Challenges Facing the Russian Defense Establishment."

17. G.P. Lannon, "Russia's New-Look Army Reforms and Russian Foreign Policy," *The Journal of Slavic Military Studies* 24, no. 1 (2011): 26–54.

18. P. Baev, "Military Reforms against Heavy Odds," in A. Åslund, S. Guriev, and A. Kuchins, eds., *Russia after the Global Economic Crisis* (Washington, DC: Peterson Institute for International Economics, 2010), 169–185.

19. Ibid.

20. D. Gorenburg, "The firing of Anatoly Serdyukov," *Russian Military Blog*, November 6, 2012, http://russiamil.wordpress.com/2012/11/06/the-firing-of-anatoly-serdyukov/ (accessed January 5, 2013).

21. More in S. Blank, ed., *Russian Military Politics and Russia's 2010 Defense Doctrine* (Carlisle: Strategic Studies Institute, 2010).

22. S.J. Main, *The Mouse That Roared, or the Bear That Growled? Russia's Latest Military Doctrine* (Wiltshire: Defence Academy of the United Kingdom, 2010); M. de Has, "Russia's New Military Doctrine: A Compromise Document," *Russian Analytical Digest*, no. 78, May 4, 2010.

23. M. Galeotti, ed., *The Politics of Security in Modern Russia* (Farnham: Ashgate, 2010); R. Legvold, ed., *Russian Foreign Policy in the 21st Century and the Shadow of the Past* (New York: Columbia University Press, 2007).

24. J. W. Parker, "Russia's Revival: Ambitions, Limitations, and Opportunities for the United States," *INSS Strategic Perspectives*, no. 3 (2011), 20–24. See also B. Lo, *Axis of Convenience. Moscow, Beijing, and the New Geopolitics* (Washington, DC, London: Brookings Institution Press and Chatham House, 2008).

25. See for instance C. King and R. Menon, "Prisoners of the Caucasus. Russia's Invisible Civil War," *Foreign Affairs,* July/August 2010, 20–34; M. Laruelle, *Russian Policy on Central Asia and the Role of Russian Nationalism* (Washington, DC: The Central Asia-Caucasus Institute, 2008).

26. Parker, "Russia's Revival: Ambitions, Limitations, and Opportunities for the United States," 14–17.

27. "Maritime Doctrine of Russian Federation 2020," July 27, 2001, English version available at http://www.oceanlaw.org/downloads/arctic/Russian_Maritime_Policy_2020.pdf (accessed May 28, 2012).

28. M. Barabanov, *Sovremennoe sostoianie i perspektivy razvitiia rossiskogo flota* [Current state and prospects for the development of the Russian fleet] (Moscow: Center for Defense Information, 2006).

29. M. Lapenkova, "Russia Wants All Technology on French-Built Mistrals," *Defense News,* June 11, 2010, http://www.defensenews.com/story.php?i=4667273 (accessed May 28, 2012).

30. "Three Companies in Barents Russia Up for Privatization," *Barents Observer,* November 18, 2010, http://www.barentsobserver.com/three-companies-in-barents-russia-up-for-privatization.4848844–16179.html (accessed May 28, 2012).

31. For more details, see http://flot.com/nowadays/structure/north/ (accessed May 28, 2012).

32. D. Rudolph, "The Arctic Military Environmental Cooperation (AMEC) Program's Role in the Management of Spent Fuel from Decommissioned Nuclear Submarines," in *Scientific and Technical Issues in the Management of Spent Fuel of Decommissioned Nuclear Submarines* (Dordrecht: NATO Science Series II, Mathematics, Physics and Chemistry, 2006).

33. K. Zysk, "Russia and the High North. Security and Defence Perspectives," in S. Holtsmark and B.A. Smith-Windsor, eds., *Security Prospects in the High North: Geostrategic Thaw or Freeze?* (Rome: NATO Defense College, 2009), 102–129; K. Zysk, "Geopolitics in the Arctic: The Russian Security Perspective," *Climate of Opinion. The Stockholm Network's Energy and Environmental Update,* no. 12 (2009): 7–9.

34. V. Patrushev, "Flotu neobkhodimy remont i modernizatsiia [The fleet must be repaired and modernized]," *Nezavisimaia gazeta,* October 06, 2006, http://nvo.ng.ru/armament/2006–10–06/6_flot.html (accessed May 28, 2012).

35. "Russian navy's regeneration plans," *IISS Strategic Comments,* February 2011, http://www.iiss.org/en/publications/strategic%20comments/sections/2011-a174/russian-navys-regeneration-plans-f9c4 (accessed October 17, 2012).

36. "Severnyi flot," *Vlast',* no. 7 (760), February 25, 2008, http://www.kommersant.ru/doc.aspx?DocsID=856043 (accessed May 28, 2012).

37. "Russian Plans to Upgrade Three Nuclear-Powered Cruisers by 2020," *RIA Novosti,* July 25, 2010, http://en.rian.ru/mlitary_news/20100725/159939020.html (accessed May 28, 2012).

38. J. W. Kipp, "The Russian Navy Recalibrates Its Oceanic Ambitions," *Free Republic,* October 30, 2009, http://www.freerepublic.com/focus/news/2375147/posts (accessed May 28, 2012).

39. "Modernized Destroyer Back at Northern Fleet Base," *Barents Observer,* February 18, 2011, http://www.barentsobserver.com/modernized-destroyer-back-at-northern-fleet-base.4886962–116321.html (accessed May 28, 2012).

40. "VMF Rossii popolnitsia novymi korabliami [Russia's naval fleet will be reinforced with new ships]," *Severnyi Flot,* January 11, 2010, http://www.severnyflot. ru/news.php?extend.1961 (accessed May 28, 2012).

41. N. Petrov, "The Russian Navy Gets Ambitious," *RIA Novosti,* August 1, 2007, http://www.spacedaily.com/reports/The_Russian_Navy_Gets_Ambitious_999.html.

42. P. Podvig, ed., *Russian Strategic Nuclear Forces* (Boston: MIT Press, 2004).

43. "State-of-the-Art Nuclear Submarines to the Russian Navy," *Barents Observer,* June 19, 2009, www.barentsobserver.com/state-of-the-art-nuclear-submarines-to-the-russian-navy.4608935–58932.html.

44. "APL Kareliia 22 ianvaria budet peredana VMF Rossii [The submarine *Karelia* will be turned over to the Russian navy on January 22]," *Severnyi Flot,* January 11, 2010, http://www.severnyflot.ru/news.php?extend.1964 (accessed May 28, 2012).

45. "Sineva Extended Range Launch," *Russianforces.org,* October 11, 2008, http://russianforces.org/blog/2008/10/sineva_extended_range_launch.shtml (accessed May 28, 2012).

46. P. Felgenhauer, "The Bulava SLBM and the US-Russian Arms Talks," *Eurasia Daily Monitor* 6, no. 232, December 17, 2009.

47. Ibid.

48. Petrov, "The Russian Navy Gets Ambitious," 49. A list of failures and successes can be accessed "Russian strategic nuclear forces," http://russianforces.org/navy/slbms/bulava.shtml (accessed May 28, 2012).

49. O. Nekhai, "Bulava Missile System to Be Put into Service Soon," *Voice of Russia,* December 30, 2011, http://english.ruvr.ru/2011/12/30/63191450.html (accessed May 28, 2012).

50. P. Baev, "Russia's Arctic Policy and the Northern Fleet Modernization," *Russie. Nei.Visions,* n. 65, 2012, http://www.ifri.org/?page=contribution-detail&id=7264 (accessed May 28, 2012).

51. "Gazprom and RF Navy Ink Cooperation Agreement," *Gazprom Press Release,* November 24, 2005, http://old.gazprom.ru/eng/news/2005/11/18373.shtml (accessed May 28, 2012).

52. For more details, see K. Åtland, "Russia's Northern Fleet and the Oil Industry—Rivals or Partners? A Study of Civil-Military Relations in the Post-Cold War Arctic," *Armed Forces & Society* 35, no. 2 (2009): 362–384.

53. Ibid.

54. "Northern Fleet," *Global Security,* no date, http://www.globalsecurity.org/military/world/russia/mf-north.htm (accessed May 28, 2012).

55. D. Gorenburg, "Russian Naval Deployments a Return to Global Power Projection or a Temporary Blip?" *PONARS Eurasia Policy Memo,* no. 57, May 2009.

56. K. Zysk, "Russian Military Power and the Arctic," *Russian Foreign Policy, EU–Russia Centre's Review,* no. 8 (2008): 80–86.

57. K. Åtland and T. Pedersen, "The Svalbard Archipelago in Russian Security Policy: Overcoming the Legacy of Fear—or Reproducing It?" *European Security* 17, no. 2 (2008): 227–251.

58. "Rossiia usilivaet voenno-morskoe prisutstvie v Arktike [Russia strengthens naval presence in the Arctic]," *Natsional'naia bezopasnost'*, July 18, 2008, http://nationalsafety.ru/n18964 (accessed May 28, 2012).

59. I. Facon, and M. Asencio, *Le Renouveau de la puissance aérienne russe* [The renewal of Russian air power] (Paris: Foundation for Strategic Research, 2010), 115.

60. Russia unilaterally suspended its long-range strategic aviation patrols in 1992.

61. "Samolety-raketonostsy VVP RF vedut patrulirovanie v raionakh Arktiki [Military planes carry out patrols in Arctic regions]," *RIA Novosti*, July 9, 2008, http://www.militaryparitet.com/teletype/data/ic_teletype/2746/ (accessed May 28, 2012).

62. A. Stukalin, "Bears and Blackjacks Are Back. What Next?" *Moscow Defense Brief*, no. 4 (22), 2010, http://mdb.cast.ru/mdb/4–2010/item4/article1/ (accessed May 28, 2012).

63. Stukalin, "Bears and Blackjacks Are Back. What Next?"

64. P. Baev, "Russia's Arctic Policy. Geopolitics, Mercantilism, and Identity-Building," *FIIA Briefing Paper*, no. 73, December 2010, 23.

65. "Russia's Air Defense 'Responds' to All Aircraft Near its Airspace," *RIA Novosti*, July 9, 2010, http://en.rian.ru/military_news/20100709/159750083.html (accessed May 28, 2012).

66. "Less Russian Military Aircraft in the Vicinity of Norwegian Airspace," *Barents Observer*, January 7, 2011, www.barentsobserver.com/index.php?id=4869459 (accessed May 28, 2012).

67. T. Pettersen, "Jet Fighters from the Norwegian Air Force Identified a Lot More Russian Military Airplanes outside Norway in 2012 than in the Previous Years," *Barents Observer*, January 3, 2013, http://barentsobserver.com/en/security/2013/01/more-russian-military-aircraft-outside-norway-03–01 (accessed January 5, 2013).

68. T. Pettersen, "Russia Reorganizes Support and Administration Troops," *Barents Observer*, November 30, 2012, http://barentsobserver.com/en/security/2012/11/reorganizes-support-and-administration-troops-30–11 (accessed January 5, 2013).

69. More details can be found in *Mezhdunarodnaia situatsiia vokrug Arktiki i sostoianie rossiiskoi priarkticheskoi infrastruktury* [The international situation in the Arctic and the state of Russian Arctic infrastructure] (Moscow: Tsentr politicheskoi informatsii, 2010).

70. "General Shamanov: Rossiia gotovitsia k voine za Arktiku [General Shamanov: Russia is ready for war in the Arctic]," *Polit.ru*, June 24, 2008, http://www.polit.ru/news/2008/06/24/getready.html (accessed May 28, 2012).

71. R. McDermott, "Russia Planning Arctic Military Grouping," *Eurasia Daily Monitor* 6, no. 72, April 15, 2009, http://www.jamestown.org/single/?no_cache=1&tx_ttnews%5Btt_news%5D=34857 (accessed May 28, 2012).

72. T. Pettersen, "Motorized Infantry Brigade to Northern Fleet," *Barents Observer*, November 26, 2012, http://barentsobserver.com/en/security/2012/11/motorized-infantry-brigade-northern-fleet-26–11 (accessed December 6, 2012).

73. "Osnovy gosudarstvennoi politiki Rossiiskoi Federatsii v Arktike na period do 2020 g. i dal'neishuiu perspektivu [Fundamentals of state policy of the Russian Federation in the Arctic for the period to 2020 and future prospects]," *Sovet Bezopasnosti*, September 19, 2008, http://www.scrf.gov.ru/documents/98.html (accessed May 28, 2012). See also K. Zysk's comments, "Russian National Security Strategy to 2020," *Geopolitics in the High North*, June 15, 2009, http://www.geopoliticsnorth.org/index.php?option=com_content&view=article&id=84&limitstart=2 (accessed May 28, 2012).

74. "Rossiia sozdaet otdel'nuiu gruppirovku voisk v Arktike [Russia creates a separate military grouping in the Arctic]," *Grani.ru*, March 27, 2009, http://grani.ru/Politics/Russia/m.149100.html (accessed May 28, 2012).

75. "Russia Enhances Control in the Arctic," *Barents Observer*, March 2, 2011, http://www.barentsobserver.com/russian-enhances-control-in-the-arctic.4891451-58932.html (accessed May 28, 2012).

76. "Agreement On Cooperation on Aeronautical and Maritime Search and Rescue in the Arctic," May 2011, http://www.arctic-council.org/index.php/en/about-us/task-forces/282-task-force-on-search-and-rescue (accessed May 28, 2012).

77. S.T. Wezeman, "Military Capabilities in the Arctic," *SIPRI Background Paper*, March 2012, http://books.sipri.org/files/misc/SIPRIBP1203.pdf (accessed May 28, 2012).

78. Speech by Norway's Foreign Minister Jonas Gahr Støre, "Current Strategic Challenges in the High North," January 29, 2009, http://www.norway-nato.org/news/0204_High_North/ (accessed May 28, 2012).

79. D. Trenin, "Russia Redefines Itself and Its Relations with the West," *Washington Quarterly* 30, no. 2 (2007): 104.

Chapter 7

Resource Nationalism vs. Patterns of Cooperation

Due to its geographic location, the economic stakes associated with development of the Arctic's natural resource wealth are particularly significant for Russia. As much as 20% of its GDP and 22% of its exports are generated north of the Arctic Circle.[1] In terms of resources, the country produces about 95% of its natural gas, 75% of its oil, and large volumes of nickel, tin, platinum, and gold in Arctic regions. With the Siberian Arctic shelf stretching to a width of 1,200 kilometers or more, Russia also has a continental shelf area of 6.2 million square kilometers,[2] even discounting claims currently before the CLCS. To this must be added the wealth of the seabed, and the potential exploitation of the water column, in particular the fish stocks.

Interpreting the Arctic as a key economic resource is the main driver of Russia's interest in the region, even trumping its security objectives. The "Energy Strategy for Russia up to 2020," ratified in 2003, defines the Barents Sea, Kara Sea, and the Yamal Peninsula as strategic for the country's future. The energy sector, which drives the entire Russian economy, faces severe reductions in production and low rates of regeneration. As a result, it must turn quickly to the Arctic, but the changing patterns of the world hydrocarbons market call Russia's strategy into question. The country is also banking on the metallic mineral industries, which had always been a mainstay of the Soviet economic structure. After the deep industrial crisis of the 1990s, this sector boomed during much of the 2000s thanks to rising global prices for major metals. The current high demand for rare earth metals could also ensure comfortable revenues for the state budget in the decades to come. Finally, given the substantial demand in Asian markets, the importance of the fishing industry cannot be discounted; it also carries symbolic weight for Russia, as the Soviet Union always considered itself a world fishing power.

However, Moscow's plan to transform the Arctic into the "Russian Federation's leading strategic resource base"[3] by 2020 is still mostly a declaration of intent. The transition from idea to reality is always more complex, longer, and more costly than expected, and success will not necessarily be forthcoming. The Russian authorities seem to vacillate between playing the card of resource nationalism—a trend that became ever more pronounced as the 2000s wore on, especially with the rise in the world price of hydrocarbons—and opting for modes of cooperation that would open the region to foreign firms, and therefore to investments and technology transfer. Despite a wavering policy in this matter and a volatile business climate, international oil firms are looking to enter the Russian market, which offers both resources and profitable returns on investments. It is therefore likely that, in the medium term, patterns of cooperation will win out, but it remains to be seen how they will impact the transformation of the Russian legal and political system.

Beyond the Metrics of the "Arctic Bonanza"

In 2000, the U.S. Geological Survey (USGS) estimated that 25% of the world's remaining undiscovered oil and gas resources were in the Arctic. These figures have long been debated, for example, by the consulting firm Wood Mackenzie in *The Future of the Arctic: A New Dawn for Exploration*, which offered the more cautious assessment that the Arctic contained 29% of the world's undiscovered gas reserves and 10% of its oil.[4] More regionally focused analysis enabled the USGS to make a more precise estimation in 2008. It contended that the Arctic contained only 13% of the world's remaining undiscovered oil reserves, but up to 30% of its gas reserves. If correct, this would mean that 90 billion barrels of oil, 1,669 trillion cubic feet of natural gas, and 44 billion barrels of natural gas liquids may yet be found in the Arctic, of which approximately 84% is located in offshore areas. More than 70% of undiscovered natural gas is estimated to lie in three areas in particular: the West Siberian Basin, the East Barents Basin, and Arctic Alaska.[5]

These statistics are often used to back up geopolitical and commercial hype. Arctic reserves, for example, have been viewed as the new Eldorado for the international oil companies (IOCs) in their competition with nationalized oil companies (NOCs), although most of the Arctic deposits are under state control.[6] Whatever the actual figures, the proportions confirm that Russia will largely dominate the production of Arctic hydrocarbons, with between 60 and 70% of reserves: the natural gas reserves are almost all in the Russian part of the Arctic, whereas oil is more evenly distributed, with considerable reserves in the North American sector.

These statistics need to be viewed with caution, however. The USGS sometimes has been criticized for overestimating the quantity of reserves. One critique is that the unreliability of information on Arctic hydrocarbons is too

Table 7.1

The 2008 U.S. Geological Survey Estimates of Undiscovered Oil and Gas of Russia's Northern Regions

Provinces	Oil, bill. barrels	Total gas, bill. cubic ft.	Natural gas liquids, bill. barrels	Bill. barrels of oil equivalent
West Siberian Basin	3,659	651,498	20,328	132,571
East Barents Basin	7,406	317,557	1,422	61,755
Yenisei-Khatanga Basin	5,583	99,964	2,675	24,919
Laptev Sea Shelf	3,115	32,562	867	9,409
Barents Platform	2,055	26,218	278	6,704
Eurasia Basin	1,342	19,475	520	5,108
North Kara Basins and Platforms	1,807	14,973	390	4,693
Timan-Pechora Basin	1,667	9,062	202	3,380
Lomonosov-Makarov	1,106	7,156	191	2,491
Lena-Anabar Basin	1,912	2,106	56	2,320
North Chukchi-Wrangel Foreland Basin	85	6,065	106	1,203
Vikitskii Basin	98	5,741	101	1,156
Northwest Laptev Sea Shelf	4,488	119	1,039	
Lena-Vilyuy Basin	376	1,335	35	635
Zyryanka Basin	47	1,505	40	338
East Siberian Sea Basin	19	618	10	133
Total for Russia	30,277	1,200,223	27,340	257,854

Source: K.J. Bird, R.J. Charpentier, D.L. Gautier, D.W. Houseknecht, T.R. Klett, J.K. Pitman, T.E. Moore, C.J. Schrenk, M.E. Tennyson, and C.J. Wandrey, "Circum-Arctic Resource Appraisal: Estimates of Undiscovered Oil and Gas North of the Arctic Circle," U.S. Geological Survey, Fact Sheet 2008-3049, 2008, http://pubs.usgs.gov/fs/2008/3049.

often ignored and many experts tend to take U.S. Geological Survey estimates as conclusive, even though they are clearly labeled as unconfirmed.[7] Very little exploratory drilling has been conducted in the majority of potential Arctic fields, while seismic and acoustic tests and geologic modeling cannot provide a basis for reliable estimates. Hence, *resources* do not necessarily translate into *reserves* for the simple reason that they may not be extractable. Moreover, *estimated* reserves are not necessarily *proven* reserves. Finally, proven reserves may not always be commercially *recoverable*, especially given current changes in the global market. Indeed, the USGS report does not take into account economic considerations linked to the costs of exploration and development.

Furthermore, the report does not include small deposits, or unconventional sources, such as coal bed methane, gas hydrate, shale oil and shale gas, and tar sands, which are in the process of transforming the world market. Peak

Oil theory stated that the annual production of oil and gas is soon set to start decreasing rapidly due to the depletion of world reserves. But thanks to new discoveries and even more to new technologies, the known magnitude of reserves continues to rise and has even doubled since the 1980s.[8] New technology is unlocking unconventional oil and gas reserves. The environmental risks caused by horizontal drilling and hydraulic fracturing, which have lead many countries, in particular in Europe, to enact moratoriums on shale extraction, could probably be overcome in the near future. This shale revolution shifts in part the geography of production and energy geopolitics.[9] It is likely to curtail somewhat the general interest aroused by the Arctic reserves, which are expensive to extract given their remoteness and difficult environmental conditions. The International Energy Agency (IEA) calculates for instance that the cost of exploiting Arctic resources is between US$40 and US$100 per barrel, whereas for Middle Eastern reserves it is between US$10 and US$40.[10] Below a world oil price of US$120 a barrel, the majority of Arctic deposits are thus not commercially recoverable.

These changes in the global market are likely to have huge collateral implications for Russia. Indeed, the United States is projected to surpass Russia as the world's largest gas producer by 2015, overtake Saudi Arabia and Russia as the world's top oil producer by 2017, and become a net exporter of oil by 2030 according to IEA estimates.[11] Europe's dependency on Russia's gas should also decline in the years to come. Lastly, China has recoverable gas resources similar to those of the United States and has a strong interest in developing its own shale gas production in order to bypass American maritime domination over the Pacific. The Gulf countries, and in particular Saudi Arabia, could see their margin for maneuver drastically reduced, given declining American interest in Middle Eastern energy. The prospects for Russia are also bleak, as oil and gas revenues provide an important part of the state budget, from 20 to 40% depending on the calculations. The Kremlin initially exhibited signs of denial, decrying the shale revolution on the basis of environmental concerns, and refuting the changes under way in Europe, in particular the possible reduced Polish and Ukrainian autonomy in the energy sphere as a result of development of their domestic shale gas deposits.[12] However, since 2012, the Russian government has indicated that the country should encourage domestic shale oil production. Putin urged Gazprom to revise its export policy, as the "shale revolution" and the development of liquefied natural gas had the potential to seriously erode the country's export revenues.[13]

Technological developments are also rapidly altering the prospects of Arctic oil and gas. Here the ultimate outcome is still uncertain and subject to speculation. It seems, however, that hydraulic fracturing (fracking) technology

—which uses pressurized fluids to fracture oil- and gas-bearing rocks and open channels for the hydrocarbons to flow toward the surface—can in part revolutionize the market. Indeed, traditional methods of oil extraction have recovered only about 40% of reserves in the ground. With the new fracking technology, large quantities of oil suddenly become commercially profitable. If the full potential of this technology is realized over the coming years, this could postpone Arctic development by several decades. Russian firms also realize the potential of hydraulic fracturing to prolong the productive lives of existing oil and gas fields and are today looking to develop fracking so that they can continue to exploit West Siberian deposits that are rich in infrastructure and have already proved very profitable.[14] The cost/benefit analyses will therefore not necessarily weigh in favor of Arctic development.

Despite these revolutions Russia still considers that its future as an energy power lies in the Arctic. Over 80% of its gas and 70% of its oil reserves are in the Arctic regions.[15] Two-thirds of these resources are situated in Russia's western Arctic, in the Barents and Kara Seas, and in the Timan-Pechora basin, with about 8.2 billion tons of hydrocarbons. Major possible fields also exist in the Okhotsk Sea, on the Kamchatka Peninsula, and in the Laptev Sea.[16] Minor oil and gas deposits have been discovered in the onshore territories near the Bering Sea. Finally, the deep-water plateau between the Lomonosov and Mendeleev Ridges, at the core of Russia's territorial claims to the UN Commission on the Limits of the Continental Shelf, may prove to be a promising area in the more distant future. Russia's Ministry of Natural Resources states that the country's Arctic territories contain around 80 billion tons of hydrocarbon deposits or 586 billion barrels of oil equivalent (boe). The Ministry for Industry and Energy calculates that Russia could be extracting upwards of 110 million tons of oil and 160 billion cubic meters (bcm) of gas from the Arctic shelf by 2030. However, an increasing number of dissenting voices can be heard, of those who do not subscribe to the excitement accorded the supposed "Arctic bonanza."[17] The geological data for most offshore Russian reserves are insufficient. Only the western part of the Arctic is well known, and according to Bellona, even there only 9 to 12% of the Barents Sea reserves have been explored.[18] Even the figures advanced by Russian sources are contradictory: the 2007 Arctic scientific expedition put forward figures that are only one-fifth of those usually estimated for the Barents and Kara Seas (up to 48.8 billion barrels of oil).[19]

Russia's Oil and Gas Strategies in the Arctic

The Soviet Union was the largest oil producer in the world, with an oil peak at 569 million tons per year, or 11.4 million barrels per day (mbd), in the late Soviet era. With the industrial collapse production plunged by nearly 50% in the first half of the 1990s. Between 1999 and 2004, output shot back up at a rate of 8.5% a year. Since then growth has slowed to 1.5% a year. In the 2000s, Russia was the world's second-largest producer of oil after Saudi Arabia and, in 2009, eclipsed the latter with a production of 9.9 mbd of oil,[20] even though it has smaller reserves.[21] In 2012, Russia produced more than 10 mbd, and the authorities seem resolute about maintaining this course of tapping its reserves and developing unconventional resources, and supporting the dynamism of the main national company, Rosneft.[22]

Most of Russia's oil resources are located in western Siberia (the Samotlor, Priobskoe, Prirazlomnoye, Mamontovo, Malobalykskoe, and Surgut fields) in the Khanty-Mansi autonomous district. In the coming years, declining western Siberian production will be complemented by increased output from Sakhalin, in the Okhotsk Sea, which is expected to become the major driver of growth in Russia's oil production in the near term. In the longer term, untapped oil reserves in Eastern Siberia, the Caspian Sea, Yamal Peninsula, and the Timan-Pechora region could play a larger role. However, the future appears to be challenging and, according to IEA, "these new projects may only be able to offset declining output from aging fields and not result in significant output growth."[23] The "General Outline of Development of the Oil Sector of the Russian Federation until 2020," issued at the end of 2010, concludes that the domestic oil sector is at a critical stage. Without timely and fundamental reforms, Russia's oil output will fall far short of what would be needed to meet growth targets—nearly 30% by 2020, and over 60% by 2030. The key conclusions are that the so-called brownfield renaissance of the first half of the 2000s is over, but that the resource base for further greenfield development is in "critical condition."[24] From now until 2030, Russian forecasts estimate an increase in production of only 40 million tons, while the IEA predicts a decrease of 40 million tons.[25]

While forecasts for Russia's oil tend to be unanimous in terms of the serious obstacles to increase future production, the set of forecasts for the future of gas is more contrasted. Russia holds the largest natural gas reserves in the world (1,567 trillion cubic feet [tcf] or 44 trillion cubic meters [tcm] according to British Petroleum).[26] For a long time it was the world's largest producer, but the United States has recently closed the gap. Indeed, depending on the methods of calculation—Russian production numbers include flared gas, which is not the case with American figures—Russia has now been overtaken by the United States: according to the IEA, the former produced 757 bcm against 769 for the latter in 2011.[27] Russia is still the world's largest exporter of gas (196 bcm in 2011[28]), but it is again set to be overtaken very soon by the United States. Its main exports are of dry (pipeline) natural gas, whereas the rising gas powers are increasingly wagering on shale and other unconventional gas (with exports in the form of LNG). Despite Russia's lagging behind in new technologies and in the development of unconventional reserves, its ambitions are substantial. With the exploitation of Arctic deposits, the Energy Strategy forecasts output attaining 900 bcm by 2030. This goal was further adjusted to 1 trillion cubic meters, which constitutes almost a doubling of production compared to 2010 and includes investments of more than US$400 billion.[29]

However, Russian production is facing multiple challenges and stagnated throughout the 2000s. The state corporation Gazprom, both producer and exporter, sells about 550 bcm per year, but its own production is in sharp decline and projected to be only 344 bcm in 2020. Only private companies like Novatek and Lukoil have contributed to increasing volumes in recent years.[30] The state-controlled conglomerate has been incapable of investing in research and development, delaying the exploitation of new deposits, and has been unable to respond to recent developments in the world market.[31] It has relied on the captive markets of Central Asia, which it is on the verge of losing to China, and has increased production solely by buying the shares of some of its privately owned competitors, Novatek and Itera. In 2009, Russia's production reached the lowest level since 1992, falling by more than 4 tcf or 17% year over year. Gazprom's long-term strategy is heavily criticized by the Kremlin itself, which nevertheless substantially profits from the financial revenues it generates.

The largest gas fields were discovered in the 1960s and put into production in the 1970s in the Yamalo-Nenets autonomous region, the world's largest natural gas producing area, which accounts for approximately 90% of Russia's current natural gas production, 45% of its total reserves, and 20% of the world's gas production. Since this date, the gas industry has centered on the super-giant fields in the Nadym-Pur-Taz region—the Urengoy, Yamburg, and Medvezhye fields account for over half of Russian gas production. They are linked to European Russia and Europe via about 50,000 kilometers of oil pipelines and 150,000 kilometers of gas pipelines. Since the 1990s, however, these three fields have registered a dramatic reduction in production. With their progressive depletion, Russia could see its onshore hydrocarbon interests move even farther north and eventually offshore. Production in the Medvezhye field has already shifted steadily northward to the Kara Sea. In the eastern part of the Barents Sea, too, some oil is extracted from the Kolguev Island fields.[32] The Zapolyarnoe field, whose reserves are estimated at 3.5 trillion cubic meters of gas and some 80 million tons of gas condensate and oil, is probably the last non-Arctic site to be put into operation in this region. At the end of 2012 it produced its first trillion cubic meters of gas. Its entry into full design capacity—130 billion cubic meters per year—making it the most productive field in Russia, was celebrated with great fanfare by the authorities at the start of 2013.[33]

In addition to Zapolyarnoe, Gazprom has pinned its hopes on the Yamal Peninsula and its adjacent offshore areas, with approximately 16 tcm of explored and preliminary estimated gas reserves and nearly 22 tcm of in-place and forecast gas reserves.[34] The Yamal reserves are therefore envisaged as supporting an annual production level comparable to that which Gazprom currently delivers to the domestic market. It alone could account for as much as 200 bcm of gas production per year by 2020, and 360 bcm per year by 2030.[35] In 2008, Gazprom launched the Yamal megaproject, which is supposed to reach its full production capacity of 115 bcm annually in 2017, together with development of the Bovanenkovo deposit, whose first comprehensive gas treatment unit was commissioned in 2012.[36] The main challenge for this project is the total absence of infrastructure on the peninsula, but the deposits may be linked to the nearby Nadym-Pur-Taz network. Gazprom plans to build more than 12,000 kilometers of new pipelines and 27 compressor stations, as well as the Yamal-Europe gas pipeline, with a capacity of 33 bcm, extending more than 4,000 kilometers to Germany.[37] If Arctic shipping develops, delivering LNG by tankers could ease pressure on Russia's aging overland pipeline system and mitigate the risks of building new pipelines on thawing permafrost.[38] The development focus will shift to adjacent offshore reserves once the onshore fields have peaked, possibly around 2030.

In the future, the bulk of Russia's hydrocarbon reserves will be situated offshore on the continental shelf, with a much smaller percentage located onshore. The first of these is the Prirazlomnoye oil field in the Pechora Sea, a southeastern extension of the Barents Sea. Located south of Novaya Zemlya, and about 60 kilometers from the shore of the Varandey terminal, it has oil reserves of 610 million barrels. Production is planned to start in 2014, more than a decade behind schedule, due to major technical problems, regular postponements, multiple changes of ownership, as well as scandals linked to its possibly environmentally insecure drilling activity. Oil will be exported via tanker, with storage and shipping facilities in the Murmansk and Arkhangel'sk regions, while the shipyard Sevmash will handle repairs and the testing of equipment.[39] Other licenses have been awarded to tracts in the Pechora Sea, for example the Medynsko-Varandey section with 163 million tons of recoverable oil reserves, and Kolokolmor-Pomor with 300 million tons.

The development of Prirazlomnoye would have been, at least on paper, followed by that of the Shtokman gas field in the Barents Sea, one of the world's largest natural gas fields, located about 600 kilometers north of the Kola

Peninsula. Its reserves are estimated at 3.8 tcm of natural gas and more than 37 million tons of gas condensate, and it has a projected annual production of around 90 bcm of gas. A portion of the gas would flow southward by pipeline to the Murmansk region, and then via the Kola Peninsula to Volkhov in the Leningrad region, where it would connect with the Nord Stream pipeline (Vyborg terminal) for transmission to continental Europe along the floor of the Baltic Sea. The other part would be liquefied at an LNG plant to be constructed at Teriberka on the Kola Peninsula. In theory Shtokman could meet total European demand for seven years and is expected to produce for 50 years.[40] However, given the current export market for natural gas, the development of Shtokman has been put on hold (see below). Should the outlook improve, output from Shtokman could be followed by that from the satellite fields of Ledov, Ludlovsk, Fersmanov, Murmansk, Severo-Kildin, and Demidov. The "Grey Zone" once in dispute between Norway and Russia is also very rich in hydrocarbons, and the bilateral treaty on the delimitation of the Barents Sea, signed in 2010, lifted the moratorium on exploration of the continental shelf that had been in place since the 1980s. It is estimated that about 30% of all undiscovered Norwegian resources lie in the Barents Sea,[41] especially in the Fedynsky High, which is believed to contain between 10 and 12 billion tons of oil.[42]

Farther east, Trebs and Titov are among the most promising oil prospects in the Timan-Pechora province, with reserves estimated at 78.9 million tons (578 million barrels) and 63.4 million tons (465 million barrels) of oil, respectively.[43] In the 2020s, other fields of the Pechora Sea, such as Dolgin and Medin, could come on line. The large fields in the Ob'–Taz Bay, situated 40 kilometers from the coast, constitute a special case because of the very shallow water and its complex composition—half salt, half freshwater.[44] Some of these fields could be brought into production by the end of the 2010s by Gazflot, the Gazprom subsidiary for offshore extraction. The large fields of the Kara Sea, with potential reserves of four tcm—especially the massive Rusanov and Leningrad gas and condensate fields, which may contain more hydrocarbons than the giant Shtokman field—will not commence production before 2030. Other complex hydrocarbon deposits have also been found on the Yamal shelf: Nyarmey, Skuratov, and Severo-Karasaev. The reserves of the South Kara Sea, the EPNZ-1, EPNZ-2, and EPNZ-3 fields, are supposed to be as rich as those in the North Sea. Rosneft's then chief executive Eduard Khudainatov stated that they contained five billion tons of oil and 3,000 bcm of gas,[45] but the very limited degree of exploration means these figures are unconfirmed. In the future, the development of hydrocarbon deposits on the Magadan shelf area and in the western Kamchatka sector of the Pacific Ocean is also envisaged.[46] For the fields in the East Siberia and Laptev Seas, meanwhile, no operating structure has yet been put into place.

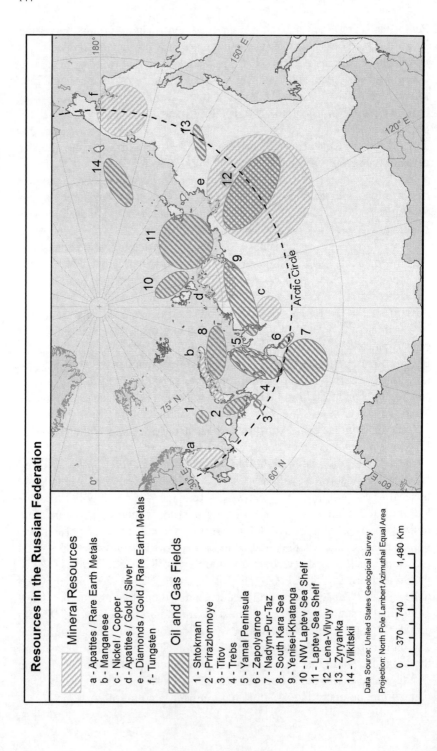

Resources in the Russian Federation

Mineral Resources

a - Apatites / Rare Earth Metals
b - Manganese
c - Nickel / Copper
d - Apatites / Gold / Silver
e - Diamonds / Gold / Rare Earth Metals
f - Tungsten

Oil and Gas Fields

1 - Shtokman
2 - Prirazlomnoye
3 - Titov
4 - Trebs
5 - Yamal Peninsula
6 - Zapolyarnoe
7 - Nadym-Pur-Taz
8 - South Kara Sea
9 - Yenisei-Khatanga
10 - NW Laptev Sea Shelf
11 - Laptev Sea Shelf
12 - Lena-Vilyuy
13 - Zyryanka
14 - Vilkitskii

Data Source: United States Geological Survey

Projection: North Pole Lambert Azimuthal Equal Area

0   370   740   1,480 Km

The Costs and Risks of Arctic-Based Energy

Without revisiting the changes in the world market that have made the Arctic reserves less attractive, numerous other challenges increase the costs of exploiting them and heighten the risk of an Arctic-based energy strategy for Russia. First, exploiting Arctic fields is technically challenging. Drilling under extreme conditions requires specific equipment and knowledge. For the Prirazlomnoye field, Sevmorneftegaz is working on a rig that will be capable of operating in temperatures as low as -50°C and able to withstand the impact of ice packs.[47] Despite the accomplishments to date, the Russian oil and gas industry still needs to catch up with its Western competitors in terms of technology and expertise, particularly offshore, which is a totally new domain for it. In 2006, Russia launched a "Strategy for Exploring and Developing the Oil and Gas Potential of the Continental Shelf of the Russian Federation until 2020."[48] According to the latter date, the country plans to have built 60 new oil rigs and an even larger number of submarine installations. A major obstacle is that for the time being, Russia is still far from possessing the necessary know-how to build and operate platforms at such high latitudes. Numerous technical issues have therefore delayed current projects for almost a decade. Both at Prirazlomnoye and at Shtokman, plans for the construction of platforms must take into account such hazards as icebergs and extreme wave heights. Shtokman requires the construction of ice-capable production platforms in more than 300 meters of water. The site is also still beyond the range of helicopters, which poses significant problems for search and rescue systems, and it is vulnerable to seasonal pack ice and storms. Prirazlomnoye is located in an area that is ice-free for just 110 days a year, meaning that its stationary platform must be ice-resistant.[49] And the Barents and Pechora Seas are "tame" compared to the extreme climates that would be encountered during operations farther east.

The question of financing is also a tricky one for Russia. There has long been a lack of investment to upgrade aging delivery systems, in particular pipelines and energy-inefficient processing plants. Accordingly, the cost of modernizing the entire Soviet-era energy infrastructure will be huge. The International Energy Agency has calculated that Russia's energy industry would need to raise an estimated $900 billion over the next 25 years just to *maintain* current oil and gas production levels.[50] To this sum, Moscow must add the costs associated with Arctic exploration and exploitation. In 2008, Rosneft president Sergei Bogdanchikov himself calculated that developing Russia's continental shelf would require about $2 trillion of investment through 2050.[51] Part of these investments needs to be made in the coming decade, but the returns will not be immediate. Whereas some fields will be operational around 2030, those in high latitudes or very remote regions might not be until 2050–2060.

In addition, Russia's strategy assumes that its oil and dry natural gas will continue to be in high demand in the decades to come. In 2011, Russia exported around 7 million barrels per day (mbd) of oil. Of this, 80% was destined for European markets, particularly Germany and the Netherlands, 12% for Asia, and 5% for the United States.[52] Not only is the latter no longer a potential importer but European demand in the years to come remains unpredictable. To complement the Soviet-era Druzhba network linking Western Siberia to Europe via Ukraine and Belarus, the Russian state monopoly Transneft built the Baltic Pipeline System (BPS), which transports oil from Timan-Pechora, West Siberia, Volga-Urals, and Kazakhstan to the Gulf of Finland. However, exports to Asia, in particular China, probably offer the only prospect for guaranteed growth in the years ahead. The new Eastern Siberia—Pacific Ocean (ESPO) oil pipeline, more than 4,800 kilometers long and stretching from the Irkutsk region to the Pacific, is designed to transport as much as 80 million tons per year. New oil loading terminals in the ports of Nakhodka, (Koz'mino and De-Kastri (exporting Sakhalin output), opened in 2009.[53] ESPO's route has been completed by an extension to Daqing, China. The Zapolyarye-Purpe Pipeline, whose construction began in March 2012, will be the first section to link the Arctic deposits of the Yamal Peninsula to the Asia market via the ESPO.

In the gas sector, Russia exported more than 7 tcf of natural gas in 2011, two-thirds of which went to Europe, and one-third to CIS countries.[54] Whereas the United States is no longer a potential destination for Russian exports, export to Europe remains important not only in market terms but also relative to geopolitical weight: Russia is seeking to bypass transit countries (mostly Ukraine) by building new gas pipelines that will reach Europe directly; that is, the North Stream (55 bcm) inaugurated in 2011, the Blue Stream (16 bcm, although it seems to have been a commercial failure), and the South Stream (63 bcm), which is set to become operational by 2015. Here again, energy demand in China and India will mitigate the decline of the European market and turn Russia increasingly toward Asia, even if the energy partnership with Beijing is difficult.[55] But this geo-economic change will come at a high price, as Russia's gas fields and infrastructure currently are heavily oriented toward Europe, and the reorientation toward Asia entails massive investments and thus rising costs. New production from the Yamal Peninsula is therefore crucial to satisfy both domestic requirements and export consumers in coming years, but Gazprom risks being penalized for delaying the necessary investments.[56] Despite projected Asian demand, Russia also must prepare for a contingency involving a reduction in overall world demand for oil and the need to diversify its export portfolio to include more natural gas, LNG, and electricity.

Last but not least, growing operations in fields located in fragile ecological areas, onshore or off, come with environmental concerns. The Arctic Monitoring and Assessment Program, established to implement components of the Arctic Environmental Protection Strategy, studied multiple links between hydrocarbon exploitation and environmental risks, ranging from oil spills to changes in the migration of marine mammals.[57] Aging Soviet-era infrastructure poses increased risks, as the big oil spill of 1994 in the Komi Republic demonstrated. International legislation such as the United Nations Convention on the Law of the Sea (UNCLOS), the International Convention for the Prevention of Pollution from Ships (MARPOL 73/78), and the Convention for the Protection of the Marine Environment in the North-East Atlantic (OSPAR) regulates offshore drilling platforms (for instance, they cannot interfere with navigational freedom in recognized sea lanes) and obliges companies to partly remove structures once fields are exhausted and to minimize the accidental discharge of harmful substances and marine pollution.[58] However the risks remain very significant; and the World Wildlife Fund has called for a moratorium on new offshore oil development in the Arctic until the gap in oil spill response is filled.[59]

Foreign Actors and the Russian State: Competition or Cooperation?

The potential that lies below the ground has long been an attraction for Russian state and private companies, as well as foreign ones, and will probably continue to be in the future (despite the recent decline in interest). But to make this potential a reality, the Kremlin needs to successfully handle two contradictory logics—one of exclusion and the other of cooperation. It seeks to maintain control over its strategic wealth for purposes of sovereignty, but cannot exploit these riches without massive foreign participation.

After the collapse of the Soviet Union, the Russian government terminated state funding for geological expeditions, and domestic exploration has been very limited since. The level of knowledge about new fields is therefore low. In the 2000s, the partly privatized exploration service Arktikshelfneftegaz returned to the control of the Federal Agency for State Property Management, and the budget allocated to exploration is planned to increase from $25 million in 2005 to 100 million in 2020.[60] Nonetheless, very few exploration licenses have been granted. Gazprom obtained one for the Dolgin oil field, in the Pechora Sea; Severneftegaz, controlled jointly by Gazprom Neft and Novatek, has three geological exploration licenses for the Kola coast.[61] In light of the costs of exploratory drilling in remote regions with practically no infrastructure, Russia is in need of foreign investments; an exploration well in a new region may cost $10–12 million, as opposed to $3–4 million in a mature region.[62] In 2012, Igor Plesovskikh, head of the Federal Agency for Subsoil Use, admitted that the country needs to spend a total of $15 billion a year on geological exploration in order to maintain its production levels, while it is currently spending only one-third that amount.[63]

Russia's need for technology transfers and outside investments has not prevented the emergence of a strong "resource nationalism." Since the beginning of the 2000s, the country has undergone a process of recentralizing its oil and gas companies. Sibneft and Yukos returned to state ownership amid well-publicized scandals and the imprisonment of Mikhail Khodorkovsky. What is more, Russia reaffirmed its sovereignty over reserves, using allegations of environmental violations to force Shell, Mitsui, and Mitsubishi to sell 50% of their shares plus one to Gazprom in the Sakhalin-2 consortium.[64] The overall share of output of state companies rose from 4.8% in 2003 to 39.7% in 2008, while the share of private companies declined from 72.6 to 43.9%.[65] This trend is not unique to Russia. National companies currently control about 80% of global oil and gas reserves, a fact that is pushing privately held international companies to compete harder for—or be marginalized from—new deposits. A global trend of increased state control over natural resources is thus becoming ascendant.[66]

The Russian authorities are aware of the need to improve the country's business climate, which currently penalizes efforts to increase investments in the hydrocarbons sector. In the second half of the 2000s, the Kremlin acknowledged that the Russian fiscal regime was unattractive for foreign firms, and that the exploration phase—a high-risk investment—needed more appealing terms. At the end of 2007 it decided to create incentives for foreign companies. Longer exploration license periods (from 7 to 10 years) were granted, a two-year exemption was placed on the payment of some customs duties and taxes, and there was a possibility of obtaining combined exploration and production licenses.[67] Although some might have expected the global economic crisis of 2008 to have impeded Russia's ambitions of sovereignty and revived the need for foreign collaboration,[68] this has not actually been the case.

In 2008, new legislation on "Foreign Investment in Strategic Sectors" classified 40 industries as strategic to the national security.[69] Ranging from arms, hydrocarbons, and precious metals to agriculture, fishing, and seafood, it requires foreign companies to gain explicit permission from governmental authorities in order to invest in more than a certain level of shares. In the energy sector, resources classified as "of federal significance" (oil reserves of more than 70 million tons and gas deposits of more than 50 bcm) cannot have foreign holdings exceeding 50%.[70] While foreign firms are able to enter into partnerships with national companies, the former have their holdings in an operating company, not the deposit itself. Russia has therefore separated access from ownership through a so-called special-purpose vehicle, which makes it easier for the government to dispossess foreign firms and conduct retroactive operations.[71] Foreign companies, meanwhile, continue to add the assets acquired in Russia into their total reserve calculations, although legally they do not own them. In April 2012, however, a government decree outlined a fiscal reform package providing incentives for the development of Russian offshore fields, including some for geological exploration.

These measures also make the position of Russian private companies, such as Lukoil, TNK-BP, Surgutneftegas, and Novatek, more difficult, as they do not wish to finance geological studies and the drilling of appraisal wells without first obtaining state guarantees of an exploration license. They are therefore pushed to specialize in new technologies like LNG instead of engaging in the raw exploitation of deposits. The 2012 "State Program for the Development of the Continental Shelf in the period up to 2030" states that the exploitation of the Arctic continental shelf is reserved for state companies, namely Rosneft and Gazprom, which are allowed to bid for 80% of it. The remaining 20% is available to firms with at least 50% state-controlled shares that have done five years of work in the Arctic—which none have.[72] Several debates over the wisdom of according priority to state-run corporations have divided political elites. The Minister of Natural Resources, Yuri Trutnev, has for example acknowledged on several occasions that the preference given to national oil companies over international oil companies or national private companies has not born any fruit, but on the contrary has impeded the development of the Arctic shelf.[73]

Despite these drastic conditions, the main majors involved in the international "Arctic race" and Russian private firms have sought to establish themselves in this market. In 2012, Lukoil, for instance, announced it was ready to invest $2.7 billion in geological exploration on the continental shelf, especially in remote areas such as the Laptev, East Siberian, and Chukchi Seas.[74] Among foreign companies, Statoil and Norsk Hydro, which merged into Statoil in 2007, have particular knowledge of deep-water oil drilling in Arctic regions due to their experiences with the Snøhvit and Ormen Lange fields. ExxonMobil is also an experienced operator in Alaska and northern Canada, while Shell is a major player in the Athabasca oil sands project in northern Alberta.[75] As for BP, it is a prominent player in Alaska and has concluded multiple agreements with Rosneft.[76] Involvement in the main Russian fields has therefore been shared among the aforementioned players. Only

Prirazlomnoye (property of Gazprom Neft Shelf) has no foreign participation. Western companies have declined to participate in the project, finding it too risky or commercially unattractive. Gazprom is also the only owner of the site for the Yamal megaproject, but it is increasingly cooperating with Novatek, Russia's largest private gas producer, which holds 51% of the Yamal LNG plant. In 2011, Novatek signed a partnership agreement with Total, Europe's third-largest oil company, according to which Total will buy 12% of Novatek. This means that it will control 20% of the Yamal LNG project, or about one billion barrels of proven and probable reserves. The LNG will begin to be produced in 2016 and will be transported by tanker.[77]

Two other major sites under development—Shtokman and the South Kara Sea—both had or have foreign participation, albeit in fits and starts. In 2007, Statoil and Total signed an operating agreement with Gazprom and its wholly owned subsidiary Sevmorneftegaz, Shtokman's owner, in which Total and Statoil controlled 25% and 24%, respectively, of the Shtokman Development AG company.[78] Although Shtokman was a major element in the Russian-Norwegian partnership in the Arctic, changes in the world market and economic downturn in Europe have jeopardized this alliance. In August 2012 Statoil relinquished its 24% share in Shtokman and, in so doing, any hope for a return on the $1.5 billion it has invested.[79] The Norwegian firm objects to the lack of tax exemptions offered by the Russian government, which would have been necessary to render the project economically viable, and was unconvinced by the development models proposed by Gazprom. Moreover, new deposits discovered in the Norwegian part of the North Sea have made the partnership with Gazprom less attractive. Statoil nonetheless remains a key actor in the Barents Sea, after having signed a deal with Rosneft to exploit the Perseevsky field. For its part, Gazprom has delayed the opening of Shtokman, posing complications for Total, and will have to find new partners ready to invest in a project costing an estimated astronomical sum of $30 billion.

BP has also experienced complications operating in Russia, but has continued to strengthen its position in this market. In 2011, it signed with Rosneft a new Arctic Cooperation Agreement on the development of the South Kara Sea, as part of a wider Arctic Protocol between the two companies for deposit exploration in East Siberia and Chukotka.[80] However, the agreement quickly broke down as a result of a legal dispute over BP's ability to do business independently in Russia outside the framework of the joint venture TNK-BP, (in part controlled by the AAR consortium Alfa, Access, and Renova, led by Mikhail Fridman, Viktor Vekselberg, and Leonid Blavatnik), which exploits deposits in West Siberia, the Volga-Urals, and East Siberia. Subsequent to this dispute, BP sold 50% of the shares it owned in the profitable TNK-BP to

Rosneft for about $27 billion. In what is presented as the "deal of the century," signed at the end of 2012, Rosneft has become the world's largest publicly traded oil producer, and BP has more than 10% stake in the new supermajor. This unprecedented agreement has turned the British giant into the biggest single shareholder in Rosneft after the Russian government and ties it closely to Russian political circles via the person of Igor Sechin, the head of Rosneft.[81] This deal enables BP to distance itself from the Deepwater Horizon disaster in the Gulf of Mexico and invest massively in Russia, possibly by reviving the Arctic agreement. For its part, ExxonMobil has entered into a historic partnership with Rosneft for the joint exploration of the Kara Sea fields (and some in the Black Sea), in exchange for the Russian firm's access to some North American deposits.[82] More modestly, the Indian state-owned ONGC, which controls about 20% of the shares in Sakhalin-1, has been in negotiation with Bashneft to participate in the operation of the Trebs and Titov fields. Finally in 2011, the largest crude oil and natural gas producer in Germany, Wintershall, was able to access some of the Urengoy fields, in exchange for which Gazprom will participate in North Sea projects with its German counterpart.[83]

A balance must also be struck between the Russian companies. The failed merger between the two majors, Gazprom and Rosneft, in 2005 created tensions within the ruling elite, who have vested personal interests in both. As a result, the two companies have had to learn to share the market. However, Rosneft's dynamism now stands in stark contrast to Gazprom's increasing weakness, and this unstable balance is obvious in their Arctic activities. Their official domains of competence, Gazprom for gas and Rosneft for oil, tend to overlap increasingly in the case of offshore fields. Rosneft for instance extracts the gas from Sakhalin, while Gazprom has a monopoly on its export. The companies' geographical strongholds—Gazprom's in the Barents Sea and Rosneft's in the Far East—are also becoming less relevant. Both have deposits to exploit in the Kara Sea and seek new ones in the Okhotsk Sea.[84] Their relationship is an important element of the internal balance in Russia, with direct implications on the political consensus among elites. The same goes for national private companies. Lukoil, TNK-BP, Novatek, Gunvor, and Surgutneftegas all play a significant role in the distribution of dividends from oil and gas among elites as well, and they are becoming increasingly aggressive in the conquest of new markets through more innovative policies and greater openness to international cooperation.

The Arctic as a Mineral Eldorado?

The subsoil and continental shelf of Arctic regions are also rich in nonferrous and precious minerals, including zinc, copper, tin, nickel, diamonds, gold, and silver. As with hydrocarbons, estimates are difficult to extrapolate into confirmed figures, but some contend that as much as 90% of the world's reserves of nickel and cobalt, 60% of copper, and 96% of platinum, are located in the Arctic—mainly in Russia and northern Canada, but also partly in Alaska.[85]

Two of Russia's regions are particularly rich with mineral resources: Sakha-Yakutia and the Kola Peninsula. Sakha-Yakutia is already well known for its diamond mines: 90% of all Russian diamonds and 24% of Russia's gold is mined in Sakha. A new deposit was discovered in 2012, with estimated reserves of $3.5 billion. The state company Alrosa, which will probably be privatized in the years ahead, is the largest diamond producer in the world, and Russia ranks second in sales after South Africa. The Kola Peninsula is particularly rich in minerals because of geological particularities dating from the Second Ice Age. There are large quantities of minerals, from apatites (used as a source of phosphorus in fertilizer production) to aluminum, as well as titanium, rare metals, ceramic raw materials, mica, and precious stones. The northern part of the peninsula has huge deposits of nickel and also contains large reserves of precious stones such as amazonite and amethyst.[86] Gold and silver can be found near the Taimyr Peninsula and in the northern part of Yakutia; apatites also in Taimyr Peninsula, Sakha, and Chukotka; nickel and copper around Noril'sk and the Kola Peninsula; tungsten in northern Yakutia and Chukotka; manganese in Novaya Zemlya; and tin, chromium, and titanium in Yakutia. Meanwhile, the Russian Arctic's bountiful coal deposits are not likely to be exploited, as coal is among the most widely distributed minerals in the world, and one of the cheapest.[87]

This subsoil wealth has tremendous potential value, but figures are difficult to calculate because the price of extraction is partly unknown and, like hydrocarbons, profitability depends on world prices. The Soviet Union first started exploring the Arctic for minerals in the 1930s. From the second half of the decade, Gulag mines in Vorkuta and Noril'sk allowed the country to extract large quantities of the minerals necessary for its massive industrialization. Today, more than twenty-five centers of mining activities operate in the Russian Arctic.[88] The main one, the Norilsk-Talnakh, is the largest nickel-copper-palladium complex in the world, with current known reserves in excess of 1.8 billion tons.

Privatized at the beginning of the 1990s, Noril'sk Nickel later merged with Severonickel and Pechenganickel on the Kola Peninsula to create one of the world's largest mining consortiums. It is now the world's largest producer of nickel and palladium, and a leading producer of platinum and copper. It also produces various valuable byproducts, such as cobalt, chromium, rhodium, silver, gold, iridium, ruthenium, selenium, tellurium, and sulfur.[89] Noril'sk Nickel also plays an important role in Russian agriculture: three-quarters of the phosphate fertilizer in the country is manufactured from apatite concentrate located in the Khibiny deposit on the Kola Peninsula. Nepheline is used in the manufacture of soda and potash for the chemical industry.[90] In a few years, Noril'sk Nickel has become one of the most important private actors of the Russian Arctic, and one of the most dynamic in terms of exports. In 2010 it shipped 10,000 metric tons of metal and coal to Asia and plans to double its shipments by 2016.[91]

While in coming decades technically challenging deep-seabed mining operations are likely to be considered, a major unknown is the future role Russia will play in the domain of rare earth elements. The 17 metals defined as rare earths have important technological applications and are essential to the production of such devices as televisions, mobile phones, and personal computer monitors, as well as for the manufacturing of green energy products (low-energy lightbulbs, wind turbines, hybrid cars). In addition, they are key components for the defense industry: according to the U.S. Department of Defense, rare earths are used in the production of a number of missiles including the Tomahawk cruise missile, as well as radar surveillance systems, Abrams M1A1 tanks, F15 fighter jets, and night vision equipment.[92] The rare earths market has literally skyrocketed over recent years, increasing from US$500 million in 2003 to $1.5–2 billion in 2010, when world demand was 136,100 tons but global production was only 133,600 tons, with the difference being filled by above ground stocks (recycling of used components) or inventories.[93] Global demand is set to grow considerably: it could reach between 185,000 and 210,000 tons in 2015, leading to strong price increases, despite having already risen by more than 300% between 2008 and the end of 2010.[94] According to some sources, prices for rare earths could increase by two or three times over the next 20 years.[95]

China has 36% of world reserves of rare metals but almost totally dominates the world market because it was the first to understand their importance in the 1980s, and did not hesitate to ramp up production, despite the fact that it has particularly negative consequences for the environment. Accounting for 95% of world production, China has imposed severe restrictions on rare earths exports over recent years. It authorizes the sale abroad of a mere 25% of its production as compared with 75% only a few years ago.[96] Beijing has justified this decision by the necessity to apply further legal restrictions to this industry, in particular due to its environmental consequences. Rare earths are thus an international strategic issue. China's decisions have caused the relevant industries in Japan (one of the largest importers in the world), South Korea, Europe, and the United States to consider alternative products and suppliers. The search for new, economically viable deposits spans the entire globe from Greenland and South Africa to the CIS countries and North America.

With the second largest explored rare earth reserves in the world (and perhaps the first in terms of potential reserves), Russia could eventually challenge China's monopoly.[97] Moscow was not planning to develop rare earth mines until 2030, but international pressure, especially from Japanese firms, has been mounting. Russia possesses two main deposits. The Lovozero mine, in the northern Murmansk region, has an estimated 80 million tons of ore reserves that can be surface-mined. It could produce a wide range of rare earths, especially the very uncommon eudiyalite; for now, however, it is focused on magnesium production. The Tomtor deposit in Yakutia has an exceptional level of rare earth content in its ore of 12%. Its proven reserves amount to 150 million tons, and the possible reserves come close to exceeding the rest of the world's reserves combined. The apatite ore of the Kola Peninsula could also contain rare earth metals.[98]

Hydrocarbons are therefore far from the only source of Arctic subsoil wealth. Moscow could generate revenues not only from oil and gas, but also from ores, especially rare earth metals, the future of which may be more stable in terms of price and demand than hydrocarbons.

Hopes for Reviving the Fishing Industry

In addition, the Arctic has a huge marine fauna that could be exploited. Among the world's major traded resources, fish is often a forgotten figure in the statistics, despite its growing role in commerce. Between 1976 and 2006, the global trade volume of fish quadrupled, from 7.9 to 31 million tons.[99] An increasing world population, improving diet, changes in Western eating patterns, the emerging middle class in China, Japanese passion for seafood, and improved freezing techniques—all account for the explosion in demand and have helped to internationalize what was once a regional market. But this success is not without its risks: 75% of straddling and high seas fish stocks are overexploited, or even depleted.[100] Some common species such as tuna and cod have now become endangered in many of their habitats.

Fishing is also a crucial geopolitical issue. The prices that Asian gourmets are willing to pay for some rare fish, as with Bering crab in the West, promote illegal, unregulated, and unreported (IUU) fishing, and aggressive behavior between competing fishing vessels. Furthermore, fishing is not only profitable, but an industry that provides jobs. This is essential for countries like Norway or Japan, where the protection of jobs is a critical component of public policy. Several skirmishes between fishing vessels, albeit largely innocuous, have degenerated into open diplomatic spats, even within the European Union—between France and Spain, for instance—or in nearby countries such as Norway and Iceland. The risks of conflict are even higher in Asia, where Japanese, Chinese, and South Korean ships are willing to take huge risks to bring back large catches.[101] International governance of the industry is thus key to avoiding an escalation of tensions. International law and the numerous existing fisheries agreements must take both soft and hard security issues into account, combine the interests of coastal states with those of new players in the market, and make decisions using information on fish stocks that is sometimes incomplete or disputed.[102]

Climate change also alters the situation and introduces new uncertainties. Fish stocks can *a priori* adapt to climate change as well as to some degree of pollution, but the transformation of marine ecosystems means that they will move farther north with warmer waters, into new areas where bilateral regulations no longer apply. In addition, melting ice could open up new areas to unregulated fishing. At present, the Arctic's share in global fisheries has been stable at 4% between 1975 and 2006, equaling 3.5 million tons per year.[103] But these figures may increase. Cod in the Barents Sea and pollock in the Russian Far East represent roughly 25% of the global catch of whitefish. Moreover, krill represent a valuable resource for the chemical and pharmaceutical sectors, which are growing worldwide, especially in Asia.

Russia is striving to become again a fishing power. The Russian coastline is the world's second longest after Indonesia, and the country's exclusive economic zone (EEZ) covers an area of 7.6 million square kilometers, including access to 12 seas and three oceans. Due to the importance of its exclusive economic zone, the Soviet Union was a major player in the world fishing industry. From the 1950s, the USSR sought to develop industrial fishing to compensate for the deficiencies of its animal husbandry sector. The catch totaled 10.3 million tons in 1975, putting Russia in second place overall behind Japan. In the 1990s, however, the Russian fisheries collapsed; the fleets were divided up and partially privatized. It was not until 2010 that Russian catches matched 1991 levels; with a catch of 4.1 million tons, Russia today ranks sixth in the world.[104] This amounts to only 4–5% of the total world catch, but does not include fish caught illegally. The Russian Federal Fisheries Agency (*Rosrybolovstvo*) hopes that the catch will rise to 4.7 million tons in 2014.[105] Three-quarters of the fish caught are from within the territorial, internal, and EEZ waters of Russia; the EEZs of foreign states account for only 15% (and the high seas 10%) of the reported catch.[106] In contrast with the Soviet period, when trawlers could be found as far afield as Africa and Latin America, Russian industrial fishing is today largely limited to its national waters, as the trawlers are too old and fuel-inefficient to sail the high seas. Pressures on stocks in the Russian EEZ have therefore increased to dangerous levels.[107]

According to current definitions, the Russian marine zone in the Arctic includes several ecosystems, but overall consists of two ecoregions, the Bering and Barents Seas. The geographical distribution of catches breaks down to about 40% in the northeast Atlantic Ocean, mainly in the Barents Sea, and 56% in the northwest Pacific Ocean, mostly in the Bering and Okhotsk Seas. The most important unloading ports in the Pacific are Vladivostok and Nakhodka, followed by Nevel'sk, Korsakov, Magadan, and Petropavlovsk-Kamchatskii; in the Atlantic region they include Murmansk, Arkhangel'sk, and Belomorsk.[108]

In the Barents Sea, Russian fishing is regulated by the Russian-Norwegian Fisheries Commission, created to replace the Northeast Atlantic Fisheries Convention, and by the Grey Zone Agreement, which was replaced by the 2010 bilateral treaty. Russian-Norwegian cooperation is considered to be successful in terms of the reasonable management of Atlantic cod stocks and Norwegian spring-spawning herring. Quotas are evenly split between the two countries and both exchange extensive scientific information, make their stocks public, and even grant access to Barents Sea fisheries to some non-coastal states.[109] Moscow and Oslo also adhere to annual quotas as recommended by the International Council for the Exploration of the Sea.[110] On account of the above, the cod stocks of the two countries are considered among the healthiest on the planet; although illegal fishing is also practiced, especially on the Russian side.[111]

Cooperation has also been successful in resolving once-frequent tensions between the two countries. In 1998, 2001, 2005, and 2007, the Norwegian Coast Guard seized Russian trawlers fishing illegally in the Fisheries Protection Zone off the Svalbard archipelago. All of these incidents were resolved peacefully, although in 2001, Moscow responded to the seizure of the trawler *Chernigov* in contested waters by deploying the *Severomorsk* warship. In 2005, the Russian trawler *Elektron* refused to be subjected to arrest when apprehended by the Norwegian Coast Guard and "kidnapped" coast guard personnel by forcing them into Russian waters.[112]

These localized tensions have never degenerated into conflict. Some problems remain unresolved, however, as evidenced by protests against the territorial treaty that Moscow and Oslo signed in 2010. The two main Russian fisheries associations, the Association of Seafood Industries, Entrepreneurs, and Exporters and the Council of Fishing Industry Workers, argued that the treaty undermines rights guaranteed by the Russian-Norwegian Fisheries Commission and forbids them from fishing in waters that were once common but now belong to Norway (the western part of the former Loophole).[113] But this view is not unanimous: the Russian Federal Fisheries Agency stated, on the contrary, that the bilateral agreement and the continuation of the joint Fisheries Commission evidenced support for Russia's fishing interests.[114] It is likely that tensions between Russian and Norwegian fishing vessels will not disappear in coming years, but the mechanisms of peaceful resolution are operational and cooperation prevails on both sides.

In the Bering Sea, the tensions are more numerous and could escalate more rapidly, as there are fewer mechanisms of peaceful resolution. Despite the absence of a definitive legal resolution, fishing is not a cause of major tensions between Russia and the United States. The two countries claim ownership of 92% of the Bering Sea within their territorial waters and EEZs. The remaining part, the Central Bering Sea, is known as "the Donut Hole," and is considered international waters,[115] much like the "Peanut Hole" in the Sea of Okhotsk. An agreement signed in 1992 concerning the regulation of fisheries in high seas beyond their respective EEZs enables both countries to take advantage of the sea's fish stocks.

Fishing in the Bering Sea, one of the most dangerous seas in the world because of its unpredictable weather, is extremely profitable. On the U.S. side, the commercial fisheries catch is worth approximately $1 billion annually, while Russian Bering Sea catches are worth approximately $600 million each year.[116] The Bering Sea is also significant in terms of the geopolitics of fishing. Over half of the seafood consumed in the United States comes from the Bering Sea, and American fishermen are sometimes tempted to leave U.S. waters to monitor the crab stocks in Russian waters;[117] for Russian fishermen, on their part, command over Asian markets is very enticing. A veritable black market of Alaskan pollock and Bering crab, among other species, exists, which encompasses the Russian Far East, Japan, South Korea, and China. It is estimated that illegal fishing and poaching accounts for over half of the fish caught in the Russian part of the Bering Sea.[118]

From food self-sufficiency to industrial revival and export possibilities, issues related to fishing are of central importance. Like other Europeans, Russians are consuming more fish, but most of it is imported. Whereas populations on or close to the Pacific Ocean have some access to local catches from Russian trawlers, the European zones of the country mainly eat exported fish products that have been deep-frozen. Revitalizing national fisheries could therefore help increase food self-sufficiency and reduce imports. The export market to Asia is also very promising, as it is growing exponentially and could bring considerable revenues for Russian fishermen. For now, Moscow is selling raw materials to Chinese processing plants, which then sell the finished product in Korea or Japan. The development prospects of domestic agribusiness are therefore significant, especially in the Far East. Finally, the fishing industry directly employs over 100,000 people and likely around one million indirectly, a blessing that the Kremlin wants to preserve, especially given the clout of the fishing lobbies in the Far East and Kamchatka Peninsula.[119]

Despite the potential, the Russian fishing fleet is in urgent need of an overhaul. In the 1990s, state investment in the fisheries collapsed, exacting a heavy toll. The size of the Russian fleet plummeted by half: today it includes only 2,500 fishing vessels, 50 floating processing plants, and nearly 400 transport ships.[120] Two-thirds of fishing vessels still in operation no longer conform to safety standards and have exceeded their legal lifespan. They lack the capacity to fish off the coast in high seas and do not possess modern catching and freezing equipment. The privatized fishing companies, which buy their vessels abroad, do not have the finances to renew their trawler fleets, whereas the state-run fleets are used to having their needs met through state subsidies. According to the director of the Russian Federal Fisheries Agency, 62 Norwegian vessels are able to take as many fish as 400 Russian ones.[121] For Moscow, the modernization of an aging fleet is no longer on the agenda; the goal is a completely new fleet. But here again, the necessary investments have been slow to arrive. The first steps were taken in 2010, when shipyards were officially ordered to build vessels equipped with modern technology, but thus far only a few units have been commissioned.[122]

Major legislative activity is also a work in progress. The State Committee for Fisheries, allegedly very corrupt, has undergone several administrative restructurings, but with little success. In 2003, the Duma ratified a concept for the development of the fishing industry of the Russian Federation until 2020, and in 2004, the fisheries administration was recentralized. In 2007, the State Committee for Fisheries was restored as a specific (unaffiliated) institution and placed under the direct control of the central government, rather than the Ministry of Agriculture.[123] And in 2008, fish and seafood were included in the list of "strategic resources." Laws were also amended in 2010; hitherto, Russian ships were asked to follow customs procedures for fish caught in the Russian EEZ, which had the effect of forcing trawlers to unload at sea or in ports in Europe.[124] In any event, Russian trawlers continue to try to sell their catches abroad, for higher prices. The issue of overfishing in the Russian EEZ also has to be addressed. Beginning in 2011, there has been open discussion about creating a state fishing corporation tasked with centrally managing the overhaul of the fleet and processing plants.[125] A bill to promote aquaculture is also being studied.[126] An amnesty on trawlers built or repaired outside of Russia, which hitherto were obliged to pay significant taxes upon entering Russian territorial waters, is also to be decided. There is thus much room for improvement in the domestic fishing industry, but this demands clear political and financial choices by the central government.

Russia's position with respect to Arctic economic opportunities has two dimensions. Cooperation with foreign countries is in Moscow's interest, but the fear of losing sovereignty is often perceived as offsetting any of the advantages accrued. Nevertheless, the prospect of profitability in joint economic pursuits does tip the scale in favor of international cooperation. Russian oil and gas fields cannot be developed by Gazprom and Rosneft alone: technological needs, for instance in LNG, require the participation of foreign players, as seen on the Yamal Peninsula. Russian firms have great expertise when it comes to onshore fields, but not so much offshore, and are therefore obliged to acquire foreign technologies, which is precisely what is happening in Sakhalin, for example. Russian private actors such as Novatek are more innovative, accept the need to take risks, and are open to international cooperation. The cooperative pattern also recurs in other economic sectors. For fisheries, the modernization of the fleet cannot be achieved without the purchase of technology from abroad. Despite regular tensions among trawlers, Moscow has developed constructive joint-fishery relations with Norway and the United States. Only the domain of mineral extraction has remained immune from a large-scale foreign presence, and remains among Russia's most opaque economic sectors.

Russia's Arctic economic prospects are paradoxical. They presuppose a favorable combination of elements over which Moscow does not have leverage—changes in the world hydrocarbon market, unexpected energy competition from new technologies or unconventional resources, world prices for minerals, laws protecting endangered fish stocks, and the level of demand in Europe and Asia—and domestic capabilities that were largely destroyed or rolled back in the 1990s. For the oil and gas industries as well as in mineral extraction and fishing, existing infrastructure must be upgraded and new operations developed. Maintaining Soviet infrastructure at the same time as creating new logistics for the twenty-first century dramatically increases the costs. Falling behind rising powers such as China and India, and also lagging in the acquisition of new technological knowledge, Russia's great power status depends on its increased ability to exploit the riches of the Arctic. A widespread impression among Russian ruling elites is that there is "no other choice" for Russia's future but to pursue such an Arctic policy. The country hopes nonetheless that new technologies such as oil fracking can save the day. This would in fact make it possible to postpone Arctic investments and to continue to live on the Soviet legacy of infrastructure investment in more temperate West Siberia, thereby avoiding the difficult choice between resource nationalism and international cooperation.

Notes

1. A. Oreshenkov, "Arctic Square of Opportunities," *Russia in Global Affairs*, December 25, 2010, http://eng.globalaffairs.ru/number/Arctic-Square-of-Opportunities-15085 (accessed January 6, 2013).

2. Speech of President Medvedev at a meeting of the Russian Security Council

on Russia's National Interests in the Arctic, Moscow, September 17, 2008, http://eng.kremlin.ru/text/speeches/2008/09/17/1945_type82912type82913_206564.shtml (accessed January 6, 2013).

3. "Osnovy gosudarstvennoi politiki Rossiiskoi Federatsii v Arktike na period do 2020 g. i dal'neishuiu perspektivu [Fundamentals of state policy of the Russian Federation in the Arctic for the period to 2020 and longer-term prospects]," *Sovet bezopasnosti Rossiiskoi Federatsii*, September 2008, http://www.scrf.gov.ru/documents/98.html.4 (accessed January 6, 2013).

4. R. Halpern, "'Above-Ground' Issues Affecting Energy Development in the Arctic," *ITA Occasional Paper,* August 2007, 5.

5. K.J. Bird, R. Charpentier, D.L. Gautier, D.W. Houseknecht, T.R. Klett, J.K. Pitman, T.E. Moore, C.J. Schrenk, M.E. Tennyson, and C.J. Wandrey, *Circum-Arctic Resource Appraisal: Estimates of Undiscovered Oil and Gas North of the Arctic Circle.* Reston: U.S. Geological Survey, Fact Sheet 2008-3049, 2008, 1, http://pubs.usgs.gov/fs/2008/3049 (accessed January 6, 2013).

6. P.F. Johnston, "Arctic Energy Resources and Global Energy Security," *Journal of Military and Strategic Studies* 12, no. 2 (2010): 1–20.

7. K. Offerdal, "High North Energy. Myths and Realities," in S. Holtsmark and B.S. Smith-Windsor, eds., *Security Prospects in the High North: Geostrategic Thaw or Freeze?* (Rome: NATO Defense College, 2009), 151–178. See also D.L. Gautier, K.J. Bird, R. Charpentier, A. Grantz, D.W. Houseknecht, T.R. Klett, T.E. Moore et al., "Assessment of Undiscovered Oil and Gas in the Arctic," *Science* 324, no. 5931 (2009): 1175–1179.

8. Yu. Morozov, "The Arctic: The Next 'Hot Spot' of International Relations or a Region of Cooperation?" Carnegie U.S. Global Engagement Program, December 16, 2009, http://www.carnegiecouncil.org/resources/articles_papers_reports/0039.html (accessed January 6, 2013).

9. P. Stevens, "The 'Shale Gas Revolution': Hype and Reality," *Chatham House Report,* September 2010, http://www.chathamhouse.org/sites/default/files/public/Research/Energy,%20Environment%20and%20Development/r_0910stevens.pdf (accessed January 6, 2013).

10. International Energy Agency, *World Energy Outlook 2008,* 2008219, http://www.iea.org/textbase/nppdf/free/2008/weo2008.pdf (accessed January 6, 2013).

11. International Energy Agency, *World Energy Outlook 2012*.

12. G. Little, "How Would the Development of Shale Gas Resources in Ukraine Impact Europe's (energy) Security?" in *Energy and the Environment: Conventional and Unconventional Solutions.* Proceedings of the 29th USAEE/IAEE North American Conference, Calgary, Canada, October 14–16, 2010.

13. "Russia Increasingly Worried about US 'Shale Revolution'," *Russia Today,* October 24, 2012, http://rt.com/business/news/russia-shale-gas-usa-110/ (accessed January 6, 2013).

14. B. Westenhaus, "New Fracking Technology to Bring Huge Supplies of Oil and Gas to the Market," *Oilprice.com,* January 16, 2012, http://oilprice.com/Energy/Natural-Gas/New-Fracking-Technology-To-Bring-Huge-Supplies-Of-Oil-And-Gas-To-The-Market.html (accessed January 6, 2013). I thank Robert Orttung for bringing this aspect to my attention.

15. Gautier et al., "Assessment of Undiscovered Oil and Gas in the Arctic," 1178. *Science* 324, no. 5931 (2009): 1175–1179.

16. S.M. Yenikeyeff and T. Fenton Krysiek, "The Battle for the Next Energy Fron-

tier: The Russian Polar Expedition and the Future of Arctic Hydrocarbons," *Oxford Energy Comment,* August 2007, 2.

17. P. Baev and D. Trenin, *The Arctic. A View from Russia, 2010* (Washington, DC: Carnegie Endowment for International Peace, 2010), 21–24.

18. "Development of Offshore Oil and Gas Reserves on the Arctic Shelf," *Bellona,* no date, http://www.bellona.org/reports/report/1197342150.13 (accessed January 6, 2013).

19. P. Baev, *Russia's Race for the Arctic and the New Geopolitics of the North Pole* (Washington, DC: The Jamestown Foundation, October 2007), 6.

20. International Energy Agency, "Russia," http://www.eia.gov/countries/cab. cfm?fips=RS (accessed January 6, 2013).

21. Russia's proven oil reserves are estimated at 74 billion barrels, which amounts to 20 years' worth of reserves and 5.6% of global reserves, while Saudi reserves total 264 billion barrels. See *BP Statistical Review of World Energy* (London: BP, June 2010), 6.

22. "Rosneft Helps Russia's Oil Output to Post-Soviet High," *Reuters,* November 2, 2012, http://www.reuters.com/article/2012/11/02/us-russia-oil-idUSBRE-8A109E20121102 (accessed January 6, 2013).

23. International Energy Agency, "Russia," http://www.eia.gov/countries/cab. cfm?fips=RS (accessed January 6, 2013). For a similar sobering assessment of the challenges of developing more remote fields in the Arctic, East Siberia, and Far East, see T. Gustafson, *Wheel of Fortune: The Battle for Oil and Power in Russia* (Cambridge, MA: The Belknap Press of Harvard University Press, 2012), 449–479.

24. Proekt "General'naia skhema razvitiia neftianoi otrasli Rossiiskoi Federatsii na period do 2020 g. [General outline of the development of the oil sector of the Russian Federation until 2020]," website of the Prime Minister, October 28, 2010, http:// premier.gov.ru/events/news/12784/ (accessed January 6, 2013).

25. Information provided by Adnan Vatansever, "Russia's Energy Strategy Abroad," lecture at the Institute for European, Russian, and Eurasian Studies, George Washington University, Washington, DC, March 24, 2011.

26. *BP Statistical Review of World Energy 2010,* 22. The figures vary depending on the source; those of the International Energy Agency are not the same as BP's.

27. "United States to Overtake Russia as Top Gas producer: IEA," *Alarabiya,* June 5, 2012, http://english.alarabiya.net/articles/2012/06/05/218675.html (accessed January 6, 2013).

28. "Russian 2012 Gas Exports to Fall 5 Percent Says Minister," *RIA Novosti,* November 20, 2012, http://en.rian.ru/business/20121120/177607931.html (accessed January 6, 2013).

29. "Russia to Invest over $400bln in Gas sector by 2030," *RIA Novosti,* October 11, 2010, http://en.rian.ru/business/20101011/160915781.html (accessed January 6, 2013).

30. A. Aslund, "Gazprom: Challenged Giant in Need of Reform," in A. Aslund, S. Guriev, and A. Kuchins, eds., *Russia after the Global Economic Crisis* (Washington, DC: Peterson Institute for International Economics, 2020), 153.

31. For more on Gazprom's strategies, see J.P. Stern, *The Future of Russian Gas and Gazprom* (Oxford: Oxford University Press, 2005).

32. More in A. Bambulyak and B. Frantzen, *Oil Transport from the Russian Part of the Barents Region* (Svanvik: Svanhold Environmental Center, 2005).

33. "Zapolyarnoye Becomes Most Productive Field in Russia—130 Billion Cubic Meters per Year," Gazprom, January 15, 2013, http://www.gazprom.com/press/news/2013/january/article154079/ (accessed January 6, 2013).

34. Yamal Megaproject, http://www.gazprom.com/about/production/projects/mega-yamal/ (accessed January 6, 2013).

35. Speech by Minister of Industry and Energy Viktor Khristenko in the State Duma, February 14, 2007.

36. See Gazprom, "Bovanenkovo," http://www.gazprom.com/about/production/projects/deposits/bm/ (accessed January 6, 2013).

37. See Europol Gaz s.a., http://www.europolgaz.com.pl/english/gazociag_zakres.htm (accessed January 6, 2013).

38. I. Øverland, "Russia's Arctic Energy Policy," International Journal, Autumn 2010, 873–876.

39. "Oil Resources on Russia's Euro-Arctic Shelf," Bellona, no date, http://www.bellona.org/reports/report/1197333526.49 (accessed January 6, 2013).

40. See details on the Shtokman website at http://www.shtokman.ru/project/ (accessed January 6, 2013).

41. "Facts 2008—The Norwegian Petroleum Sector," Norwegian Petroleum Directorate, 2008, http://www.npd.no/en/Publications/Facts/Facts-2008/ (accessed January 6, 2013).

42. "Rossiia zastolbit Arktiku [Russia 'columnizes' the Arctic]," Vzgliad, September 17, 2008.

43. "Russia's Lukoil May Join Bashneft to develop Giant Trebs, Titov Oilfields," RIA Novosti, March 15, 2011, http://en.rian.ru/business/20110315/163015542.html (accessed January 6, 2013).

44. "Oil and Gas Raw Material Base on Russia's Arctic Shelf," Bellona, no date, http://www.bellona.org/reports/report/1197291722.54 (accessed January 6, 2013).

45. T. Carlisle, "Russia's Rosneft to be BP's Largest Shareholder," The National, January 16, 2011, http://www.thenational.ae/business/energy/russias-rosneft-to-be-bps-largest-shareholder (accessed January 6, 2013).

46. N. Dobronravin, "Maritime Issues in Russian Energy Politics," Centrum Balticum, 2010, http://www.centrumbalticum.org/files/408/Dobronravin_www.pdf (accessed January 6, 2013).

47. See "Kompleksnyi plan deistvii po realizatsii Strategii izucheniia i osvoeniia neftegazovogo potentsiala kontinental'nogo shelfa Rossiiskoi Federatsii na period do 2020 [Integrated plan of action on realization of a strategy for exploring and developing the oil and gas potential of the continental shelf of the Russian Federation until 2020]," Ministry of Natural Resources and Ecology, http://www.mnr.gov.ru/part/?act=more&id=646&pid=45 (accessed January 6, 2013).

48. R. Kefferpütz, "On Thin Ice? (Mis)interpreting Russian Policy in the High North, CEPS Policy Brief, no. 205 (February 2010), 4.

49. OffshoreTechnology.com, "Prirazlomnoye Oilfield—Russian Federation," http://www.offshore-technology.com/projects/Prirazlomnoye (accessed January 6, 2013).

50. N.J. Watson, "The Money Gap," Petroleum Economist, January 1, 2006, www.petroleum-economist.com/Article/2733074/The-money-gap.html (accessed January 6, 2013).

51. N. Skorlygina, "Sergei Bogdanchikov nyrvul na zolotoe dno [Sergei Bogdanchikov dove for the golden bottom]," Kommersant, April 21, 2008, http://www.kommersant.ru/Doc/885039 (accessed January 6, 2013).

52. International Energy Agency, "Russia," September 18, 2012 http://www.eia.gov/countries/cab.cfm?fips=RS (accessed January 6, 2013).

53. W. Konończuk, "The East Siberia/Pacific Ocean (ESPO) Oil Pipeline: A Strategic Project—An Organisational Failure?" *Center for Eastern Studies Commentaries*, no. 12, 2008.

54. International Energy Agency, "Russia."

55. A. Barnes, "Russian-Chinese Oil Relations: Dominance or Negotiation?" *PONARS Eurasia Policy Memo*, no. 124, 2010.

56. L. Solanko, and P. Sutela, "Too Much or Too Little Russian Gas to Europe?" *Eurasian Geography and Economics* 50, no. 1 (2009): 58–74.

57. More details in *AMAP Oil and Gas Arctic 2007* (fifth AMAP State of the Arctic Environment Report), May 1, 2008, http://www.amap.no/workdocs/index.cfm?dirsub=%2FOGA%20Overview%20Report&sort=default (accessed January 6, 2013).

58. K.N. Casper, "Oil and Gas Development in the Arctic: Softening of Ice Demands, Hardening of International Law," *Natural Resources Journal* 49 (2009): 825–881.

59. "Calls for Immediate Arctic Oil Drilling Moratorium Grow," *WWF*, July 14, 2010, http://www.wwf.org.uk/wwf_articles.cfm?unewsid=4071 (accessed January 6, 2013).

60. Yu. P. Trutnev, "O povyshenii effektivnosti osvoeniia uglevodorodnykh resursov kontinental'nogo shelfa Rossiiskoi Federatsii [On increasing the effectiveness of the development of hydrocarbon resources of the continental shelf of the Russian Federation]," *Geoinform.ru*, http://www.geoinform.ru/?an=trutnev_ru (accessed January 6, 2013).

61. A. Moe and L. Rowe, "Petroleum Activity in the Russian Barents Sea. Constraints and Options for Norwegian Offshore and Shipping Companies," *Fridtjof Nansen Institute Report*, no. 7 (2008): 7–8.

62. I thank Clifford Gaddy for sharing this information with me.

63. B. Aris, "BP-Rosneft Hailed," *The Telegraph*, November 27, 2012, http://www.telegraph.co.uk/sponsored/russianow/business/9706001/bp-rosneft-deal-hailed.html (accessed January 6, 2013).

64. Today, ExxonMobil, ONGC (Indian Oil and Natural Gas Corporation), and Rosneft affiliates operate Sakhalin-1 (Chayvo, Odoptu, and Arkutun-Dagi fields), while Shell, Mitsui, a Mitsubishi subsidiary, and Gazprom work on Sakhalin-2 (Piltun-Astokhskoe oil field and the Lunskoe natural gas field). The Sakhalin-1 project involves the construction of a 220-kilometer pipeline across the Tatar Strait to the De-Kastri oil terminal, whereas Sakhalin-2 includes the first LNG plant in Russia; both are crucial for Moscow's capacities to reach East Asian markets. For details, see M. Bradshaw, "A New Energy Age in Pacific Russia: Lessons from the Sakhalin Oil and Gas Projects," *Eurasian Geography and Economics* 51, no. 3 (2010): 330–359.

65. C. Locatelli and S. Rossiaud, "Russia's Gas and Oil Policy: the Emerging Organizational and Institutional Framework for Regulating Access to Hydrocarbon Resources," *International Association for Energy Economics*, no. 1 (2011): 23.

66. A. Myers Jaffe, *The Changing Role of National Oil Companies in International Energy Markets* (Houston: James A. Baker III Institute for Public Policy of Rice University, April 2007); P. Johnston, *The Energy Security Impact of Oil Nationalization* (Ottawa: Canadian Centre for Operational Research and Analysis, October 2009).

67. The exploration phase may indeed prove to be of interest to foreign companies

if there is the prospect of obtaining a license if the results are positive. Moe and Rowe, "Petroleum Activity in the Russian Barents Sea," 5.

68. P. Hanson, "Russian Energy Policy and the Global Crisis," *Energy Economist*, no. 336 (2009): 5–7.

69. J.R. Heath, "Strategic Protectionism? National Security and Foreign Investment in the Russian Federation," *George Washington International Law Review* 41 (2009): 101–138.

70. A. Moe and E. Wilson Rowe, "Northern Offshore Oil and Gas Resources: Russian Policy Challenges and Approaches," Fridtjof Nansen Institute Working Paper, June 2008, 2, http://www.fni.no/russcasp/WP-Moe%26Wilson.pdf (accessed January 6, 2013).

71. R. Heath, "Strategic Protectionism?"

72. "'Gazprom' i 'Rosneft' mogut do fevral'a poluchit' litsenzii na shel'f [Before February Gazprom and Rosneft can receive licenses to the shelf]," *Arctic-info.ru*, January 18, 2013, http://www.arctic-info.ru/News/Page/-gazprom-i-rosneft_-mogyt-do-fevrala-polycit_licenzii-na-sel_f (accessed January 6, 2013).

73. K. Mel'nikov and A. Gudkov, "Pravitel'stvo priotkroet shel'f [Government slightly opens the shelf]," *Kommersant*, March 1, 2012, http://www.kommersant.ru/doc/1883820 (accessed January 6, 2013).

74. "Lukoil gotov investirovat' v geologorazvedku shel'fa Arktiki 2.7 mlrd dollarov [Lukoil is ready to invest $2.7 billion in geological exploration of the Arctic shelf," *Golos Rossii*, October 25, 2010, http://rus.ruvr.ru/2012_10_25/LUKOJL-gotov-investirovat-v-geologorazvedku-shelfa-Arktiki-2-7-mlrd/ (accessed January 6, 2013).

75. ExxonMobil, *Arctic Leadership*, 2008, http://www.exxonmobil.com/Corporate/files/news_pub_poc_arctic.pdf (accessed January 6, 2013).

76. *BP in the Arctic and Beyond*, no date, http://www.bp.com/liveassets/bp_internet/russia/bp_russia_english/STAGING/local_assets/downloads_pdfs/g/BP_in_Arctic_eng.pdf (accessed January 6, 2013).

77. A. Shiryaevskaya, and S. Bierman, "Total to Buy US$4 Billion Novatek Stake, Enter Yamal Project," *Business Week*, March 3, 2011, http://www.businessweek.com/news/2011-03-03/total-to-buy-4-billion-novatek-stake-enter-yamal-project.html (accessed January 6, 2013).

78. Moe and Rowe, "Petroleum Activity in the Russian Barents Sea," 5.

79. A. Staalesen, "Statoil Exits Shtokman," *Barents Observer*, August 7, 2012, http://barentsobserver.com/en/energy/statoil-exits-shtokman-07–08 (accessed January 6, 2013).

80. Moe and Rowe, "Petroleum Activity in the Russian Barents Sea," 5.

81. L. Harding, "Igor Sechin: Rosneft's Kremlin Hard Man Comes Out of the Shadows," *The Guardian*, October 18, 2012, http://www.guardian.co.uk/business/2012/oct/18/igor-sechin-rosneft-kremlin-hard-man-shadows (accessed January 6, 2013).

82. C. Belton, "Exxon and Rosneft Seal Arctic Deal," *Financial Times*, April 18, 2012, http://www.ft.com/cms/s/0/8b0c869e-8977-11e1-85af-00144feab49a.html#axzz2IItq64RB (accessed January 6, 2013).

83. "Gazprom Comes to North Sea," *Barents Observer*, March 11, 2011, http://www.barentsobserver.com/gazprom-comes-to-north-sea.4896753-16178.html (accessed January 6, 2013).

84. Moe and Wilson Rowe, "Northern Offshore Oil and Gas Resources," 119.

85. M. Shestopalov, "Vektor ustremlenii—Arktika [A vector of aspiration—the Arctic]," *Vozdushno-kosmicheskaia oborona*, no. 6 (2008), 18.

86. G.P. Glasby and Yu. L. Voytekhovsky, "Arctic Russia: Minerals and Mineral Resources," *Geoscientist* 20, no. 8 (2010): 16–21.

87. J.S.P. Loe, *Driving Forces in Russian Arctic Policy* (Pöyry Management Consulting, January 2011), 16.

88. M. Smelror, "Mining in the Arctic," *Arctic Frontiers*, January 25, 2011, 5.

89. See detailed information on the company's website, http://www.nornik.ru/en/investor/fact/ (accessed January 6, 2013).

90. "Murmansk Region," *Kommersant*, no date, http://www.kommersant.com/t-54/r_5/n_398/Murmansk_Region/ (accessed January 6, 2013).

91. I. Khrennikov, "Russia's Norilsk Plans to Invest $370 Million to Double Arctic Shipments," *Bloomberg.com*, June 28, 2011, http://www.bloomberg.com/news/2011–06–28/russia-s-norilsk-plans-to-invest-370-million-to-double-arctic-shipments.html (accessed January 6, 2013).

92. "Rare Earth Elements: Not So Rare, Especially in Mongolia," *EsDalanZurgaa*, July 29, 2011, http://english.esdalanzurgaa.mn/2011/07/29/rare-earth-elements-not-so-rare-especially-in-mongolia/ (accessed January 6, 2013).

93. Marc Humphries, *Rare Earth Elements: The Global Supply Chain* (Washington, DC: Congressional Research Service, 2012), 3.

94. "La Chine et les terres rares: bataille mondiale pour les métaux précieux, [China and the rare earths: The global battle for precious metals]," *La Tribune*, November 10, 2010, http://www.latribune.fr/actualites/economie/international/20101110trib000571640/la-chine-et-les-terres-rares-bataille-mondiale-pour-les-metaux-precieux.html (accessed January 6, 2013).

95. Sergei Smirnov, "Redkie metally i zemli daiut GMK redkii shans [Rare metals and earths will offer the mining and metallurgical industry a rare chance]," *Investkz.com*, no. 3, 2011, http://www.investkz.com/journals/78/863.html (accessed January 6, 2013).

96. J.C.K. Daly, "Mongolia's Rare Earth Reserves Draw Foreign Investor Interest," *Central Asia and Caucasus Analyst*, June 8, 2011, http://cacianalyst.org/?q=node/5572 (accessed January 6, 2013).

97. M. Mongomery, "Russia May Challenge China's Rare Earth Dominance," *Rare Earth Investing News*, March 2, 2011.

98. I. Rubanov, "REM Stakes: A Rare Chance for Russia," *Expert Magazine*, February 7, 2011, http://indrus.in/articles/2011/02/07/rem_stakes_a_rare_chance_for_russia_12134.html (accessed January 6, 2013).

99. F. Asche and M.D. Smith, *Trade and Fisheries: Key Issues for the World Trade* (Geneva: World Trade Organization, Staff Working Paper ERSD-2010-13, 2010), 7.

100. OECD, *Strengthening Regional Fisheries Management Organizations* (Paris: OECD Publishing, 2009), 17.

101. S. Clarke, "Illegal Fishing in the Exclusive Economic Zone of Japan," *MRAG Working Paper*, August 24, 2007, http://www.mrag.co.uk/Documents/IUW_Japan.pdf/ (accessed January 6, 2013); Zou Keyuan, "Implementing the United Nations Convention on the Law of the Sea in East Asia: Issues and Trends," *Singapore Year Book of International Law* (Singapore: National University of Singapore, 2005), 37–53.

102. O. Schram Stokke, ed., *Governing High Seas Fisheries. The Interplay of Global and Regional Regimes* (Oxford: Oxford University Press, 2001).

103. B. Rudloff, "The EU as Fishing Actor in the Arctic. Stocktaking of Institutional Involvement and Exiting Conflicts," *SWP Working Papers*, July 2010, 11.

104. "Russian Fisheries back on Old Heights," *Barents Observer*, March 9, 2011,

http://www.barentsobserver.com/russian-fisheries-back-on-old-heights.4895784–16179.html (accessed January 6, 2013).

105. "Rosrybolovstvo ozhidaet rosta vylova ryby v RF k 2014 na 17 percent, do 4,7 million ton [Russian Federal Fisheries Agency expects growth of the fish catch in the Russian Federation by 17% by 2014, to 4.7 million tons]," *Fish.gov.ru*, March 17, 2011, http://www.fish.gov.ru/DocLib3/%D0%BD%D0%BE%D0%B2%D0%BE%D1%81%D1%82%D1%8C004668.aspx (accessed January 6, 2013).

106. FAO, *National Fishery Sector Overview. The Russian Federation* (Rome: United Nations Food and Agriculture Organization, 2007), 2.

107. A.-K. Jørgensen, "Recent Development in the Russian Fisheries Sector," in E. Wilson Rowe, ed., *Russia and the North* (Ottawa: University of Ottawa Press, 2009), 89.

108. FAO, *National Fishery Sector Overview. The Russian Federation*, 3.

109. O. Schram Stokke, L.G. Anderson, and N. Mirovitskaya, "The Barents Sea Fisheries," in O.R. Young, ed., *The Effectiveness of International Environmental Regimes: Causal Connections and Behavioral Mechanisms* (Cambridge: MIT Press, 1999), 91–154.

110. "Barents Region Set the Bar for Success in Fishing," *Barents Observer*, May 19, 2010, http://barentsobserver.custompublish.com/barents-region-sets-the-bar-for-success-in-fishing.4785234–16149.html (accessed January 6, 2013).

111. WWF, *Analysis of Illegal Fishery for Cod in the Barents Sea* (Moscow: World Wildlife Federation-Russia, 2005).

112. K. Åtland and K. Ven Bruusgaard, "When Security Speech Acts Misfire: Russia and the *Elektron* Incident," *Security Dialogue* 40, no. 3 (2009): 333–353.

113. N. Zhuravleva, "Postepenno nas vydaviat ottuda [Gradually they will expel us from there," *Vzgliad*, October 27, 2010, http://vz.ru/economy/2010/10/27/442890.html (accessed January 6, 2013).

114. "Delimitation Agreement No Threat for Russian Fishermen," *Barents Observer*, November 29, 2010, http://www.barentsobserver.com/delimitation-agreement-no-threat-to-russian-fishermen.4855148–16179.html (accessed January 6, 2013).

115. *Fishery Management Plan for Fish Resources of the Arctic* (Anchorage: North Pacific Fishery Management Council, August 2009).

116. For more details, see *The International Bering Sea Forum*, http://www.beringseaforum.org/issues.html (accessed January 6, 2013).

117. R. Howard, *The Arctic Gold Rush: The New Race for Tomorrow's Natural Resources* (London and New York: Continuum, 2009), 97.

118. A. Vaisman, *Trawling in the Mist: Industrial Fisheries in the Russian Part of the Bering Sea* (Moscow: World Wildlife Federation, 2001).

119. Anonymous discussions at the Far East Branch of the Russian Academy of Sciences, Department of Geography and Natural Resources, Petropavlovsk-Kamchatskii, October 18, 2010.

120. "Rybolovnyi flot RF za 10 let sokratilsia pochti v dva raza [The fishing fleet of the Russian Federation for 10 years has been reduced almost by half]," *Shipbuilding.ru*, July 30, 2002, http://shipbuilding.ru/rus/news/russian/2002/07/30/fish/ (accessed January 6, 2013).

121. "Putin Set on Reviving Domestic Fisheries," *Barents Observer*, April 19, 2010, http://www.barentsobserver.com/putin-set-on-reviving-domestic-fisheries.4774586–16149.html (accessed January 12, 2013).

122. "Rossiia v etom godu nachnet obnovliat' rybolovnyi flot [Russia this year will begin to renovate its fishing fleet]," *Rosbalt*, September 1, 2010, http://www.rosbalt. ru/business/2010/09/01/767677.html (accessed January 6, 2013).

123. Jørgensen, "Recent Development in the Russian Fisheries Sector," 95–99.

124. "Russian Fisheries Back on Old Heights."

125. "Rosrybolovstvo izuchaet vozmozhnost' sozdaniia infrastrukturnoi rybolovnoi korporatsii [The Russian Federal Fisheries Agency studies the possibility of creating a fisheries infrastructure corporation]," *Fish.gov.ru*, March 17, 2011, http://www.fish. gov.ru/DocLib3/%D0%BD%D0%BE%D0%B2%D0%BE%D1%81%D1%82%D1% 8C004667.aspx (accessed January 6, 2013).

126. S. Maksimov, "Akvakul'tura v ozhidaniia zakona [Aquaculture in expectation of a law]," *Fishnews.ru*, March 16, 2011, http://www.fishnews.ru/rubric/zakon-ob-akvakulture/3527 (accessed January 6, 2013).

Chapter 8

Unlocking the Arctic? Shipping Along the Northern Sea Route

The question of sea lanes of communication, that is, maritime routes between ports used either for trade, logistics, or military forces, constitutes an important element of state security and of the global geopolitical (im)balance. American supremacy on the seas is considered a central component of U.S. global security. Control of the main straits of Hormuz, Malacca, Gibraltar, and the Bosporus, of the choke points between the Atlantic, Pacific, and Arctic Oceans, and of the Suez and Panama Canals, makes it possible to exert pressure on certain states and to privilege others. Given that three-quarters of world trade is conducted via the sea, and in light of new factors of instability such as piracy, the oceans have once again become important in international affairs after having been somewhat forgotten at the end of the Cold War.

The prospect of three new sea lanes of communication in the Arctic thus takes on special significance. The Northwest Passage, which runs from the Bering Strait, past the northern Alaskan and Canadian coasts, to the Atlantic between Labrador and Greenland, connects the Atlantic Ocean with the Pacific Ocean without having to go through the Panama Canal to or round Cape Horn. The Northeast Passage, meanwhile, skirts the northern Russian coast, thus linking the Atlantic and Pacific, and obviating the detour via the Suez Canal or the Cape of Good Hope. A third potential sea lane, the so-called Arctic Bridge, directly crosses the middle of the Arctic Ocean, connecting Eurasia with North America. Of these three sea lanes of communication, only the third, a high-latitude one, presents no legal problems, as it crosses mainly international waters that are not subject to the claims of state sovereignty, but it will probably not open for many decades, if ever. The other two routes, although still little used, are topics of more debate. The melting of the icecap is not proceeding as quickly on the Canadian side as on the Russian. Russia will therefore be the first country to be affected by the prospect of ice-free Arctic navigation. Since 2007, its navigation season—that is, not requiring the presence of an icebreaker—has extended to two whole months, at least in theory. In August 2008, both the Northeast and Northwest passages were simultaneously open for the first time in recorded history and this situation is bound to recur with increasing regularity.

Depending on what methods of calculation are used and on trends in climate that are still unknown, forecasts fluctuate considerably with regard to the prospects of navigation in Arctic ice-free waters. Some assert that the Arctic Ocean will be ice-free in summer as early as 2015. Accordingly, Arctic routes may be open to four months of navigation without an icebreaker in the foreseeable future. The eventual disappearance of summer ice could means that parts of the Arctic will face conditions more similar to those that prevail in the Baltic Sea today.[1] However, the majority of forecasts are more cautious. The Arctic Monitoring and Assessment Program (AMAP) foresees, for instance, a summer shipping season along Russia's coasts that will extend from the current 30 days to an estimated 90 to 100 days by 2080. In any case, it will probably still take around 20 years until conditions become suitable for regular transits. Large-scale, year-round transit operations will barely be possible until the ice cover disappears for most of the year, and this does not seem realistic until at least 40 to 60 years from now.[2] However, private shipping companies and many states, coastal or otherwise, are following closely the still-unfolding race for the new Arctic sea lane. For Russia, the stakes are multiplied, as the Northeast Passage is not only a communication lane open to foreign trade but a strategic domestic issue, a key component of the country's regional development.

Sovereignty Issues in the Russian Straits

The legal status of the Arctic passages is based on multiple texts that are subject to diverse interpretations. It depends on the classification of the waters (internal, territorial, adjacent waters, exclusive economic zone, and open sea), the status of the archipelagos crossed, the access points to other seas, the question of whether, historically, these waters were internal ones or were used for international navigation, and so on. In addition to the International Maritime Organization's legislation, the 1982 Law of the Sea Convention (UNCLOS) states that the regulations for straits used for international navigation are subordinate to those of ice-covered areas.[3] Coastal states can thus impose limitations on navigation when ice conditions increase the risks of accidents or of pollution from spills. Both Canada and Russia view these passages as having historically belonged to them, and oppose international opinion, in particular that of the United States, which argues that they are international waters. Whatever the legal status, the passages are open to foreign commercial traffic, but state prerogatives are more significant if they are recognized as national straits. The state has the right to apply "special conditions" in accordance with the extent of ice coverage and particularly in cases of severe weather conditions. Ships must give advanced notification, apply for guidance, and comply with national laws. In the second case, that of international waters, all ships enjoy the right of transit passage without having to ask for the authorization of any specific body; the littoral states can only enforce fishing and environmental regulations, fiscal and anti-smuggling laws, as well as laws designed to ensure the safety of ships at sea.[4]

The Canadian debate with the United States over the Northwest Passage has shaped Canadian public opinion since the 1960s, but the polemic has intensified recently with increased media focus on the Arctic. U.S. vessels and nuclear submarines are used to traveling unannounced through Canadian Arctic waters, but the trip of U.S. icebreaker *Polar Sea* in 1985 resulted in a diplomatic incident. Ottawa regularly makes unilateral declarations of sovereignty over the Northwest Passage, and the Canadian Parliament passed a bill to this effect in 2006.[5] The issue seems above all a symbolic one: relations between the United States and Canada are good, and both are committed to North American continental security and defense in the NATO framework. Moreover, Canadian military presence in the High Arctic waters is possible only thanks to U.S. icebreakers—the last Canadian icebreaker, the *Labrador*, was decommissioned in 1987, but a new one is under construction. Both countries have signed the 1988 Agreement on Arctic Cooperation, which resolves the practical issues but provides no solutions in regard to questions of sovereignty. The importance of the Northwest Passage for Canadian nationhood, and U.S. arguments asserting the right of free circulation in the world's seas, reduce the possibilities of legal compromise.[6]

Russia also must take into account international discontent concerning its definition of the Northeast Passage as an internal strait. In contrast to the Northwest Passage, *Sevmorput'* (the Northern Sea Route, NSR) has predominantly been used only by Russia, an argument that plays in favor of Moscow's claims. Some parts of the route were mentioned since the time of Ivan the Terrible as internal waters and referred in Russia as "bay waters." However, the route was traversed in its entirety for the first time in 1878–1879 by the Swede Otto Nordenskjöld, and then again in 1893 by the Norwegian Fridtjof Nansen. At the start of the twentieth century, the use of icebreakers opened up new possibilities, such as the hydrographic expedition of the Glacial Arctic Ocean in 1905. Traffic on the *Sevmorput'* reached its peak in the Soviet period with commercial navigation becoming a fairly regular occurrence along it in the second half of the 1930s. This was in large part due to Stalin's emphasis on developing the Far North, particularly through Gulag forced labor. The route was also used during the Second World War by Soviet supply ships and armed vessels, and was more extensively developed during the decades of the Cold War with the construction of surveillance stations, missile launching bases, and polar military aerodromes.

The dispute over the legal status of the strait began during the Cold War, in particular in 1965, when the U.S. Coast Guard icebreaker *Northwind* set out to traverse the Vilkitskii Strait between the Kara and Laptev Seas, and continues to this day. Moscow defines the Northern Sea Route as "a historically existing national unified transport route of the Russian Federation in the Arctic,"[7] and therefore considers it to be under its exclusive jurisdiction. Although Russia's Arctic coastline stretches more than 14,000 kilometers across the Barents, White, Kara, Laptev, and East Siberian Seas, the *Sevmorput'* proper is considered to lie between the port of Kara, at the western entry of the Novaya Zemlya straits, and Provideniia Bay, at the southern opening of the Bering Strait, which makes a total length of 5,600 kilometers. The Barents Sea is therefore not a part of the *Sevmorput'* legal regime. The latter includes nearly 60 straits, the main ones being the Vilkitskii, Shokalski, Dmitri Laptev, and Sannikov Straits, running through three archipelagos, Novaya Zemlya, Severnaya Zemlya, and the New Siberian Islands.[8] The legal definition is thus made more complex, as there is not one single shipping channel per se; rather, there are multiple lanes, and the NSR passes through waters of different status: internal, territorial, and adjacent waters, exclusive economic zone, and the open sea. Indeed the course of the route depends upon whether the ship passes close to the coastline or farther out, or chooses to bypass Severnaya Zemlya. In 1978, a Soviet cargo ship escorted by an icebreaker passed north of the New Siberian Islands, in High Arctic seas, confirming that the straits can be avoided when suitable ice conditions prevail. As a result of accumulated pack ice in the straits, the route may also include sea lanes that are situated beyond Russia's 200-nautical mile EEZ, but which Moscow continues to regard as under its jurisdiction.[9]

Russia is also in disagreement with international opinion on the classification of internal and territorial waters.[10] In 1985, the Soviet Union drew a total of more than 400 straight baselines along its Arctic coastline,[11] the majority being situated within the 12 miles of territorial waters from the archipelagos. Waters enclosed by baselines are conventionally assimilated into internal waters without any right of innocent passage for foreign ships, but the 1958 Convention on the Territorial Sea, to which the Soviet Union is a signatory member, stipulates that the right of innocent passage continues to apply to internal waters that were once territorial waters or part of the high seas.[12] The process of "territorializing" the Soviet Arctic waters also led Moscow to decree the White Sea, Kara Sea, and part of the Barents Sea as Soviet internal waters, which it had already done for the Laptev and East Siberian Seas. However, the international community did not validate this decision. No legal text had set a precedent for this definition, and in fact Soviet practice did not enforce sovereignty by requiring ships or planes to request permission to enter this part of the sea or the air space above it.[13]

The first offer to open the Northern Sea Route to international shipping was made by Moscow early in 1967 during the *détente* years, without ever becoming a reality. The offer was repeated in 1987 by Mikhail Gorbachev in his Murmansk speech, and the route was formally opened to foreign use in 1991, just a few months before the collapse of the Soviet Union. The norms for using it were specified in the "Regulations for Navigation on the Seaways of the NSR" (1991), the "Guide for Navigation through the NSR," and the "Regulations for the Design, Equipment, and Supply of Vessels Navigation in the NSR" (1995). Today, Russia has every interest in transforming the *Sevmorput'* into a sea lane that is open to foreign trade. The maintenance of its own Arctic fleet, in particular of the icebreakers, and of port infrastructure is extremely costly, and additional revenues are therefore welcome. The more international navigation grows, the lower the costs will be for intra-Russian trade.

Despite the debates surrounding the legal status of the waters being transited, Russian territorial waters are subject to the right of innocent passage, and the Law of the Sea Convention requires that treatment of foreign vessels be non-discriminatory. Russia is thus legally unable to ask for fees to transit through its Arctic waters, but may establish regulations governing passage of vessels in ice-covered areas, especially in accordance with environmental protection and safety laws (civil liability regulations for damage arising from vessel-source oil pollution). In 2012, the Duma passed a long-awaited "Law on the Northern Sea Route," which stipulates conditions of transit and demands new insurance requirements, under which responsibility for possible environmental damage and pollution is ascribed to ship owners, and which set costly tariffs for assistance and logistical information.[14] These binding rules have been validated by major international insurance companies, but have been refuted by the United States, which deems that acceptance of such would be tantamount to recognizing Russia's sovereignty beyond its territorial waters. These costly services—icebreaker assistance, sailing master services, radio communication, and hydrographic information—are provided by the Marine Operation Headquarters and the Northern Sea Route Administration, which has been based in Arkhangel'sk beginning in 2013. If it widely recognized that coastal states should not be solely financially responsible for costs associated with transit, it seems that thus far only foreign vessels are paying for it, and that Russian ships are exempt, which in legal terms can be regarded as a discriminatory measure.[15] The International Chamber of Commerce has therefore expressed its concerns and recalled that the UNCLOS regime on straits used for international navigation should take precedence over the rights of coastal states.[16]

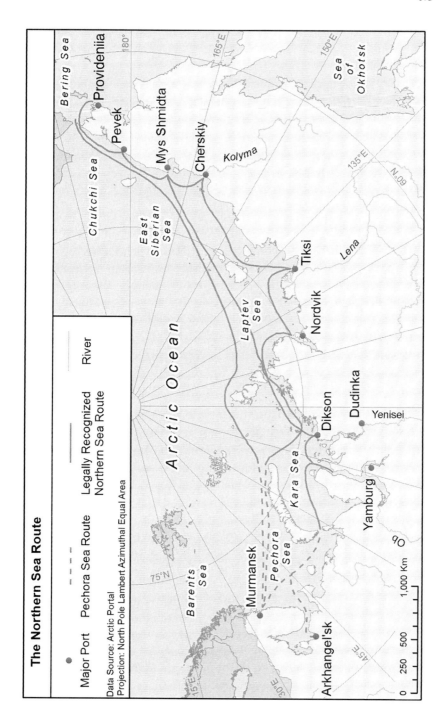

The Northern Sea Route

Major Port   Pechora Sea Route   Legally Recognized Northern Sea Route   River

Data Source: Arctic Portal
Projection: North Pole Lambert Azimuthal Equal Area

Hopes for an International Trade Lane via the Northern Sea Route

The question of opening Arctic trade routes and of their profitability has been studied by several programs, beginning with the International Northern Sea Route Programme (INSROP) in the 1990s,[17] and continuing with the Arctic Operational Platform (ARCOP) and the Japan Northern Sea Route-Geographic Information System (JANSROP-GIS). Numerous feasibility studies, some of which are published, while others are classified, have also been conducted by the main shipping companies. In 2009, the Norway-based Tschudi Shipping Company opened the Centre for High North Logistics, which aims to become the main logistical and informational gateway for NSR use.[18] Shipping along the Northern Sea Route can be either destinational (having an entry or arrival port along the NRS), which means regional or trans-Arctic shipping, or transitory, which means crossing the route from two points not within the NRS. This distinction is important, as it does not include the same categories of ships (transit shipping must involve very large tonnage tankers to be profitable) and invokes different commercial profitability strategies and logistical challenges.

The prospect of a new commercial Europe-Asia trade route is one of the most hyped themes related to the Arctic. On paper an ice-free Arctic could make the transportation of commodities to international markets easier and significantly reduce transportation costs by cutting the distance from Western Europe to Japan or China by 20 to 40%. All Asian cities north of Hong Kong could reach Europe more rapidly via the Arctic than via the Suez Canal. The potential benefits brought about by the opening the Northern Sea Route are therefore of greater interest for Japan, Korea, and China than for India. For instance, the route between Hamburg and Yokohama through the Suez Canal (18,350 kilometers) would be reduced to 11,100 kilometers by using the Northern Sea Route, which in theory reduces the sailing time from 22 to 15 days. The route between Rotterdam and Shanghai, meanwhile, would be reduced from 22,200 kilometers (via the Cape of Good Hope) to 14,000 using the NSR.[19] The volatile situation in the Middle East, especially since the "Arab Spring" of 2011, the overburdening of the Suez Canal, rising tensions in the Strait of Hormuz and, more importantly, growing piracy in the Horn of Africa, all encourage the development of new alternatives.

Transit from Russia to the North American continent would also be made shorter by crossing the Arctic, both eastward along the NSR as well as via a westward route (depending on the destination). Murmansk is only 9,600 kilometers from Vancouver via the Bering Strait, but is 16,000 kilometers via the Panama Canal. In 2007, Russia and Canada both evoked the concept of an "Arctic Bridge" connecting the port of Churchill in Manitoba to Murmansk via Iceland-Greenland.[20] The project had already been mooted some years before; OmniTRAX, a major railroad operator that owns the Churchill port, had been in negotiations with the Murmansk Shipping Company on this issue. In 2007 and 2008, the first shipments of Russian fertilizer from Kaliningrad purchased by the Farmers of North America cooperative in Saskatoon arrived in Churchill from the Kola Peninsula.[21] This possible Arctic bridge has piqued the interest of many shipping companies.

In 1990, six voyages—with an approximate duration of 25 days each— were completed along the NSR. In 1997, only two ships sailed the entire passage, with freight totaling a mere 30,000 tons. The cargoes consisted mainly of fertilizers, metal, and timber exported from Finland and Sweden to Japan, as well as processed agricultural products transported to Europe from China and Thailand. In the second half of the 2000s, with the confirmation of the icecap's retreat, an increasing number of shipping companies tested the viability of the route.[22] The year 2009 proved to be the test year for Europe-Asia transit: two ships from the Germany-based Beluga Shipping sailed from South Korea to Rotterdam and were the first foreign ships able to cross the NSR without using icebreakers.[23] In July 2010, two Russian ice-class tankers carrying 27,000 tons of diesel oil sailed from Murmansk to Pevek.[24] In August of the same year, the state-run shipping company Sovcomflot sent its first shipment of gas condensate on the *Baltica* to Ningbo in China. In September, the Norwegian ship *Nordic Barents*, freighted by Nordic Bulk Carriers and the Tschudi Shipping Company, was the first bulk carrier with a non-Russian flag to use the Northern Sea Route, transporting iron ore to China.[25] These journeys are set to grow rapidly in number. In 2011, a record number of 34 vessels sailed the route, although this was surpassed in 2012 with 46 vessels transporting a total cargo of 1.2 million tons—a 53% increase from 2011, including the first LNG freight, which was sent by Statoil to Japan.[26]

These trade and transit prospects are especially interesting for the Asian nations, which are very dependent upon energy supplies coming through the Hormuz and Malacca straits, and whose trade is mainly directed toward the United States and Europe. Upon the collapse of the Soviet Union, a Japanese team set out to the Arctic and participated in the International Northern Sea Route Programme, a large Russian-Norwegian-Japanese research project conducted between 1993 and 1999.[27] At the time, Tokyo was considering using the NSR to transport its nuclear fuel to reprocessing facilities in Europe, but those plans seem to have been abandoned. Today, growing numbers of Japanese research centers are active participants in international polar stations, and shipping companies are increasingly interested in the possibilities afforded by the NSR. South Korea displays a similar interest. While its Arctic scientific research is less developed than that of China or Japan, its naval construction sector is cutting-edge. In 2007, Samsung Heavy Industries delivered a shuttle tanker weighing 70,000 tons that is able to navigate through Arctic sea and pack ice at a speed of 2.8 knots, a feat that has been recognized as a technological breakthrough.[28] However, the most advanced Asian country is undoubtedly China, whose Arctic strategy is of a larger scale.

Ice Without Hype: The Harsh Realities of Arctic Shipping

Drawing a lane of communication on a map or a globe does not suffice to demonstrate its viability. Developing a new shipping route depends upon a set of complex practical and technical conditions, as well as factors of predictability and existing competing modes of transport. These elements combine to reduce the NRS's prospects of operability and profitability.

Traveling along the NSR poses a number of significant challenges. Firstly, the disappearance of the ice-cap during the summer does not mean that the Arctic Ocean will become ice free in the proper sense of the term. Ice can quickly form in very different locations; there will still be icebergs; and the danger of collision will be considerable. Ice can take ships by surprise and reduce the predictability of the journey. Year-to-year variations in the presence of ice will continue to severely hinder the scheduling of the shipping season and its smooth operation. Climate change is also not likely to make the situation of navigation any easier: the polar night will not disappear, temperatures will continue to be extremely cold, periods of rain and fog will increase, and visibility will be reduced. Hazards linked to winds and waves will intensify. There will also likely be an increase in the frequency of ice storms and in the intensity of spray freezing, as well as coastal erosion as a result of substrates loosened by the thawing of permafrost.[29] Lastly, depending upon the thickness of the ice, ship speed through ice floes will vary between two and five knots, considerably lengthening travel times.

In addition, travel in an extreme climate is expensive. The ice conditions in the straits separating the Severnaya Zemlya archipelago and the New Siberian Islands from the Russian mainland are difficult to negotiate even for icebreakers. Straits tend to accumulate large ice masses that may block the progress of vessels. The ships must travel in convoys that are often subject to long waiting times and immobility. The shallowness of the shelf areas— less than 100 meters in the Kara Sea and about 50 meters in the Laptev and East Siberian Seas—also sets limits on the drafts of ships. In the Sannikov Strait the maximum depth is a mere 13 meters, and the Laptev Strait is even shallower: eight meters.[30] This excludes passage by ships with conventional hulls larger than 20,000 deadweight tons (dwt), and in any case ships cannot be larger than the nuclear-powered icebreakers used to open the route. A large number of the world's container ships are already too large for the Suez or Panama Canal, and the booming trade between China and the West has fueled the development of even larger container ships.[31] As a result of these very specific conditions, shipping companies would have to charter specific ice-class vessels with double hulls and to train teams in operating in circumpolar environments. Technological innovations are emerging in this domain. The Finnish shipbuilders Aker Arctic (formerly Kvaerner Masa-Yards) have designed a new type of dual-purpose vessel that has the same open sea characteristics as other ships in its class, but is combined with the breaking capacity of a powerful icebreaker.[32]

On a strictly financial level, several barriers must also be taken into account and the administrative procedure of transiting the NSR is time-consuming. Russia demands that foreign ships pay fees for chartering icebreakers and for obtaining weather and ice reports, and that they hire two Russian pilots to guide them in the straits and pay for clean-up costs after accidents. The ice-breaking fee depends on ship size (the larger the ship, the lower the per ton tariff), ice class, the route, and the level of support required. In the 2000s, the fee was increased to an average of $23 per ton of cargo in order to maintain and modernize the icebreakers.[33] These expenses are considered too costly by the main international shipping companies. But fees are set based on the current cargo flow, such that should the cargo flow increase to 40 million tons or more per year, the fees could probably fall to around $1 per ton.[34]

Furthermore, the requisite insurance for an Arctic trip puts an added strain on budgets. As in Antarctica, shipping in the Arctic is among the most expensive in the world. Presently, the NSR has no real operational rescue system, the number of ports able to host ships in need of repairs is insufficient, and the risks of collision are considerable, as the lanes of direction are not defined, not even in the Barents Sea, which already sees a fair amount of traffic.[35] Even though vessel fuel efficiency and reduced distances may, on paper, appear to be one of the drivers of NSR development, the route also has major disadvantages, such as its seasonality, its excessive technological costs, and its unpredictability. For world container transit the "just-in-time" issue is an overriding one, while the time required for an Arctic transit can never be guaranteed. This does not encourage shipping companies to develop their own Arctic fleets and to train personnel in circumpolar navigation unless the route can become functional year-round. And even combining a summer route via the NSR with a winter route via the Suez Canal would create planning challenges with respect to the development of the vessel fleet.[36]

In terms of environmental protection, maritime traffic in the Arctic region will increase the likelihood of accidents. In July 2010, two oil tankers belonging to the Murmansk Shipping Company collided along the NSR, fortunately without causing too much damage.[37] But the pollution of sea waters and Arctic coastlines could have an unprecedented impact on already weakened systems. Around 20% of marine pollution originates from ships, drilling platforms, and other maritime installations. The new law "On Management of Radioactive Waste," signed in 2011 after several postponements, puts Russia's national radioactive waste management system into line with the requirements of the Joint Convention on the Safe Management of Spent Nuclear Fuel and on the Safe Management of Radioactive Waste, and is therefore an encouraging sign of the Kremlin's awareness of the risks of carrying nuclear waste into the Arctic environment.[38] Apart from the risks of accidents, it is also necessary to take into account the possibility of invasive species entering the Arctic eco-system, the disturbance of mammal life by the movement and noise created by ships, and an increase in the levels of low-lying ozone, as ship exhausts pump pollutants into the still pristine environment. Growing economic activity in the Arctic thus multiplies the risks of oil spills (during exploration, exploitation, storage, and/or shipping; accidental releases in harbors and terminals; accidents on the major transportation routes), spillages of hazardous waste, radioactive releases associated with shipboard nuclear power plants and nuclear waste storage facilities, accidents at drilling platforms such as fires and explosions, as well as of accidental releases of heavy metals and diverse chemical compounds.[39] Moreover, there are over 12 million empty barrels and fuel containers still remaining in the Russian Arctic, 3% of which are potentially dangerous.[40]

Under these conditions, questions concerning the securitization of navigation are crucial, especially in a region that will have to manage a number of different vessels ranging from icebreakers, tankers, bulk carriers, and tug-barge combinations to fishing vessels, cruise ships, and research vessels. What is more, the Arctic tankers will essentially transport hydrocarbons and minerals, and not manufactured products, so the environmental risk in case of accident is even higher. These issues are being discussed within the International Maritime Organization (IMO), as is the possibility of implementing voluntary guidelines for ships operating in Arctic ice-covered waters, or even the future implementation of a binding Polar Code.[41] In this way, the EU, several non-EU member states, and the International Association of Classification Societies (IACS) have developed non-mandatory Unified Requirements for their members that address ship construction standards for the Polar Classes, which are defined in the IMO Guidelines.[42]

The implementation of strategies of prevention and training for emergency situations in the Arctic is also a core activity of the Emergency Prevention, Preparedness, and Response (EPPR) Group of the Arctic Council. Russia, represented by the Ministry of Emergency Situations (EMERCOM), is particularly active in questions of search and rescue (SAR) systems.[43] Search and rescue capabilities are in place in Murmansk and Arkhangel'sk for the western part of the Arctic, and in Vladivostok and Petropavlovsk-Kamchatskii for the eastern part. The Murmansk Basin Emergency Rescue Service (MBERS) and the company Ekospas-Murmansk are the two agencies in the region responsible for cleaning up after emergency situations involving oil and gas. The international cooperation framework is also well developed. The Barents Rescue Cooperation, for instance, improves the ability of rescue services agencies to coordinate emergency and rescue issues across national borders in the Barents Region.[44] In 2012 Russia and Norway signed an agreement for a mandatory ship reporting system in the Barents Sea, the first International Maritime Organization–approved ship reporting system in the world that does not require verbal communication.[45] MBERS has also been contracted by the Rosmorport company to provide emergency rescue services in the White Sea. In the Bering Sea, regional SAR agreements between the U.S. Coast Guard and Russia's EMERCOM have improved response and coordination. The United States and Russia are also leading regional cooperation on nuclear- and radiation-related emergency management issues.

However, there is a large SAR gap along the central section of the Northern Sea Route in East Siberia, where almost no infrastructure has been set up. If the region's transit of people and commodities is lower than in the western part of the Arctic, the so-called Trans-Arctic Air Corridor, i.e., the Primorye-Kamchatka-Magadan region, is teeming with flights traveling between North America and Asia. Originally introduced in 2001, the number of flights on this route has recorded year-on-year increases of 30% and fly over extremely remote territories. The Eyjafjallajökull Volcano eruption in 2010 suddenly brought to light the importance of this air transit corridor in connecting the Eurasian and North American continents via the North Pole. This major global development therefore requires the establishment of rescue systems in the overflight regions. In order to address this security deficit, 10 new rescue centers in the Arkhangel'sk, Salekhard, Dudinkaka, Tiksi, Pevek, and Anadyr' areas, to be manned on a permanent basis by 150 personnel, and supplied with rescue and fire protection equipment, helicopters, and small boats, are to be created by 2015.[46] Russia also plans to design the next generation of its icebreaker fleet with multi-functional equipment, such as SAR helicopters and equipment for fighting offshore oil rig fires. These systems will be designed to support navigation in the NRS, but also to prepare for emergency situations stemming from air travel over the North Pole.

However, despite these projected improvements, the question remains as to how the 14,000 kilometers of Russian coastline will be monitored and patrolled, especially with the rapid change in nautical conditions as a result of climatic changes. The existing navigation aids, radio stations, and hydro-meteorological services are largely insufficient, and polar aviation brigades are unable, in the current state of affairs, to carry out rescue operations in all parts of the Russian Arctic. A large part of the central section of the Arctic coastline is reportedly not covered by radio, with the result that Moscow is obliged to purchase such information from the United States and Canada.[47] To resolve this, Russia will have to close up the immense accumulated gap in communication technologies, in particular satellite-based ones, and improve observation techniques to allow ship operators to monitor the conditions of sea and pack ice. The authorities plan to create a unified space of communica-tion in the Arctic by 2015 with the installation of Polarnet, a new-generation international telecommunications network consisting of a fiber-optic cable system. The system, also called Russian Trans-Arctic Submarine Cable System, is set up to run from Great Britain to Russia, before splitting for the United States, Japan, and China, respectively.[48]

This communication system can operate only with the aid of satellites. So far Russia's satellite network has 14 stations dedicated to the NSR, but this is viewed as the minimum requirement for route finding through the ice. Four low-orbit satellites and five geo-stationary satellites will be used for the COSPAS-SARSAT system, developed jointly by the United States, Canada, France, and Russia for maritime SAR. Whereas the GPS system is relatively dysfunctional in the Arctic for the moment, its Russian equivalent, GLO-NASS (*Global'naia navigatsionnaia sputnikovaia sistema*), a radio-based satellite navigation system developed in the 1970s, seems more effective. Since 2011 the full orbital constellation of 24 satellites was restored, offering full coverage of the Russian territory.[49] Satellite communications were a core issue of the second international forum, The Arctic–Territory of Dialogue, held in Arkhangel'sk in 2010.[50] The Russian state space agency, Roskosmos, is going to play an important role in managing the launch of several satellites to be committed to monitoring the Arctic region. This is explicitly part of plans drawn up in the Federal Space Program through 2020.[51] Cooperation between Roskosmos and Roshydromet also has increased: A new system, called the Multipurpose Space Systems Arktika, should allow Russia to ac-cumulate all the resources necessary to better monitor emergency situations and climate change in the Arctic. It will comprise three phases: first, radar monitoring; second, hydrometeorological monitoring; and, finally, mobile communications and broadcasting in the Arctic.[52]

A More Realistic Future: *The Sevmorput'* as a Domestic Route

The future of the NSR is clearly linked to destinational shipping. It includes some international shipping, mainly in the Barents Sea between the Nordic countries and Russia (timber has been exported since the 1920s by this route, as are supplies of oil and LNG to Europe today), or in the Bering Sea between Russia, the Asian countries, and the United States. However, it chiefly involves domestic shipping within Russia's regions. Indeed, the NSR constitutes a strategic internal communication route for the country. Although the Trans-Siberian railway delivers the majority of the freight circulating between the European regions, southern Siberia, and the Far East, delivery north of the Trans-Siberian or of the BAM is extremely difficult. Here again, the figures on the paper seem to speak in favor of Arctic transit. The trip between Murmansk and the Bering Strait is 5,600 kilometers along the Arctic coastline, 4,600 via the north of Severnaya Zemlya and the New Siberian and Wrangel Islands, and only 4,300 via the pole itself.[53] However, when it comes to delivering products from European Russia to the Far East, the Trans-Siberian, with a length 6,400 kilometers and only seven days of required travel, remains the quickest and most economical route.

Since Bolshevik times, the Soviet regime considered the NSR to be a key component of its strategies for economic development in the Far North and remote Siberian regions. The opening of shipping routes during the summer season was always presented as a transport priority. Since 1978, the Russian icebreaker fleet has succeeded in keeping open all year round the stretch from Murmansk to Dudinka, on the banks of the Yenisei River. Traffic moving from west to east essentially consisted of liquid fuel and coal, construction materials, and consumer goods (manufactured and food products), while returning ships were laden with timber and minerals. The link between the ocean and remote regions via rivers was conceived as a totally integrated system. In many Arctic ports, cargoes were discharged directly onto the ice in winter and in the river estuaries in the summer. A large number of 3,000-ton river-sea shallow-draught freighters and tankers were used between northern coastal ports and stations located deep in the interior; but the towing of large barges was not a developed practice in the Soviet Union.[54]

Although trans-Arctic shipping did take place during the Soviet period, transport was mainly regionalized and confined to two main routes: between Murmansk or Arkhangel'sk and the Taimyr Peninsula; and between Vladivostok and Chukotka. Between 1950 and 1980, more than 400 ice-strength-ened freighters were used in operations along the NSR on an annual basis.[55] Up until 1987, the state subsidized the *Sevmorput'* to the tune of about $400 million per year, and in the 1980s, yearly traffic accounted for nearly seven million tons. This figure declined dramatically to around 2 million tons in the 1990s.[56] In 1993, with the Russian state experiencing partial bankruptcy, the management of the *Sevmorput'* was handed over to the regions in the name of decentralization, but the latter also found themselves in dire financial straits. As a result, the NSR became seriously jeopardized as costly infrastructure was no longer maintained and security was no longer guaranteed.

By 2000, upon Putin's accession to power, the volume of NSR traffic had dropped to a mere 1.6 million tons, or a quarter of its 1980s' level. This was well below the minimal threshold—4 million tons—ensuring the profitability of the icebreakers.[57] The new president then decided to set up a new centralized service called the Administration of the Northern Sea Route, which comprises part of the Ministry of the Merchant Fleet. It manages the icebreaker services that accompany ships, and the use of nuclear energy in maritime transport. It is also in charge of the prevention and management of environmental accidents, as well as providing navigation aid systems, the monitoring of hydrographic conditions, and access to ports.[58] The modest revival of shipping since 2008 is shown by statistics on freight volumes moving through Russian Arctic ports. The main oil terminals—Arkhangel'sk, Kolguev, Mokhnatkina Pakhta, Murmansk, Ob' Bay, Varandey, Vitino—have undergone expansions and witnessed an increase of oil shipments from approximately 4 million tons of crude in 2002 to 10 million tons in 2008. In 2012, freight volume for all Russian ports (Arctic and non-Arctic) increased 5.9%, reaching 560 million tons. This growth, however, is uneven, and especially within the Arctic: while the port of Arkhangel'sk registered an increase of 20%, those of Murmansk, Vitino, Varandey, and Kandalaksha have all experienced decreases.[59]

The Northern Sea Route Administration has projected that freight volume will increase to 15 million tons by 2015,[60] largely due to domestic transport needs, and mainly on account of increasing oil-related activities but also rising exports of roundwood, lumber, pulp, and paper. Today the traffic is almost exclusively limited to the western section of the Russian Arctic coast, between Murmansk and Dudinka. With the increase in gas production and cooperation between Norway and Russia, the Barents Sea—which is not legally part of the NSR—is bound to become the most dynamic part of the Russian Arctic and the most congested with ships and vessels. Even moderate forecasts predict that transportation of oil from Russian ports on the Barents Sea could increase by 50% by 2020.[61] The West Kara Sea is also experiencing an increase in oil traffic from the West Siberian fields bound for Northern Europe, and the exploitation of the South Kara Sea deposits by Rosneft will likely accelerate this trend. Since 2000, small tankers have transported gradually increasing volumes of oil from the new Varandey terminal on the Pechora coast. Timber exports, ores, and processed metals are also shipped from the Yenisei River port of Dudinka via the Kara Sea.[62] Once the deposits of the South Kara Sea are under exploitation, and the Yamal Peninsula starts production of LNG, domestic freight could grow, up to 50 million tons by 2020.[63]

The eastern part of the Russian Arctic sees much less traffic—albeit with some notable, one-time exceptions: in 2004, several tens of thousands of tons of pipes destined for a Gazprom gas pipeline were transported by sea to Chukotka.[64] Around 60% of the incoming freight passing through the port of Igarka and ports on the Kolyma River comes directly by sea, while the rest moves at least in part along the Lena River.[65] The potential exploitation of new mineral deposits in East Siberia could revive some of the traffic, as the sites will require heavy construction materials that are easier to transport by sea. Moreover, Russian firms do not pay, or pay lower fees than foreign companies when using the services of the Marine Operation Headquarters and the Northern Sea Route Administration, or when requiring use of port infrastructure. This division of the Arctic navigation into West and East is reflected in administration of supporting services. Two private shipping companies act as Marine Operation Headquarters: the Murmansk Shipping Company, which has its operations headquarters at Dikson, is in charge of the western part; while the Far East Shipping Company (FESCO), headquartered at Pevek, is responsible for the eastern section.[66]

Modernizing the Fleet and the Shipyard Sector

At the start of the 1970s, the Soviet Union had 138 ice-class freighters in the Arctic Basin, with an aggregate deadweight of nearly 500,000 tons. At the end of the Soviet period, their number approached 350, added to which were 16 icebreakers, 8 of which were nuclear powered.[67] The first nuclear-powered icebreaker, the *Lenin*, entered into service in 1960. The other nuclear icebreakers were built at the Baltic factory in Leningrad from 1974. Their flagship, the *Arktika*, ensures year-round navigation between Murmansk and Dudinka and extends the shipping season in other Arctic regions. Shallow-draft icebreakers were also introduced to operate in rivers and their estuaries. The 1990s were harsh years devoid of finances, which witnessed the virtual dismantling of the ice breaker shipbuilding industry. From the time the atomic icebreaker *Yamal* joined the fleet in 1993, it was a full 14 years before the next such vessel, the *Fifty Years of Victory,* was launched in 2007. This hiatus will have consequences. Although Russia still has the world's largest and most powerful icebreaker fleet, it is aging: of the seven nuclear-powered icebreakers constructed in the 1970s and 1980s, all will have to be decommissioned by 2020.

Russian shipbuilders resumed work in the 2000s. The Maritime Doctrine of the Russian Federation to 2020,[68] adopted in 2001, plans the revival of maritime transportation, the development of coastal port infrastructure, and the upgrading of maritime trade and mixed (river-sea) shipping.[69] It is accompanied by another ambitious document entitled the Strategy for the Development of Port Infrastructure by 2030, the program of which is to be implemented by the state-run corporation Rosmorport. Icebreakers are a key priority in ensuring implementation of the doctrine: six nuclear icebreakers, four of the heavy *Arktika* class and two of the shallow-draft *Taimyr* class, are charged with maintaining the NSR. In 2009, Putin approved plans to construct three nuclear-powered icebreakers with a capacity of 60 megawatts (MW) to be ready by 2020, a lead icebreaker with a capacity of 110 MW, as well as seven diesel-electric and four port-supporting icebreakers.[70]

However, given the time required for construction, technological lags, and the financial difficulties, Russia risks finding itself in a transition period, around 2017–2020, in which it will have only one or two operational icebreakers, an insufficient number to ensure the passage of tankers. Moreover, because of the 2008 economic downturn, Russian projects are largely behind schedule. The budget to commission a new icebreaker for active service in 2016 was received from the Ministry of Transport only in 2011.[71] In addition, to ensure year-round shipping along the polar route, Moscow needs third-generation icebreakers that are more powerful and meet the expectations of large energy companies. The Russian nuclear fleet is managed by Atomflot, the control of which was transferred from the Ministry of Transport to the State Atomic Energy Corporation Rosatom, which is itself in charge of supplying the nuclear fuel needed for the fleet. The Iceberg Central Design Office is the leading designer of icebreakers and ice-ready ships, including those propelled by nuclear power.[72] However, it is not only icebreakers that are in need of renewal, but also the Russian fleet of hydrographic ships, three-quarters of which have been in operation for over 25 years.[73]

Despite the state orders, the main actors in today's market for Arctic ships are corporations.[74] The metallurgical holding company Noril'sk Nickel, the gas corporation Gazprom, the oil enterprises Rosneft, Lukoil, and Novatek, and the two maritime companies, the Murmansk Shipping Company and the Far East Shipping Company are the main clients of the shipping industry. Because domestic shipbuilding capabilities declined dramatically during the 1990s, the Russian merchant fleet has been obliged to order 95% of its new ships from abroad and only 5% from Russian companies.[75] The market that has been lost by the domestic shipyards is thus immense—orders placed abroad amount to about $1 billion—and with it has also come the loss of knowledge; Russian yards need double the time and double the money compared to other countries to build similar ships. Many of their specialized engineers have gone to work abroad, as the shipyard market is largely international.[76]

In order to exploit the resources of the continental shelf of both the Arctic and the Caspian Sea, Russian companies claim that they will need 55 extraction platforms, floating or submarine edifices, 85 transport ships, and 140 auxiliary ships by 2030.[77] Perhaps not surprisingly, the main naval shipyards have developed a keen interest in diversifying their orders to capture some of the market for ice-ready commercial vessels. Today they are largely run according to market principles rather than by military-strategic considerations. As a sign of this change, these shipyards now fall under the Ministry of Commerce and Economic Development, and not the Ministry of Defense. The shipbuilding sector is expected to double production by 2015–2020, with civilian vessels accounting for at least one-third of total output.[78]

At the end of the 1990s, Lukoil availed itself of a new fleet of 10 ice-class oil tankers, each with a capacity of 15,000 to 20,000 tons. These tankers, which were used for the transport of crude oil, belonged to Lukoil's subsidiary, Arctic Tankers. Some were resold in the 2000s to enable purchase of the *Varandey* multi-purpose icebreaker, built by Keppel Singmarine (Singapore).[79] Since 2009 it has been deployed near the stationary sea ice–strengthened shipping platform of the Varandey terminal, ensuring safe operations during tanker loading.[80] Another terminal close to Murmansk will be able to accommodate tankers of 250,000 deadweight tonnages, onto which will be loaded the crude arriving in ice-class ships. Lukoil has also acquired majority control in the capital of the Northern Shipping Company based in Arkhangel'sk, and 51% of the shares of the Murmansk Shipping Company. The Lukoil fleet is intended to ensure the continuous year-round export of the company's oil production from the Timan-Pechora district. Today Lukoil is the main operator in the Arctic Basin, with around 200 vessels of different types.[81]

Noril'sk Nickel is itself on the verge of becoming a key actor in Arctic shipping. Since 2004 it has been building a fleet of ice-breaking cargo vessels, rendering it almost independent of icebreaker assistance. The firm concluded a contract with Finnish shipbuilder Aker Yards to develop and build 14,500-ton container ships of up to 400 TEU (twenty-foot equivalent units) capacity designed for year-round operations. The first was delivered from Finland in 2006, and four more have been being built at Aker dockyards in Germany. All are equipped with AZIPOD double-action propelling units:

each ship is independently capable of plowing stern-first through 1.5-meter thick Arctic ice at speeds of up to three knots.[82] Noril'sk Nickel therefore has an operational fleet of five icebreaking carriers capable of operating autonomously through the winter season to serve Dudinka. In 2009, the company received an exemption from the law that ensures carriers comply with Russian customs regulations, which include customs duty payments, customs support, and fixed transport routes.[83] It now transports about one million tons of goods, mainly metal products and nickel matte, as well as gas condensate from the Petlyatkin field on the Taimyr Peninsula. Also in 2009, Norilsk Nickel opened a logistics office in Rotterdam to serve the company's cargo transport interests between Dudinka and Europe.[84]

The Murmansk Shipping Company, the world's only owner of civilian nuclear-powered vessels, has sold some of its ice-class ships and since then has been supplied from abroad. For a long time it was in charge of servicing Dudinka for Noril'sk Nickel, at a time when the mining combine was without its own fleet. It also transports apatites from Kandalaksha, on the Kola Peninsula, and it services the oil terminals of Varandey, Kolguev, the Ob' estuary, and Yakutia-Sakha. At present it has about 20 ships able to transport up to 460,000 tons, and six tankers with a total capacity of 340,000 tons.[85] The Far East Shipping Company, the country's largest private intermodal transportation group, also owns icebreakers, but these are not nuclear-powered. Every year FESCO icebreakers patrol the Eastern Arctic and provide services to over 600 vessels, which deliver about two million tons of cargo. It mainly serves the ports of Chukotka and Yakutia-Sakha and has an active fleet of about 80 ships.[86] Both companies should be able to make use of a new generation of nuclear-powered ships of 60,000 kW around 2015.[87]

For its part, Gazprom is in need of more than 50 ships and floating storage facilities to exploit the Arctic shelf. It has launched plans for a large-scale construction program of 20 LNG tankers to transport production from Shtokman.[88] As a state-run corporation, it has been decided that Gazprom carriers should be built at Russian shipyards, even though it could be done more inexpensively at foreign shipyards. In any case many of the parts and materials for the vessels, from pipes to paint, will still have to be imported. In 2009, Gazprom concluded an agreement with St. Petersburg's Northern Shipyard on the production of LNG carriers and signed an agreement with Sovcomflot for shipping services. A new generation of Arctic class tanker, the *Mikhail Ul'yanov*, is scheduled to start serving the Prirazlomnoye field. Gazflot, Gazprom's offshore exploration subsidiary, is also in need of drilling capacity and geological and geophysical ships. In 1995, it ordered an Arctic platform to be built in Severodvinsk—set to play a key role in the development of Arctic offshore resources—as well as the Prirazlomnoye one, but the completion of both platforms had been delayed several times and incurred additional costs. They finally were delivered in 2011.[89]

The state-run company Sovcomflot, one of Russia's largest infrastructure companies—25% of whose shares the state plans to privatize—operates a fleet of about 150 vessels with a total deadweight exceeding ten million tons. It is the largest operator of Arctic shuttle tankers and ice-class natural gas carriers, and already has a dozen ice-class 1A tankers.[90] It has commissioned its third 70,000 dwt dual-purpose tanker for use along the NSR. It specializes in the transport of crude oil to Europe, the use of floating storage facilities, and the delivery of drilling rigs and production platforms using specialized vessels. In 2011, Novatek, Russia's largest independent gas producer and second-largest natural gas producer overall, signed an agreement with Atomflot to secure reliable supply routes for the delivery of materials and the technological infrastructure necessary to construct its surface facilities and LNG plant on the Yamal Peninsula.[91]

To meet these pressing needs, in 2007 Moscow launched a "Development Strategy for the Naval Industry for 2020," and in 2008, a "Federal Targeted Program in the Development of Civilian Marine Engineering."[92] The government has planned investments of more than $5.5 billion for the development of shipyards between 2010 and 2015.[93] Alongside aviation and space, nautical activities are one of the three priority areas the Kremlin has identified in order to revive its domestic industry; Russian ambitions have been slow to become reality, however. The hope is to transform the shipyards into a competitive industry by 2016 and, in addition to exports, to be able to respond to a large share of domestic needs. If the scheduled year of 2016 seems highly optimistic, a revival is nonetheless under way in the main shipyards. Putin's recentralization strategies have yielded a new holding, the state-run Unified Shipbuilding Corporation (OSK), combining the Northern Center for Shipbuilding and Ship Repairs—that is, Russia's two main shipyards, Sevmash and Zvezdochka, both based in Severodvinsk—as well as smaller yards and associated production companies; the Western Center for Shipbuilding in Saint Petersburg, which includes the Admiralty yards, several smaller yards, and part of the Northern Yard (*Severnaya verf'*); Far East Shipbuilding and the Rubin Central Design Bureau for Marine Engineering; and the firm Iceberg, which is in charge of designing new Arctic vessels.[94] Although state-run, the Unified Shipbuilding Corporation has clashed many times with the Ministry of Defense over the building of the submarine *Aleksandr Nevski*.[95]

Despite the massive state recentralization process, three of the most important yards are still privately owned: the Vyborg Shipyard and, in part, the Northern Yard and the Baltic Factory (*Baltiiskii zavod*) in St. Petersburg. Their owners are all close associates of Putin's inner circle, and the policies they pursue remain in total consonance with the Kremlin's choices. The Vyborg shipbuilding company, which has very close ties to Gazprom, specializes in building small- and medium-tonnage vessels and offshore drilling rigs. It has experience in semi-submersible floating drilling and production platforms, and plans to build stationary production platforms and deep sea jack-ups.[96] The Northern Yard and the Baltic Factory, both created in Tsarist times, are owned by the private investment company United Industrial Corporation (OPK), which also has majority share in Iceberg. Both are specialized in large nuclear vessels, such as the *Fifty Years of Victory*, and have recently built two diesel-electric icebreakers, including the *Moskva*, which has been commissioned by Rosmorport. They are also in charge of constructing four Orlan nuclear cruisers and are expecting orders for large tankers.[97]

The OPK's ambitious aim is to set up a modern and compact world-class shipyard by merging the existing facilities of the Northern Yard and the Baltic Factory. This will be done by revamping and re-equipping the existing facilities and building new ones, which will mean that OPK is able to produce the full gamut of ships of up to 300,000 tons in deadweight, something it would like to do in partnership with the South Korean company Daewoo Shipbuilding and Marine Engineering (DSME).[98] Specializing in small coastal vessels, the new site could theoretically build 30 corvettes, 30 frigates, 66 escort squadrons, and 30 auxiliary vessels by 2020. The challenge of this new shipbuilding project is immense, and there are conflicting interests between private and public actors; indeed, competition between both yards has long been headline news.[99] Construction of post-Soviet Russia's first floating nuclear power plant, which began at Sevmash but was transferred to the Baltic facility, was initiated at the end of 2009. It is the first of eight floating nuclear power plants to be built, and will be delivered to Viliuchinsk in Kamchatka.[100]

The St. Petersburg- and Vyborg-based yards may play a central role in projects involving foreign clients, although the technological level of the Severodvinsk yards was higher in Soviet times, and Sevmash is still Russia's largest submarine yard. Today Sevmash and Zvezdochka are in charge of building Borey-class submarines: the *Aleksandr Nevski*, which was moved to Sevmash's floating dock at the end of 2010, and the forthcoming *Vladimir Monomakh*. Zvezdochka has also built a series of carrier vessels for the shallow waters of the Barents Sea, the White Sea, and the Sea of Azov. Russia's border guard service has additionally commissioned a series of small patrol vessels for coastal surveillance.[101] Both yards also deal with repairs to atomic cruisers such as the *Admiral Rakhimov* and nuclear submarines such as the *Pantera*. Several ships and submarines decommissioned from the Russian army are used at Sevmash in cooperative programs with the United

States and NATO.[102] To cope with the collapse of domestic military demand, since 1997 both yards have initiated cooperation with the Indian Ministry of Defense, which ordered the modernization and transformation of a cruiser/ aircraft carrier and several Soviet diesel-electric submarines. But it has had to deal with multiple delays, surplus costs, and technological issues. The Indian Navy recommissioned a diesel-electric submarine, the *Sindhuvidjay*, in 2008,[103] but had to wait until 2012 to receive the cruiser/aircraft carrier, the former *Admiral Gorshkov*, renamed the *Vikramaditya*.[104] In 2003, Zvez-dochka won the right to independently conduct business operations abroad. Using its status, it sold over $30 million worth of military spare parts to foreign companies in 2009, mainly in India and China.[105]

Since the 1990s, when military orders dropped by 95%, Sevmash and Zvezdochka have been forced to diversify their output. In 2005, 33% of Sev-mash orders came from the Ministry of Defense, 30% from the oil industry, and 25% from foreign companies. In terms of production for civilian use, the building of trawlers, tug boats, and various types of passenger vessels makes up an increasingly important part of their portfolio. Nonetheless, several of their projects have been either partly or completely unsuccessful—these have included the so-called "Arctic Platform," an 85,000-ton ice-resistant oil platform intended for the Prirazlomnoye field, and the aborted contract with Norwegian Dan Odfjell for a series of 12 chemical tankers, Sevmash's largest civilian contract.[106] Sevmash has nonetheless succeeded in renovating cruise ships such as the *Alushta*; transforming a submarine into a museum; and building a fish factory for the American company Sea Wing; several piers for the Swedish company Promar; and floating docks, barges, yachts, and frigates. The shipyard is also involved in the construction of several types of platforms planned for the Pechora Sea or the Shtokman site. Together with Noril'sk' Nickel, it has explored the possibility of converting Typhoon submarines for the purpose of transporting nickel from Dudinka to Mur-mansk. It also collaborates with foreign companies such as Conoco, Total, and Halliburton, and is involved in extraction activities at the Ardalin and Khariagin deposits in the Nenets autonomous district. Finally, it provides pipelines to several national companies, such as Transneft, several Lukoil subsidiaries, Surgutneftegaz, and Yuganneftegaz.[107]

Zvezdochka is more advanced in its civilian conversion and has even retrained its staff in activities (e.g., the processing of precious stones) that are totally unrelated to its primary expertise. It has also managed to penetrate the civilian seafaring market. Since the early 1990s, it has won tenders from Dutch companies like Swets Shipping and Trading, has received orders for a series of tugboats from Damen Shipyards, and now works closely with Finnish and Norwegian companies. It has built metal elements destined for

Statoil, Kvaerner Oil and Gas, and Aker Solutions, and has expanded its partnership with Moss Maritime, a Norwegian leader in maritime technology. Domestically, Zvezdochka works with major Russian energy companies and is also part of the Union of Producers of Oil and Gas Equipment. The plant is also well known for its construction of 50010 trawlers, considered the best in their class in terms of Russian-built vessels. Zvezdochka's strategy seems to be paying off—orders for 2011 were 71% higher than for the previous year, and it maintains nearly 300 vessels at the plant.[108]

Despite the shipyard industry revival throughout the 2000s, Russian companies have found it difficult to be competitive in a now widely globalized market, in which Nordic countries, as well as some Asian ones such as South Korea or China, control a large part of the production. Russian firms will therefore have to create their own specific niches of excellence, which in all likelihood will be linked to Arctic shipping or dual-purpose ships, if they want to remain market players.

The idea that Arctic shipping might come to replace or rival the main commercial sea lanes has produced a lot of hype, fueled by epics from the history of navigation. Private firms involved in the "shipping race" have set themselves far more limited goals. Their interest in Arctic shipping lies largely in its potential either as an area of research and innovation, whose repercussions for the industry will go far beyond Arctic transit, or as a specific commercial niche that, albeit limited in size, satisfies precisely identified market needs. If the ice does not melt as expected, the Arctic route will be too difficult to use and therefore not viable commercially. But even if the Arctic becomes an ice-free ocean, the technological challenges, the financial cost, and unpredictability do not guarantee its transformation into a major trading route. Its geographical location between Europe, America, and Asia-Pacific does not, in and of itself, suffice to impact market-based principles; shipping companies presently prefer their tankers to traverse more southerly seas rather than risk Arctic transit. Only catastrophist scenarios forecasting unprecedented destabilization of the Middle East, disturbance in the traffic of the Suez Canal or the Hormuz Strait, an epidemic of piracy, or blockages in the Indian Ocean and the Malacca Strait could force shipping companies to suddenly turn toward the Arctic.

Barring such events, it is likely that the NSR will never be a world-class international transit lane and will remain a destinational one, of interest only to certain sectors of world trade. The actors that will specialize in Arctic traffic will chiefly be Asian companies as China, Japan, and South Korea seek to become less dependent upon the southern straits and diversify their supplies, even at a higher cost. Their concerns are thus more geopolitical than purely commercial. Other actors include German and Nordic companies, which are targeting destinational transit to and from Russia. The transported goods on the NSR will mostly consist of hydrocarbons, minerals, and wood, the exploitation of which are booming, but not manufactured goods such as textiles or (less still) appliances of any kind.

For Russia, the stakes are of an entirely different nature: the NSR is above all a domestic route, and a driving part of its strategies devised for developing the Siberian regions. Climate change or not, Moscow hopes to revive the Arctic Route, and is in theory ready to pay the price to overcome the necessary technological challenges. Destinational traffic is indeed bound to play a growing role in the energy-based revival of the Arctic regions. It could even render the use of the main rivers less costly, making it possible to more effectively supply some Siberian populations. Moscow would also like to recover its know-how in the shipyard industries, as well as its human capital: Russian engineers, who are well trained, have largely gone abroad chasing more attractive salaries, and the generation gap is immense. Russian companies, both public and private, all of which are linked to the gas and oil sector with the exception of Noril'sk Nickel, will play a driving role in the future of Arctic shipping. The NSR will therefore be used for ends that are more commercial than military, and become one of the main venues of cooperation between the public and private sectors, and between foreign and national actors. Although the NSR is highly unlikely to become a very busy trade route, the high potential for accidents, the fragile ecosystems, and the increasingly international character of shipping will force Moscow to emphasize soft security issues alongside growing international cooperation, the latter mainly focused on search and rescue systems.

Notes

1. "Arctic Shipping 2030: From Russia with Oil, Stormy Passage, or Arctic Great Game?" (Oslo: *ECON Report* no. 2007–070, 2007), 11.

2. C.L. Ragner, "The Northern Sea Route," in T. Hallberg, ed., *Barents—ett gränsland i Norden* [Barents—a borderland of the Nordic countries] (Stockholm: Arena Norden, 2008), 127.

3. K. Bartenstein, "The 'Arctic Exception' in the Law of the Sea Convention: A Contribution to Safer Navigation in the Northwest Passage?" *Ocean Development & International Law* 42, no. 1–2 (2011): 22–52.

4. W.E. Butler, *The Northeast Arctic Passage* (Alphen aan den Rijn: Sijthoff & Noordhoof International Publishers, 1978).

5. M. Carnaghan and A. Goody, "Canadian Arctic Sovereignty," text submitted to the Canadian Parliament, January 26, 2006, http://www.parl.gc.ca/Content/LOP/researchpublications/prb0561-e.htm (accessed May 26, 2012).

6. E. Elliot-Meisel, "Politics, Pride, and Precedent: The United States and Canada in the Northwest Passage," *Ocean Development & International Law* 40, no. 2 (2009): 204–232.

7. "Law on the Internal Sea Waters, Territorial Sea, and Adjacent Zone of the Russian Federation," July 31, 1998, http://www.un.org/depts/los/LEGISLA-TIONANDTREATIES/PDFFILES/RUS_1998_Act_TS.pdf (accessed January 9, 2013).

8. Listed in W. Dunlap, *Transit Passage in the Russian Arctic Straights* (Durham: International Boundaries Research Unit, University of Durham, 2002), 26–34.

9. Ibid.

10. O.R. Young, *Arctic Politics. Conflict and Cooperation in the Circumpolar North* (Hanover, London: Dartmouth College, 1992), 162. See also W. E. Butler, "Soviet Maritime Jurisdiction in the Arctic," *Polar Record*, no. 16 (1972): 418–421; and A.L. Kolodkin and M.E. Volosov, "The Legal Regime of the Soviet Arctic: Major Issues," *Marine Policy*, no. 14 (1990): 163–167.

11. W. Ostreng, *The Soviet Union in Arctic Waters* (Honolulu: Law of the Sea Institute, 1987), 35.

12. "Convention on the Territorial Sea and the Contiguous Zone," signed in Geneva on April 29, 1958, entered into force on September 10, 1964, http://untreaty.un.org/ilc/texts/instruments/english/conventions/8_1_1958_territorial_sea.pdf (accessed January 9, 2013).

13. B.R. Posen, "The U.S. Military Response to Soviet Naval Developments in the High North," in J. Svarre, and K. Nyblom, eds., *The Military Buildup in the High North: American and Nordic Perspectives* (Lanham: University Press of America, 1986), 46.

14. "Zakon 'O vnesenii izmenenii v otdel'nye zakonodatel'nye akty RF v chasti gosudarstvennogo regulirovaniia torgovogo moreplavaniia v akvatorii Severnogo morskogo puti' [Law 'On the inclusion of changes in separate legislative acts of the Russian Federation in part of the state regulation of commercial navigation in the waters of the Northern Sea Route']," July 28, 2012, published in *Rossiiskaia gazeta*, July 30, 2012, http://www.rg.ru/2012/07/30/more-dok.html (accessed January 9, 2013).

15. I.V. Stepanov and P. Ørebech, *Legal Implications for the Russian Northern Sea Route and Westward in the Barents Sea* (Oslo: Fridtjof Nansens Institute, 2005), 10.

16. International Chamber of Shipping, "Position Paper on Arctic Shipping," 2012, http://www.ics-shipping.org/ICS%20Position%20Paper%20on%20Arctic%20Shipping.pdf (accessed January 9, 2013).

17. W. Østreng, ed., *The Natural and Societal Challenges of the Northern Sea Route. A Reference Work* (Dordrecht: Kluwer Academic, 1999).

18. See the website of the Center for High North Logistics, http://www.chnl.no (accessed January 9, 2013).

19. *North Meets North. Navigation and the Future of the Arctic* (Reykjavik: Iceland Ministry for Foreign Affairs Working Group, 2005), 9 and 21.

20. Yu. Evdokimov, Yu. Batskikh, and A.V. Istomin, "Severnyi morskoi put': problem, vozmozhnosti, perspektivy vozrozhdeniia [The Northern Sea Route: Problems, possibilities, and prospects for revival]," *Ekonomicheskaia nauka sovremennoi Rossii*, no. 2 (2000): 101–112.

21. "Port Of Churchill Welcomes First-Ever Ship From Russia," *OmniTRAX*, October 17, 2007, http://www.omnitrax.com/media-center/news/07–10–17/port-of-churchill-welcomes-first-ever-ship-from-russia.aspx (accessed January 9, 2013).

22. H. Schøyen and S. Bråthen, "Bulk Shipping via the Northern Sea Route versus via the Suez Canal: Who will gain from a Shorter Transport Route? An Explorative Case Study." Paper presented at the 12th World Conference on Transportation Research (WCTR), July 11–15, 2010, Lisbon, Portugal.

23. "Trailblazer Beluga," *TradeWinds*, September 5, 2008, 18, http://www.beluga-group.com/uploads/media/2008_09_08_TradeWinds_Trailblazer.pdf (accessed January 9, 2013).

24. "SCF Baltica Arrives in Pevek—the First Stage of the Arctic Voyage is Over," *Sovcomflot*, August 25, 2010, http://www.scf-group.com/npage.aspx?did=71730 (accessed January 9, 2013).

25. "Historic Sea Route Opens through the Arctic to China," *Marine News*, February 27, 2010, http://marine-news.net/Historic_sea_route_opens_through_the_Arctic_to_China-i18448.html.

26. T. Pettersen, "46 vessels through Northern Sea Route," *Barents Observer*, November 23, 2012, http://barentsobserver.com/en/arctic/2012/11/46-vessels-through-northern-sea-route-23–11 (accessed January 9, 2013).

27. For the main findings of the program see C.L. Ragner, ed., *The 21st Century—Turning Point for the Northern Sea Route?* (Oslo: Kluwer Academic Publishers, 2000).

28. "Arctic Shuttle Tanker," Samsung website, http://www.shi.samsung.co.kr/Eng/product/ship_prd01.aspx (accessed January 9, 2013).

29. Roshydromet, *Strategic Prediction for the Period up to 2010–2015 of Climate Change Expected in Russia and its Impacts on the Sectors of the Russian National Economy* (Moscow: Roshydromet, 2006), 20–22.

30. Miaojia Liu, and J. Kronbak, "The Potential Economic Viability of Using the Northern Sea Route (NSR) as an Alternative Route between Asia and Europe," *Journal of Transport Geography* 18, no. 3 (2010): 441.

31. *North Meets North. Navigation and the Future of the Arctic*, 26–27.

32. See the Aker Arctic website, http://www.akerarctic.fi/ships.htm (accessed January 9, 2013).

33. Liu and Kronbak, "The Potential Economic Viability of Using the Northern Sea Route (NSR) as an Alternative Route between Asia and Europe," 440.

34. Arctic Council, *Arctic Marine Shipping Assessment 2009 Report* (Akureyri: Arctic Council, 2009), 117.

35. Information provided by Captain Stephen M. Carmel, from Maersk Line, CSIS Arctic Working Group, Washington, DC, March 8, 2011.

36. V.C. Khon, I.I. Mokhov, M. Latif, V.A. Semenov, and W. Park, "Perspectives of Northern Sea Route and Northwest Passage in the Twenty-First Century," *Climatic Change* 100, no. 3–4 (2010): 757–768.

37. "Tankers Collide in the Northeast Passage," *Siku News*, July 19, 2010, http://www.sikunews.com/News/Russia/Tankers-collide-in-the-Northeast-Passage-7829 (accessed January 9, 2013).

38. "Russian Radioactive Waste Law Signed," *World Nuclear News*, July 15, 2011, http://www.world-nuclear-news.org/newsarticle.aspx?id=30417.

39. See Emergency Prevention, Preparedness and Response Working Group (EPPR) http://eppr.arctic-council.org/ (accessed January 9, 2013).

40. International Conference on "Prevention and Elimination of Emergency Situations in the Arctic," Anadyr, Russia, August 19–20, 2009.

41. "Working Towards a Mandatory Polar Code," *ASOC Briefing*, October 20, 2010, http://www.asoc.org/storage/documents/IMO/ASOC_Polar_Code_Briefing_October_2010.pdf (accessed January 9, 2013).

42. See the International Association of Classification Societies,http://www.iacs.org.uk/publications/publications.aspx?pageid=4&sectionid=3 (accessed January 9, 2013).

43. S. Steinicke and S. Albrecht, "Search and Rescue in the Arctic," *SWP Policy Papers,* no. 5, 2012, http://www.swp-berlin.org/fileadmin/contents/products/arbeits-papiere/WP_FG2_2012_Steinicke_Albrecht.pdf (accessed January 9, 2013).

44. "The Barents Sea's Emergency Rescue Organizations," *Bellona,* http://www.bellona.org/reports/report/1196949957.81 (accessed January 9, 2013).

45. T. Pettersen, "Mandatory Ship Reporting System in the Barents Sea," *Barents Observer,* November 29, 2012, http://barentsobserver.com/en/arctic/2012/11/mandatory-ship-reporting-system-barents-sea-29-11 (accessed January 9, 2013).

46. "Glava MChS nazval kliuchevye zadachi dlia arkticheskikh avariino-spasatel'nykh tsentrov [Head of the MChS named key tasks for Arctic aviation rescue centers]," *Arctic-info.ru,* January 18, 2013, http://www.arctic-info.ru/News/Page/glava-mcs-nazval-klucevie-zadaci-dla-arkticeskih-avariino-spasatel_nih-centrov (accessed January 9, 2013).

47. "Rossiia usilivaet voenno-morskoe prisutstvie v Arktike [Russia strengthens naval presence in the Arctic]," *Natsional'naia bezopasnost',* July 18, 2008, http://nationalsafety.ru/n18964 (accessed January 9, 2013).

48. On Polarnet, see http://polarnetproject.ru (accessed January 9, 2013).

49. S. Shrivastava, "Russian GLONASS an Answer to American GPS?" *The World Reporter,* April 21, 2011, http://www.theworldreporter.com/2011/04/russian-glonass-answer-to-american-gps.html (accessed January 9, 2013).

50. Author's attendance at the Second International Forum, Arkhangel'sk, September 19–21, 2010. See also "NIS GLONASS prezentoval tekhnologii GLONASS na vtorom Mezhdunarodnom Arkticheskom Forume v Arkhangel'sk [GLONASS technology presented at second International Arctic Forum in Arkhangel'sk]," *NIS-Glonass,* September 22, 2011, http://www.nis-glonass.ru/press/news/694 (accessed January 9, 2013).

51. "Gosudarstvennaia programma Rossiiskoi Federatsii 'Kosmicheskaia deiatel'nost' Rossii na 2013–2020 gody' [State Program of the Russian Federation on 'Space Activity of Russia for 2013–2020']," *Roskosmos,* December 28, 2012, http://www.federalspace.ru/main.php?id=24 (accessed January 9, 2013).

52. European Commission, *Space and the Arctic, Joint Communication to the European Parliament and the Council Developing a European Union Policy towards the Arctic Region: Progress since 2008 and Next Steps.* Brussels: European Commission, June 26, 2012, http://eeas.europa.eu/arctic_region/docs/swd_2012_183.pdf (accessed January 9, 2013).

53. A.V. Istomin, "Rol' severnogo morskogo puti v khoziaistvennom razvitii i osvoenii severnykh territorii [The role of the Northern Sea Route in the agricultural development and conquest of northern territories]," *Sever promyshlennyi,* no. 6–7 (2007), http://www.helion-ltd.ru/rolofsevmorput (accessed January 9, 2013).

54. J. Drent, "Commercial Shipping on the Northern Sea Route," *The Northern Mariner/Le Marin du nord* III, no. 2 (1993): 8.

55. W. Ostreng, "Looking Ahead to the Northern Sea Route," *Scandinavian Review* 90, no. 2 (2002): 77.

56. A.V. Istomin, "Rol' severnogo morskogo puti v khoziaistvennom razvitii i osvoenii severnykh territorii. [The role of the Northern Sea Route in the agricultural development of northern territories]," *Sever promyshlennyi,* no. 6–7 (2007).

57. P. Thorez, "La Route maritime du Nord. Les promesses d'une seconde vie [The Northern Sea Route: Promise of a second life]," *Le Courrier des Pays de l'Est,* no. 2 (2008): 58.

58. A.V. Istomin, "Severnyi morskoi put': organizatsionno-ekonomicheskie osnovy vozrozhdenia i razvitiia [The Northern Sea Route: Logistical and economic principles of revival and development]," *Formirovanie osnov sovremennoi strategii prirodopol' zovaniia v evro-arkticheskom regione* [Formation of the foundations for a current strategy of natural resource use in the Euro-Arctic region] (Murmansk: Akademiia nauk, 2005), 471–481.

59. "Gruzooborot arkticheskikh morskikh portov Rossii v 2012 snizilsia na 5,7% [Freight traffic of the Arctic ports of Russia in 2012 fell by 5.7%]," *Arctic-info.ru*, January 15, 2013, http://www.arctic-info.ru/News/Page/gryzooborot-arkticeskih-morskih-portov-rossii-v-2012-gody-snizilsa-na-5–7 (accessed January 9, 2013).

60. T. Mishina, "Bor'ba za Arktiku. Chto dast regionu razvitie severnogo sudokhod-stva [Struggle for the Arctic. What the development of northern shipping will yield]," *Rossiiskaia gazeta*, January 29, 2011, http://www.rg.ru/2011/01/27/reg-dvostok/perevozki.html (accessed January 9, 2013).

61. "Arctic Shipping 2030: From Russia with Oil, Stormy Passage, or Arctic Great Game?" 14.

62. "Varandey Terminal Boosted Profit," *Barents Observer*, June 3, 2010, http://www.barentsobserver.com/varandey-terminal-boosted-profits.4789555–16178.html (accessed January 9, 2013).

63. *North Meets North. Navigation and the Future of the Arctic*, 14.

64. Thorez, "La Route maritime du Nord, " 58.

65. Ragner, "The Northern Sea Route," 14 and 17.

66. Ibid., 120.

67. *Arctic Transportation System of Export of Oil from the North-West Russia* (St. Petersburg: Central Marine Research, 2003), 12.

68. "Maritime Doctrine of Russian Federation to 2020," July 27, 2001, http://www.oceanlaw.org/downloads/arctic/Russian_Maritime_Policy_2020.pdf; Russian version at http://nvo.ng.ru/wars/2001–08–03/4_sea_doctrina.html (accessed January 9, 2013).

69. Ibid.

70. N. Petrakov, "Russia Makes a Step Forward in the Battle for the Arctic," *Russia Today*, July 24, 2009, http://rt.com/politics/press/nezavisimaya/russia-makes-a-step-forward-in-battle-for-the-arctic/en/ (accessed January 9, 2013).

71. "Rosatom v 2011 g. ozhidaet pervogo zakaza na novyi atomnyi ledokol dlia Sevmorputi [In 2011 Rosatom expects the first order for a new atomic icebreaker for the Northern Sea Route]," *Rosatom*, December 6, 2010, http://www.rosatom.ru/wps/wcm/connect/rosatom/rosatomsite/journalist/atomicsphere/7acdcb8044f1c20d882ec a6fd126209c (accessed January 9, 2013).

72. See http://www.iceberg.sp.ru (accessed January 9, 2013).

73. A. Komaritsyn, "Rol' i zadachi voennoi gidrografii v ekonomicheskom osvoenii shel'fa Arkticheskikh morei Rossii [Role and tasks of military hydrography in the economic development of Russia's Arctic shelf]," *Flot.com*, no date, http://flot.com/science/nh1.htm (accessed January 9, 2013).

74. This trend already was evident at the beginning of the 2000s. See *Arctic Transportation System of Export of Oil from the North-West Russia.*

75. "Sudostroitel'nyi kompleks OPK gotov k uchastiiu v gosudarstvenno-chastnom partnerstve [United Industrial Corporation shipbuilding complex ready to participate in state-private partnership]," *Okean Pribor*, May 15, 2008, http://shipbuilding.ru/rus/news/russian/2008/05/15/opk/ (accessed January 9, 2013).

76. "Esli Rossiia ne podgovit kadry, to na osvoenii severnogo shel'fa budut rabotat' aziaty [If Russia does not train personnel, then Asians will work on development of the shelf]," *Regnum*, 12 December 2006, webpage no longer available.

77. Speech by Minister of Industry and Energy Viktor Khristenko in the State Duma, February 14, 2007, "Ob osnovykh napravleniiakh gosudarstvennoi promyshlennoi politiki i ee realizatsiia v sudostroitel'noi otrasli [On basic directions of state industrial policy and its realization in the shipbuilding sector]," *Fishnews.ru*, February 15, 2007, http://www.fishnews.ru/news/1485 (accessed January 9, 2013).

78. Yu. Zaitsev, "Russia Set to Overhaul Its Arctic Fleet," *RIA Novosti*, April 9, 2007, http://en.rian.ru/analysis/20070409/63375060.html (accessed January 9, 2013).

79. "Lukoil's Arctic Fleet Welcomes Ice-Breaker Varandey," *Rustocks*, February 3, 2009, http://www.rustocks.com/index.phtml/pressreleases/1/113/17420?filter=2009 (accessed January 9, 2013).

80. "10 million Tons Shipped from Varandey Oil Terminal," *Barents Observer*, January 26, 2010, http://www.barentsobserver.com/index.php?id=4725304 (accessed January 9, 2013).

81. It possessed a smaller number during the mid-2000s; see A. Bambulyak and B. Frantzen, *Oil Transport from the Russian Part of the Barents Region* (Svanvik: Svanhovd Environmental Centre, 2005), 22.

82. Arctic Council, *Arctic Marine Shipping Assessment 2009 Report*, 82–83.

83. "Norilsk Nickel Completed Creation of Its Own Arctic Fleet," *Nornik*, February 26, 2009, http://www.nornik.ru/en/press/news/2372/ (accessed January 9, 2013).

84. "Busy for Norilsk Nickel's Fleet," *Barents Observer*, January 6, 2010, http://barentsobserver.custompublish.com/busy-for-norilsk-nickels-fleet.4670013–16149.html (accessed January 9, 2013).

85. "Murmanskoe morskoe parokhodstvo [Murmansk marine steamship line]," http://fleet.msco.ru/ (accessed January 9, 2013).

86. FESCO, http://www.fesco.ru/index.html (accessed January 9, 2013).

87. Thorez, "La Route maritime du Nord," 57.

88. "Gazprom: Dlia stroitel'stva arkticheskogo flota u Rossii nedostatochno moshchnostei [Russia has insufficient capacity for construction of the Arctic fleet]," *Rosbalt*, June 24, 2009, http://www.baltinfo.ru/2009/06/24/Dlya-stroitelstva-ark-ticheskogo-flota-u-Rossii-nedostatochno-moschnostei—Gazprom-91342 (accessed January 9, 2013).

89. "Russia: Platform Reaches Prirazlomnoye Field in Pechora Sea," *Offshoreenergytoday.com*, August 29, 2011, http://www.offshoreenergytoday.com/russia-platform-reaches-prirazlomnoye-field-in-pechora-sea/ (accessed January 9, 2013).

90. See the company's website, http://www.sovcomflot.ru/default.aspx?anim=1&ln=RU (accessed January 9, 2013).

91. "Russia: Novatek and Atomflot Sign Cooperation Agreement," *LNG World News*, February 2, 2011, http://www.lngworldnews.com/russia-novatek-and-atomflot-sign-cooperation-agreement/ (accessed January 9, 2013).

92. "Strategiia razvitiia sudostroitel'noi promyshlennosti na period do 2020 g. i na dal'neishuiu perspektivu [Strategy for the development of the shipbuilding industry for the period to 2020 and its future prospects]," Ministry of Industry and Trade, September 7, 2007, http://www.minpromtorg.gov.ru/ministry/programm/5 (accessed January 9, 2013).

93. "Sovcomflot Strategy for 2010–2015 Approved by the Board of Directors," *Sovcomflot*, December 21, 2009, http://www.sovcomflot.ru/npage.aspx?did=57531 (accessed January 9, 2013).

94. A. Moe and L. Rowe, "Petroleum Activity in the Russian Barents Sea. Constraints and Options for Norwegian Offshore and Shipping Companies," *Fridtjof Nansen Institute Report*, no. 7 (2008): 18.

95. A. Kolesnikov, "K borty OSK prishvartovalis 280 milliardov [280 billion tied up in OSK]," *Kommersant*, November 10, 2011, www.kommersant.ru/doc/1812186 (accessed January 9, 2013).

96. See http://vyborgshipyard.ru/en/?p=en_catalog (accessed January 9, 2013).

97. "Sudostroitel'nyi kompleks OPK gotov k uchastiiu v gosudarstvenno-chastnom partnerstve."

98. "Dominanta gosudarstvennogo podkhoda [The fundament of the state approach]," *Arsenal. Voenno-promyslennoe obozrenie*, no. 4, 2008, http://rusarm.com/arhiv/n4_2008/dominanta_gosudarstvennogo_podhoda/ (accessed January 9, 2013).

99. A. Gritskova and E. Kiseleva, "Ot Baltzavoda otchalil gendirektor [The Baltic Factory cast off a general director]," *Kommersant*, no. 191 (4008), October 21, 2008, http://www.kommersant.ru/pda/kommersant.html?id=1044809 (accessed January 9, 2013).

100. "Assembling of Floating Nuclear Power Plant Started," *Barents Observer*, June 19, 2009, http://www.barentsobserver.com/index.php?id=4591370&xxforceredir=1&noredir=1 (accessed January 9, 2013).

101. See Zvezdochka's website, http://www.star.ru/index.php?page=130 (accessed January 9, 2013).

102. See Sevmash website, http://www.sevmash.ru/?id=2857&lg=ru (accessed January 9, 2013).

103. See Sevmash website, http://www.star.ru/index.php?page=133 (accessed January 9, 2013).

104. "Admiral Gorshkov Delivery to India in 2012," *Hindustan Times,* April 21, 2009, http://www.hindustantimes.com/Admiral-Gorshkov-delivery-to-India-in-2012-Russia/Article1-402682.aspx (accessed January 9, 2013).

105. "Tsentr sudoremonta Zvezdochka postavit v 2009 g. inozakazchikam zapchasti dlia remonta voennykh korablei na summu 30 millionov dollarov [Zvezdochka ship repair center in 2009 receives a total of 30 million dollars in foreign orders for the repair of military vessels]," *Korabel.ru*, September 7, 2009, http://www.korabel.ru/news/comments/tsentr_sudoremonta_zvezdochka_postavit_v_2009_godu_inozakazchikam_zapchasti_dlya_remonta_voennih_korabley_na_summu_30_mln_dol.html (accessed January 9, 2013).

106. See Sevmash website, http://www.sevmash.ru/?id=753&lg=ru (accessed January 9, 2013).

107. Ibid.

108. "Huge State Orders for Zvezdochka Shipyard," *Barents Observer*, March 3, 2011, http://www.barentsobserver.com/huge-state-orders-for-zvezdochka-shipyard.4892173–58932.html (accessed January 9, 2013).

Conclusion

As stated by the Canadian explorer and ethnologist of Icelandic descent, Vilhjalmur Stefansson (1879–1962), "there are two kinds of Arctic problems, the imaginary and the real. Of the two, the imaginary are the most real."[1] Indeed, in many various ways, Arctic affairs are marked by statistical hype and utopian hopes, as well as rooted in national imaginaries. However, Arctic affairs do not merely involve the placement of old topics in a new territory. The region, precisely because it is largely uncharted territory, is bound to give rise to innovative solutions, as the classic axioms of international affairs will not always yield satisfactory answers here. This can be seen, for example, in the establishment of the collective search and rescue system, which comprises the first binding, soft security agreement to have been ratified by the Arctic Council, or in the American proposal to create an Arctic Coast Guard Forum.[2]

If, thus far, all the Arctic stakeholders have adhered to and praised the existing legal framework, it is nonetheless likely that in the coming years the need for new regional platforms or new, more binding legislation will arise. The Arctic will present specific challenges that go beyond the current framework of international debate. Some states may decide to bypass the United Nations Convention on the Law of the Sea (UNCLOS) in the event of a failure to effectively delimit the continental shelf; tensions may also arise from non-Arctic actors that wish to have a recognized right to oversee the future of the region; the absence of a framework for discussing the region's security issues could increase the odds of conflicts; and the unpredictability of Arctic resources could pressure both private and public actors to move forward without adequate preparation for the risks entailed. Although these challenges would not seem to involve the hydrocarbon deposits, which essentially fall under national jurisdictions, fishing could become an element of tension, especially with the increasing scarcity of specific species and the still-booming Asian demand.

Though Arctic affairs will probably never lie at the center of international tensions, as do other regions of the world such as the Middle East, they will remain important in terms of regional projections of power. The Arctic is an unrivaled theater for testing notions of soft power or of peaceful leadership. Symbols here are just as important as realities on the ground. Moreover, although they are largely internationalized, Arctic questions are paradoxically shaped by domestic agendas above all else. While it is a minor stake for the United States, the Arctic will remain firmly on the Canadian agenda and could increase in importance as part of the debate over the future of the trans-Atlantic commitment. Europe as a whole, although more oriented toward the Mediterranean Basin and the Eastern Partnership, will probably push for more integration between Arctic and Nordic affairs. For Norway in particular, the Arctic is destined to remain a major element of its identity on the international and regional scenes. It is, however, Russia for which the underlying stake in the Arctic is most vital.

As seen from Moscow, the Arctic is an important piece of Russia's statehood puzzle. The country's quest to regain its superpower status—essentially defined by the recognition accorded by the other stakeholders—will continue to involve the Arctic region: the mere presence of its nuclear arsenal there makes it a key element of the much sought-after parity with Washington. More generally, the Kremlin hopes for a positive outcome from its role in regional bodies such as the Arctic Council and the Barents Euro-Arctic Council. Along these lines, it has actually succeeded in changing its image in what is an uncertain geopolitical context, because the shadow cast by NATO's presence allows a doubt to hover as to the absence of the potential for conflict in the region. Moscow sees the Arctic as a new space in which it is possible to express an identity that is more consensual with the international community—the rest of the post-Soviet space is in fact more conflictual in terms of geostrategic influence, whether it be Ukraine, the Caucasus, or Central Asia—and to test out its soft power tools. Russia has succeeded in building many forms of cooperation in terms of search and rescue systems, knowledge production and sharing, and legal debate. For the present, however, it has failed to become a proactive stakeholder on environmental and climate change–related issues, on the status of indigenous peoples, and on the long-term sustainability of human resources in the Arctic.

The role of the Asian countries could alter the shape of Russia's Arctic theater, both strategically and commercially, and its integration into the Asia-Pacific region. Relations with Japan and South Korea may well develop in the name of greater Arctic cooperation. Increasing Chinese shipping on the Northern Sea Route could open up new possibilities for Russia's resource development strategies for the Yamal fields and potentially also those of the South Kara Sea, to say nothing of lesser-known fields in East Siberia, all of which will likely find more clients in Asia than in Europe. Chinese traders and migrants are still rare north of the BAM route, but the interest in Arctic resources, in particular in trade with Yakutia-Sakha, could grow in magnitude in the years ahead. However, the sentiment that China presents a strategic risk, which has already found expression in relation to Chinese economic activities in the Far East, could work to hamper Russia-Chinese cooperation in the Arctic. Such a partnership, which is often defined as an "axis of convenience," is indeed paradoxical in many regards,[3] and the Arctic is set to become one of its new drivers.

Unique in many ways, the Arctic is an extraordinary window on Russia as a whole. It sheds light on the past: patterns of colonization and human settlement, the notion of *osvoenie* (mastery) of the territory, and the contemporary "memory wars" between Russians and indigenous peoples all illustrate the weight of the imperial past. The Arctic's contemporary development has its roots in the authoritarian Soviet management of human capabilities, industrial gigantism, and resource mismanagement. The Arctic sheds light on the present too: whenever it is promoted by the presidential administration, it is subject to intense state attention, yet it remains largely absent from public debates and people's everyday preoccupations. Indeed, the interest that the Russian authorities have shown for it wavers between none at all and hyperbole, between being a periphery and being in the media limelight. The prism through which the Arctic is seen is twofold. It is above all a statehood symbol of Russia's international status as a great power, of the immensity of its territory, of the withdrawal of its population toward the European regions and of the imbalance between a potential "Nordic identity" and the burden of the South (the North Caucasus region). But it is also one element among others of the strategies of Putin's inner circle in terms of connecting their political and business interests.

Lastly, the Arctic sheds light on Russia's long-term future. In its report on climate change in Russia, the U.S. National Intelligence Council states that the country "is reaching a point where serious deterioration of its physical and human capital is a major obstacle to sustainable economic growth and Russia's capacity to adapt and protect its people will be tested out to 2030."[4] Adaptive capacity presumes a certain level of decentralization in order to enable local and regional governments to respond flexibly to challenges and to allow decision-makers to interpret information. It needs to make it possible for human capital to inform, predict, and manage challenges and to provide better decision-making in support of sustainability and competence-building in emergency response. Russia is relatively well prepared in terms of its emergency response capacity, with a relatively efficient Ministry of Emergency Situations; but it is not similarly positioned in terms of environmental planning and prevention, decentralization, or sustainability, and has put its human capital at risk. In addition, extreme weather events or technological/ ecological catastrophes can prompt political discontent by undermining the image of the state as a good manager of technology.

More importantly, Russia faces growing challenges in implementing its economic development strategies. The authorities have to deal with the rising costs associated with maintaining Soviet-era infrastructure and diminishing human and technological capacities while simultaneously looking to develop new sectors for investment. The Russian state therefore tends to look for ways to camouflage its deficiencies while simultaneously trying to overcome them—opening itself to international cooperation without which it cannot modernize its industries, but seeking to avoid having to pay a political price. In the Arctic, Moscow has had to learn to manage the rather classical contradiction between the imperatives of competitiveness, which imply more openness to industrial partnerships with foreign companies, and considerations of sovereignty.

The country cannot remain a major power without energy and mineral resources, which constitute the backbone of its economy. Even if the strategies of modernization that former President Dmitri Medvedev[5] proposed—which have remained mere rhetoric until now—had been implemented and Russia transformed into a kind of post-industrial economy focused on services and the high-tech sector, the Russian state would have to spend enormous amounts from its budget for at least two decades to finance structural economic changes. The necessary funds for such changes would still have to come from its hydrocarbons rent.[6] Yet, the enormous energy revenues needed for modernization cannot be maintained without immediate massive investments of hundreds of billions of dollars in currently deteriorating infrastructure. The still high price of oil and the rapid emergence of new technologies, such as oil fracking, could spell some bright years ahead for Russia, despite the drastic changes in the world gas picture. The real issue for Moscow is what to do with its energy rent: is it simply an additional source of revenue for the artificial boosting of standards of living or a tool to be used for innovation? An oil and gas-based economy is not outdated if the hydrocarbons industries are fundamentally high-tech, and if some diversification strategies are implemented thanks to the oil revenues. An Arctic-based economy can therefore turn out to be either a way of postponing the need for an in-depth reformation of the country's structure or an engine of Russia's modernization.[7]

Today's Russia must also manage the heritage of its Soviet past in terms of human resources, while simultaneously breaking free from old patterns. Russia is "Europeanizing" massively: its material (GDP per capita) and social and cultural wealth (education, travel abroad, access to the media) is mostly concentrated in the country's European regions. The rest of its territory is either in economic and social crisis (Siberia, Arctic regions, and Far East) or in huge political crisis (North Caucasus). The imbalance in population issues intersects with that of territory: in the European parts of Russia people are richer, younger, and healthier; in the Siberian regions people are poorer, older, and not as well cared for and in the North Caucasus, the population is poorer, if not older.

The question remains whether a sparsely populated territory presents a risk for national security and border stability. Because Australia is an island and Canada has a unique relationship with the United States and has no other neighbors, these countries do not view their low-population zones as problematic. However, this is not the case for Russia: the authorities' aim to repopulate the Far East at the border with China is rather revealing of this perception of "invasion," whether conceived in demographic or economic terms. The Arctic regions, however, do not face the same imaginary peril, even though it is likely that China's growing role in the high latitudes will provoke some anxiety. Chinese presence in the Arctic, and the potential involvement of Chinese firms in Russia's Far North, is understood as both a chance and a challenge for Russia.[8]

The statement that the Russian population is "too small" compared to the size of the country—even if it is "too big" in terms of the level of productivity[9] —will probably remain part of the discursive agenda for quite some time. Whatever the case, the Russian Federation of today is not the Soviet Union of yesterday. Freedom of movement is spontaneously driving the Russian population toward the western and southern areas of the country, leaving the eastern and northern regions deserted. The Russian state will not again turn into an authoritarian regime with a capacity to forcibly send its population into zones deemed inhospitable. It will be pushed by the lack of workforce, and by market mechanisms, to shift from labor-intensive methods to labor-saving technologies, with increasing labor immigration coming from the southern republics. Siberia in general and the Arctic in particular will remain border resources, to be considered separate from the rest of the Russian mainland. If the authorities shift to this perspective on development patterns, the need for increasing infrastructure for human settlement will be less pressing, and therefore less costly.

Rethinking the role of the Arctic in twenty-first-century Russia thus presumes that the ruling elites open a public debate on the notion of connectedness, and that the emphasis on economic development is focused on technology, communications, and transportation as opposed to size and location.[10] As such, the Arctic could see the emergence of a new Russia, or a resurgence of the old. Regardless of the chosen strategy, Russia's Arctic is anything but a unified region. The absence of a comprehensive federal policy specifically designed for all the Arctic provinces confirms, as if it were needed, that the region is not conceived by the Kremlin as a unity per se, but as belonging to different regional contexts. Indeed, there exist multiple Arctics in Russia, all of which have very different economic and demographic outlooks, and a developed Far North will coexist with a non-profitable one.

The Murmansk-Arkhangel'sk Arctic, a European Transborder Region

The western part of the Russian Arctic, which stretches from Murmansk to Arkhangel'sk, is a rather well-defined region. Administratively it is part of the Northwestern Federal District, which includes Moscow and St. Petersburg as well as the Barents Sea's shipping lanes, which do not belong to the Northern Sea Route. The region is relatively well-connected to both Moscow and St. Petersburg, and the large majority of its population consists of ethnic Russians. It also benefits from well-developed infrastructure: the region hosts Russia's main naval shipyards and the Northern Fleet; in the west, its ports are ice-free year-round; and several nuclear power plants as well as mining industries are active there. Whereas during the Soviet period, its proximity to Finland and Norway turned it into an outpost of the Cold War, the dynamism of relations between Russia and the Nordic countries has since deeply transformed the region, as have the prospects for the exploitation of hydrocarbons. In terms of domestic geopolitics, the Murmansk-Arkhangel'sk region, despite its specific geographic and climatic conditions, is likely to become part of Russia's "West"—that is, of the set of regions whose economies interact and are interlinked with those of its European neighbors.[11] This Arctic region, linked to the Baltic one, is bound to become a driving force in Russia's relationship with Europe through the "Northern Dimension." An initiative in the European Union regarding the cross-border and external policies covering the Nordic countries, Baltic states, and Russia, the Northern Dimension, first proposed by Mikhail Gorbachev and Finland president Urpo Kivikari, provides a good example of constructive cooperation between all the stakeholders in the North.[12]

   This European Arctic can further be divided into three sub-regions: Murmansk and the Kola Peninsula; the Republic of Karelia, which has access to the White Sea through the Baltic-White Sea Canal; and Arkhangel'sk. The future of the Kola Peninsula is that of the trans-border European region, while Arkhangel'sk, even if it becomes integrated into the same trend, remains more remote and will have some time to wait before it can benefit from the same level of cross-border activities. Economic development is progressing throughout the region, although at different rates in different places. The ice-free ports of Murmansk, Severomorsk, and Kandalaksha have been renovated as part of the modernization of the Northern Fleet. Murmansk and Kandalaksha are the main commercial ports of the Russian western Arctic, with many trawlers unloading their catch there, and the region is considered to be one of the richest in terms of fishing.[13] The port of Murmansk also hosts the Russian atomic icebreaker fleet. Further, the mining industry will continue to develop, as the Kola Peninsula is particularly rich in rare minerals. If it becomes a reality, the exploitation of Shtokman gas field should serve to make the entire region more dynamic as well. The small port of Teriberka/Vidyaevo would become the terminus of a pipeline connecting the gas fields to the continent, running along 570 kilometers of sea bed. A transport and technological complex has been planned for the port, including an unloading terminal, a factory for producing liquefied natural gas, and installations for preparing the gas for transport overland. An overland gas pipeline between Vidyaevo and Volkhov, about 1,300 kilometers in length, is planned to link to the network connecting with Europe and should enable the industries of the region to switch to gas.[14]

The region's future is strongly influenced by the relationship with its Nordic neighbors. Transborder cooperation has developed between Russia, Finland, and Norway, the aim of which is to increase cross-border activity and to unify transportation routes. The Barents Euro-Arctic Transport Area (BEATA) plans to improve road, air, and rail transport linkages between the Nordic countries and the northwest regions of Russia, and to develop joint security projects on the external maritime connections.[15] In 2007, Moscow and Oslo set up a Vessel Traffic Center to facilitate the exchange of data between the Norwegian and Russian maritime transport authorities.[16] Many cross-border projects between Finnish and Russian Karelia and between Finnish and Norwegian Lapland and the Murmansk region have taken shape. Not being part of the EU, Norway has implemented a simplified system of multi-entry visas for persons living near the border, called Pomor visas, and this has led to a veritable boom in transborder tourism.[17] A Pomor Zone for joint industry and commerce, with Kirkenes as the main center, has also been created.[18]

In Arkhangel'sk, meanwhile, transformations have been much slower. The region's economy is dominated by the naval industries of Sevmash and Zvezdochka at Severodvinsk, Russia's Nuclear Naval Construction Center, and the fishing industry. Administratively, the region also controls Novaya Zemlya and the Franz Joseph Land archipelago, and could therefore also see military and commercial activities develop much farther north.[19]

The port of Arkhangel'sk, Russia's first port, created in 1584, is today in competition with Murmansk. It would like to host the Northern Fleet if it is moved in order to free up Murmansk solely for commercial activities. The Arkhangel'sk port is in the process of being renovated in order to cope with the revival of large-scale commercial fishing, but above all to manage the transit of hydrocarbons through the Arctic. It now has an oil-loading terminal as well as a Belokamenka floating storage unit for oil that arrives from the Timan-Pechora fields. The region can also take pride in the Plesetsk cosmodrome, which is likely to play a central role in the development of satellite navigation in the Arctic, as well as in a new federal Arctic university.[20]

The Mineral- and Hydrocarbon-Rich Central Arctic

Farther east, stretching from the Urals to the Taimyr Peninsula, a second Arctic displays an economic unity through its wealth of hydrocarbons and minerals but has no administrative unity. It includes the three autonomous districts of Nenets, Yamalo-Nenets, and Taimyr, to which can be added the Komi Republic and its mines, and the autonomous district of Khanty-Mantsi, which partly belongs to the same hydrocarbons-related industrial base. The Nenets district is attached to the Arkhangel'sk region and therefore comprises the easternmost part of the Northwestern Federal District. The Yamalo-Nenets and Khanty-Mansi districts are under Tyumen's administration, which is itself part of the Ural Federal District. And the Taimyr district was established as part of the Krasnoyarsk region, in the Siberian Federal District.

This second Arctic region is set not only to be Russia's center of extraction in the twenty-first century, but also, because of the demand for transport, it will play a key role in destinational shipping along the Arctic routes. Its infrastructure is essentially directed toward the western, European regions, and not toward Asia. This orientation, due to historical reasons, could nonetheless be reversed in the decades to come, as the main future markets are bound to be Asian and not European ones. The region hosts numerous industrial towns, such as Noril'sk and Vorkuta, which have specialized in mineral extraction since the 1930s, and includes others such as Khanty-Mansiisk that embody the oil boom of the 2000s, and, albeit more modestly, Nar'yan-Mar, Noyabrsk, and Novyi Urengoy. It is also the key Arctic/subarctic region in terms of indigenous groups, since the Nenets and other less populous groups live there and increasingly interact with industrial actors.

The region's industrial revival has fostered numerous infrastructure projects. Some of the local administrations, in this case the Tyumen' region, Cheliabinsk farther to the south, as well as the Nenets and Yamalo-Nenets districts, have initiated a huge project called "Urals Industrial—Urals Polar." It plans to build a new industrial and infrastructure complex to ensure the connection between the Arctic/subarctic regions and the old industrial core of the Central and Southern Urals, and thus facilitate the export of resources to Europe.[21] The Belkomur railway project was, for instance, conceived in order to connect the railway infrastructures of Finland and Norway with the Trans-Siberian by linking together several small individual rail lines in the expanse between Arkhangel'sk and Perm', over a distance of more than 1,500 kilometers. Designed to facilitate the transportation of industrial products both to the east and to the west, the Belkomur railway will be one of the first large infrastructure projects with Chinese participation.[22]

Lastly, a new Ob'–Bovanenko line of nearly 600 kilometers, the north-ernmost railway in the world, became operational in 2010, and links the Bovanenko deposit with the extant section of the so-called Transpolar Mainline. The Salekhard–Igarka railway, an unfinished line dating from the Gulag period, was partly completed in the 1970s in order to link up the deposits of Novyi Urengoy and Yamburg, and its western extension to Vor-kuta has remained functional. Since 2010, work has been under way on the Salekhard–Nadym section. In addition, a railway line from Noril'sk, which is totally cut off from the national network, connects the mining towns of Talnakh and Kayerkan with the port of Dudinka more than 300 kilometers away. It has not carried passengers since the end of the 1990s, but it still transports minerals and has been modernized by Noril'sk Nickel.

In terms of port infrastructure, only Dudinka, which was privatized by Noril'sk Nickel, is developed to any extent, whereas the other ports are wait-ing for a potential boom in Arctic resources to take off. Simultaneously a sea and river port, Dudinka has the largest docking capacity anywhere along the Northern Sea Route, with nine posts along a quay 1.7 kilometers in length, added to which are 20 others allocated for river boats. Shipping between Dudinka and Murmansk, which takes place year-round, mainly consists of mineral and timber exports. Compared to Dudinka, the other ports of the region are found wanting. The port of Nary'an-Mar in the Nenets district, situated 100 kilometers from the mouth of the Pechora River, will prob-ably be turned into an oil port with the exploitation of the Timan-Pechora reserves.[23] The port of Amderma, which opens onto the South Kara Sea, has only a limited function, receiving construction materials and coal. Moscow has planned to revive its activities by building a railway from Vorkuta, and the exploitation of the South Kara Sea deposits could also provide a stimulus. The settlement of Indiga, situated farther west, could well become a deep-water port for the transshipment of cargo and industrial exports from the Komi Republic.[24] The small capital of the Yamalo-Nenets district, Salekhard, has a modest level of port activity, as do Kharasavey, Yamburg, and Novyi Port: these ports specialize in oil products, and have hedged their bets on the development of the Ob'-Taz' deposits.[25] Activities at the port of Dikson, meanwhile, have pretty much dried up, whereas Khatanga is primarily used only by Noril'sk Nickel.[26]

The Sakha Arctic: Looking Both North and South

The republic of Yakutia-Sakha, in the Lena River basin, forms a third Arctic on its own. Part of the Far East Federal District, it is the largest autonomous Arctic republic in area, with more than 40% of its territory above the Arctic Circle. It is presented as a model of harmonious relations between the Yakuts and ethnic Russians; each constituted about 45% of the population in the 2002 census.[27] The republic has tried to develop its own Arctic brand by hosting numerous international conferences on the subject, and by promoting its indigenous culture and its network of environmentally protected areas. However, the political establishment is distinctly dominated by ethnic Russians, and resource extraction lies at the core of the republic's development strategies. The diamond, gold, and tin ore mining industries are the major focus of the local economy, dominated by the Alrosa diamond company.[28] Yakutia-Sakha advertises its geographical position as a way of campaigning for a revival of the Northern Sea Route, but also, and above all, of opening itself to the Asia-Pacific region. It seeks to develop its economic links with southern Siberia, in particular the Irkutsk region, and with the Primorye (Far East) territory, which serves as its path of access to China, a direction in which it does not conceal commercial ambitions.[29]

The Yakut administration traditionally presents the Northern Sea Route as its "Arctic road of life."[30] It calls for the improvement of port infrastructure on its Arctic coastline between the mouth of the Anabar River and that of the Kolyma. It hopes to revive its main port, Tiksi, located on the Arctic coast to the south of the Lena River delta, which has fallen into partial disrepair, and that of Zelenyi Mys located on the Kolyma River, which has been practically shut down. Both ports are open only seasonally. In view of this, the Sakha government has proposed to sponsor an Arctic rescue center with modern technology and transport, in order to exploit its proximity to the geophysical observatory and the fleet of Roshydromet, part of which is based at Tiksi.[31] The prospect of cross-continental transit of Asian ships has created great hopes for the development of the republic's Arctic coastline, which at present is among Russia's most isolated.[32] For the whole of Yakutia-Sakha, the confluence of the republic's northward-flowing rivers with the Arctic Ocean is conceived as affording a means of unified transport.[33] Indeed, most freight is still transported along the Lena River and its tributaries, the Vilyui and Aldan, and also via the Yana, Indigirka, and Kolyma Rivers.[34]

Other transport modes are also being developed. In 2008, the federal highway "Kolyma" connecting Yakutsk with Magadan was opened for year-round use. An 800-kilometer-long railway line connecting the capital Yakutsk to the BAM (the so-called Amur-Yakutsk line, or AYAM), thus serving as a connection with southern Siberia, is in the process of completion (the line is planned to be fully operational in 2014). This will make it possible to allow scattered populations to travel between regions, to export mineral products from Sakha to Asia, and, in exchange, to obtain Chinese goods at the lowest possible price. It is likely that of the two Sakha strategies—one directed toward the north, and the other south—the latter will prove to be commercially more dynamic.

The Bering Arctic: Winning Out From the American and Asian Neighborhoods?

The fourth Russian Arctic is that of Chukotka and Kamchatka, which includes the country's Pacific façade, which opens onto the Bering, Chukchi, and Okhotsk Seas. Part of the Far East Federal District, this Arctic is probably the most marginalized. It has a particularly small population, has experienced an acute migration crisis since the 1990s, has a high unemployment rate among those ethnic Russians that have remained, and its indigenous peoples have been forced to resume their traditional livelihoods due to the lack of central subsidies. Whereas this region's proximity to the United States made it a point of tension during the Cold War, Moscow now dreams of exploiting more peaceful ties with Alaska, and even more so with Asia. Asian dynamism is the only opportunity for the region's economic revitalization, but this presupposes that transcontinental shipping via the Arctic really does take off, and that the fishing industry revives, which is far from certain. The population of this fourth Arctic is essentially composed of ethnic Russians and Ukrainians, while there are a statistically small number of indigenous peoples; the presence of Chinese migrants is currently limited for the time being to the border regions of Amur and Primorye.

There are still too many unknowns concerning the region's prospects for subsoil resource development, so it is too early to place any hope in a hydrocarbons- or minerals-based economic revival. But other dimensions of development have to be taken into account. Growing Arctic tourism, coupled with eco-tourism and volcano-viewing on the Kamchatka Peninsula, harbors the potential to revitalize some small settlements in the most isolated regions. The growing use of the Trans-Arctic Air Corridor also requires the development of rescue systems in the overflight regions. The administration of Chukotka has for instance proposed to create a Crisis Management Center and Rescue Center to be based in Anadyr' under the control of the Ministry of Emergency Situations.[35]

However, the main regional economic project remains the transformation of the port of Petropavlovsk-Kamchatskii in the Avacha Bay into a hub for North Pacific trade.[36] The port has maintained its industrial fishing activities, but on a lesser scale than during the Soviet period.[37] Part of the Pacific Fleet is stationed there, as well as at Viliuchinsk, albeit under the command of Vladivostok. Prospects of a trade boom, however, seem limited: not even the southernmost ports of Vladivostok and Nakhodka, whose geographical location is clearly more advantageous, are able to rival the major Asian ports, which are mostly based in southern seas. Petropavlovsk-Kamchatskii's own location on a peninsula makes the transport of goods to the continent both costly and technically challenging.[38] Meanwhile, the world's northernmost port of Pevek, on the Arctic coast of Chukotka, was all but deserted by its population in the 1990s.[39] It still serves as an outlet for the gold extracted from the Kolyma basin, one of the only industries that has remained active in Chukotka, but which operates only in summer. Projects to revive the port will not be able to make any substantial headway, because it is exclusively seasonal and its infrastructure old. The Bilibino nuclear power plant, likewise the northernmost in the world, has been in operation since the 1970s[40] but offers no prospects for economic development.

Any kind of port development is based on the capacity to connect with remotely situated territories deep in the country. Hitherto, wintertime ice roads (*zimniki*) built on the frozen surfaces of rivers have been the main transportation system between remote settlements, but climate change could have the effect of rendering such means of transport obsolete. Railway projects are more likely to materialize, although the harsh climatic conditions and increased thawing of the permafrost present considerable technological problems. The Amur-Yakutsk rail line could, for instance, be extended to Uelen in Chukotka, which is Russia's easternmost settlement. The possibility has also been raised of building a 5,000-kilometer railway line to connect the port of Petropavlovsk-Kamchatskii to the Siberian continent and to the Primorye. This line would join the BAM and then the Trans-Siberian, but the project appears unrealistic in view of the actual freight opportunities, and would involve an enormous detour to bypass the northern Sea of Okhotsk and access Kamchatka via the Magadan region. The Russian Transport Development Strategy for 2030 also plans the construction of a railway line connecting Russia to Alaska via a tunnel beneath the Bering Strait (less than 100 kilometers wide). An investment promotion agency, InterBering, has been created to promote this utopian project: the agency calculates its cost at around $100 billion, for a potential of 100 million tons of freight.[41] The hope of Vladimir Yakunin, the CEO of Russian Railways, to see a passenger railway line running between New York and London via Siberia, seems to be seriously detached from reality.[42]

The Arctic illustrates Russia's current dilemma between population and space. This is not a new choice for the country: "geography as a destiny" is a recurring issue that has resurfaced at different moments in Russia's history since the nineteenth century. The mental geography of the country will deeply change in the years to come, and the idea that size and location confer international stature to Russia must be reformulated, with emphasis shifting to the efficiency, productivity, and well-being of the population. However the incumbent regime still refuses to engage in any head-on reforms of the political and economic system: its memory of the trauma of the 1990s and fears of further disintegration of the country, with, as a corollary, yet another disappearance from the international arena, have created pressure to maintain the status quo. The present situation is still supported by large sections of the population, which share with the authorities the idea of a progressive but not revolutionary transformation. This consensus, challenged by parts of the new middle and upper classes, is based on the regular increase in living standards and the state's ability to manage, for better or for worse, the Soviet legacy, endemic corruption, and implementation deficiency. Russia is therefore wagering on its ability to postpone any radical changes: the need for these changes is not denied, but simply pushed further into the future, in the hope that in the years to come, there will be more leeway in which to achieve reforms, all the while maintaining political and social stability. The Arctic occupies a flagship position in this postponement strategy, but the cost of an Arctic-centered development model is probably higher than is estimated by the Russian authorities, and the relevance of this choice could be brutally undermined by developments in the international and domestic arenas.

Notes

1. Quoted in H.A. Conley, T. Toland, J. Kraut, and A. Østhagen, "A New Security Architecture for the Arctic. An American Perspective," *CSIS Europe Report*, (Washington, DC: Center for Strategic and International Studies, January 2012), 1.
2. Ibid.
3. I. Danchenko, E. Downs, and F. Hill, "One Step Forward, Two Steps Back? The Realities of a Rising China and Implications for Russia's Energy Ambitions," *Brookings Policy Paper*, no. 22, August 2010; M.A. Smith, *The Russo-Chinese Energy Relationship* (Shrivenham: Defence Academy of the United Kingdom, October 2010).

4. *Russia. The Impact of Climate Change to 2030.* (Washington, DC: National Intelligence Council, 2009), 3.

5. M.A. Smith, *Medvedev and the Modernisation Dilemma* (Shrivenham: The Defence Academy of the United Kingdom, no. 15, 2010).

6. C. Gaddy, and B.W. Ickes, "Resource Rents and the Russian Economy," *Eurasian Geography and Economics* 46, no. 8 (2005): 559–583.

7. For more on this point, see T. Gustafson, *Wheel of Fortune: The Battle for Oil and Power in Russia* (Cambridge, MA: The Belknap Press of Harvard University Press, 2012), 480–501.

8. V.N. Konyshev, and A.A. Sergunin, "Osvoenie prirodnykh resursov Arktiki: puti sotrudnichestva Rossii s Kitaem v interesakh budushchego [Mastering Arctic natural resources: Ways for a Russia-China cooperation in the interests of the future]," *Prioritety Rossii* 38, no. 180 (2012): 2–9.

9. F. Hill and C. Gaddy, *The Siberian Curse: How Communist Planners Left Russia Out in the Cold.* (Washington, DC: Brookings Institute Press, 2003), 187.

10. See for instance *Reshaping Economic Geography* (Washington, DC: The World Bank, 2009).

11. See M. Tykkyläinen and V. Rautio, eds., *Russia's Northern Regions on the Edge: Communities, Industries, and Populations from Murmansk to Magadan* (Helsinki: Aleksanteri Institute 2008).

12. D.A. Lanko, "Russian Debate on the Northern Dimension Concept." Paper presented to the 6th Pan-European International Relations Conference, "Making Sense of a Pluralist World," Torino, Italy, September 12–15, 2007.

13. "Murmanskaia oblast' [Murmansk region]," *Morskaia kollegiia,* no date, http://www.morskayakollegiya.ru/primorskie_regio/arktika/murmanskaja_obla (accessed April 26, 2012).

14. "Gas Resources on Russia's Euro-Arctic Shelf," *Bellona,* no date, http://www.bellona.org/reports/report/1197337371.03 (accessed January 16, 2013).

15. "Transport and Communication," *Barents Info,* no date, http://www.barentsinfo.org/?DeptID=3641 (accessed January 16, 2013).

16. L.S. Voronkov, *Geopolitical Dimensions of Transport and Logistics Development in the Barents Euro-Arctic Transport Area (BEATA)* (Kirkenes: Barents Institute, 2009).

17. See the "borders" section of the *Barents Observer* website for details, http://barentsobserver.com/en/sections/borders (accessed January 16, 2013).

18. "Welcome to Kirkenes!" *Barents Observer,* no date, http://www.barentsobserver.com/index.php?id=542804 (accessed January 16, 2013).

19. See http://www.morskayakollegiya.ru/primorskie_regio/arktika/arhangel/ (accessed April 26, 2012).

20. A. Shalevyi, "Rossiia konsolidiruet svoi pozitsii v Arktike [Russia consolidates its position in the Arctic," *Barents Observer,* April 22, 2010, http://www.barentsobserver.com/enefnnecn-neoefefnefereceaecnnemn-nesefec-eiefemecnecec-es-eneoneceoem.4777757–16149.html (accessed January 16, 2013).

21. See the website Ural Industrial—Ural Polar Corporation, http://www.en.cupp.ru/about_project.html (accessed January 16, 2013).

22. A. Staalesen, "China Jumps aboard a Russian Arctic-Bound Train," *Barents Observer,* November 27, 2012, http://barentsobserver.com/en/arctic/2012/11/china-jumps-aboard-russian-arctic-bound-train-27–11 (accessed January 16, 2013).

23. "Nenetskii avtonomnyi okrug [Nenets autonomous district]," *Morskaia kollegiia,* no date, http://www.morskayakollegiya.ru/primorskie_regio/arktika/nenetskij_avtono/ (accessed April 26, 2012).

24. "Future Bases for the Northern Sea Route Pointed Out," *Barents Observer*, December 17, 2010, http://www.barentsobserver.com/future-bases-for-the-northern-sea-route-pointed-out.4863371–16288.html (accessed January 16, 2013).

25. "Iamalo-Nenetskii avtonomnyi okrug [Yamalo-Nenets autonomous district]," *Morskaia kollegiia*, no date, http://www.morskayakollegiya.ru/primorskie_regio/arktika/jamalo-nenetskij/ (accessed April 26, 2012).

26. "Taimyskii avtonomnyi okrug [Taimyr autonomous district]," *Morskaia kollegiia*, no date, http://www.morskayakollegiya.ru/primorskie_regio/arktika/tajmyr-skij_dolga/ (accessed April 26, 2012).

27. For a review of the situation in the 1990s, see U.A. Vinokurova, "The Ethnopolitical Situation in the Republic of Sakha (Yakutia)," *Anthropology & Archeology of Eurasia* 34, no. 1 (1995): 60–98 and V. Robbek, "Language Situation in the Yakutia Republic (Sakha)," in E. Kasten, ed., *Bicultural Education in the North: Ways of Preserving and Enhancing Indigenous Peoples' Languages and Traditional Knowledge* (Münster: Waxmann Verlag, 1998), 113–122. See also D. Gorenburg, *Minority Ethnic Mobilization in the Russian Federation* (Cambridge: Cambridge University Press, 2003).

28. T. Argounova-Law, "Diamonds. A Contested Symbol in the Republic of Sakha (Yakutia)," in E. Kasten, ed., *Properties of Culture, Culture as Property. Pathways to Reform in Post-Soviet Siberia* (Berlin: Dietrich Reimer Verlag, 2004), 257–265.

29. Anonymous discussions with Russian scholars in Vladivostok, October 11, 2010.

30. V. Chlenov, "Arkticheskaia doroga zhizni [Arctic road of life]," *Parlamentskaia gazeta na Dal'nem Vostoke*, no. 9 (252), 2008, http://www.parldv.ru/index.php?mod=art_show&id_art=391 (accessed January 16, 2013). This term refers to the Ladoga Road, which enabled Leningrad to survive the Nazi blockade during the Second World War.

31. T. Uttal, "The Tiksi Hydrometeorological International Facility for Atmospheric, Terrestrial, and Ocean Observations." Paper presented at the 11th Conference on Polar Meteorology and Oceanography, May 2–5, 2011, Boston. http://ams.confex.com/ams/11Polar/webprogram/Paper188852.html (accessed January 16, 2013).

32. "Respublika Sakha," *Morskaia kollegiia*, no date, http://www.morskayakollegiya.ru/primorskie_regio/arktika/respublika_saha-/ (accessed April 26, 2012).

33. Chlenov, "Arkticheskaia doroga zhizni."

34. A.V. Istomin, "Rol' severnogo morskogo puti v khoziaistvennom razvitii i osvoenii severnykh territorii [The role of the Northern Sea Route in the agricultural development and conquest of northern territories]," *Sever promyshlennyi*, no. 6–7 (2007).

35. International Conference "Prevention and Elimination of Emergency Situations in the Arctic," Anadyr', August 19–20, 2009.

36. "Proekt razvitiia porta Petropavlovsk-Kamchatskii v kachestve khaba vostochnoi chasti Severnogo morskogo puti [Plan for development of the port of Petropavlovsk-Kamchatskii as a hub of the eastern part of the Northern Sea Route]," *Sever Dal'nego Vostoka*, September 10, 2010, http://severdv.ru/news/show/?id=43721 (accessed April 26, 2012).

37. Personal observation during fieldwork in Petropavlovsk-Kamchatskii, October 19, 2010.

38. T. Mishina, "Bor'ba za Arktiku. Chto dast regionu razvitie severnogo sudokhod-stva [Struggle for the Arctic. What the development of northern shipping will yield],"

Rossiiskaia gazeta, January 29, 2011, http://www.rg.ru/2011/01/27/reg-dvostok/perevozki.html (accessed April 26, 2012).

39. M. Krans, "Russia's Northern Sea Route: Just a Dotted line on the Map?" *RIA Novosti*, May 23, 2007, http://en.rian.ru/analysis/20070523/65989859.html (accessed April 26, 2012).

40. V.M. Abramov, A.V. Bondarenko, A.A. Vaimugin, L.V. Gurevich, V.V. Dolgov, O.V. Komissarov, M.E. Minashin et al., "Bilibino Nuclear Power Station," *Atomic Energy* 35, no. 5 (1973): 977–982.

41. See the Interbering website, http://interbering.com/ (accessed April 26, 2012).

42. Ibid.

Bibliography

Abramov, V.M., Bondarenko, A.V., Vaimugin, A.A., Gurevich, L.V., Dolgov, V.V., Komissarov, O.V., Minashin, M.E. et al., "Bilibino Nuclear Power Station," *Atomic Energy* 35, no. 5 (1973): 977–982.

ACIA Report—Arctic Climate Impact Assessment: Impacts of a Warming Arctic. Cambridge: Cambridge University Press, 2004.

Aitamurto, K., "Russian Paganism and the Issue of Nationalism: A Case Study of the Circle of Pagan Tradition," *Pomegranate: The International Journal of Pagan Studies* 8, no. 2 (2006): 184–210.

Alekseev, M., "Migration, Hostility, and Ethnopolitical Mobilization: Russia's Anti-Chinese Legacies in Formation," in B. Ruble and D. Arel, eds., *Rebounding Identities*. Washington, DC: Woodrow Wilson Center Press, 2006, 116–148.

Anderson, A., *After the Ice: Life, Death, and Geopolitics in the New Arctic*. New York: Smithsonian Books, 2009.

Anderson, D.H., "The Status under International Law of the Maritime Areas around Svalbard," *Ocean Development & International Law* 40, no. 4 (2009): 373–384.

Andreinko, Y., and Guriev, S., *Determinants of Interregional Mobility in Russia: Evidence from Panel Data*. Moscow: New Economic School, 2003.

Anisimov, O. and Reneva, S., "Permafrost and Changing Climate: The Russian Perspective," *Ambio* 35, no. 4 (2006): 169–175.

Anisimov, O.,Velichko, A., Demchenko, P., Eliseev, A., Mokhov, I., and Nechaev, V., "Effect of Climate Change on Permafrost in the Past, Present and Future," *Atmospheric and Oceanic Physics* 38, no. 1 (2002): 25–39.

Antrim, C.L., "The Next Geographical Pivot. The Russian Arctic in the Twenty-first Century," *Naval War College Review* 63, no. 3 (2010): 15–37.

Arctic Council, *Arctic Marine Shipping Assessment 2009 Report*. Akureyri: Arctic Council, 2009.

Arctic Monitoring and Assessment Programme, *Oil and Gas Arctic 2007*. Oslo: AMAP, 2008.

Arctic Transportation System of Export of Oil from the North-West Russia. St. Petersburg: Central Marine Research and Design Institute, 2003.

Argounova-Law, T., "Diamonds. A Contested Symbol in the Republic of Sakha (Yakutia)," in E. Kasten, ed., *Properties of Culture, Culture as Property. Pathways to Reform in Post-Soviet Siberia*. Berlin: Dietrich Reimer Verlag, 2004, 257–265.

Armstrong, T., *Russian Settlement in the North*. Cambridge, UK: Cambridge University Press, 1965.

Asche, F. and Smith, M.D., *Trade and Fisheries: Key Issues for the World Trade*. Geneva: World Trade Organization, Staff Working Paper ERSD-2010-13, 2010.

Aslund, A., Guriev, S., and Kuchins, A., *Russia After the Global Economic Crisis*. Washington, DC: Peterson Institute for International Economics, 2010.

Åtland K., "Mikhail Gorbachev, the Murmansk Initiative, and the Desecuritization of Interstate Relations in the Arctic, Cooperation and Conflict," *Journal of the Nordic International Studies Association* 43, no. 3 (2008): 289–311.

———. "Russia's Northern Fleet and the Oil Industry—Rivals or Partners? A Study of Civil-Military Relations in the Post-Cold War Arctic," *Armed Forces & Society* 35, no. 2 (2009): 362–384.

Åtland, K. and Pedersen, T., "The Svalbard Archipelago in Russian Security Policy: Overcoming the Legacy of Fear—or Reproducing It?" *European Security* 17, no. 2 (2008): 227–251.

Åtland, K. and Ven Bruusgaard, K., "When Security Speech Acts Misfire: Russia and the Elektron Incident," *Security Dialogue* 40, no. 3 (2009): 333–353.

Baev, P., *Russia's Race for the Arctic and the New Geopolitics of the North Pole*. Washington, DC: The Jamestown Foundation, October 2007.

———. "Russia's Arctic Policy. Geopolitics, Mercantilism, and Identity-Building," *FIIA Briefing Paper*, no. 73, December 2010.

———. "Russia's Arctic Policy and the Northern Fleet Modernization," *Russie.Nei. Visions*, no. 65, 2012.

Baker, B., "Law, Science, and the Continental Shelf: The Russian Federation and the Promise of Arctic Cooperation," *American University International Law Review* 25, no. 2 (2010): 251–281.

Bambulyak, A. and Frantzen, B., *Oil Transport from the Russian Part of the Barents Region*. Svanvik: Svanhovd Environmental Center, 2005.

Barabanov, M., *Sovremennoe sostoianie i perspektivy razvitiia rossiskogo flota* [Current state and prospects for the development of the Russian fleet]. Moscow: Center for Defense Information, 2006.

Barany, Z., *Democratic Breakdown and the Decline of the Russian Military*. Princeton: Princeton University Press, 2007.

Barnes, A., "Russian-Chinese Oil Relations: Dominance or Negotiation?" *PONARS Eurasia Policy Memo*, no. 124, 2010.

Bartenstein, K., "The 'Arctic Exception' in the Law of the Sea Convention: A Contribution to Safer Navigation in the Northwest Passage?" *Ocean Development & International Law* 42, no. 1–2 (2011): 22–52.

Bassin, M., Ely, C., and Stockdale, M.K., eds., *Space, Place, and Power in Modern Russia: Essays in the New Spatial History*. DeKalb: Northern Illinois University Press, 2010.

Bird, K.J., Charpentier, R.J., Gautier, D.L., Houseknecht, D.W., Klett, T.R., Pitman, J.K., Moore, T.E., Schrenk, C.J., Tennyson, M.E., and Wandrey, C.J. *Circum-Arctic Resource Appraisal: Estimates of Undiscovered Oil and Gas North of the Arctic Circle*. Reston: U.S. Geological Survey, Fact Sheet 2008-3049, 2008.

Black, J., *Maps and Politics*. London: Reaktion Books Ltd., 1997.

Blakkisrud, H. and Hønneland, G., eds., *Tackling Space: Federal Politics and the Russian North*. Lanham, Oxford: University Press of America, 2006.

Blank, S., ed., *Russian Military Politics and Russia's 2010 Defense Doctrine*. Carlisle: Strategic Studies Institute, 2010.

Bonifazi, C., Okolski, M., Schoorl, J., and Simon, P., eds., *International Migration in Europe: New Trends and New Methods of Analysis*. Amsterdam: Amsterdam University Press, 2008.

BP Statistical Review of World Energy. London: BP, June 2010.

Budenko, M.I., *Vliianie cheloveka na klimate* [The influence of mankind on climate]. Leningrad, 1972.

Butler, W.E., "Soviet Maritime Jurisdiction in the Arctic," *Polar Record*, no. 16 (1972): 418–421.

———. *International Straits of the World: Northeast Arctic Passage.* Alphen aan den Rijn: Sijthoff & Noordhoff, 1978.

———. *The Northeast Arctic Passage.* Alphen aan den Rijn: Sijthoff & Noordhoof International Publishers, 1978.

Byers, M., *Who Owns the Arctic? Understanding Sovereignty Disputes in the North.* Vancouver: Douglas and McIntyre, 2009.

Campbell, C., "China and the Arctic: Objectives and Obstacles," U.S.-China Economic and Security Review Commission Staff Research Report, April 13, 2012.

Caracciolo, I., "Unresolved Controversy: The Legal Situation of the Svalbard Islands Maritime Areas; an Interpretation of the Paris Treaty in Light of UNCLOS 1982." Paper presented at the International Conference on Disputed Territory & Maritime Space, Durham University, April 2, 2010.

Carbon Disclosure Project, "Public Procurement Programme 2010," London, AEA Europe 2010.

Carrère d'Encausse, H., *L'Empire éclaté: la révolte des nations en URSS* [The broken empire: The revolt of nations in the USSR]. Paris: Flammarion, 1978.

Casper, K.N., "Oil and Gas Development in the Arctic: Softening of Ice Demands, Hardening of International Law," *Natural Resources Journal* 49 (2009): 825–881.

Centre for Analysis of Strategies and Technologies, *Russian Defense Industry and Arms Trade: Facts and Figures.* Moscow: Centre for Analysis of Strategies and Technologies, 2010.

Charap, S., "Russia's Lackluster Record on Climate Change," *Russian Analytical Digest*, no. 79, 2010, 11–16.

Chestin, I.E. and Colloff, N.A., eds., *Russia and Neighbouring Countries: Environmental, Economic and Social Impacts of Climate Change.* Moscow: WWF and Oxfam, 2008.

Clarke, S., "Illegal Fishing in the Exclusive Economic Zone of Japan," *MRAG Working Paper*, 2007.

Climate Change in Russia: Research and Impacts. London: Climate Change Risk Management, May 2008.

Conley, H.A., and Kraut, J., "U.S. Strategic Interests in the Arctic. An Assessment of Current Challenges and New Opportunities for Cooperation," *CSIS Europe Program Working Paper*, April 2010.

Conley, H.A., Toland, T., Kraut, J., and Østhagen, A., "A New Security Architecture for the Arctic: An American Perspective," *CSIS Europe Report*, January 2012.

Crate, S.A., "Co-Option in Siberia: The Case of Diamonds and the Vilyuy Sakha," *Polar Geography* 26, no. 4 (2002): 418–435.

Danchenko, I., Downs, E., and Hill, F., "One Step Forward, Two Steps Back? The Realities of a Rising China and Implications for Russia's Energy Ambitions," *Brookings Policy Paper*, no. 22, August 2010.

Daucé, F. and Sieca-Kozlowski, E., *Dedovshchina in the Post-Soviet Military. Hazing of Russian Army Conscripts in a Comparative Perspective.* Stuttgart: Ibidem Verlag, 2006.

De Has, M. "Russia's New Military Doctrine: A Compromise Document," *Russian Analytical Digest*, no. 78, May 4, 2010.

De Tinguy, A., *La Grande Migration. La Russie et les Russes depuis l'ouverture du rideau de fer* [The great migration. Russia and the Russians since the opening of the Iron Curtain]. Paris: Plon, 2004.

Derrick, M., "The Merging of Russia's Regions as Applied Nationality Policy: A Suggested Rationale," *Caucasian Review of International Affairs* 3, no. 3 (2009): 317–323.

Dienes, L., "Reflections on a Geographic Dichotomy: Archipelago Russia," *Eurasian Geography and Economics* 43, no. 6 (2002): 443–458.

Dobrolyubova, J., *Climate Change Effects and Assessment of Adaptation Potential in the Russian Federation*. Moscow: Russian Regional Environmental Centre, November 19–20, 2007.

Dobronravin, N., *Maritime Issues in Russian Energy Politics*. Turku: Centrum Balticum, 2010.

Dolatat-Kreutzkamp, P., "An Arctic (Cold) War: Alarming Developments or Empty Rhetoric?" *European Centre for Energy and Resource Security Newsletter*, no. 4 (2011): 1–5.

Drent, J., "Commercial Shipping on the Northern Sea Route," *The Northern Mariner/ Le Marin du nord* III, no. 2 (1993): 1–17.

Dressler, A. and Parson, E.A., *The Science and Politics of Global Climate Change: A Guide to the Debate*. Cambridge: Cambridge University Press, 2010.

Dronin, N. and Kirilenko, A., "Climate Change and Food Stress in Russia: What If the Market Transforms as It Did During the Past Century?" *Climatic Change* 86 (2008): 123–150.

Dugin, A., *Misterii Evrazii* [The mysteries of Eurasia]. Moscow: Arktogeia, 1991.

———. *Giperboreiskaia teoriia. Opyt ariosofskogo issledovaniia* [Hyperboreal theory. An experiment in ariosophic investigation]. Moscow: Arktogeia, 1993.

Dunlap, W., *Transit Passage in the Russian Arctic Straights*. Durham: International Boundaries Research Unit, University of Durham, 2002.

Eberstadt, N., "Russia's Peacetime Demographic Crisis: Dimensions, Causes, Implications," *NBR Report*, May 2010.

———. "The Security Consequences of Democratic Decline," Paper presented at the international conference on "Matching Ambitions and Realities: What Future for Russia?" Canadian Security Intelligence Service (CSIS), Ottawa, May 6–7, 2010.

Elferink, A.G., "The Law and Politics of the Maritime Boundary Delimitation of the Russian Federation, Part 1," *The International Journal of Marine and Coastal Law* 10, no. 4 (1996): 525–561.

———. "The Law and Politics of the Maritime Boundary Delimitation of the Russian Federation, Part 2," *The International Journal of Marine and Coastal Law* 11, no. 1 (1997): 5–35.

Elliot-Meisel, E., "Politics, Pride, and Precedent: The United States and Canada in the Northwest Passage," *Ocean Development & International Law* 40, no. 2 (2009): 204–232.

Emmerson, C., *The Future History of the Arctic*. New York: Public Affairs, 2010.

European Commission, *Space and the Arctic, Joint Communication to the European Parliament and the Council Developing a European Union Policy towards the Arctic Region: Progress since 2008 and Next Steps*. Brussels: European Commission, June 26, 2012.

Evdokimov, Yu., Batskikh, Yu., and Istomin, A.V., "Severnyi morskoi put': problemi, vozmozhnosti, perspektivy vozrozhdeniia [The Northern Sea Route: problems, possibilities, and prospects for revival]," *Ekonomicheskaia nauka sovremennoi Rossii*, no. 2 (2000): 101–112.

ExxonMobil, *Arctic Leadership*, 2008. www.exxonmobil.com/Corporate/files/news_pub_poc_arctic.pdf

Facon, I. and Asencio, M., *Le Renouveau de la puissance aérienne russe* [The renewal of Russian air power]. Paris: Foundation for Strategic Research, 2010.

Fairhall, D., *Cold Front: Conflict Ahead in Arctic Waters*. London, New York: I.B. Tauris, 2010.

FAO, *National Fishery Sector Overview. The Russian Federation*. Rome: United Nations Food and Agriculture Organization, 2007.

Feshbach, M., *Russia's Health and Demographic Crises: Policy Implications and Consequences*. Washington, DC: Chemical & Biological Arms Control Institute, 2003.

Forsyth, J., *A History of the Peoples of Siberia: Russia's North Asian Colony 1581–1990*. Cambridge: Cambridge University Press, 1994.

Frolov, A.F., *Doklad ob osobennostiakh klimata na territorii Rossiiskoi Federatsii za 2011 god* [Report on the distinctive features of climate on the territory of the Russian Federation in 2011]. Moscow: Roshydromet, 2012.

Frost, O., *Bering: The Russian Discovery of America*. New Haven and London: Yale University Press, 2003.

Gaddy C. and F. Hill, *The Siberian Curse: How Communist Planners Left Russia Out in the Cold*. (Washington, DC: Brookings Institute Press, 2003), 187.

Gaddy, C. and Ickes, B.W., "Resource Rents and the Russian Economy," *Eurasian Geography and Economics* 46, no. 8 (2005): 559–583.

Gaddy, C., and Kuchins, A., "Putin's Plan: The Future of 'Russia Inc.,'" *The Washington Quarterly* 31, no. 2 (2007): 117–129.

Galeotti, M., ed., *The Politics of Security in Modern Russia*. Farnham: Ashgate, 2010.

Gautier D., Bird, K.J., Charpentier, R., Grantz, A., Houseknecht, D.W., Klett, T.R., Moore, T.E. et al., "Assessment of Undiscovered Oil and Gas in the Arctic," *Science* 324, no. 5931 (2009): 1175–1179.

Glasby, G.P. and Voytekhovsky, Yu. L., "Arctic Russia: Minerals and Mineral Resources," *Geoscientist* 20, no. 8 (2010): 16–21.

Godzimirski, J.M., "Grand enjeux dans le Grand Nord. Les relations Russie-Norvège et leurs implications pour l'Union européenne [Grand challenges in the High North. Russian-Norwegian relations and their implications for the European Union]," *Russie.NEI.Visions*, no. 25, December 2007.

Gorenburg, D., *Minority Ethnic Mobilization in the Russian Federation*. Cambridge: Cambridge University Press, 2003.

———. "Russian Naval Deployments: A Return to Global Power Projection or a Temporary Blip?" *PONARS Eurasia Policy Memo*, no. 57, May 2009.

Górski, T., "A Note on Submarine Ridges and Elevations with Special Reference to the Russian Federation and the Arctic Ridges," *Ocean Development & International Law* 40, no. 1 (2009): 51–60.

Gottemoeller, R. and Tamnes, R., eds., *High North: High Stakes*. Bergen: Fagbokforlaget, 2008.

Grajauskas, R., "What Is New in Russia's 2009 National Security Strategy?" *Eastern Pulse* 6, no. 21 (2009).

Gustafson, T., *Wheel of Fortune: The Battle for Oil and Power in Russia*. Cambridge, MA: The Belknap Press of Harvard University Press, 2012.

Halpern, R., "'Above-Ground' Issues Affecting Energy Development in the Arctic," *ITA Occasional Paper*, August 2007.

Hanson, P., "Russian Energy Policy and the Global Crisis," *Energy Economist*, no. 336 (2009): 5–7.

Heath, J.R., "Strategic Protectionism? National Security and Foreign Investment in the Russian Federation," *George Washington International Law Review* 41 (2009): 101–138.

Heinapuu, A., "Finno-Ugric peoples in Russia. Territorial or Cultural Autonomy," *2004 Estonian Ministry of Foreign Affairs Yearbook*. Tallinn: Tallinn Foreign Affairs Ministry, 2004, 71–75.

Heleniak, T., "Out-migration and Depopulation of the Russian North during the 1990s," *Post-Soviet Geography and Economics* 40, no. 3 (1999): 281–304.

———. "Regional Distribution of the Muslim Population of Russia," *Eurasian Geography and Economics* 47, no. 4 (2007): 426–448.

———. "Population Perils in Russia at the Beginning of the 21st Century," in S. Wegren, and D. Herspring, eds., *After Putin's Russia: Past Imperfect, Future Unknown*. Lanham: Rowman & Littlefield, 2009, 133–158.

———. "The Role of Attachment to Place in Migration Decisions of the Population of the Russian North," *Polar Geography* 32, no. 1–2 (2009), 31–60.

———. "Population Change in the Periphery: Changing Migration Patterns in the Russian North," *Sibirica: Interdisciplinary Journal of Siberian Studies* 9, no. 3 (2010): 9–40.

Henriksen, T. and Ulfstein, G., "Maritime Delimitation in the Arctic: The Barents Sea Treaty," *Ocean Development & International Law* 42, no. 1–2 (2011): 1–21.

Herd, G.P. and Aldis, A., *Russian Regions and Regionalism: Strength through Weakness*. London: Routledge, 2002.

Hill, F. and Gaddy, C., *The Siberian Curse: How Communist Planners Left Russia out in the Cold*. Washington, DC: Brookings Institution Press, 2003.

Hirsch, F., *Empire of Nations. Ethnographic Knowledge and the Making of the Soviet Union*. Ithaca: Cornell University Press, 2005.

Hoggan, J. and Littlemore R., *Climate Cover-Up: The Crusade to Deny Global Warming*. Toronto and Vancouver: Greystone, 2009.

Holtsmark, S. and Smith-Windsor, B.A., eds., *Security Prospects in the High North: Geostrategic Thaw or Freeze?* Rome: NATO Defense College, 2009.

Horensma, P., *The Soviet Arctic*. London: Routledge, 1991.

Howard, R., *The Arctic Gold Rush: The New Race for Tomorrow's Natural Resources*. London and New York: Continuum, 2009.

Hulme, M., *Why We Disagree About Climate Change: Understanding Controversy, Inaction and Opportunity*. Cambridge: Cambridge University Press, 2009.

"Indigenous Peoples—Excluded and Discriminated," *Human Rights Report*, no. 43, 2006.

Indzhiev, A., *Bitva za Arktiku. Budet li sever russkim?* [The Battle for the Arctic. Will the North Be Russian?]. Moscow: Iauza, Eksmo, 2010.

Institute of Stability and Development, *Cross-Border Cooperation on the EU's Eastern Border—Learning from Finnish and Norwegian Experience*. Prague: Institute of Stability and Development, 2012.

International Chamber of Shipping, "Position Paper on Arctic Shipping," 2012.

International Energy Agency, *World Energy Outlook 2008.*

Ioffe, G. and Zayonchkovskaya, Zh., *Immigration to Russia: Why It Is Inevitable, and How Large It May Have to Be to Provide the Workforce Russia Needs.* Washington, DC: National Council for Eurasian and East European Research, NCEEER Working Paper, January 2011.

IPCC (International Panel on Climate Change). *Climate Change 2007: Synthesis Report,* Geneva: Intergovernmental Panel on Climate Change, 2007.

———. *Contribution of Working Group I to the Fourth Assessment Report of the Intergovernmental Panel on Climate Change.* Cambridge: Cambridge University Press, 2007.

Istomin, A.V., "Severnyi morskoi put': organizatsionno-ekonomicheskie osnovy vozrozhdenia i razvitiia [The Northern Sea Route: Logistical and economic principles of revival and development]," in *Formirovanie osnov sovremennoi strategii prirodopol'zovaniia v evro-arkticheskom regione* [Formation of the foundations for a current strategy for natural resource use in the Euro-Arctic region]. Murmansk: Akademiia nauk, 2005, 471–481.

———. "Rol' severnogo morskogo puti v khoziaistvennom razvitii i osvoenii severnykh territorii [The role of the Northern Sea Route in the agricultural development and conquest of northern territories]," *Sever promyshlennyi,* no. 6–7 (2007).

Jakobson, L., "China Prepares for an Ice-Free Arctic," *SIPRI Insights on Peace and Security,* no. 2, 2010.

———. "China and the Arctic: Cautious but Determined." Paper presented at the International Studies Association (ISA) Convention, San Diego, April 1–4, 2012.

———. "Northeast Asia Turns Its Attention to the Arctic," *NBR Analysis Brief,* December 2012.

Jensen, L.C. and Hønneland, G., "Framing the High North: Public Discourses in Norway after 2000," *Acta Borealia* 8, no. 1 (2011): 37–54.

Jensen, O. and Vigeland Rottem, S., "The Politics of Security and International Law in Norway's Arctic Waters," *Polar Record* 46, no. 236 (2010): 75–83.

Johnston, P.F., *The Energy Security Impact of Oil Nationalization.* Ottawa: Canadian Centre for Operational Research and Analysis, October 2009.

———. "Arctic Energy Resources and Global Energy Security," *Journal of Military and Strategic Studies* 12, no. 2 (2010): 1–20.

Jokat, W., Uenzelmann-Neben, G., Kristoffersen, Y., and Rasmussen, T.M., "Lomonosov Ridge—A double-sided continental margin," *Geology* 20, no. 10 (1992): 887–890.

Judah, B. and Wilson, A., "The End of the Putin Consensus," *ECFR Policy Memo,* March 2012.

Kappeler, A., *The Russian Empire: A Multi-Ethnic History.* New York: Longman, 2001.

Kefferpütz, R., "On Thin Ice? (Mis)interpreting Russian Policy in the High North," *CEPS Policy Brief,* no. 205, February 2010.

Khon, V.C., Mokhov, I.I., Latif, M., Semenov, V.A., and Park, W., "Perspectives of Northern Sea Route and Northwest Passage in the Twenty-First Century," *Climatic Change* 100, no. 3–4 (2010): 757–768.

King, C. and Menon, R., "Prisoners of the Caucasus. Russia's Invisible Civil War," *Foreign Affairs,* July/August 2010, 20–34.

Koivurova, T., "Alternatives for an Arctic Treaty—Evaluation and a New Proposal," *European Community & International Environmental Law* 17, no. 1 (2008): 14–26.

————. "Governance of Protected Areas in the Arctic," *Utrecht Law Review* 5, no. 1 (2009): 128–159.

————. "Limits and Possibilities of the Arctic Council in a Rapidly Changing Scene of Arctic Governance," *Polar Record*, no. 46 (2010): 146–156.

Kolodkin, A.L. and Volosov, M.E., "The Legal Regime of the Soviet Arctic: Major Issues," *Marine Policy*, no. 14 (1990): 163–167.

Kononczuk, W., "The East Siberia/Pacific Ocean (ESPO) Oil Pipeline: A Strategic Project—An Organisational Failure?" *Center for Eastern Studies Commentaries*, no. 12 (2008).

Konyshev, V.N. and Sergunin, A.A., *Arktika v mezhdunarodnom politike. Sotrudnichestvo ili sopernichestvo?* [The Arctic in international affairs: Cooperation or Competition?] (Moscow: RISI, 2011).

Konyshev, V.N., Sergunin A.A., "Osvoenie prirodnykh resursov Arktiki: puti sotrudnichestva Rossii s Kitaem v interesakh budushchego [Mastering Arctic natural resources: Ways for a Russia-China cooperation in the interests of the future]," *Prioritety Rossii* 38, no. 180 (2012): 2–9.

Korppoo, A., "Russia and the Post-2012 Climate Regime: Foreign Rather than Environmental Policy," *FIIA Briefing Paper*, no. 23, November 24, 2008.

————. "The Russian Debate on Climate Doctrine, Emerging Issues on the Road to Copenhagen," *Finnish Institute for International Affairs Briefing Paper*, no. 33, June 5, 2009.

————. "Russia's Climate Policy Fails to Raise Hopes," *Finnish Institute for International Affairs Papers*, June 19, 2009.

Korppoo, A., Karas, J., and Grubb, M., eds., *Russia and the Kyoto Protocol. Opportunities and Challenges*. London: Chatham House, 2006.

Kotlowski, A., "Russian Energy Strategy and Transit Routes in Eastern Europe," *Oil, Gas and Energy Law Intelligence* 7, no. 2 (2009): 1–31.

Kozlova, N., "Strashnei vsego—pogoda v dome. Sovet bezopasnosti ob ugrozakh i problemakh, kotorye neset izmenenie klimata [The most fearful of all—the weather at home. Security Council on the threats and problems which climate change brings]," *Rossiiskaia gazeta*, no. 136(57), March 19, 2010.

Koz'menko, S. and Kovalev, S., "Morskaia politika v Arktike i sistema natsional'noi bezopasnosti [Maritime policy in the Arctic and the national security system]," *Morskoi sbornik* 8 (2009): 57–63.

Kuchins, A., *Alternative Futures for Russia to 2017*. Washington, DC: Center for Strategic and International Studies, 2007.

Lanko, D.A., "Russian Debate on the Northern Dimension Concept." Paper presented to the 6th Pan-European International Relations Conference, "Making Sense of a Pluralist World," Torino, Italy, September 12–15, 2007.

Lannon, G.P., "Russia's New-Look Army Reforms and Russian Foreign Policy," *The Journal of Slavic Military Studies* 24, no. 1 (2011): 26–54.

Laruelle, M., *Russian Eurasianism. An Ideology of Empire*. Washington, DC: Woodrow Wilson Press/Johns Hopkins University Press, 2008.

————. *Russian Policy on Central Asia and the Role of Russian Nationalism*. Washington, DC: The Central Asia-Caucasus Institute, 2008.

————. *In the Name of the Nation. Nationalism and Politics in Contemporary Russia*. New York: Palgrave, 2009.

————. "The Ideological Shift on the Russian Radical Right: From Demonizing the West to Fear of Migrants," *Problems of Post-Communism* 57, no. 6 (2010): 19–31.

———. "Conspiracy and Alternate History in Russia: A Nationalist Equation for Success?" *The Russian Review* 71, no. 4 (2012): 565–580.

———. "Larger, Higher, Farther North . . . Geographical Metanarratives of the Nation in Russia," *Eurasian Geography and Economics* 53, no. 5 (2012): 557–574.

Laruelle, M., ed., *Labor Migration and Social Upheaval as the Face of Globalization in Central Asia*. Leiden: Brill, 2013.

Ledeneva, A.V., in Legvold, R., ed., *Russian Foreign Policy in the 21st Century and the Shadow of the Past*. New York: Columbia University Press, 2007.

Lemeshko, N., "Climate Change, Vulnerability, and Adaptation in Agriculture. The Situation and State of Art in Russia," *ADAGIO International Symposium*, Vienna, June 22–24, 2009.

Lemeshko, N. and Nikolaev, M., "Climate Change, Vulnerability, and Adaptation in Agriculture. The Situation and State of Art in Russia," *ADAGIO International Symposium*, Sofia, March 10–11, 2008.

Lioubimtseva, E., "Russia's Role in the Post-2012 Climate Change Policy: Key Contradictions and Uncertainties," *Forum on Public Policy*, Spring 2010, 1–18.

Liu, Miaojia and Kronbak, J., "The Potential Economic Viability of Using the Northern Sea Route (NSR) as an Alternative Route between Asia and Europe," *Journal of Transport Geography* 18, no. 3 (2010): 434–444.

Lo, B., *Axis of Convenience. Moscow, Beijing, and the New Geopolitics*, Washington DC, London: Brookings Institution Press and Chatham House, 2008.

———. "Medvedev and the New European Security Architecture," *CER Policy Brief,* July 2009.

Locatelli, C. and Rossiaud, S., "Russia's Gas and Oil Policy: The Emerging Organizational and Institutional Framework for Regulating Access to Hydrocarbon Resources," *International Association for Energy Economics*, no. 1 (2011): 23–26.

Loe, J.S.P., *Driving Forces in Russian Arctic Policy*. Pöyry Management Consulting, January 2011.

Löwy, M., "Marxists and the National Question," *New Left Review* I, no. 96 (1976).

Macnab, R., "Use It or Lose It in Arctic Canada: Action Agenda or Election Hype?" *Vermont Law Review* 34, no. 1 (2009): 1–14.

Main, S.J., *The Mouse That Roared, or the Bear That Growled? Russia's Latest Military Doctrine*. Wiltshire: Defence Academy of the United Kingdom, 2010.

———. *If Spring Comes Tomorrow . . . Russia and the Arctic*. Shrivenham: Defence Academy of the United Kingdom, 2011.

Makarychev, A., "New Challenges to Russian Federalism," *PONARS Eurasia Policy Memo*, no. 75, 2009.

Mansoor, A. and Quillin, B., eds., *Migration and Remittances: Eastern Europe and the Former Soviet Union*. Washington, DC: The World Bank, 2006.

March, L., "Nationalism for Export? The Domestic and Foreign Policy Implications of the New 'Russian Idea'," *Europe-Asia Studies* 64, no. 3 (2012): 401–425.

Martin, T., *The Affirmative Action Empire. Nations and Nationalism in the Soviet Union, 1923–1939*. Ithaca, London: Cornell University Press, 2001.

Martynova, E.P. and Novikova, N.I., *Tazovskie nentsy v usloviiakh neftegazovogo osvoeniia* [The Taz Nenets under conditions of oil and gas development]. Moscow: RAN, 2012.

Mazhitova, G., Karstkarel, N., Oberman, N., Romanovsky, V., and Kuhry, P., "Permafrost and Infrastructure in the Usa Basin (Northeast European Russia): Possible Impacts of Global Warming," *Ambio* 33, no. 6 (2004): 289–294.

McCannon, J., *Red Arctic: Polar Exploration and the Myth of the North in the Soviet Union, 1932–1939*. Oxford: Oxford University Press, 1998.

McGhee, R., *The Last Imaginary Place. A Human History of the Arctic World*. Chicago: The University of Chicago Press, 2005.

McKinsey and Co., *Pathways to an Energy and Carbon Efficient Russia*. Moscow: McKinsey & Co. Inc., 2009.

Melvin, N. and Klimenko, E., "Russia's Arctic Strategy in the Context of Its Eurasian Security Policies." Paper presented at the Annual Meeting of the International Studies Association (ISA), San Diego, April 1–4, 2012.

Mezhdunarodnaia situatsiia vokrug Arktiki i sostoianie rossiiskii priarkticheskoi infrastruktury [The international situation in the Arctic and the state of Russian Arctic infrastructure]. Moscow: Tsentr politicheskoi informatsii, 2010.

Moe, A., Fjærtoft, D., and Øverland, I., "Space and Timing: Why Was the Barents Sea Delimitation Dispute Resolved in 2010?" *Polar Geography* 34, no. 3 (2011): 145–162.

Moe, A. and Rowe, L., "Petroleum Activity in the Russian Barents Sea. Constraints and Options for Norwegian Offshore and Shipping Companies," *Fridtjof Nansen Institute Report*, no. 7, 2008.

Moe, A. and Wilson Rowe, E., "Northern Offshore Oil and Gas Resources: Russian Policy Challenges and Approaches." Fridtjof Nansen Institute Working Paper, June 2008.

Monmonier, M., *Drawing the Line: Tales of Maps and Cartocontroversy*. New York: Henry Holt & Co., 1996.

Myers Jaffe, A., *The Changing Role of National Oil Companies in International Energy Markets*. Houston: James A. Baker III Institute for Public Policy of Rice University, April 2007.

Nansen, F., *Through Siberia—the Land of the Future*. New York: Frederick A. Stokes Co., 1914 (republished by Books for Libraries Press, 1972).

Nihoul, J.C.J. and Kostianoy, A.G., eds., *Influence of Climate Change on the Changing Arctic and Sub-Arctic Condition*. New York: Springer, 2009.

NOAA (National Oceanic and Atmospheric Administration) *Arctic Report Card. Update for 2010*, 2010.

———. *State of the Arctic*, October 2006.

Nordquist, M.H., Norton Moore, J., and Skaridov, A.S., eds., *International Energy Policy, the Arctic and the Law of the Sea*. Leiden, Boston: Martinus Nijhoff, 2005.

North Meets North. Navigation and the Future of the Arctic. Reykjavik: Iceland Ministry for Foreign Affairs Working Group, 2005.

North Pacific Fishery Management Council, *Fishery Management Plan for Fish Resources of the Arctic*. Anchorage: North Pacific Fishery Management Council, August 2009.

Norwegian Petroleum Directorate, *Facts 2008—The Norwegian Petroleum Sector*, 2008.

Nurminen, J. and Lainema, M., *A History of Arctic Exploration: Discovery, Adventure, and Endurance at the Top of the World*. London: Conway, 2010.

O'Loughlin, J., Toal, G., and Kolossov, V., "The Geopolitical Orientations of Ordinary Russians: A Public Opinion Analysis," *Eurasian Geography and Economics* 48, no. 2 (2006): 129–152.

O'Loughlin, J. and Talbot, P., "Where in the World Is Russia? Geopolitical Perceptions and Preferences of Ordinary Russians," *Eurasian Geography and Economics* 46, no. 1 (2005): 23–50.

OECD, *Strengthening Regional Fisheries Management Organizations*. Paris: Organisation for Economic Co-operation and Development, 2009.

Oreshenkov, A., "Severnaia ledovitaia diplomatiia [Northern Arctic Diplomacy]," *Rossiia v global'noi politike*, no. 4 (2009).

———. "Arctic Diplomacy," *Russia in Global Affairs*, no. 8 (2009).

———. "Arctic Square of Opportunities," *Russia in Global Affairs*, December 25, 2010.

Orttung, R., ed., *Russia's Arctic Cities: State Policies, Resource Development, and Climate Change*, forthcoming.

Osherenko, G. and Young, O.R., *The Age of the Arctic: Hot Conflicts and Cold Realities*. Cambridge: Cambridge University Press, 2005.

Østreng, W., *The Soviet Union in Arctic Waters*. Honolulu: Law of the Sea Institute, 1987.

———. "Looking Ahead to the Northern Sea Route," *Scandinavian Review* 90, no. 2 (2002): 78–79.

Østreng, W., ed., *The Natural and Societal Challenges of the Northern Sea Route. A Reference Work*. Dordrecht, Netherlands: Kluwer Academic, 1999.

Överland, I., "Russia's Arctic Energy Policy," *International Journal*, Autumn 2010, 865–878.

Palamar, N.G., "Nekotorye aspekty pogranichnogo razgranicheniia mezhdu Rossiiskoi Federatsiei i SShA [Some Aspects of Boundary Differentiation between the Russian Federation and the United States of America]," *Znanie, Ponimanie, Umenie*, no. 6 (2009).

Parker, J.W., "Russia's Revival: Ambitions, Limitations, and Opportunities for the United States," *INSS Strategic Perspectives*, no. 3 (2011).

Parsons, M.A., Godøy, Ø., LeDrew, E., de Bruin, T.F., Danis, B., Tomlinson, S., and Carlson, D.,"A Conceptual Framework for Managing Very Diverse Data for Complex, Interdisciplinary Science," *Journal of Information Science* 37, no. 6 (2011): 555–569.

Pedersen, T., "The Svalbard Continental Shelf Controversy: Legal Disputes and Political Rivalries," *Ocean Development & International Law* 37, no. 3–4 (2006): 339–358.

Perelet, R., Pegov, S., and Yulkin, M., "Climate Change. Russia Country Paper," in *Fighting Climate Change: Human Solidarity in a Divided World. Human Development Report*. Washington, DC: United Nations Development Programme, 2008.

Petrov, A.N., "Lost Generations? Indigenous Population of the Russian North in the Post-Soviet Era," *Canadian Studies in Population* 35, no. 2 (2008): 269–290.

Pilkington, H., Omel'chenko, E., and Garifzianova, A., *Russia's Skinheads. Exploring and Rethinking Subcultural Lives*. London: Routledge, 2010.

Podvig, P., ed., *Russian Strategic Nuclear Forces*. Boston: MIT Press, 2004.

Posen, B.R., "The U.S. Military Response to Soviet Naval Developments in the High North," in J. Svarre and K. Nyblom, eds., *The Military Buildup in the High North: American and Nordic Perspectives*. Lanham: University Press of America, 1986, 45–59.

Pribylovskii, V., *Kooperativ Ozero i drugie proekty Vladimir Putina* [The Ozero Cooperative and other projects of Vladimir Putin]. Moscow: Algoritm, 2012.

Prokhorov, P., "'Gaagskaia vaktsina' ot 'sindroma Siuarda'" [The "Hague vaccine" against "Seward's syndrome"], *Sankt-Peterburgskie vedomosti*, no. 137, July 28, 2006.

———. "How Do We Divide the Barents Sea?" Paper presented at the Northern Research Forum, October 4, 2006.

Pykhtyn, S., "Kak prodavali Aliasku: temnaia storona russko-amerikanskikh otnoshenii s 1824 po 1867 god [How Alaska Was Sold: The Dark Side of Russian-American Relations from 1824 to 1867]," *Moskva*, no. 8 (2005): 144–165.

Radvanyi, J., *La Nouvelle Russie. Géographie économique, régions et nations, géopolitique* [The new Russia: Economic geography, regions and peoples, geopolitics]. Paris: Masson, Armand Colin, 1996.

Ragner, C.L., ed., *The 21st Century—Turning Point for the Northern Sea Route?* Oslo: Kluwer Academic Publishers, 2000.

———. "The Northern Sea Route," in T. Hallberg, ed., *Barents—ett gränsland i Norden* [Barents—a borderland of the Nordic countries]. Stockholm: Arena Norden, 2008, 114–127.

Raviot, J.-R., "Géographie politique de la Russie en 2010 [Political geography of Russia in 2010]," *Hérodote*, no. 138 (2010).

Repnikova, M. and Balzer, H., "Chinese Migration to Russia: Missed Opportunities," *WWICS Eurasian Migration Paper*, no. 3 (2010).

Riddell-Dixon, E., "Canada and Arctic Politics: The Continental Shelf Extension," *Ocean Development & International Law* 39, no. 4 (2008): 343–359.

Risse, T., Ropp, S.C., and Sikkink, K., eds., *The Power of Human Rights: International Norms and Domestic Change*. Cambridge: Cambridge University Press, 1999.

Robbek, V., "Language Situation in the Yakutia Republic (Sakha)," in E. Kasten, ed., *Bicultural Education in the North: Ways of Preserving and Enhancing Indigenous Peoples' Languages and Traditional Knowledge*. Münster: Waxmann Verlag, 1998, 113–122.

Roberts, K., "Jets, Flags, and a New Cold War? Demystifying Russia's Arctic Intentions," *International Journal*, Autumn 2010, 957–976.

Roshydromet, *Strategic Prediction for the Period up to 2010–2015 of Climate Change Expected in Russia and its Impacts on the Sectors of the Russian National Economy*. Moscow: Roshydromet, 2006.

———. *Assessment Report on Climate Change and its Consequences in Russian Federation. General Summary*. Moscow: Roshydromet, 2008.

Ross, C. and Campbell, A., *Federalism and Local Politics in Russia*. London: Routledge, 2010.

Rothwell, D.R. and Joyner, C.C., "Polar Oceans and the Law of the Sea," in A.G. Oude Elferink and D.R. Rothwell, eds., *The Law of the Sea and Polar Maritime Delimitation and Jurisdiction*. Leiden, Boston: Martinus Nijhoff Publishers, 2001, 1–22.

Rothwell, D.R., *The Polar Regions and the Development of International Law*. Cambridge: Cambridge University Press, 1996.

Ruble, B.A., Koehn, J., and Popson N.E., eds., *Fragmented Space in the Russian Federation*. Washington, DC: Woodrow Wilson International Center for Scholars and Johns Hopkins University, 2011.

Rudloff, B., "The EU as Fishing Actor in the Arctic. Stocktaking of Institutional Involvement and Exiting Conflicts," *SWP Working Papers*, July 2010.

Rudolph, D., "The Arctic Military Environmental Cooperation (AMEC) Program's Role in the Management of Spent Fuel from Decommissioned Nuclear Submarines," in *Scientific and Technical Issues in the Management of Spent Fuel of Decommissioned Nuclear Submarines*. Dordrecht: NATO Science Series II, Mathematics, Physics, and Chemistry, 2006.

Russia. The Impact of Climate Change to 2030. A Commissioned Research Report. Washington, DC: National Intelligence Council, 2009.

"The Russian Navy's Regeneration Plans," *IISS Strategic Comments*, February 25, 2011.

Sakhalin Indigenous Minorities Development Plan, First Five-Year Plan (2006–2010), Sakhalin Energy Investment Company Ltd., 2006.

Sakwa, R., *Putin, Russia's Choice*. London: Routledge, 2007.

———. "Putin's Leadership: Character and Consequences," *Europe-Asia Studies* 60, no. 6 (2008): 879–897.

———. *The Crisis of Russian Democracy. The Dual State, Factionalism, and the Medvedev Succession*. Cambridge: Cambridge University Press, 2011.

Sale, R. and Potapov, E., *The Scramble for the Arctic: Ownership, Exploitation and Conflict in the Far North*. London: Frances Lincoln, 2010.

Sasgen, P., *Stalking the Red Bear: The True Story of a U.S. Cold War Submarine's Covert Operations Against the Soviet Union*. New York: St. Martin's Press, 2009.

Schmidt, G. and Wolfe, J., *Climate Change: Picturing the Science*. New York: W.W. Norton & Company, 2009.

Schøyen, H. and Bråthen, S., "Bulk Shipping via the Northern Sea Route versus via the Suez Canal: Who Will Gain from a Shorter Transport Route? An Explorative Case Study." Paper presented at the 12th World Conference on Transportation Research (WCTR), July 11–15, 2010, Lisbon, Portugal.

Schram Stokke, O., ed., *Governing High Seas Fisheries. The Interplay of Global and Regional Regimes*. Oxford: Oxford University Press, 2001.

Shebarshin, L., "Oni bez nas prozhivut, a my bez samikh sebia—net [They will survive without us, but we won't without ourselves]," *Ekonomicheskie strategii*, no. 6 (2000): 36–49.

Shestopalov, M., "Vektor ustremlenii—Arktika [A vector of aspiration—the Arctic]," *Vozdushno-kosmicheskaia oborona*, no. 6 (2008): 16–24.

Shnirelman, V., *'Tsepnoi pes rasy': divannaia rasologiia kak zashchitnitsa 'belogo cheloveka'* ["The watch dog of race": A couch-based raciology in defense of the "white man"]. Moscow: SOVA, 2007.

———. *Intellektual'nye labirinty: ocherki ideologii v sovremennoi Rossii* [Intellectual labyrinths: Essay on ideology in contemporary Russia]. Moscow: Academia, 2004.

Slezkine, Yu., *Arctic Mirrors. Russia and the Small Peoples of the North*. Ithaca, London: Cornell University Press, 1994.

Smelror, M., "Mining in the Arctic," *Arctic Frontiers*, January 25, 2011.

Smith, M.A., *Medvedev and the Modernisation Dilemma*. Shrivenham: The Defence Academy of the United Kingdom, November 2010.

———. *The Russo-Chinese Energy Relationship*. Shrivenham: The Defence Academy of the United Kingdom, October 2010.

Söderlund, P., *The Dynamics of Federalism in Russia*. Helsinki: Åbo Akademi University Press, 2006.

Solanko, L. and Sutela, P., "Too Much or Too Little Russian Gas to Europe?" *Eurasian Geography and Economics* 50, no. 1 (2009): 58–74.

Solovyev, E.G., "Geopolitics in Russia, Science or Vocation?" *Communist and Post-Communist Studies* 37, no. 1 (2004): 85–96.

Solum Whist, B., "Norway and Russia in the High North: Clash of Perceptions," *Security Brief*, no. 1, 2008.

Spears, J., "The Snow Dragon Moves into the Arctic Ocean Basin," *China Brief* 11, no. 2 (2010).

Spielman, B., "An Evaluation of Russia's Impending Claim for Continental Shelf Expansion: Why Rule 5 Will Shelve Russia's Submission," *Emory International Law Review* 23 (2009): 309–349.

Steinicke, S. and Albrecht, S., "Search and Rescue in the Arctic," *SWP Policy Papers*, no. 5, December 2012.

Stepanov, I.V., Ørebech, P., and Brubaker, R.D., *Legal Implications for the Russian Northern Sea Route and Westward in the Barents Sea*. Oslo: Fridtjof Nansen Institute, 2005.

Stern, J.P., *The Future of Russian Gas and Gazprom*. Oxford: Oxford University Press, 2005.

Stevens, P., "The 'Shale Gas Revolution': Hype and Reality," *Chatham House Report*, September 2010.

Stritzel, H., "Towards a Theory of Securitization: Copenhagen and Beyond," *European Journal of International Relations* 13, no. 3 (2007): 357–383.

Stukalin, A., "Bears and Blackjacks Are Back. What Next?" *Moscow Defense Brief*, no. 4 (22) (2010).

Thompson, N., "Administrative Resettlement and the Pursuit of Economy: The Case of Chukotka," *Polar Geography* 26, no. 4 (2002): 270–288.

———. *Settlers on the Edge: Identity and Modernization on Russia's Arctic Frontier*. Vancouver and Toronto: University of British Columbia Press, 2008.

Thorez, P., "La Route maritime du Nord. Les promesses d'une seconde vie [The Northern Sea Route: Promise of a second life]," *Le Courrier des Pays de l'Est*, no. 2 (2008): 48–59.

Timtchenko, L., "The Russian Arctic Sectoral Concept: Past and Present," *Arctic* 50, no. 1 (1997): 29–35.

Trenin, D., "Russia Redefines Itself and Its Relations with the West," *Washington Quarterly* 30, no. 2 (2007): 95–105.

Trenin, D. and P. K. Baev, *The Arctic: A View from Russia*. Washington, DC: Carnegie Endowment for International Peace, 2010.

Tunander, O., "Geopolitics of the North: Geopolitik of the Weak. A Post–Cold War Return to Rudolf Kjellén," *Cooperation and Conflict* 43, no. 2 (2008): 164–184.

Tykkyläinen, M. and Rautio, V., eds., *Russia's Northern Regions on the Edge: Communities, Industries, and Populations from Murmansk to Magadan*. Helsinki: Aleksanteri Institute, 2008.

UNEP, *Policy Implications of Warming Permafrost. Nairobi: United Nations Environment Programme*, 2012.

UNHRC, *Assessment for Yakut in Russia*. United Nations Human Rights Council, Minorities at Risk Project, December 31, 2003.

Vaisman, A., *Trawling in the Mist: Industrial Fisheries in the Russian Part of the Bering Sea*. Moscow: World Wildlife Federation, 2001.

Vasil'kova, T.N., Evai, A.V., Martynova, E.P., and Novikova, N.I., *Korennye malochis tlennye narody i promyshlennoe razvitie Arktiki* [Indigenous small-numbered peoples and the industrial development of the Arctic]. Moscow: Shchadrinskii dom pechati, 2011.

Vendil Pallin, C. and Westerlund, D., "Russia's War in Georgia: Lessons and Consequences," *Small Wars and Insurgencies* 20, no. 2 (2009): 400–424.

Verzhbitsky, V., Frantzen, E., Savostina, T., Little, A., Sokolov, S.D., and Tuchkova, M.I., "Russian Chukchi Sea," *GeoExpro*, September 10, 2008.

Vinokurova, U.A., "The Ethnopolitical Situation in the Republic of Sakha (Yakutia)," *Anthropology & Archeology of Eurasia* 34, no. 1 (1995): 60–98.

Voitolovsky, G.K., "Nereshennye problemy Arkticheskogo morepol'zovaniia [Unresolved problems of Arctic navigation]," *Vestnik MGTU*, no. 1 (2010): 90–104.

Voronkov, L.S., *Geopolitical Dimensions of Transport and Logistics Development in the Barents Euro-Arctic Transport Area (BEATA)*. Kirkenes: Barents Institute, 2009.

Vylegzhanin, A., "Agreement between the USSR and the USA about the Line of the Demarcation of the Maritime Spaces of 1990: Different Assessments of Interim Application," unpublished manuscript.

Vylegzhanin, A.N. and Zilanov, V.L., *Spitsbergen. Legal Regime of Adjacent Marine Areas*. Portland, OR: Eleven International Publishing, 2007.

Waisberg, P.D., "Emerging Configurations of Indigenous Status in Post-Soviet Russia." Paper presented at the Annual Meeting of American Association for the Advancement of Slavic Studies, Pittsburgh, November 21–24, 2002.

Watson, N.J., "The Money Gap," *Petroleum Economist*, January 1, 2006.

Wenger, A., Langenbach, S, and Orttung, R., "The Role of Hydrocarbons in Maritime Claim-Making: Patterns of Conflict & Cooperation," unpublished manuscript.

Wezeman, S.T., "Military Capabilities in the Arctic," *SIPRI Background Paper*, March 2012.

Wilson Rowe, E., "Russian Regional Multilateralism: The Case of the Arctic Council," in E. Wilson Rowe and S. Torjesen, eds., *The Multilateral Dimension in Russian Foreign Policy*. London: Routledge, 2008, 142–152.

———. "Who is to Blame? Agency, Causality, Responsibility, and the Role of Experts in Russian Framings of Global Climate Change," *Europe-Asia Studies* 61, no. 4 (2009): 593–619.

———. "International Science, Domestic Politics: Russian Reception of International Climate Change Assessments," *Environment and Planning D: Society and Space* 30, no. 4 (2012): 711–726.

Wilson Rowe, E., ed., *Russia and the North*, Ottawa: University of Ottawa Press, 2009.

Wites, T., "Depopulation of the Russian Far East. Magadan Oblast. A Case Study," *Miscellanea Geographica*, vol. 12 (2006): 185–196.

Wood, A., ed., *Siberia: Problems and Prospects for Regional Development*. London: Croom Helm, 1987.

Wood, D., *The Power of Maps*. New York: The Guilford Press, 1992.

World Bank. *Reshaping Economic Geography*. Washington, DC: The World Bank, 2009.

———. *Russian Federation, Reducing Poverty through Growth and Social Policy Reform*. Washington, DC: World Bank, 2005.

WWF (World Wildlife Federation). *Analysis of Illegal Fishery for Cod in the Barents Sea*. Moscow: World Wildlife Federation-Russia, 2005.

――――. The *Impact of Climate Change on the Russian Arctic and Paths to Solving the Problem*. Moscow: World Wildlife Federation-Russia, 2008.

――――. *Arctic Climate Feedbacks: Global Implications*. Oslo: World Wildlife Federation International Arctic Program, 2009.

Yenikeyeff, S.M. and Fenton Krysiek, T., "The Battle for the Next Energy Frontier: The Russian Polar Expedition and the Future of Arctic Hydrocarbons," *Oxford Energy Comment*, August 2007.

Young, O.R., *Arctic Polities: Conflict and Cooperation in the Circumpolar North*. Hanover, London: Dartmouth College, 1992.

――――. ed., *The Effectiveness of International Environmental Regimes: Causal Connections and Behavioral Mechanisms*. Cambridge, MA: MIT Press, 1999.

――――. "Arctic Governance—Pathways to the Future," *Arctic Review on Law and Politics*, no. 1 (2010): 164–185.

Zaionchkovskaia Zh.A., Vendina, O.I., Mkrtchyan, N.V., Tyrukanova, E.V., Ivanova, T.D., and Gelbras, V.G., *Immigranty v Moskve* [Immigrants in Moscow]. Moscow: Tri kvadrata, 2009.

Zaionchkovskaia, Zh.A. and Vitkovskaia, G.S., eds., *Postsovetskie transformatsii: otrazhenie v migratsiiakh* [Post-Soviet transformations and their impact on migrations]. Moscow: Tsent migratsionnykh issledovanii, 2009.

Zamiatina, N. and Yashunskii, A., "Severa kak zona rosta dlia Rossiiskoi provintsii [The North as a place of growth for Russia's provinces]," *Otechestvennye zapiski*, no. 5 (2012): 227–239.

Zellen, B. Scott, *Arctic Doom, Arctic Boom? The Geopolitics of Climate Change in the Arctic*. Santa Barbara, Denver, Oxford: ABC Clion, 2009.

Znamenski, A., "History with an Attitude: Alaska in Modern Russian Patriotic Rhetoric," *Jahrbücher für Geschichte Osteuropeas* 57, no. 3 (2009): 346–373.

Zou Keyuan, "Implementing the United Nations Convention on the Law of the Sea in East Asia: Issues and Trends," *Singapore Year Book of International Law*. Singapore: National University of Singapore, 2005, 37–53.

Zysk, K., "Russian Military Power and the Arctic," *Russian Foreign Policy, EU–Russia Centre's Review*, no. 8 (2008): 80–86.

――――. "Geopolitics in the Arctic: The Russian Security Perspective," *Climate of Opinion: The Stockholm Network's Energy and Environment Update*, no. 12 (2009), 7–9.

――――. "Russian National Security Strategy to 2020," *Geopolitics in the High North*, June 15, 2009.

――――. "Russia's Arctic Strategy: Ambitions and Constraints," *Joint Force Quarterly*, no. 57 (2010): 103–110.

Index

244 INDEX

About the Author

Marlene Laruelle is Director of the Central Asia Program and a Research Professor of International Affairs at the Institute for European, Russian, and Eurasian Studies (IERES), The Elliott School of International Affairs, The George Washington University, Washington DC. She has published on Russia's political and social trends, identity issues, nationalism, citizenship, and migration. She is the author of several books including *Russian Eurasianism: An Ideology of Empire* and *In the Name of the Nation: Nationalism and Politics in Contemporary Russia.*